Designing Effective Instruction for Secondary Social Studies

THOMAS L. DYNNESON
University of Texas of the Permian Basin

RICHARD E. GROSS
Stanford University

Merrill, an imprint of
Prentice Hall
Englewood Cliffs, New Jersey   Columbus, Ohio

Library of Congress Cataloging-in-Publication Data

Dynneson, Thomas L.
    Designing effective instruction for secondary social studies /
Thomas L. Dynneson and Richard E. Gross
        p.   cm.
    Includes bibliographical references and index.
    ISBN 0-02-331221-1
        1. Social sciences—Study and teaching (Secondary)   I. Gross,
Richard E. II. Title
    H62.D87 1995
    300'.72—dc20

94-34090
CIP

Editor: Bradley J. Potthoff
Production Editor: Patricia A. Skidmore
Text Designer: STELLARViSIONS
Production Buyer: Patricia A. Tonneman
Electronic Text Management: Marilyn Wilson Phelps, Matthew Williams, Jane Lopez,
    Karen L. Bretz

This book was set in Dutch and Swiss by Prentice Hall and was printed and bound by
R.R. Donnelley & Sons. The cover was printed by Phoenix Color Corp.

 © 1995 by Prentice-Hall, Inc.
A Simon & Schuster Company
Englewood Cliffs, New Jersey 07632

Printed in the United States of America

10 9 8 7 6 5 4 3 2 1

ISBN: 0-02-331221-1

Prentice-Hall International (UK) Limited, *London*
Prentice-Hall of Australia Pty. Limited, *Sydney*
Prentice-Hall of Canada, Inc., *Toronto*
Prentice-Hall Hispanoamericana, S. A., *Mexico*
Prentice-Hall of India Private Limited, *New Delhi*
Prentice-Hall of Japan, Inc., *Tokyo*
Simon & Schuster Asia Pte. Ltd., *Singapore*
Editora Prentice-Hall do Brasil, Ltda., *Rio de Janeiro*

Preface

According to Aristotle:

> Mankind are by no means agreed about the things to be taught, whether we look
> to virtue or to the best life. . . . Should the useful in life, or virtue, or the higher
> knowledge be the aim of training?. . . . (and). . . . about the means of education
> there is no agreement."[1]

Many secondary methods books have been written describing the characteristics of the social studies and prescribing how the subject should be taught within the schools. Some of these textbooks continue to serve as reference books for classroom instruction once students become qualified teachers. We intend this volume to serve both as a basic methods textbook for teacher candidates and also as a curriculum and instruction resource for social studies teachers who want to improve their planning and teaching skills. To enhance the reference value of the text, we have included substantive issues pertaining to curriculum and to designing, developing, and executing instruction.

To begin planning instruction, teachers must be able to prioritize commonly agreed-upon learning goals in light of the characteristics of the subject matter, pupil attributes, mandated program requirements, accepted principles regarding good pedagogical practice, available instructional materials, recognized needs of students, and the desires of the teacher. In addition, teachers should encourage students to study societal events from many different points of view and to use reflective and critical thinking skills in connection with contemporary social issues and concerns.

---

[1] *The Works of Aristotle, Politica*, Book VIII, ch. 2, trans. Benjamin Jowett, vol. X (Oxford: Clarendon, 1921), 1,338.

A Model for Instruction

Currently, there are systems approaches or models for planning curriculum, designing instruction, and executing instruction. It is not our intention to provide a new design model or a comprehensive review of design literature or to go beyond the current understandings related to instructional design. Our purpose is to provide social studies teachers with a simple process they can use to organize social studies curriculum, instruction, and methods courses in a more systematic way.

Subsequently, this volume is based on the following premises regarding planning instruction for the social studies classroom:

- *Premise 1:* Teacher training in the social studies can be improved through the use of a methods textbook that is organized according to an integrated organizational structure. This text, therefore, is formatted according to a five-part sequential pattern for the presentation of the "social studies." This presentation attempts to (1) provide basic information about the social studies as a field of instruction and (2) present this information in a manner that can be used to improve the social studies curricula and methodology through the application of certain design principles, recommendations, and a model for planning and executing instruction.

- *Premise 2:* The best organizational pattern for designing social studies curriculum and instruction is a deductive format that begins with the foundations of the field (historical and ideological) and ends with the means for presenting instruction.

Such a social studies approach should present the history and the ideologies that have influenced the field in order to provide students with an understanding of the issues and the concerns that have brought it to its current position as an instructional field in the schools. Following an exploration of subject matter, including the disciplines, elements of content, and components of instruction, the book should conclude with a model and examples for planning and presenting courses, units, and lessons to students.

- *Premise 3:* A social studies text devoted to curriculum and methods should focus on various approaches for organizing subject matter and the structure (content and methodologies) of the disciplines that are characteristic of the field.

More often than not, those who seek to become social studies teachers are not familiar with the social studies approaches that are characteristic of the field. As a result, teachers often are unable to distinguish between one social studies program and another. In addition, beginning teachers generally are unfamiliar with several of the core disciplines that have contributed to subject-matter content in the field. Therefore, it is important that a social studies methods textbook review these disciplines, their approaches, and their uses for teaching in the social studies classroom.

- *Premise 4:* Social studies education volumes should emphasize the elements of content (concepts, skills, and values) that are characteristic of the content of the field.

One of the most critical aspects of social studies instruction rests on the teacher's ability to plan and present key concepts, target skills, and core values to students. If prospective teachers are trained in the nature and characteristics of these elements, they may be better equipped to develop more effective instructional presentations for their students.

- *Premise 5:* Social studies methods texts should emphasize the components of instruction to promote a more systematic understanding of the interrelationship between objectives, motivation, strategies, activities, materials, and evaluation.

The components of instruction should be used to help focus the teacher's classroom presentations and learning activities on the objectives that have been formulated for teaching. This focus should promote a higher level of consistency within and between the components of instruction as well as throughout the instructional setting. Materials provide the resources as well as an organizational structure for subject-matter content; therefore, materials help to determine the nature of instruction and also greatly influence the teacher's classroom presentation. Subsequently, the teacher must be able to modify materials when they are not suitable for the students and be able to select additional materials for specific needs that are not being met by regular classroom materials. In addition, the teacher should be skilled at designing and constructing materials that will aid in their classroom presentations.

- *Premise 6:* Books on social studies curriculum and instruction methods books should contain a specific model for design-based instruction that can be used as a guideline for designing, developing, and executing courses, units, and lessons.

In recent years, teachers have been encouraged to adapt certain procedures for presenting content to students. But more important still is the need for an organizational structure based on a step-by-step systematic model for designing, developing, and presenting courses, units, and lessons.

Text Organization

Based on our premises for an effective presentation for teaching the social studies, we have structured our text to have five integrated parts. This design explores the selected social studies issues and ideas and, at the same time, guides teachers in the design, development, and implementation of appropriate social studies education.

A description of the role of each of these parts follows:

Part One—Ideological and Historical Concerns: Perceptions and Origins

This part of the book explores the perceptions and the origins of social studies instruction and contains an overview of the research literature in social studies education. This literature also serves as a resource for formulating new ways of organizing instruction.

Part Two—The Selection and Organization of Subject Matter: Designing Instruction According to Approaches and Disciplines

Part Two explores the selection of subject matter from history, social science, and related disciplines. It describes the characteristics of these disciplines and their applied uses within the social studies curriculum, particularly in regard to the study of American heritage and the acquisition of the skills needed to study the people and places of the world. It also presents the characteristics of these disciplines and their use in describing the American political and economic systems and the sociological, psychological, and anthropological concerns related to American cultures, institutions, and individual groups.

Part Three—The Selection and Organization of Subject-Matter Elements: Designing Instruction According to Concepts, Skills, and Values

This part of the book explores the selection and organization of subject matter according to the elements of content (concepts, skills, and values) that serve as the building blocks of instruction and the means for helping students acquire critical thinking skills and values.

Part Four—The Selection and Organization of Instructional Components: Objectives, Motivation, Strategies, Activities, and Evaluation

Part Four explores the selection and organization of the components of instruction, including: the experiences, behaviors, and capabilities that students need in order to deal with subject-matter knowledge; the role of objectives within the instructional setting; influences that affect the motivation for learning; descriptions of how teachers present instruction and how they provide students with appropriate learning experiences; criteria used in the textbook selection process; and the organization and construction of supplemental materials and media that are needed to support teacher presentations. It also describes the use of a systematic plan for evaluation, the techniques for assessing students, and the wise use of test results.

Part Five—The Design-Based Instruction: Designing, Developing, and Implementing Courses, Units, and Lessons

This part of the text explores how the elements of instruction are implemented according to effective teaching concerns and a nine-step model for designing, developing, and implementing courses, units, and lessons. It reviews the teacher's role in promoting effective instruction, meeting student needs, and setting up classroom conditions that facilitate learning and features the nine-step model with specific examples for planning and presenting courses, units, and lessons.

Text Goals

The goals of the five-part organizational approach are to help you:

- Recognize the historical and ideological basis on which social studies instruction is based
- Address the issues and problems associated with designing, developing, and executing instruction according to the principles of scope, sequence, continuity, integration, focus, and balance
- Describe the different approaches of the social studies in regard to the selection and organization of disciplinary content
- Organize the elements of subject-matter content (concepts, skills, and values) into effective presentation patterns for students
- Provide learning experiences that will encourage students to advance in their capacities, attitudes, and sense of self-confidence in their ability to learn outside of the classroom
- Ensure that learning materials will be appropriate for students according to their levels of maturity, experience, and ability.

The Appendices: Practical Teaching Workshops

Designing Effective Instruction for Secondary Social Studies is devoted to modeling a somewhat unique approach to social studies education. Our organization and emphases are based on longtime experience and careful thought as to an optimum social studies program. It is why, in addition to the five-part text structure, we have also included appendices that include detailed workshops for precertified and experienced teachers. This feature is designed to help methods instructors assist teachers in acquiring design skills related to social studies lessons and units.

Meeting National Standards

Current national activities in numerous disciplinary fields are characterized by the identification of basic standards. We cannot predict the results of this somewhat new (at least in terminology) movement. We cannot disagree with the need to identify the fundamentals of each subject-matter area; teachers have long been misled to attempt superficial coverage of a mass of selected details in their courses. But we believe that, even with the development of related assessment devices, the creation of so-called national standards and the desire by some to impose these on schools and teachers, the true success of reshaped or reformed social studies courses will ultimately depend on the abilities and insights of classroom teachers. There, on the "front lines" of education, the knowledge, creativity, and motivation of these instructors working directly with learners will be the ultimate force toward reaching vital national objectives. The truly competent social studies mentor will be the crucial factor in attaining standards. Thus, it remains essential that these teachers have the understandings and skills which *Designing Effective Instruction for Secondary Social Studies* explicates and promotes.

Acknowledgments

We would like to acknowledge the following individuals for their assistance, encouragement, and suggestions in the development and refinement of this manuscript:

- Our wives, Barbara J. Dynneson and Jane Gross: confidantes, advisors, reactors, and editors
- Bob L. Taylor, University of Colorado
- James L. Barth, Purdue University
- Robert C. Rhodes, The University of Texas of the Permian Basin
- The Publication and Media staff, including Travis Woodward, Mark Newport, and Eugenia Worontsoff
- Julie Neal, student assistant
- Vickie Bevers, Bowie Jr. High
- Maudine D'Laine Young, student

Thomas L. Dynneson
Richard E. Gross

Contents

PART TWO
The Selection and Organization of Subject Matter   47

3
History and Geography: The Story of People, Places, and the Past   49

4
Political Science and Economics:
The Systems and Processes of Society   75

5
The Behavioral Sciences: Sociology,
Psychology, and Anthropology   99

PART FOUR
The Selection and Organization of Instructional Components   193

9
The Identification and Formulation of Instructional Objectives   195

10
Motivating Student Learning   213

11
Instructional Strategies and Activities   229

12

The Evaluation, Selection, and Development of Instructional Materials   265

13

Assessing Instructional Effectiveness and Learning Outcomes   285

PART ONE

Ideological and Historical Concerns:

PERCEPTIONS AND ORIGINS

What knowledge, skills, and values do social studies teachers need in order to become professional practitioners?

Over time, social studies educators have argued about the great social issues and how to address them in the classroom. More importantly, social studies educators have long debated the issue of how to best educate youth so they can lead successful lives in the United States. Modern instructional programs are based on philosophical, psychological, and ideological perspectives. To appreciate current and future instructional programs, you need to study varying perspectives in the history of the field. It is also important to understand the variety of philosophies that have contributed to social studies curriculum and teaching practices. Indeed, much of what is claimed as innovation is often cradled in the practices of the past.

One reason for founding the National Council for the Social Studies was to provide social studies teachers with a clearinghouse for ideas on how the social studies should be organized and taught in the schools. As a result of the work of the Council, social studies educators have been able to share many ideas and practices that have helped to enhance the further development of the social studies curriculum.

Ironically, schools have proven to be resistant to many of the ideas and practices that have been so popular with the leaders of the field. Paradoxically, the schools as institutions tend to cling to their traditional practices in spite of internal and external pressures that have attempted to move them. Those of you just entering this field need to understand the nature of social studies and its relationship to American society. In addition, this background on the cultural and historical forces that led to the development of current instructional programs is critically important to both beginning and experienced teachers.

The best instructional programs for the social studies do not consist of narrow single subjects or isolated, simplified presentations to young people. The best programs are orchestrated to address the physical, intellectual, and sociological needs of children and youth within the context of American society. As such, appropriate social studies education should rest at the heart of basic general education in our schools today.

The next two chapters will help prepare you to accept the challenge of providing your students with the best integrated, multidisciplinary instruction that will prepare them to be citizens in the "real world."

Perceptions, Ideologies, and Approaches Within the Social Studies

INTRODUCTION

In this chapter you will learn that the social studies is a complex and often confounding instructional area that is not easily understood by those just entering the teaching profession. Scholars who have spent years studying the history and development of the social studies acknowledge the difficulties of attempting to make clear sense of it; however the social studies can be understood by examining its goals, definitions, related terms, outlooks, ideologies, and approaches. These elements are the results of the traditions and influences that affect the development of educational institutions and policies.

Perceptions include those outlooks that are held by social studies educators regarding the best possible means for educating youth for their roles and responsibilities as citizens of their communities, nation, and world. *Ideologies* consist of the systematic bodies of beliefs about the workings of society; this includes the role that social studies education should play in society, based on broader comprehensive theories of human nature and learning. *Approaches* include applied stratagems for enacting instructional practices that embody the beliefs, values, and principles that were stated in the ideologies and theories of education applied to the field of social studies education. Because of the varied perceptions, ideologies, and approaches that have been applied to social studies education, a state of chaos is claimed to be characteristic of this instructional field. Professors Barr, Barth, and Shermis (1977), for example, contend that: "The field of social studies is so caught up in ambiguity, inconsistency, and contradiction that it represents a complex educational enigma. It has also defied any final definition acceptable to all factions of the field" (p. 1).

In time, you will begin to appreciate the complexities of the field as you delve deeper into the professional issues and problems that characterize the social studies profession. For example, the following list of goals is provided to help you realize something of the breadth and depth of social studies education.

The Goals of the Social Studies

The overall instructional goals of the social studies are often related to the following concerns:

- To prepare students for a changing world
- To broaden students' perspectives and understanding of the community, state, nation, and world
- To provide students with the knowledge, skills, and abilities they need in both their personal and public lives
- To help students relate to and understand the subject matter content of history and the social sciences including knowledge, skills, and values that are characteristic of social studies subject matter
- To contribute to the students' understanding of what it means to live in a complex and pluralistic society
- To provide students with an understanding of the means and processes of a representative form of government
- To encourage students to participate in the affairs of society and to work toward establishing a "good" society
- To promote important social goals associated with democratic living

The literature of the social studies has long acknowledged that its core value is a broadly defined citizenship education along with a relatively large number of goals associated with knowledge, skills, and values related to the content of the social science disciplines. According to Professor Saxe (1991), from its beginning the core of the social studies curriculum has been mainly concerned with socialization and citizenship education. Morrissett and Haas (1982) summarized the following social studies purposes associated with the content and pedagogical attributes of the field: knowledge, thinking skills, democratic beliefs, participation skills, civic action, problem solving, and social skills.

What Do You Think?

Program design must accommodate fundamental course aims and purposes. Can you suggest one or more goals for the social studies that are not included in the previous list? What crucial factors can you cite to support your addition(s) as major goals for the social studies curriculum?

In a 1992 official position statement, the National Council for the Social Studies (NCSS), recognized the disagreements and the diverseness of social studies goals and accepted locally set goal and programs over an attempt to establish a specific set of national goals, although in 1994 it was preparing a national statement.

> Among both social studies teachers and the general public there is disagreement about the relative importance of major social studies goals and content strands. Consequently, there never has been and may never be agreement on a single scope and sequence as the basis for a national social studies curriculum. Recognizing this, the NCSS curriculum guidelines state that goals-setting and program development should be undertaken locally in response to locally perceived needs. (p. 215)

One of the indirect results of this position may be to place a greater responsibility on teachers for identifying local social studies goals, and as a consequence, for developing programs.

Questions Regarding Social Studies Instruction

As an instructional area or field of the school curriculum, the social studies is complicated because the field lacks a clear understanding regarding a definitive organizational structure, clarity of purpose, explicit instructional agreements, or a conclusive professional status. In spite of these ambiguities, the social studies has provided an important instructional dimension to the education of American students, especially regarding their social education. In light of these concerns, the following questions are briefly explored to help you to focus on current concerns and influences in the social studies.

What Is "Social Studies"?

This question has no clear and definitive answer. For the past seventy-five years or more, social studies teachers have debated this question; most agree that the social studies is the study of humankind from a multitude of perspectives. Later, this question will be more meaningful in connection with the varying definitions for the term *social studies* that have been proposed.

Why Should the Social Studies Be Taught?

Every subject taught within the school curriculum must be justified according to its importance to society and its educational goals. While the term *social studies* recently has been used to label a host of disciplines and approaches that focus on human activity, the importance of the social studies must be defined according to the goals, applications, and functions that are assigned to it. In most societies, the study of history and its related social science disciplines educates youth about the heritage, customs, and traditions of society. The social studies is also assigned the important task of socializing students for their future responsibilities as citizens.

How Should the Social Studies Be Taught?

Teaching methods are usually determined by four important elements: the characteristics of the content, acceptable instructional practices, the nature of the instructional materials, and the learning attributes of the students. In addition, the means of instruction should include a consideration of the level of competence of teachers and the characteristics of the learner, including age, sex, and social background.

When Should the Social Studies Be Taught?

This question relates to the placement of courses and content elements within the curriculum. Social studies educators tend to disagree about the placement of courses and elements, but traditionally, certain subjects have been taught in the elementary school, junior high school, and high school. This issue often centers on "scope and sequence" debates regarding the best social studies framework or curriculum by grade level. A scope and sequence pattern involves curriculum design elements regarding the "range" and the "order" of topics. These design elements are arranged into patterns within the curriculum framework or outline. The scope and sequence pattern shown below is an example of a pattern that has greatly influenced secondary social studies curriculum.

Grade (Sequence)	Topic (Scope)
7th	State history and geography
8th	U.S. history and government with an emphasis on the period after the Civil War
9th	Civics, world geography, or state history
10th	World history or modern history
11th	U.S. history
12th	Contemporary problems related to the study of government, economics, psychology or sociology, and social science electives

In general, then, four factors must be considered in determining when the social studies should be taught:

1. *Scope and sequence patterns.* These include the range and order of topics to be taught.
2. *Student characteristics.* These include the level of mental and social maturity, prior experiences, culture and language ability, and innate intellectual ability.
3. *Values and philosophical and historical traditions.*
4. *Legal requirements.*

These influences help to determine the goals of instruction, the placement of topics, the patterns of presentation, and the basis for evaluating instruction.

WHAT WOULD YOU DO?

A scope and sequence design should reflect developmentally appropriate goals, content, definitions, and civic and personal needs, as well as recommended instructional approaches. What process would you use to generate a workable series of social studies offerings from grade one through high school? You may wish to display the elements of this process in the form of a chart.

Where Should the Social Studies Be Taught?

Social studies can be taught in a variety of settings inside and outside the classroom. Within the classroom, students can learn social studies content in large or small groups or individually. Social studies can be learned in either a competitive or cooperative environment, but a cooperative social arrangement is usually preferred to be consistent with the values and goals of the social studies. Within school, social studies can be taught in the classroom, library, or resource center. Outside school, social studies can be taught within the local community or in more distant places. Perhaps the most important place where social studies is learned is within the family and related social settings.

Is Social Studies a Discipline?

Most would agree that the answer is no; however, the possibility of becoming a discipline has been addressed and debated for many years. This debate began with the formation of The National Council for the Social Studies in the 1920s (Gross & Dynneson, 1983). In 1963 Samuel P. McCutchen delivered his presidential address to the forty-second annual meeting of the National Council for the Social Studies. His address centered on the need for social studies to become a discipline, thus revealing some insights into the focus of the social studies. McCutchen outlined the basis for the social studies discipline and suggested that it should be based on the following major elements:

1. The societal goals of the United States
2. The heritage and values of Western civilization
3. The dimensions and interrelationships of today's world
4. A specific process of rational inquiry and the tenets of good scholarship

Over the years social studies literature has included periodic articles that continue to address the ideological foundations of a social studies discipline in connection with the acceptance of an "official" definition for the social studies. In 1993, for example, James Barth published an article in which he outlined the following four basic beliefs that should represent the ideological foundation and focus of the social studies:

1. Social studies is citizenship education.
2. Social science and humanities concepts are integrated across disciplines for instructional purposes.

TO BE OR NOT TO BE A DISCIPLINE?

What are the basic elements that characterize a domain as a discipline? Do you accept the idea that the social studies in themselves should be considered as a separate discipline? Why or why not?

3. The proper content of the social studies consists of persistent and contemporary social and personal conflicts, issues, and problems expressed as concepts, topics, and themes.

4. Citizenship education requires the practice of problem solving and decision making throughout a social studies curriculum. (p. 57)

Barth goes on to state that if these are basic beliefs, then this definition of social studies would logically follow:

Social studies is the interdisciplinary integration of social science and humanities concepts for the purpose of practicing problem solving and decision making for developing citizenship skills on critical social issues.

This debate also suggests that the focus of the social studies is on societal issues that were expressed in the age of social reform known as the "Progressive Era." While new voices express new concerns related to the changing scene of American society, many of the debates over ideology center on definitions and on the inability of educators to agree on the content of the social studies.

The Definitions of the Social Studies

The term *social education* first appeared at the end of the nineteenth century when Conway MacMillan, a University of Minnesota professor, suggested that the schools be responsible for helping to promote and develop the social individual. The social individual was a person sensitive to the needs of the group as opposed to the promotion of self-interest (Saxe, 1991). The term *social studies* was first used by Thomas Jesse Jones as early as 1905, and in 1913 the term *social studies* was formally used as the name of the official Committee on

Social Studies as a part of the National Education Association report on the Reorganization of Secondary Education (Saxe, p. 16). By 1916 the term *social studies* was emerging as an acceptable term among educators as it was applied to the teaching of history and related subjects within the school curriculum. The term, according to Saxe, evolved into its present form according to the following transition:

> Beginning with social studies as rooted in the social sciences for the purpose of attending to social welfare, the term evolved into social studies grounded in social sciences for the purpose of directly educating future citizens. (p. 18)

The term *social studies* developed out of a curricular need to provide a descriptive label that would serve a curricular purpose:

> Simply put, social study was a helpful, descriptive phrase like "nature study," employed to describe the use of the social sciences in the schools for the development and nurturing of young citizens. (p. 20)

As a comprehensive label or umbrella term that included several disciplines, the "social studies" is not easily defined and to date, no single official definition has been agreed upon among social studies educators.

Since the inception of social studies, a number of definitions have been advanced in an attempt to unify the field and to clarify the term. Most of these definitions suggest that the social studies consists of a federation of academic subjects that focus on the study of people, especially in connection with the study of American society. Over the years, definitions of the term have changed to reflect changing interests and concerns. John U. Michaelis (1992) categorized definitions according to their emphasis on subject matter, society, and students. Irving Morrissett and John D. Haas (1982) point out that most attempts to define the term fall short of the criteria that Webster uses for such definitions by simply failing to define what the social studies is.

> Actually, very few of the proffered definitions would pass muster with Webster. Most preferred definitions of the social studies focus on the principal purposes of the social studies or on the methods used in social studies, bypassing a description of what social studies is (or are). A true definition tells what something is, not what it does or how it is accomplished. (p. 17)

The following definitions suggest something of the range of meanings that have been used to describe the social studies:

> The term "social studies" indicates materials whose content as well as aim is predominantly social. The social studies are the social sciences simplified for pedagogical purposes. (Wesley & Wronski, 1964, p. 3)

. . . a fusion or integration of the social sciences. (Wilson, 1933, p. 5; *First Yearbook of the National Council for the Social Studies*, pp. 118–131)

The social studies are . . . those [disciplines] whose subject matter relates directly to the organization and development of human society, and of man as a member of social groups. (Dunn, 1916, p. 9)

Social studies consist of adaptations of knowledge from the social sciences for teaching purposes at the elementary and secondary levels of education. (*Thesaurus of ERIC*, 1987, p. 226)

Social studies (are) that part of the school's general education program which is concerned with the preparation of citizens for participation in a democratic society. (Shaver, 1967, pp. 588–592, 596)

The social studies is an integration of experience and knowledge concerning human relations for the purpose of citizenship education. (Barr, Barth, & Shermis, 1977, p. 69)

An inter-disciplinary field of learning, drawing upon the concepts and means of the social sciences and related areas; it features problem-focused inquiry, ethical decision making, and personal/civic action on issues vital to students and society. (Gross, 1990, p. 14)

. . . a basic subject of the K–12 curriculum that derives its goals from the nature of citizenship in a democratic society that is closely linked to other nations and peoples of the world; draws its content primarily from history, the social sciences and, in some respects, from the humanities and science; and is taught in ways that reflect an awareness of the personal, social, and cultural experiences and developmental levels of learners. (NCSS, 1983; *Social Education, 48*, p. 251)

. . . primarily concerned with the study of those human relationships believed to be most important in developing responsible citizenship. It explores relationships and interactions of people in selected cultures and areas, with attention to the past, the present, and the future. It fosters the intellectual, social, and personal development of students in order to develop competence in preparing in decision making and other human activities. (Michaelis, 1988, p. 3)

In essence, social education represented a broad view of education based on social science, whereas social studies, although sharing the purpose of education based social science, was defined as a specific field of study within the general school curricula given over entirely to citizen preparation. (Saxe, 1991, p. 11)

One of most recent definitions adopted by the National Council for the Social Studies (NCSS, 1992; also in *Social Education)* states that:

Social Studies is the integration of history, the social sciences, and the humanities to promote civic competence. Within the school program, social studies provides coordinated, systematic study drawing upon such disciplines as anthropology, archeology, economics, geography, history, law, philosophy, political science, psychology, religion, and sociology, as well as appropriate content from the

WHAT'S YOUR POSITION?

Which of the definitions of the social studies field presented above do *you* accept? Explain why. If you do not agree with any of the definitions, propose a statement more satisfying.

humanities, mathematics and natural sciences. The primary purpose of social studies is to help young people develop the ability to make informed and reasoned decisions for the public good as citizens of a culturally diverse, democratic society in an interdependent world. (p. 213)

Because the social studies is characterized by conflicting goals and definitions, we have constructed the following definition that can be used in support of instructional design.

Social Studies is an integrated, broad field of learning, drawing upon the concepts and processes of history, the social sciences, and related areas; it features problem-focused inquiry, ethical decision making, and personal or civic action on issues vital to individuals and their society.

We hope that this definition will help interested educators distill the goals of instruction and design and plan effective instruction for students.

Related Definitions

Several related terms are also associated with the term *social studies* (Gross, 1990). Because these terms are used throughout the book to describe special topics of interest within the social studies, we will review them now to help you understand them prior to their use in the text.

- *Social Science.* The field of scholarly investigation that deals with human society and its characteristic elements. It is usually organized into branches of study, such as geography, political science, economics, psychology, sociology, and anthropology. (History, often viewed as a humanity, may or may not be included.)
- *Citizenship Education.* A total program that sometimes extends to related or cooperative experiences beyond the school. These programs

contribute particularly to the development of political or civic under-standings, skills, values, and actions in individuals and groups.

- *Behavioral Science.* Refers to those social sciences heavily devoted to the scientific collection of original data that reflects the direct behavior of individuals or small groups. The typical components are anthropology, psychology, and sociology.
- *Social Education.* A term that encompasses all school activities that enhance an individual's social competence.

Perceived Program Needs

Frequently, educators make recommendations for program design based on their perception of the nature of society, children, and subject matter content. During the 1930s, educators became involved in a great curriculum contro-versy regarding the "needs" approach in education, that is, what needs should be addressed by education. By the 1950s educators had identified three approaches that could be taken:

- teaching those things that had always been taught
- teaching those elements of knowledge (concepts, skills, and values) that adults need to cope with life in American society
- teaching to the needs of students or selecting those aspects of knowl-edge, skills, and values that are appropriate to the current lives of their students

Many educators were greatly divided by this issue and disagreed with the idea of developing a curriculum around the perceived, current needs of stu-dents (Taba, 1962):

> A special storm center was created around the problem of whether the individual or the social needs should have supremacy in determining curriculum content, and whether the studies of children and adolescents were sufficient as the basis for curriculum development. (p. 285)

In addition, some educators proposed that curriculum content should serve broad social needs. For example, during the era of the Great Depression, edu-cational reconstructionists such as Harold Rugg (1947) proposed social stud-ies programs that would re-educate American youth and thereby contribute to the reconstruction of American society. Most ideological positions are based on educating American students according to three factors: societal needs, child needs, and content needs.

Societal Needs

Educational programs are formulated to meet the needs of society by addressing the social, economic, and political education of students. Because of the complex nature of American society, however, there are few norms or traditions that every educator supports as a subject of study. As members of a pluralistic society, U.S. citizens do not share common racial and cultural backgrounds that might otherwise unite the nation. Differences in religion, cultural values, and language tend to divide Americans along ethnic and cultural identities. At the same time, as citizens, we do share a common outlook, an acceptance of a representative form of government, support for the U.S. Constitution, shared values associated with our democratic system of beliefs, and participation in a vast and complex economic system. An accessible nationwide media has also been influential in creating a shared common outlook. Consequently, educational programs tend to reflect both the similarities and diversity of American society.

In 1979, John Haas described the conservative interpretation of the relationship between the social studies and American society as one of "Conservative Cultural Continuity" (CCC) in which the social studies is assigned the role of socializing American youth to the "American way of life." Morrissett and Haas (1982) summarize this approach in the following statement:

> The CCC position relies heavily on tradition in Western civilization and in American society; on history as selected facts and events that enhance the prestige of the United States as the fulfillment and culmination of Western culture; on political science as the justification of the superiority of American republican democracy as a form of government and for the idealization of the citizen as the repository of power; and on political and economic geography to legitimize national destiny, state destiny, imperialism, and the U.S. capitalist economic system. The CCC approach ensures the perpetuation of a society's myths, ceremonies, and rituals, especially as these celebrate the socio-politico-economic status quo, the current conception of growth and progress, and an extreme gradualism as the preferred mode of social change. (p. 21)

This view is further echoed by Barr, Barth, and Shermis (1977), who describe the purpose of the social studies as follows:

> Social studies has functioned as a mirror for our society. Our society believes and acts as though it must perpetuate its beliefs, values, customs, and traditions—as, of course, do all societies. Schools function as just this vehicle for transmission;

and, of all of the school subjects, the social studies most insistently lends itself to being the repository of societal values and traditions. (p. 9)

Other authors have taken the position that the social studies can and should become an agent of social change and reconstruction. For example, Harold Rugg emphasized the reform of American society through educational means (Gross & Dynneson, 1983):

> According to this approach, the schools would become the agent for building a new society. Harold Rugg is one of the major educators associated with this approach. He spent a lifetime attempting to develop a curriculum that would help change American society. (pp. 25–26)

In light of this position, American society seems to be involved in a constant process of change, and as society changes, so should the teaching of the social studies. Therefore, changes in American society lead to changes in the social studies because the content of the social studies is, to some extent, influenced by current social, political, and economic conditions.

Thus, from within the large body of social studies literature, we learn that the social studies is seen from varied and competing perspectives with a wide range of conservative and liberal views. At the same time, the curriculum often lags behind societal changes. Today the social studies curriculum in many respects resembles the curriculum of fifty years ago. In many cases the current needs of society may be altered before school programs change; therefore, the social studies instructional programs seldom accommodate current conditions, let alone future needs. (A case in point is the isolated hour per week devoted to current events in many social studies classrooms.)

Child Needs

In addition to addressing societal needs, instructional programs also reflect educators' perceptions of the needs of children and the conditions of their lives. Even though these needs and conditions are varied and diverse, we must keep in mind that the social studies is an important aspect of socialization in which students are encouraged to acquire the knowledge, skills, and values that characterize American society.

Educators' perceptions of children's needs are reflected in their goals of instruction. The instructional programs and design patterns on which the goals are based represent attempts to transform theory into practice. Keep in mind that theory is derived from educational philosophy and is concerned with the nature of human beings—including how they learn and should be taught. In addition, theory is also derived from historical experience as in the tradition of instruction according to custom and practice.

For example, traditional theory was based on the idea that subject matter should be selected partly for the purpose of disciplining (training) the child's mind. However, child-centered theory was based on the notion that teachers were expected to address their students' personal needs within the instructional setting. At the same time, students were encouraged to work together cooperatively because cooperation was considered important as a way to advance collective decision making; decision making was considered a shared responsibility of teachers and students. In the social studies, the child-centered ideology was emphasized in the Progressive Era and in the life-adjustment movement of the 1930s and 1940s. This perspective was expressed in a more radical form in A.S. Neill's approach to child rearing as asserted in his book *Summerhill*.

Within the educational setting, needs are determined by tradition and by the educational programs that have been developed according to the goals of instruction. Once known, the gap between the desired state of affairs and the reality of the situation should be determined. In most situations, *needs assessment* is a process of comparing the goals of instruction with the content of the instructional program to determine how compatible the goals are to societal needs, student needs, and content needs. Student needs are determined through various forms of pre-instructional information including pre-instructional assessments and various means for gathering background information about each student.

Content Needs

During the twentieth century, American educators have expressed different positions regarding what students needed to know, do, and believe. The content needs issue centers on the question: *"What knowledge, skills, and values do students need to succeed in American society?"* Educators have answered this question in different ways. For example, some suggest that students need an information base as well as a set of essential skills for the continuous acquisition of knowledge. Other educators believe that students need to learn a process for solving problems so that they can better manage their public and private affairs. Still others believe that content must address students' needs to learn to cooperate and participate in the community and national affairs in order to help develop a "good" society. Because of the different answers given to this question, different instructional approaches were devised to resolve the issue of content needs.

Diverse Program Approaches

The social studies include several program approaches that reflect various beliefs regarding how to solve problems associated with societal, child, and

Can You Reach Agreement?

Can your class agree on a program rationale for social studies that balances the three areas of emphasis just suggested—disciplinary accent, amount of cognitive skills, and citizenship needs?

content needs. Content needs usually are addressed in a **rationale** (ideological position) **statement** on which the instruction is based, including the program approach that will be emphasized throughout instruction. This statement describes what is important in instruction and is the basis for writing instructional objectives. Subsequently, the priorities of instruction are identified in the rationale statement. So are the important elements (concepts, skills, and values) and components of design (objectives, motivation, strategies and activities, and evaluation). Also included are the instructional approaches (disciplinary, cognitive development, or citizenship) (Taba, 1962) that will be emphasized to address the question: *"What knowledge, skills, and values do students need to succeed in American society?"*

The diverse program approaches even further emphasize that social studies is a broad teaching field with differing points of view regarding what constitutes an ideal instructional program. As we mentioned earlier, some of these different points of view are ideological in nature, especially regarding the learning needs related to content. In addition, educational approaches represent educational values, some of which have persisted over time. These values are sometimes the subject of debate in educational organizations and institutions. Varying program approaches in the social studies emphasize basic issues such as the following:

- the extent to which disciplines should be emphasized
- the extent to which cognitive skills should be emphasized
- the extent to which citizenship education should be emphasized

These three approaches are described in the following sections.

Disciplinary Approaches

Disciplinary approaches are based on the belief that the social studies offers a means by which a discipline should be taught by modifying the content according to the age, experience, or maturity of the child. Throughout the nineteenth and twentieth centuries, the teaching of discrete courses in history, geography, and government was a common practice. In the Progressive Era and again in the 1960s, this practice was somewhat modified by the proponents of an integrated multidisciplinary approach, who tried to broaden the teaching of a single discipline. They advocated an instructional strategy in which a core discipline (a single discipline such as geography or economics) was supplemented with the content of the other social science disciplines.

In the 1930s educators had experimented with a variety of cross-field approaches in which the content from the social sciences was integrated with content from the humanities or sciences. This "fusion" of teaching fields was exemplified in "block" programs and various forms of the "core curriculum." At the heart of "fusion" was a progressive idea or principle that all knowledge is related or integrated. Therefore, separate disciplinary approaches were opposed because they had so departmentalized knowledge that students were unable to make connections across subject matter lines. Nevertheless, disciplinary approaches continue to thrive today. They consist of two basic organizations: the single-discipline approach and the integrated multidisciplinary approach.

The *single-discipline* approach tends to focus instruction on a discrete, usually indepth study of history, geography, government, and economics. The most distinguishing characteristic of this approach is its emphasis on content knowledge, methodological (disciplinary) processes, and various analytical skills through which topics and problems can be studied (Barr, Barth, & Shermis, 1977).

> Social scientists assume that there is a highest value—and that is the knowledge inherent in the disciplines. Stated briefly, it is better to know than not to know, to possess knowledge than to be ignorant. And, since they assume that the most valuable knowledge resides in the discipline, it is good for young people to possess such knowledge. (p. 79)

Therefore, students should be presented with the "structure of disciplines" (knowledge) of the subject. The structure of a discipline, according to some authorities (Chapin & Gross), consists of a conceptual framework and methods of inquiry.

> The structure of a discipline has two fundamental components or parts: (1) the *conceptual framework*, or the fundamental concepts, generalizations, and principles of the field; and (2) the *methods of inquiry* and research used by the scholars of the field. (p. 131)

Thus, the single-discipline (social science) approach applied to the teaching of geography would, for example, require the student to master concepts related to location, place, and space relationships within regions. In addition, among other concepts, the student would be expected to use maps and aerial photos in resolving geographic problems or clarifying a geographic relationship. Geography processes or methods of inquiry would be taught to students, and these processes would serve as classroom tasks and activities. Barr, Barth, and Shermis (1977) describe the reasoning behind this approach:

> In brief, then, social science teachers and curriculum-makers select valid concepts, problems, and processes from their disciplines. They organize them into a systematic introduction of social science knowledge, appropriate to students' ages and understanding. Out of the knowledge selected and organized by informed teachers will come, it is hoped, a more enlightened understanding of the world as it is and a better quality of citizenship. . . . (p. 79)

As a result of this approach, various teaching strategies and learning activities would resemble processes used by historians and social scientists in acquiring new information or in answering questions. The single-discipline approach also emphasizes scientific objectivity in the study of issues or problems; therefore, students are expected to express a reasonable level of skepticism regarding the claims, solutions, or conclusions regarding the complexities of the social world. An important goal of the disciplinary approach is to discipline the mind as well as to acquire content knowledge. Mental discipline includes the ability to resist the natural tendency to jump to conclusions or to make snap judgments about an event before it is completely examined. Therefore, a disciplinary approach is considered an important means of helping youth learn to withhold their judgments until they can examine factual information. Unfortunately this approach, especially in the hands of poorly prepared teachers, also has lead to the rote learning of content and to parroting memorized chunks of subject matter. In some courses of wide breadth, such as history, the urge to cover large amounts of information leads to content surveys and superficial treatment that promotes little, if any, worthwhile understandings and no skills except memorization.

Citizenship, according to this approach, is based on the ability of students to acquire a social science perspective that they can apply to decisions related to their responsibilities as citizens in a democratic society. According to Barr, Barth, and Shermis (1977), proponents of this approach claim that emphasizing social science content, skills, and values helps students to solve the social, economic, and political problems that they will confront as adults.

> The purpose of social studies defined as social science—which we shall simplify and refer to as Social Science—is that young people shall acquire the knowledge, skills, and devices of particular social science disciplines to the end that they become effective as citizens. (pp. 61–62)

The *integrated multidisciplinary approach* differs from the single-discipline approach in that it attempts to combine content from two or more of the social studies disciplines into an instructional approach. According to this approach, one discipline (for example, history, geography, or economics) is used as the core discipline, while the content from the other disciplines enriches and supplements the core. This approach was preferred by academicians who recognized the limitations of a single-discipline approach for pre-collegiate students. Lawrence Senesh (1971) proposed an "orchestrated" approach (a model integrated multidisciplinary approach) to advance the teaching of the social sciences within the social studies curriculum.

> In every grade we develop units in which different disciplines are called upon to play the dominant analytical role. We develop units in which the political scientists play the solo role, with the others playing supporting roles. We develop units in which the economist plays the solo role, while the other social scientists play accompanying roles; and so on. If this interplay among the different instruments of the social sciences is well done, the result is a well-orchestrated curriculum. (p. 27)

The recent recommendation by the National Commission on the Social Studies in the Schools (1989) seems to support an integrated multidisciplinary approach in which history and geography are to serve as the core of a subject-centered curriculum.

Cognitive Development Approaches

An important goal of the social studies is to develop cognitive skills (skills related to the ability to think in a systematic way). Cognitive skills are emphasized in the disciplinary approaches as a means of helping students deal with disciplinary content and societal issues. Also, cognitive skills taught as an instructional approach are sometimes called *reflective thinking.*

The reflective thinking approach is considered an important skill area in which students are required to learn one or more processes to solve a dilemma or a predicament. These processes are taught in the form of a model or an applied step-by-step method that guides the student through a specific procedure. In this approach, teachers play the role of guide as the student is expected to resolve the predicament. In addition, the teacher serves as a problem poser, resource source, individual advisor, and a tester or challenger of outcomes. The goal of reflective thinking is to help the student acquire "insight" through the processes of research and reasoning as opposed to expository teaching approaches in which information is directly presented to students. In addition, reflective thinking is an approach that shifts some of the learning responsibilities from the teacher to the student. Each variation of reflective thinking requires that students learn different or particular intellectual skills.

Do You Have an Opinion?

In your opinion, what is the major reason(s) that skill development has been largely overlooked by many social studies teachers in planning the content and emphasis of their courses?

The unfortunate slow and limited acceptance by teachers of this form of organization and instruction is related to a number of factors including the following: teachers' lack of experience with this approach in their own schooling, failure of social studies textbooks to organize and include problem-oriented content, the continued reliance on traditional disciplinary organization (and lectures) in college and university academic courses, failure to emphasize a skill-centered focus in teacher education offerings, tentativeness and lack of sure answers that can easily be assessed in testing and for grading, fear of controversial topics and heated classroom situations, and opposition to the schools' treatment of certain problems by various publics. (For a more detailed description, see the section on "Problem Settings" in Chapter 11.)

Socialization Through Citizenship Approaches

Faced with the complexities of the new industrial age at the beginning of the twentieth century, educators viewed with alarm the breakdown of family and community. Some reform-minded educators reacted by trying to replace the disciplinary approach in the social studies with a more socially relevant approach. Citizenship approaches were aimed at helping students adjust to American life and to live more productive and successful lives in spite of the changes, poverty, and chaotic conditions of the times. The educational reforms that followed were based on the progressive principles stated in the 1918 Seven Cardinal Principles of Education relating to health, citizenship, vocational preparation, ethical development, and the worthy use of leisure time as well as the fundamental processes or academic subjects described under disciplinary approaches. Based on the needs of students, these principles promoted a new social education that attempted to help students deal with contemporary social problems within their communities and understand the requirements of democratic citizenship.

Social studies instruction has been designed around the special interests and needs of students to help them to understand and face the conditions of life in American society. During the 1940s, a *life-adjustment* curriculum was proposed as a way to provide greater educational opportunities for the majority of students who were not planning to go to college (Pulliam, 1991). Life-adjustment curricula attempted to meet the needs of students by providing them with practical educational experiences. This approach has been attributed to progressive educators who attempted to apply the educational theories of John Dewey. A number of these programs associated with the life-adjustment movement were vocational in nature (Cremin, 1964); but proponents of issue-centered programs saw them as necessary for all learners (Fersch, 1955).

Also, in the 1940s and early 1950s blocks-of-time programs, core curriculums, and common learning courses expressed a general education approach that included social studies components. Common learnings courses often provided for high school students who were taking general education rather than college preparation courses. Segments of the common learning courses were aimed at helping students examine occupational choices and to help them understand some of the skills needed as workers and as consumers. Because these programs were loosely organized, students often were encouraged to pursue some of their own interests and to achieve some degree of self-realization. More recent expressions of humanistic and personalized approaches include Head Start programs, various individualized studies schemes, multicultural studies, values clarification exercises, environmental studies, a concern for individual rights and responsibilities, emphasis on ethical and moral development, global studies, and programs designed for at-risk students, often with vocational elements and part-time work experiences.

Citizenship education approaches tend to be value centered. Also, the citizenship education approach has characteristically emphasized the historic or traditional societal values associated with the evolving American way of life. In addition, this approach emphasizes fundamental democratic principles and ethics. Also, a citizenship education approach frequently emphasizes the development of problem-solving and critical thinking skills. These skills are applied in ways that encourage students to confront historic and contemporary issues and problems.

The citizenship education position is aimed at helping students become worthy citizens of the United States. The approaches of citizenship education are based on the belief that democratic American citizenship is more than an accident of birth. It requires that students adopt the shared cultural traits of their society including a knowledge of its commonly agreed to (social, economic, and political) systems, technologies, values and beliefs, standards of appropriate and acceptable behaviors, and the general consensus on the nature of a fair and just society. The most frequent method of instruction associated with citizenship education combines persuasion (through presentation, description, discussion, logic, analysis, and indoctrination) and aspects of critical thinking and problem solving (Barr, Barth, & Shermis).

The teaching tradition we have labeled Citizenship Transmission is dedicated to transmitting to the young a precisely defined image of society and of citizenship; yet different transmitters entertain different visions of the ideal society. But the essential point is this: the ultimate justification for wanting to transmit such an image is the guarantee of survival of society. Because of the Citizenship Transmission, teachers are never neutral vessels filled with objective information. Many of them are, in the nature of things, partisan, biased, and committed. These teachers are committed to a way of believing and acting which is designed to guarantee cultural survival. There is hardly anything more basic than this. (p. 60)

Therefore, the citizenship approach requires that students acquire the knowledge, skills, and values that are associated with society, the system of government, and a democratic way of life, and that they understand the events and influences that have contributed to current cultural conditions. According to Dynneson and Gross (1991),

In America, educating the people for citizenship was advanced by Hamilton and Jefferson as a means of assuring the establishment and continuity of the republic; therefore, citizenship in the democratic society tended to place an important and heavy burden on educational processes. In time, the public school system in America was given the mission of educating students for political literacy, including fundamental subject areas and skills related to the political system and the promulgation of democratic values. (p. 2)

Barr, Barth, and Shermis (1977) argue that even though there is a definite body of content to be mastered in the citizenship approach, according to the approach selected, "the actual content itself is not really important" (p. 77). What is important is *how* certain societal values are transmitted to students. The purpose of citizenship education is to instill in students the principles of an idealized American society. In this sense, citizenship education may be considered a reconstructionist approach. Earlier, Harold Rugg, George Counts, and other reformers wanted to use education to reconstruct American society in the wake of the Great Depression. Once an ideal society is envisioned, instructional programs would be developed to help attain that society (Rugg, 1947, Part Six).

In addition, an important goal of citizenship education is to help students develop social skills and positive social relationships, which are both essential if they are to become involved cooperatively and effectively in community affairs. In addition, students are expected to become more socially aware and knowledgeable of community, state, national, and world concerns. The value or affective elements of citizenship include a belief in social justice and a commitment to the development of a good society in which every citizen receives equal justice. This also requires the student to develop skills in and experience with resolving social, economic, and political strife through fair and rational conflict resolution.

CITIZENSHIP VS. SOCIAL STUDIES: WHICH IS WHICH AND WHICH SHOULD COME FIRST?

A continuing problem of social studies course design is the difference in the definitions of both social studies and citizenship education. Many readers may disagree with the claims of Professors Barr, Barth, and Shermis that specific content in citizenship education is relatively unimportant. Does such a position complicate or simplify the relationship and responsibilities between the social studies and civic education? How shall we determine the extent to which civic education is included in social studies? Or should it become a prime responsibility of the entire school enterprise? Can a model be devised that properly apportions the elements of citizenship education in the curriculum?

Like the term *social studies*, the term *citizenship education* is also difficult to describe and to define. Related terms such as "good" citizenship are even more confusing. Professors Barr, Barth, and Shermis (1977) express the difficulty of teaching the social studies when such perplexities exist.

> The content of social studies is a smorgasbord of this and that from everywhere; it is as confusing and vague as is the goal of citizenship, for not only do social studies educators have conflicting ideas as to how to create a "good" citizen, they cannot even agree on the meaning of the term. (p. 2)

In 1981 Professors Gross and Dynneson analyzed current social studies literature in order to list the variety of citizenship education approaches. The following box shows the results of this research: eight approaches to citizenship education.

From this examination of courses, study guides, sample units, and lessons as well as observations of civics and government teachers, we can clearly conclude that these elements of citizenship learning draw on aspects of most of the eight approaches to civic education described on page 25. Such a variety of concerns is an understandable result of the breadth of the concept of citizenship. But this very breadth may well suggest an imminent need to define citizenship more narrowly and to focus its prime responsibilities, particularly when it serves a specific purpose in the social studies program.

If, however, the eight approaches include numerous and different portions of vital civic learnings, curricular and instructional planners must have opportunities to evaluate contending program designs. Perhaps then, for example, we may gather solid evidence about whether the fundamental objectives of citizenship education can best be obtained via a single subject matter approach or through a thematic or a problem- or issue-centered one.

Citizenship as Persuasion, Socialization and Indoctrination—this approach is based on the assumption that students should be taught the norms and values of their society

Citizenship as Contemporary Issues and Current Events—this approach is based on the assumption that effective citizenship rests on an awareness of contemporary issues

Citizenship as the Study of American History, Civics, Geography and Related Social Science—this approach is based on the assumption that the discipline content of the social studies is important to the development of "good citizenship"

Citizenship as Civic Participation and Civic Action—this approach is based on the assumption that participation in community affairs is an important aspect of "good citizenship"

Citizenship as Scientific Thinking—this approach is based on the assumption that students need certain cognitive thinking skills in order to meet their future citizenship responsibilities

Citizenship as a Jurisprudence (legalistic) Process—this approach is based on the assumption that an awareness of the constitutional and legalistic process is an important aspect of democratic citizenship

Citizenship as Humanistic Development (concern for the total welfare of the student)—this approach is based on the assumption that the basic needs of the student must be met as a prerequisite to citizenship education

Citizenship as Preparation for Global Interdependence—this approach is based on the assumption that citizenship education includes an awareness and concern for world-wide needs, links, and responsibilities to humankind

Finally, the breadth of knowledge, skills, and values included in these eight approaches also reveals that citizenship education is in reality the responsibility of the total school program even though it is also a basic aim of social studies education. Therefore, civic education should be so recognized, planned, and apportioned throughout the entire educational enterprise.

CONCLUSIONS

In reading this chapter, you learned that for almost a century social studies educators have attempted to find one instructional approach that would unify the social studies field. Unfortunately, disagreement and a long-running debate about the direction of the social studies continue to characterize social studies instruction. Also, you learned that there is a very tentative agreement that citizenship education is the most acceptable emphasis for the social studies. Because citizenship education approaches include an array of orientations, almost any instructional approach might be taught under its banner. This being the case, it appears that the social studies, with its varied approaches, definitions, and orientations, is destined to remain a "smorgasbord" of approaches even with the agreement that citizenship is its core approach. At the same time, educators continue to hope that some new approach may be developed that will reorganize and unite the field.

For example, in the 1980s, Irving Morrissett and his colleagues (1982) made a valiant attempt to provide a unified approach that would accommodate a new direction through "Project SPAN." Although it was widely cited and received great attention, this proposal, as have so many others, failed to unify the social studies. It appears that before a new instructional approach can be accepted by all interested parties, it must address a multitude of cultural and educational expectations. Recall that the various points of view expressed in this chapter suggest that no single approach can entirely meet this requirement. Consequently, social studies instruction tends to represent diverse instructional emphases and subject matter compromises, none of which are accepted by all groups.

The field of social studies continues to change as does American education. While certain aspects of the field persist over time, other trends develop and fade according to the changing moods of the nation. The pendulum of change seems to swing widest between the two widely divergent ends of the ideological spectrum—that of the single-discipline approach and the more progressive and integrated student-centered social studies approach. Instructional design is influenced by changes in shifting ideological positions and perceptions.

This chapter should leave you with the impression that certain social, political, or economic conditions within American society help to determine the extent to which the social studies will emphasize one approach over another. The extremes of these positions seem to be expressed more in the form of debate and dialogue than in actual practice. In other words, you should remember that the ideological rhetoric of the social studies appears to be more a characteristic of intellectual debate at professional meetings and in professional literature than it is actually expressed as instructional practice within the schools. The practices of social studies classroom teachers are less extreme, more balanced, and less susceptible to change. While this stability has helped to protect teaching practices from the more radical or more antiquated recommendations of educational reformers, it also has worked to preserve some educational practices that have been ineffective and self-defeating. This reliance on the status quo suggests that most classroom teachers are little affected by social studies research, literature, leaders, or organizations. Therefore, commercial teaching materials such as textbooks have remained basically the same, thereby prompting few changes in instructional design.

REFERENCES

Barr, R. D., Barth J. L., & Shermis, S. S. (1977). *Defining the social studies* (Bulletin 51). Washington, DC: The National Council for the Social Studies.

Barth, J. L. (1993). Social Studies: There is a history, there is a body, but is it worth saving? *Social Education, 57,* 57.

Chapin, J., & Gross, R. E. (1973). *Teaching social studies skills.* Boston: Little Brown.

Cremin, L. A. (1964). *The transformation of the school: Progressives in American education 1876–1957.* New York: Vintage Books.

Dunn, A. W. (1916). *The social studies in secondary education.* (Bulletin no. 28). Washington, DC: U. S. Department of Interior, Bureau of Education.

Dynneson, T. L., & Gross, R. E. (1982). Citizenship education and the social studies: Which is which? *The Social Studies, 73,* 229–234.

Dynneson, T. L., & Gross, R. E. (1991). The educational Perspective: Citizenship education in American society. In R. E. Gross & T. L. Dynneson (Eds.), *Social science perspectives on citizenship education* (pp. 1–42). New York: Teachers College Press.

Fersch, G. (1955). (NCSS Curriculum Bulletin #9). *The problems approach and the social studies.* Washington, DC; also in a 1960 second edition.

Gross, R. E. (Summer, 1990). Curriculum and instruction in social studies. unpublished course manual.

Gross, R. E., & Dynneson, T. L. (1983). *What should we be teaching in the social studies?* Bloomington, IN: Phi Delta Kappa (Fastback #199).

McCutchen, S. P. (1963). A discipline for the social studies. *Social Education, 27,* 62–63.

Michaelis, J. U. (1988). *Social studies for children: A guide to basic instruction* (9th ed.). Englewood Cliffs, NJ: Prentice-Hall.

Michaelis, J. U. (1992). *Social studies for children: A guide to basic instruction* (10th ed.). Boston: Allyn & Bacon.

Morrissett, I., & Haas, J. D. (1982). Rationale, goals, and objectives in social studies. In *The Current State Of Social Studies: A Report of Project Span.* Boulder, CO: Social Science Education Consortium.

National Commission on Social Studies in the Schools (1989). *Charting a Course: Social studies for the 21st century.* Washington, DC: Author.

National Council for the Social Studies (NCSS). (1983). *In search of a scope and sequence for social studies.* Washington, DC: Author; and a preliminary report in *Social Education, 48,* 251.

National Council for the Social Studies (NCSS). (1992). *A vision of powerful teaching and learning in the social studies: Building social understandings and civic efficacy.* Washington: Position Statement of the Task Force on Standards for Teachers and Learning in Social Studies; also, included in *Social Education, 57,* 215.

Pulliam, J. D. (1991). *History of education in America.* New York: Merrill/Macmillan.

Rugg, H. (1947). *Foundations for American education.* Yonkers-on-Hudson, NY: World.

Saxe, D. W. (1991). *Social studies in schools: A History of the early years.* New York: State University of New York Press.

Senesh L. (1971). Orchestration of social sciences in the curriculum. In I. Morrissett and Stevens, W. W., Jr. (Eds.), *Social science in the schools: A search for rationale* (pp. 125–135). New York: Holt, Rinehart & Winston.

Shaver, J. P. (1967). Social Studies: The need for redefinition. *Social Education, 31,* 588–592, 596.

Taba, H. (1962). *Curriculum development: Theory and practice.* New York: Harcourt, Brace & World.

Thesaurus of ERIC, (1987). Phoenix, AZ: ORYX.

Wesley E. B., & Wronski, S. P. (1964). *Teaching social studies in high school.* Lexington, MA: D. C. Heath.

Wilson, H. E. (1933). *The fusion of the social studies in the junior high school.* Cambridge, MA: Harvard University Press; or (1931) *Some aspects of the social sciences in the schools: First yearbook of the National Council for the Social Studies.* Philadelphia: McKinley.

Origins of the
Social Studies

INTRODUCTION

In the following historical overview, we will discuss the changing nature of the social studies and the extent to which it is affected by social change in American society. The social studies as a field of study has been in existence for over seventy-five years; however, long before the term *social studies* was coined and debated, elements of social education were a part of American education. Even during the colonial period, elements of an important social education can be recognized. Following the American Revolution, new social, political, and economic institutions contributed to the eventual development of the social studies as it is currently expressed in instructional programs. In this chapter we will review the important periods of American history to identify and trace the evolution of the elements of social studies design from the past to the present.

For example, you will learn that prior to the twentieth century, social education was comprised of an assortment of elements related to religious education, geography, history, and civics. Not until the end of the nineteenth century did several discrete disciplines began to emerge and develop into what is commonly called the social sciences (Hertzberg, 1981). During this same time, higher educational requirements led to higher standards for teachers, which in turn led to the rise of professional teacher organizations. As a consequence of these events, subject matter areas would form into discrete teaching fields. Therefore, you will realize that the appearance of the social studies as a distinct field of social instruction would not occur until the early decades of the twentieth century.

English and Colonial Origins

David Saxe (1991) traces the "social studies" to an 1820s social welfare movement in Great Britain which was a product of the social problems created in part by the expanding urban and industrial culture. In American education, moral and religious training could be cited as early elements of social education dating back to the colonial period.

During the colonial period, religious instruction played a key role in the education of children. Some of the most important educational developments occurred in New England, and these patterns of education served as the basis for establishing a public school system during the decades that followed the American Revolution.

This era also was characterized by regional differences in the types of educational systems that would appear in North America. In time, this sectionalism became more important as populations grew and the institutions of society took shape. Sectionalism lead to differing value and belief systems that would eventually influence educational practices. The elements of social education that existed during the colonial period were based on sectarian instruction in the moral doctrines of the church. Biblical instruction prescribed specific moral codes (the "golden rule") of conduct and defined relationships within the family, church, and the religious state. The main ingredients of secular instruction focused on elements of geographic and historical concerns. Geography was of special interest since there were many unknowns within the physical world and at that time it was important to keep up with the constantly changing maps and extended explorations of the world. In addition, elements of English history were taught to encourage loyalty to the crown, as most educational practices were transplanted from England.

The New Republic

General education in the schools consisted of instruction in reading, writing, and arithmetic, while the home and community provided vocational training. Many of the features of public schools during the colonial period continued into the period following the American Revolution. Individuals such as Horace Mann worked to ensure that the states would provide tax-supported public schools for all students, regardless of a person's social class. During the first half of the nineteenth century, public elementary schools were founded in most of the northern states, while education in the southern states remained largely within the hands of families. Elements of social studies instruction included aspects of geography with a growing emphasis on history. Following the ratification of the U.S. Constitution, children were expected to study the characteristics and principles of the new government as well as recite the Bill of Rights. At this time, everything American came into fashion. Newly founded printing firms began to publish primers, spellers, and various textbooks for the growing numbers of public elementary schools. One of the most successful attempts to preserve moral values outside of the religious sphere was in the form of William McGuffey's readers, which "contain numerous moral lessons designed to teach appropriate behavior in a developing industrial society with increasing concentrations of wealth and expanding social divisions between the rich and the poor" (Spring, 1990, p. 143).

American textbook publishers were preferred over European printers, but the relatively small number of American firms limited the number of textbook offerings. The result of this limitation was that indirectly standardized instructional school programs were established in the nineteenth century public elementary school. While geography instruction continued to dominate social education, interest in the new republic spurred additional demand for history textbooks that included a study of ancient Western civilization. Civics was considered a part of history. Civics instruction continued to be organized with an emphasis on the Constitution, heroes of the American Revolution, and the structure and function of the government. Butts and Cremin (1953) note the huge increase in textbooks of all types during this period:

> In comparing the number of texts offered for sale in the years 1804 and 1832, one writer in the *American Annals of Education* noted that the total had risen from 93 to 407, and that the number of Spelling Books, Reading Books, and Arithmetics, [sic] had increased fourfold; of Grammars, threefold; of Geographies, sixfold; and Histories, eightfold; while a number of works have been published in branches of study which were then unknown in our school. (p. 271)

The Civil War and Aftermath

The epoch between the Civil War and World War I marked the beginning of modern education and the emergence of the modern school system (Pulliam, 1991). The Civil War settled many constitutional issues and ended slavery. By 1860 most states had accepted the idea of universal elementary education, and most states had provided or were in the process of developing tax-supported public elementary schools. During this period, the elements of social studies education came to include the important subjects of history, civics, and geography. History courses began to replace geography as an important subject to be studied. George Bancroft, a professor of history, influenced the development of history courses with a patriotic orientation, which he felt was needed to heal the nation following the Civil War. In addition, this patriotic orientation was used to help "Americanize" immigrant children into "mainstream" American culture. Bancroft helped to promote the idea of "the American Dream." Through hard work, one could find success and social mobility in the "New Eden" of America. George Bancroft's history, which exemplified a nationalistic or patriotic character, was history with a mission. Later, this "type" of history was modified by a scholarly history based on more scholarly approaches, approaches that emphasized the use of primary sources and research methodologies (Gross & Dynneson, 1983).

The emergence of the social studies parallels important social events in the twentieth century such as the formation of the common school during the last decades of the nineteenth century and the evolution of public high schools. According to Saxe (1991), social reformers during this time helped to transform American institutions, which included the schools, and educational reforms led to the emergence of the social studies.

> As education became a major issue of social reformers in the 1890s, the notion of social reform as education emerged under a common term. By the end of nineteenth century, the name for this type of development shifted from social science to social education and social studies. (p. 11)

Important social movements related to the Industrial Revolution and the urbanization of society came to dominate the politics of the nation. The changes that resulted from these movements grew out of an awareness of the nation's social problems and the attempts of progressive educators to use the schools to reform society. Massive immigration had continued to underscore the need for civic education. The social studies was singled out for an important role in educating students for modern living and for developing acceptable social values that underlay an industrial democratic society.

The most important difference between the teaching of traditional history and geography and the social studies was that from its inception, the social studies was based on three principles that would transform the old history and old geography tradition into a new hybrid social studies tradition:

1. This new tradition included history, geography, and social science content within a sociological orientation based on a social philosophy (the social welfare orientation of the British school).

2. The social studies included an instructional methodology based on the needs and characteristics of the student.

3. The social studies tradition embraced the realization that education had a social as well as an educational mission, a mission directly tied to the development of democratic citizens for American society.

In recent years, marketplace values and the need for highly trained workers have acted to displace the social orientation of the schools and to redirect

Is There a Relationship Between the Social Studies and Social Change in American Society?

Can you explain why the area of social studies emerged in the school curriculum when it did? Do any of these reasons explain why traditional subjects such as history and geography were charged with not meeting the educational needs of the era?

them into academic avenues of thought. According to some recent critics, the social studies should return to a disciplinary orientation (a scholarly form of historical and social science study) in which the facts, concepts, and generalizations of the disciplines should supersede social concerns. But, according to Saxe, from the beginning of the social education/social studies movement, the social sciences served a social purpose of social mission:

> . . . we find that the initial use and shaping of the term "social studies" was directly tied to the utilization of social science data as a force in the improvement of human welfare. (p. 17)

The connection between social studies and citizenship grew out of the need to advance the humanitarian concerns of the nineteenth century. According to this concern, "individual citizens should organize and become active participants in social welfare issues . . .". (Saxe, 1991, p. 19). The educational response to this need was to encourage the study of community civics as an important element of the social studies movement. During the Progressive Era, social reform movements attempted to address the growing social problems related to urbanism, industrialism, poverty, immigration, and corruption.

> Industrial growth carried with it the new problem of educating children in the urban slums and the need for Americanizing foreigners on a grand scale (Pulliam, p. 83).

Progressives and the Secondary School Movement

Tax-supported public high schools spread throughout the United States while the questions about the purposes of educational programs became important issues. High school enrollments dramatically increased by 1900. Over half of the states had enacted compulsory attendance laws, and public school enrollments were rapidly increasing. During this same period, John Dewey, the foremost American philosopher, helped to establish progressive education as an educational theory for educating the public. At the same time, separate social science disciplines, which were focused on specific aspects of American social life, were breaking away from the history curriculum.

The social studies curriculum evolved into a formal structure of courses and programs during this period. The social studies curriculum was greatly influenced by a series of national committees that worked on the purpose and programs of the public schools.

- *The 1893 National Education Committee of Ten (The Madison Conference)*. This committee attempted to resolve a basic question about the mission and the purpose of the emerging high schools. In their final recommendation, committee members recommended a strong academic program for students who would not go beyond the high school. History should emphasize "scientific" history over "patriotic" history. The goal of this committee was to "modernize" the secondary curriculum and to establish a set of standard history courses that would prepare college-bound students for university admission.

- *The 1899 AHA Committee of Seven*. Sponsored by the American Historical Association, the members of this committee consisted of seven eminent historians. The committee recommended that in the high school history curriculum students would learn to study events and issues through a "scientific" analytical approach in which historical evidence would be a major part of the pedagogical approach. The committee conducted a survey of schools and used the data gathered to prescribe an ideal pattern of courses to the schools.

- *The 1905 AHA Committee of Eight*. This committee consisted of eminent historians who were concerned about the teaching of history in the elementary school. They recommended that Old World history should be taught in the sixth grade as background for the American history that would be taught in the high school. According to Barr, Barth, and Shermis (1977),

The historians argued that history was the repository of the great classical ideas and ideals of humankind that were prerequisite to effective democratic citizenship, and that the task of learning this encyclopedic factual knowledge of the past was sufficiently difficult to discipline the faculties of the mind. Thus, the historians shrewdly met the concerns of the mental disciplinarians and the classicists without overtly breaking with the traditional use of history to promote good citizenship. (pp. 19–20)

- *The 1916 National Education Association (N.E.A) Commission on the Reorganization of Secondary Education—Committee on the Social Studies*. In 1912 the N.E.A. set out to provide a new curriculum structure for the nation's secondary schools. The committee was responding to social

WHY WAS A SOLO HISTORICAL PERSPECTIVE DEEMED ADEQUATE FOR THE NEEDS OF AMERICAN CITIZENS?

Why did some early Progressive education theorists believe that history, as then organized and taught, was an insufficient core of social education? Why might the study of history be considered a rear-view outlook on society? How might this view limit its application to current problems of society?

changes in the United States that had resulted from rapid urbanization and industrialization following the Civil War. At the same time, the number of immigrants arriving in the United States from southern Europe was increasing rapidly. All of these changes further stressed the social and political institutions of the nation. Traditional history had fought its way into the public school curriculum, especially thorough the efforts of the Committee of Seven. But, in light of the changing social fabric of American society, progressive educational reformers viewed history as an inadequate carrier of the social goals that they espoused. According to Saxe (1991),

> From 1902 to 1916 the battle lines were drawn between the three camps concerned with history in secondary schools: (a) those who accepted and sought the maintenance of the traditional history curriculum as written by the Committee of Seven; (b) those who criticized the program and called for revision, yet chose to remain within the general guidelines of the program; and (c) those who rejected outright and argued for the complete reformation of the discipline. . . . social studies insurgents took the initiative to bring the history curriculum in line with the push for more socially efficient and socially responsible schools. (pp. 83, 142)

Social Studies as Curriculum

The reform movement that opposed traditional history became known as the "social studies" and, while this movement failed to replace established history in the curriculum, it did open a new age in educational thought and practice in the schools. Prior to 1916, social studies teachers had been called history teachers regardless of their teaching specialty. While those who taught history in these early years found a professional home within the National Education

Association and the American Historical Association, there was a growing trend for teachers to form "councils" that more specifically addressed their needs and interests. As stated previously, on March 3, 1921, at the annual meeting of the National Education Association's Department of Superintendency held in Atlantic City, New Jersey, a small group of educators met and decided to form a national association for social studies teachers (Gross & Dynneson, 1983). At about the same time, a major power shift was occuring in American education that would open the door for a new type of social studies education that differed from the study of history and geography.

> The 1916 NEA Committee broke dramatically with tradition by assembling, for purposes of determining school curriculum, a group of scholars who were not subject matter specialists. With a few exceptions, the vast majority were public school and university educators. . . . This was the first time a national curriculum committee had been organized that was not composed largely of historians and social scientists; and for the first time, the school curriculum and the academic disciplines were considered from a far different perspective than the "add course" approach to curriculum reform. (Barr, Barth, & Shermis, 1977, p. 25)

In education, the teaching and learning principles of John Dewey were influential in leading teaching toward community-centered citizenship education, scientific inquiry, and participatory learning to support the development of this new industrial democracy. The authoritarian nature of the disciplinary approach was to be modified in favor of an applied (authentic human actions) approach that attempted to meet the needs and aspirations of typical citizens. Recall that the final report of the NEA Commission contained a list of Seven Cardinal Principles that were well grounded in progressive theory. They included the following:

- Health
- Command of fundamental processes
- Worthy home membership

ISN'T EIGHTY YEARS OF AN ESTABLISHED SCOPE AND SEQUENCE ENOUGH?

Why do you think the 1916 recommendations of the N.E.A. Commission on the Reorganization of Secondary Education has had such a long-lasting influence on the design of social studies programs in the United States?

- Vocation
- Citizenship
- Worthy use of leisure
- Ethical character

The influence of the progressive movement gave direction and meaning to the social studies, and from that time to the present, the social studies has acknowledged the foregoing principles as they try to accommodate those who espouse the more traditional values of the academician.

The Battle over the Social Studies

Education was directly influenced by the international issues and new technologies that emerged from World Wars I and II. The Great Depression also raised many social issues concerning the role of government as a regulator of society and as a mediator in class conflicts over the growing gaps between the rich and the poor. These troubled years bore witness to a continuing dialogue regarding the role and the nature of history instruction in the social studies curriculum. Conflict between traditional members of the academic community and supporters of progressive education surfaced frequently. This long and heated debate fueled various educational reform movements, and the rift between academicians and educationalists widened over time. This rift had the effect of splintering any hope of unity or consensus within the social studies and its affiliated groups. As we previously stated, the NCSS was founded by academics and educators in 1921. Even though it was partly supported by the AHA initially, it was not able to gain substantial agreement about the prime content and emphasis for the social studies (Gross & Dynneson, 1983). As late as 1995, it was still trying to reach an agreement on a definition of the field!

In 1926 the American Historical Association report on History and the Social Studies declared the teaching of history in the public schools was "candidly moribund." As a consequence, a new Commission on the Social Studies was organized under the leadership of Professor Charles Beard. At the same time, social reconstructionists attempted to reform American society, and as a result of Franklin D. Roosevelt's administration, many of these reforms were expressed in the law and in the expansion of a vast federal bureaucracy. Reconstructionist educators, including some historians, were again ready to develop an interpretation that was designed to reform society. Consequently, historians could not agree on how history should be taught in the schools. Charles Beard had attempted to address the teaching of history and the social studies in the public schools in the

?

WHAT IS "HANDS-ON AND HANDS-OFF" LEARNING?

Are there some unique social studies design and organizational features that may make historical and social science subject matter content more interesting to students than that offered by the traditional disciplinary approaches? What are these? Why would these hold greater appeal for learners?

1930s; however, his full committee failed to adopt their own document on "Conclusions and Recommendations." Many teachers were disappointed that the commission failed to agree on and recommend a basic K–12 social studies curriculum. While much of the work of the commission was well received, the attempt to replace citizenship education with a scholarly type of history and social science was doomed to failure (Gross & Dynneson, 1983). Many teachers were unhappy with the commission's failure to spell out a detailed and complete course of study. Not until 1989, when they created another National Commission on the Social Studies, did educators try to set up a similar type of study.

Reconstructionist educators also tried to introduce school reform that would reorient students to reform society. Harold Rugg, for example, developed "new" reconstructionist textbooks for the social studies. These books came under attack by conservative interests, and Rugg was labeled a "socialist." With the beginning of World War II, the appeal of social reconstruction diminished, and once again, historians began to critically re-examine how history was being taught in the public schools. Historians were especially motivated by a desire to purge the social studies of its progressive orientation.

The social studies came under the attack of university historians, including Ralph W. Robey, who examined the quality of history textbooks in the public schools; Allan Nevins, who attacked the nature of the social studies program for its integrated and weak content, calling the social studies "social slush"; and Arthur Bestor, who authored two critical books on the failure of public education in light of the growing Soviet threat. The National Council for the Social Studies responded to these charges and defended the social studies as best it could.

Reforming the Social Studies

In 1957 the success of Sputnik, the orbiting Soviet satellite, convinced many that progressive education had failed the American public. Sputnik lead to an educational reform movement in the United States that attempted to replace progressive education with a new academic education. This movement emphasized separate courses in the disciplines and advanced academic training for students of ability. After Sputnik, the times called for the inclusion of history and all of the social science disciplines in which selected aspects of each discipline could provide a broader and more balanced social studies curriculum. This broader array of topics had the effect of breaking the traditional hold that history, geography, and civics had on the social studies curriculum since its inception (Jenness, 1990). The federal government sponsored curriculum reform projects that designed and published curriculum materials, many of which were centered in the social science disciplines. According to Barr, Barth, and Shermis (1977), the government's efforts provided rich opportunities for program improvements:

> Both historians and social scientists were attracted to the field of social studies by the lure of huge federal grants for curriculum development. Almost overnight, scholars in all of the social sciences and history began curriculum development projects. Never before had an effort at social studies revision begun with such popular support and financial backing, and with such an abundance of scholars from so many academic disciplines [often] working together. And the curriculum materials they produced were both innovative and stimulating. (p. 35)

The federal government sponsored these projects through the National Science Foundation and the National Defense Education Act. Notable scholars, including Jerome Bruner, helped establish guidelines to be followed in developing new curricula through his influential book, *The Process of Education* (1963). Bruner suggested that project directors base the new social studies materials on four important principles: the structure of the discipline, readiness for learning, intuitive and analytic thinking, and motives for learning.

Ultimately, over fifty social studies projects were organized to reform the social studies curriculum. These projects were mainly disciplinary in nature and emphasized the scientific approach to problem solving (Barr, Barth, & Shermis, 1977). It was clear that much of the "new social studies" would take on a strong disciplinary orientation aimed at developing curriculum materials for teaching each of the seven social studies disciplines as separate entities. But it was also clear that the disciplinary approach required instructional materials that emphasized the "nuts and bolts" of the disciplines—facts, concepts, and generalizations (Bruner, 1963).

The group responsible for the movement away from social studies (and its emphasis on citizenship education) and toward the social sciences was the federally funded Social Science Education Consortium under the direction of Irving Morrissett. Morrissett and W. Williams Stevens, Jr. laid out the rationale for this approach in an influential book entitled *Social Science in the Schools: A Search for Rationale* (1971). In spite of the work of the consortium, though, the social science movement was not able to

HAVE YOU EXPERIENCED ANY CREATIVE CLASSROOM LEARNING ACTIVITIES?

Have you ever personally experienced a broad field, multidisciplinary social studies course that was organized and presented via a topical, thematic, or problems approach? If so, describe it and explain why you reacted positively or negatively to it.

unseat citizenship education from its traditional role as the primary goal of the social studies. The social science movement was further hindered by several influences that moved the social studies in another direction. The civil rights movement tended to focus education on the underclasses and the study of values. In addition, the social studies experienced a resurgent interest in citizenship education, an interest that continues to influence the curriculum.

Maurice Hunt and Lawrence Metcalf (1968) suggested that the social science skills and knowledge be merged with the goals of the social studies and citizenship education. They suggested that the social studies curriculum be organized around "closed areas" or topical subjects that were important to the students' understanding of society. "Closed areas" included sociological and psychological concepts treating sex, religion, morality, race, and other important social subjects that are often "closed" to discussion and debate—some of the taboos of American society. Simply stated, the social studies should deal directly with some of the most important value issues of our times. The unrest in American society unleashed by the unpopular Vietnam War further strained school programs, and in many instances, curriculum anarchy nearly evolved.

During this same period, the civil rights movement would overtake curriculum reform and became the most important social issue of the day. Consequently, the momentum shifted away from curriculum reform to issues of poverty and prejudice. By 1977 the "new social studies" movement ended because its funding had ceased, and most of the reform curriculum materials became relics of experimentation. The new emphasis in the social studies was on values and related approaches such as value clarification. In time, a subjective values education would be opposed as the social studies lost status within political and educational circles. The back-to-basics movement, with its emphasis on the three Rs, lead to a deemphasis of the social studies, especially in the elementary schools (Barr, Barth, & Shermis, 1977).

In Search of New Directions

By the mid-1970s into the 1980s, citizenship education had made an impressive comeback, and most reasonable advocates of social studies education were willing to concede that citizenship education was the accepted organizing core of the social studies. At the same time, the back-to-basic movements had discounted the importance of social studies instruction in the schools. This caused leaders of the social studies profession to search for new directions to revitalize the social studies and improve its status with the public and within the schools. Barr, Barth, & Shermis (1977) describe the continuing confusion:

> The 1970s arrived with the social studies once again under attack and still searching for identity. Looking back from our vantage point in the late seventies, it would seem that the issues that had confronted the social studies for the past 70 years [sic] were still unresolved: concerns over the question of indoctrination, conflicting goals of instruction, and disputes over content. (p. 35)

A national educational reform movement, which began with the publication of *A Nation at Risk* in 1983 and was followed by a series of similar reports, has profoundly influenced the orientation of the social studies. Critics of the social studies, including Chester Finn, then a federal education official and Diane Ravitch, a historian, responded with the Educational Excellence Network, which, among other goals, promoted the teaching of history and geography as the most important content areas of the social studies. The concerns and recommendations of these critics were based on national test results that suggested that student knowledge of American history was unsatisfactory. At the same time, reports on the weaknesses of student knowledge of geography were appearing in the media. As a result of these reports, Finn and Ravitch called for reforms that would focus the social studies curriculum on history and geography instruction. If, according to these critics, educational reforms were to be based on the outcomes of national test results, change in instruction would encourage better test results.

Those who disagreed with the critics of the social studies feared that instruction would become focused on history and geography with little room for the other disciplines of the social studies. In addition, the teaching of history and geography would emphasize dates, persons, events, and place-name knowledge, an approach that was similar to the educational practices in the social studies of a century ago (Gross, 1988). These fears also were reinforced as some states began to revise their social studies frameworks to emphasize history and geography as the core of the social studies. In 1986 the National Council for the Social Studies and cooperating associations organized a National Commission on Social Studies in the Schools. In 1989 this commission issued a final report entitled, *Charting a Course: Social Studies for the 21st Century*, which was received with a mixture of reactions because of its recommended emphasis on history in the curriculum. Some of the members of the Council believed that these recommendations signaled a return to an earlier age when history dominated the curriculum and led to an overemphasis on the memorization of names, dates, and trivial facts. Under President Bush, the role of social studies education reflected much more of a disciplinary orientation as was stated in goal 3 of educational reform known as *America 2000*. According to this recommendation:

> By the year 2000, American students will leave Grades 4, 8, and 12 having demonstrated competency in challenging subject matter including English, mathematics, science, history, and geography, and every school will ensure that all students learn to use their minds well so they may be prepared for responsible citizenship, further learning, and productive employment in our modern economy. (U.S. Department of Education, 1993, p. 57)

Currently, the membership of the Council remains divided over the direction in which the social studies seems to be going. Therefore, these issues will continue to be debated, even as new textbooks are being printed that reflect the history/geography emphasis. Citizenship, it was believed, would follow from historical and geographic knowledge and would not need special attention beyond these fundamentals. The transmission of knowledge was to supersede citizenship development as the primary goal of the social studies. These issues illustrate the fundamental differences within the social studies between what academic experts want for and expect of the social studies and what professional educators and many parents and citizens want and expect from social studies.

Today as in the past, these same ideological issues continue to be debated in connection with education reform. Today the trend in social studies is to accommodate both the supporters of traditional history and those who support the more sociologically oriented social studies. In the last decade of the twentieth century, the advocates of traditional history will provide continuing

ARE THE REFORMERS IN NEED OF REFORMING?

In recent years, reforms related to the integrated and civic value of social studies have come under increasing pressure. Why do some professionals and lay critics claim the social studies need to be reformed? Is the current attempt by disciplinary scholars to reinstitute their subjects as the core of social education appropriate and defensible? Why or why not?

criticism and call for further change in the more progressively oriented social studies programs. The proponents of a citizenship/issue-centered social education will have their counter positions to forward.

CONCLUSIONS

In this chapter you have learned that the social, economic, and political conditions that are of concern to the public help to determine the direction of educational institutions in the United States. Also in connection with Chapter 1, you have learned that educational institutions are expected to serve social needs as well as educational needs. In justifying the establishment of the common school (public school), in the 1930s Ellwood Cubberley listed the following arguments in favor of a new social education:

> . . . prevention and reduction of poverty and crime; increased work force productivity; elimination of "wrong ideas as to the distribution of wealth"; reduction of tensions between social classes; elimination of charity schools because they stigmatized a certain class in society; assimilation of immigrants; and preparation of the citizenry for the exercise of the right to vote. (Spring, 1990, p. 76)

These social goals were assigned to the public school during the early twentieth century. Social studies education is, to some extent, derived from the social thought and goals of the common school movement. An important theme that was developed in this chapter was that, from the beginning, the social studies was rooted in the problems of social transition, the problems associated with converting American society from a rural society to an urban/industrial society. This transition produced a new, complex, diverse, and somewhat chaotic social environment. Out of this environment, a social reform movement emerged under the banner of "progressivism." These reformers scrutinized every aspect of American society, including the purpose and role of educational institutions and programs in light of concerns enumerated by Cubberley above. The social studies emerged, therefore, as an aspect of a new social education.

Moreover, we discussed the united efforts of social studies educators of the early twentieth century to reform the teaching of history, geography, and government in the school and to focus instructional programs on the social concerns of the times. At the same time, educators were divided about the nature of the social studies instruction. For some, the social studies should become a means of social change; for others the social studies should become the means for including additional social science disciplines in the school curriculum. A few leaders recommended that the social studies should become a new discipline in its own right, a discipline based on the integrated content of history and the social sciences in conjunction with addressing important contemporary social problems, training in reflective thinking skills, and developing a new "scientific pedagogy." In addition, we described how a social studies vision was often thwarted by theoretical problems such as the failure of elementary and high school teachers to accept the theories and leadership of social studies educators in colleges and universities (Leming, 1989).

We also described how the ambiguity of the social studies made it a target for criticism from diverse groups that often have intimidated professionals from forwarding the concepts envisioned by its founders in 1921. All of these conflicts led to the inability to agree and define the mission, scope, and methodology of the social studies. Because most of these original problems have not yet been resolved, the social studies continues to lack the direction and unity that is so essential to the development of a social studies discipline. This lack of unity and direction is expressed in ideological differences, a multitude of approaches and recommendations, a general inability to agree on a definition for the term *social studies*, and the unfortunate failure to agree on a scope and sequence of courses for the social studies curriculum. From the inception of social studies, social studies leaders have not been able to forge the diverse interests of various groups within the field into a united discipline. In spite of these problems, the social studies field does agree on certain elements, for example, that at the core of the social studies is the need to educate American youth for citizenship.

Remember that prior to the early twentieth century, before there was such a thing as "social studies," the study of human affairs in the schools consisted of the expository study of history, geography, and related elements of civics. The progressive mission associated with citizenship education gained a new acceptance during the twentieth century. Because of citizenship education, social studies instruction was redirected to help students become effective decision makers and responsible citizens. In other words, the social studies began as a reform movement to change the character of education. These reforms attempted to make education a shared or cooperative teacher/student learning responsibility. According to this approach, teachers and students were expected to jointly explore some of the most pressing historical and modern social problems of American society.

As a result of this historical overview, you should have come to realize that social studies instructional design aimed to incorporate certain instructional elements into a comprehensive new instructional field. These elements included a study of the social problems of society and the interests and needs of individual students; a cooperative rather than competitive learning arrangement; the development of decision-making and problem-solving approaches to learning; the clarification and modification of values related to personal decision making and democratic behaviors; and the reconstruction of an idealized or "good society." Later, the citizenship education approach was interrupted by an instructional approach in which the social science disciplines attempted

HAVE YOU LEARNED ABOUT THE RELATIONSHIP BETWEEN THE SOCIAL STUDIES AND AMERICAN SOCIETY?

As a result of your reading, thinking, and discussion, what can you identify as the most helpful and valuable insights of being familiar with the history of the field of the social studies? For example, do current social phenomena such as increased immigration of non-Europeans, the disintegration of traditional family structure, serious challenges to the environment, and the erosion of worthy personal values and behaviors encourage the development of a single social studies discipline or promote the extension of social education via the study of separate disciplines?

to change the emphasis in citizenship education and to develop new instructional design components. Still later, history and geography would once again attempt to redefine citizenship and to reassert some of the same expository approaches that had dominated in the past. And the query must remain: "What proof exists that these latest reforms will lead to a design and approach that will rescue the social studies from its over three-quarter century dilemma?"

REFERENCES

Barr, R. D., Barth, J. L., & Shermis, S. S. (1977). *Defining the social studies* (Bulletin 51). Washington, DC: National Council for the Social Studies.

Barth, J. L. (1993). Social Studies: There is a history, there is a body, but is it worth saving? *Social Education 57*, 57.

Bruner, J. (1963). *The process of education.* New York: Vintage.

Butts, R. F., & Cremin, L. A. (1953). *A History of Education in American Culture.* New York: Henry Holt.

Gross, R. E. (1988). Forward to the trivia of 1890: The impending social studies program? *Phi Delta Kappan, 70*, 47–49.

Gross, R. E., & Dynneson, T. L. (1983). *What should we be teaching in the social studies?* (Fastback #199). Bloomington, IN: Phi Delta Kappa.

Hertzberg, H. W. (1981). *Social studies reform 1880–1989.* Boulder, CO: Social Science Education Consortium (project SPAN).

Hunt, M. P., & Metcalf, L. E. (1968). *Teaching high school social studies: Problems in reflective thinking and social understandings* (2nd ed.). New York: Harper & Row.

Jenness, D. (1990). *Making sense of social studies.* New York: Macmillan.

Leming, J. L. (1989). The two cultures of social studies education. *Social Education, 53*, 404–408.

Morrissett, I., & Stevens, W. W., Jr. (1971). *Social science in the schools: A search for rationale.* New York: Holt, Rinehart & Winston.

National Commission of Social Studies in the Schools. (1989). *Charting a course: Social studies for the 21st century.* Washington, DC: Author.

Pulliam, J. D. (1991). *History of education in America* (5th ed.). New York: Merrill/Macmillan.

Saxe, D. W. (1991). *Social studies in schools: A history of the early years.* New York: State University of New York.

Spring, J. (1990). *The American school 1642–1990* (2nd ed.). New York: Longman.

United States Department of Education. (1993). *America 2000: An educational strategy.* Washington, DC: Government Printing Office.

PART TWO

The Selection and Organization of Subject Matter

DESIGNING INSTRUCTION ACCORDING TO APPROACHES AND DISCIPLINES

What disciplinary understandings, background knowledge, and skills do teachers need to know to successfully design and present units, courses, and lessons to students?

As future teachers you will learn that the selection and organization of social studies subject matter takes place mainly within a curriculum plan. This plan usually is designed under the supervision of state and/or school district officials with some consultation and input from selected committees that include classroom teachers. The individuals responsible for these tasks must have an in-depth knowledge of the unique focus, strengths, and methodologies for solving problems in each of the seven social studies disciplines. As secondary social studies teachers, you also will want to be knowledgeable about these same disciplines. The chapters in Part Two of this text will help you explore how these disciplines have been used within the social studies curriculum. (Chapter 15 also contains a helpful discussion regarding curriculum issues and elements related to design.)

You may recall from Chapter 1 that the selection and organization of subject matter is often associated with instructional approaches. These approaches were developed to reflect certain ideologies and content needs based on a particular view of the nature of American society and the educational needs of American students. For example, you learned that, as a broad teaching field, the social studies includes three major instructional approaches: a disciplinary approach, a cognitive development approach, and a citizenship education approach. According to these approaches, subject matter should be selected and organized in conjunction with specific program needs. In addition, teachers may select and organize subject-matter content to meet their program needs. For example, a social studies teacher may be required or wish to use a single-discipline approach (for example, government), while in another situation the teacher may be required or wish to use a multidisciplinary approach (for example, drawing on government, economics, geography, and sociology). Similar choices may be made when disciplinary content is selected and used for training students in various cognitive thinking skills and in the various citizenship education approaches.

Therefore as a teacher, you should try to become familiar with the features of each discipline and how it is used within social studies courses, units, and lessons to understand the various content options that are available to you. This same knowledge will be useful in helping your students to understand the nature of the materials that they are studying. According to the instructional design experts Gunter, Estes, and Schwab (1990),

> Only when teachers consider the organization of content carefully and can explain the reasons for the order in which material is presented, is it possible for students to have an overall understanding of what they are learning. (p. 35)

The following three chapters describe social studies instruction from a subject-matter content perspective and explain how the characteristics, history, and use of each of the seven disciplines fit in the social studies curriculum. After studying these chapters, you should be better equipped to provide your students with the most appropriate separate-subject or integrated, multidisciplinary courses, units, and lessons.

History and Geography: The Story of People, Places, and the Past

INTRODUCTION

For many of your students, history will be an exciting story about exceptional individuals who helped to direct the course of human affairs. Well-written history can stimulate the imagination of students and motivate them to delve into the past to learn more about the real-life successes and failures of people. For most of us, history serves as a collective memory of the people that is passed on from one generation to the next. From this reservoir of knowledge, the present generation draws on the experiences of the past and, in turn, makes contributions to succeeding generations.

You will find that the importance of geography is found in a natural human fascination with both common and exotic places and with the lives of people who occupy these sites. Because many of your students are already or will become interested in the natural world, geography as a learning vehicle allows them to visit places and peoples without leaving the classroom. Through the creative use of maps, globes, pictures and films, music and dance, customs, and ceremonies, teachers can create realistic and exciting experiences for students, many of whom have never traveled beyond the confines of their immediate neighborhood.

The Study of History

History can be thought of as the river of human experience that is fed by the rivulets, creeks, streams, and tributaries of both ordinary and exceptional life events. From the stream of history, individuals draw their cultural identity and sense of integration with others, a process that allows each history student to become intimately involved with past generations. At the same time, this river of past events never repeats its exact course; but like most great streams, it tends to bend and curve in similar directions because people and conditions tend to be similar through the years. Thus, perceptive students of history can often anticipate opportunities and dangers in like situations of their own day.

The origins of history reach back to the dawn of time when stories were told and retold as legends and myths. Included in these stories are the legends and myths that explain beliefs about the origin of life and the migrations of people and tribes, and those that recount the epic tales of great heroes and leaders of the past. To be "real," history had to emerge in a written form. Written history evolved out of the need to keep official records of transactions and to record the accomplishments of rulers.

History as a systematic study of society did not begin until the work of Herodotus, the first political historian, who applied the standard of skeptical criticism to the telling of the story. Thucydides (400s B.C.) wrote his history of the Peloponnesians, and his work reflected a high-minded, accurate, and impartial description of the events. Both Herodotus and Thucydides relied on the works of earlier writers as a form of historical research that in time became the process of trained historians. Thucydides was the first scholar to write a book-length manuscript for his readers (Shotwell, 1939). Libraries of clay tablets and papyrus scrolls had been established in the Middle East long before the appearance of books.

After the fall of Rome, great historical works were not forthcoming, and the purpose of early church writings was mainly to defend the faith. However, following the Renaissance, the scientific age stimulated a new interest in "scientific" history, the "real" history that had started with Herodotus and Thucydides. During this period, Immanuel Kant began to organize and structure knowledge in systematic frameworks and helped to lay the foundation for systematic or scientific study of human events. Out of Kant's work came the idea of organizing historic facts and human events according to their relationship through time. This proved an ideal framework for the study of history. Over the years, influenced by German historians, history became less of a storytelling narrative and more of a "scientific" attempt to more accurately portray events. General agreements were reached on proper methods of reaching a more objective truth. However, "new" historians continue to appear to be reflecting not only recent discoveries but also on the times, aims, and personalities of historians and of those for whom they wrote.

Contemporary written history is characterized by many forms and styles, and the standards for judging "good" history are based on the standards of good scholarship. At the core of these standards is the historical process on which every historian is judged. Historical scholarship is based on the three-fold processes of collecting, organizing, and interpreting events within the broad context of the culture and the times. From this process, students are able to gain a perspective of the present and reach beyond themselves to experience a sense of generational existence. According to Gunter et al. (1983),

> Thus the study of history passed from a process of memorizing dates and events of little interest to the youthful student to the discipline of exercising caution in the examination of evidence and the exhilarating sense of direct contact with a living past. (p. viii)

History is an inclusive field that examines what has occurred in the past. Unlike the social sciences, history is considered to be a humanities because it is open to interpretation. Henry Johnson (1949) quotes Huizinga's statement on history: "History is the intellectual form in which a civilization renders account of itself to its past" (p. 15). And according to Lester Stephens (quoted in Hogue & Crump, 1988), history is

> a mental constriction of the past based on evidence which has been carefully subjected to tests of validity and then critically and systematically ordered and interpreted to present a story of man's interaction with other men in a society. (p. 1)

According to Henry Steel Commager (1965),

> No two histories are ever precisely alike, any more than any two poems or novels are precisely alike; if they were we should call it plagiarism. Yet over the centuries historians have worked out a number of patterns and these have come to be conventional, just as have patterns of poetry, music, and art. (p. 15)

Carl Becker and Charles Beard have both pointed out that history is the memory of things said and done; thus there are many histories that depend on numerous factors. There are at least two histories: the actual series of events that once occurred and the ideal accounts held and recounted by the people, or literary history. Literary history attempts to recover the past because the history of the people, nation, or civilization is considered a cultural treasure. Scientific history is a type of technical history that is interested in solving questions or problems that have been posed by scholars.

As with other disciplines, history serves many purposes that are important to contemporary society. Historians tend to explain the importance of history as a critical aspect of culture that serves both utilitarian or humanistic purposes. According to Saxe (1991), at the turn of twentieth century historians defended the teaching of history, as opposed to the teaching of the social sciences, on the basis of its scientific and its human qualities.

CAN YOU DEFINE HISTORY FOR YOUR STUDENTS?

Can you develop a useful definition of history for your high school students? Would you describe one or two specific examples of events that could be cited in your explanation?

> History bridged the gap between the incipient urban industrial state that degraded the individual and reduced the human being to a mere cog in the machinery of capital and finance, and the human spirit that gave each human a special quality. By utilizing the methods of science with the eloquence of literature, history took the hard edge off the sciences while celebrating humanity, a justifiable compromise. (p. 62)

The story of history is not legend, but a history based on facts and evidence. In some cases, the record of a particular event might be incomplete or may favor those who dominated society at the time of the event or even those who dominate the society now. But history is also an open record that can be modified as new information is brought to light. At the same time, as Schlesinger (1992) notes, historians are expected to protect this process and to guard against those who would rewrite history to fit some new unreality.

> The high purpose of history is not the presentation of self nor the vindication of identity but the recognition of complexity and the search for knowledge. (p. 72)

The process of history consists of three important operations in which information is collected, organized, and interpreted. The collection of history requires knowledge, patience, and often good fortune. Historians are trained in the skills of locating information. At the same time, original sources are prized over secondhand sources of information. A "good" history is measured according to the use or lack of important original sources. Therefore, historians are trained to evaluate all types of information and to seek "primary" sources when they are available. Once this information has been collected, it must be organized according to some pattern or framework. Typically, historians will use a chronological pattern. As a common practice, historians develop these patterns before or while information is being collected, and this outline will prove useful when writing the historical narrative. After the sources have been located and information has been collected according to the outline or framework, the historian is expected to interpret the meaning of the information. For example, a historian may establish a series of cause-and-effect relationships that were identified during the collection and organization of the information. These rela-

Can You Design a Clarifying or Classifying Assignment?

Prepare a specific assignment and set of directions that can introduce a high school class to the differences between primary and secondary sources and between fact and opinion.

tionships are open to interpretation, and the historian is expected to add his or her interpretation of the dynamics of the event or situation.

In recent decades, historians have begun to explore new fields with new methodologies. Many have tended to move beyond political and economic history to include issues and events such as everyday life and the roots of contemporary problems. This shift in emphasis can help make history more interesting and valuable to the average pupil or citizen. Some of the most dramatic changes have taken place in the study of social history. At one time this area of interest focused on the study of religion, education, and social reform. Downey (1982) points out that, since the 1960s, social history has focused considerable attention on social and cultural diversity.

> Although the traditional topics (religion, education, and reform) continue to receive some attention, historians during the 1960s began to pay far more attention to the history of various groups in American society—Blacks, Hispanics, Native Americans, white ethnics, blue-collar workers, and finally, women. (p. 1)

History, like the social sciences, has experienced changes in focus of study and in the processes of "doing" history. Another change has been the use of computers as an important tool for searching libraries and archives, writing and organizing

Evaluating for Multicultural Inclusion

In an era of multicultural concerns, do the historical events or periods that are generally presented in textbooks include adequate treatment of minority or ethnic involvement and contributions? Select an example of an important event that can be illustrated to reveal the need for such an inclusive approach.

notes, and writing manuscripts. The computer, however, cannot replace the trained historian, especially in terms of the research and writing skills that make the difference between excellence and a mediocre account of the past.

In the 1960s and 1970s, some states and professional groups attempted to focus on the essential contributions of history. The idea was not new. In 1923, for example, the historian Edward Cheyney attempted to formulate six "laws" of history (see the *American Historical Review*, January, 1924). But since every historical event is unique, there is grave danger in attempting to state any universal generalizations even if such conclusions are bolstered by numerous similar events and their consequences.

History has value beyond any attempt to generalize; there are clear "lessons" from past experiences. Few academics would agree with the late historian Edgar Robinson (1946) that the rush of events since 1900 has actually crowded out the past and that, along with the impact of the contemporary scene and the global widening of our relationships, "the present scene is so changed. . . that the earlier scene has few similarities and hence fewer lessons" (p. 75). If one accepts this statement, it does not negate the key role of history in the social studies curriculum, but it does provide an argument for establishing a balance in citizenship and social education with the contributions of geography and the other social sciences. As Schlesinger (1992) notes,

> Writing history is an old and honorable profession with distinctive standards and purposes. The historian's goals are accuracy, analysis, and objectivity in the reconstruction of the past. But history is more than an academic discipline up there in the stratosphere. It also has its own role in the future of nations. (p. 45)

History skills reflect the work of the scholarly historian and are specifically associated with activities related to written documents, other records, and human activities that have influenced the story of people. First, a trained historian must identify an important problem or issue that merits study. The problem or issue has occurred sometime in the past over a period of time that may not be readily known at first until an initial review of the problem is completed. The historian also may not know in the beginning where the study may lead geographically, politically, or economically. Some problems may prove to be too overwhelming and may have to be abandoned, or a more specific aspect of the problem may be pursued.

In general, the historian works within a limited time frame. A long period of time might limit the *depth* of the study and the historical narrative that should eventually culminate from it; a narrow span of years might limit the *breadth* of the study but allow the historian to dig deeply into an event of narrower scope if adequate source materials could be found. Locating resources requires a thorough search for documents pertaining to the topic of interest. For example, a historian may begin a study in a local state historical society library by reviewing newspaper articles written during the period of the event. These sources should help identify more specific clues regarding persons, groups, churches, schools, and other people or organizations that may have vital firsthand knowledge of the event. The next step is to identify and interview individuals who might have important information that is not available within libraries or, if they are deceased, their letters, records, and other information they may have left.

Assessing the importance and the credibility of the gathered sources is an important methodological skill. For example, a historian may discover that a descendant has a diary of an individual who played a key role in an event. Upon examination of the diary, the historian discovers important details that were unknown about the event. Because the diary was written by a person who witnessed and played a key role in the event, the diary is considered an important and credible source of valuable historical evidence. This is called a **primary source.** On the other hand, suppose that the historian found two newspaper accounts of the event. These are called **secondary sources.** If the two newspaper accounts are different, which account is to be believed and how can the truth be uncovered? These are some of the problems of historians which indicate the types of skills necessary to conduct historical studies. Elementary and secondary school students can learn and apply some of the skills that are used by the historian when doing historical research. These skills can be learned and practiced within the school or community setting. For example, a social studies teacher can instruct students in some of the primary history skills within an elementary or secondary history course or program. Many books are available that contain documents, copies of various reports or statements, and other primary evidence about important historical events. Some teachers focus on such a source approach to build student understanding of the historical method. Excellent examples are found in the older but fundamental book by Henry Johnson (1940).

The content of history includes information regarding the values, morals, ethics, aesthetics, and attitudes that were characteristic during each epoch or historical period. Therefore, students learn that each historical period has its own unique standards regarding the good life and the noble qualities of the good person in terms of what is worth knowing, doing, and believing. In addition, teachers can encourage students to relate historic values and attitudes to modern-day ones for comparative purposes. In addition, democratic values evolved over four centuries of continental occupation in North America and when studying U.S. history, students should be encouraged to pay close attention to the origins and development of democratic values in American society. Many historians believe that the study of history can help develop character in students. They believe that one of the most important reasons for including history in the curriculum is that history offers many examples of individuals and deeds. In other words, history is not just about past events, but about human character that has been tested by the trials of life. Schlesinger (1992) argues that value lessons may help students face present and future difficulties by giving them the courage to base their actions on moral and ethical grounds when caught in a dilemma.

CAN HISTORY AS A SCIENCE BE DEFENDED?

History often has been charged with being at best only "informed opinion." What argument or examples could you give to counter this opinion?

Properly taught, history will convey a sense of the variety, continuity, and adaptability of cultures, of the need for understanding other cultures, of the ability of individuals and peoples to overcome obstacles, of the importance of critical analysis and dispassionate judgment in every area of life.

Above all, history can give a sense of national identity. We don't have to believe that our values are absolutely better than the next fellow's or the next country's, but we have no doubt that they are better *for us*, reared as we are—and are worth living by and worth dying for. (p. 137)

The teaching of history is based on certain rationales. David Jenness (1990) describes the following reasons that are given to justify the teaching of history in the schools:

The Sake of the Present. The 1916 Commission stated that: "The past becomes educational to (children) only as it is related to the present." Teachers often justify the teaching of history as the need to understand the present, the understanding of origins as a means of making sense out of present conditions, systems, processes, attitudes, and outlooks.

History and the Cultural Purpose. This approach is based on the idea that history is seldom objective nor is it intended to be. This generally serves a cultural purpose and that purpose is to defend, advance, and develop loyalty for the culture or the society in which it is taught.

History as Past Politics. History is the record of the great men who, through force of will and the exercise of power, were able to shape and direct the development of the government and the nation that it ruled. Textbooks are noted for their encyclopedic presentation of the deed of the great movers and shakers of American life.

History as Narration. Scholars often have described history as the telling of a story of the people, culture, or nation. In this sense history serves as the collective memory of the people. Great historians are considered great story tellers and their success often depends on their ability to narrate the biographies and the events that are worth repeating in an exciting and lively fashion.

History as Collective Memory. The study of history helps to create a collective memory in the minds of students. This memory helps to create a mind set which helps students establish a common culture and common citizenship. While history is the story of the shared experiences of a people, it is more than

COULD, WOULD, AND SHOULD YOU USE HISTORY TO ENCOURAGE ETHICAL AND MORAL DEVELOPMENT?

What is the rationale for using history to help students build values, ethical qualities, and moral character? If you accept this aim, provide a specific example of how this is to be accomplished.

legend or myth. History is not fiction and does not have a plot. History is the story of individuals and groups who are caught up in the environment and the conditions of their times. (pp. 269–290)

For a very long time, history has been a core discipline of the social studies and is currently enjoying a resurgence in popularity with the development of state curriculum frameworks. During the 1990s, there was a growing attempt to reassert the dominance of history. For example, a report of the Curriculum Task Force of the National Commission on Social Studies in the Schools called *Charting a Course: Social Studies for the 21st Century* promoted the teaching of history and geography at all grade levels, thus attempting to make history and geography the core of the social studies. In spite of this dominant role of history in the social studies, Leinwand (1978) contends that "history is not so central to the curriculum as it once was. Because other disciplines have gained in ascendancy, history reigns but does not rule" (p. 11).

Presently, history is included in the social studies curriculum as American history, world history, and state history. It is taught in the elementary grades, junior high and middle schools, and in the high school. History has been taught extensively in the secondary schools. The only other social studies subject that is taught regularly, but less often than history, is government.

In spite of the renewed interest in this discipline, some long-standing instructional problems and content selection issues remain with the teaching of history in the schools. Each year and decade pile more important events and information into the accumulation of history. Curriculum makers and teachers face ever-mounting challenges concerning what to include in their courses and lessons. These conditions help account for the negative student reactions to their history courses and especially to classes in so-called World History where considerable portions of human history are often squeezed into single-year offerings. Over the years, the resulting shallow courses have continually contributed to student rankings that place history at or near the bottom of lists of courses they find interesting or valuable. Another part of the problem is that most social studies teachers have studied American history as

BREADTH OR DEPTH? WHICH IS BEST FOR TRAINING TEACHERS?

If you could choose between a semester survey course of world history or a nineteenth century world history offering, which would you prefer to study and why?

a part of their college training, but fewer have had the benefit of studying world history. Those who have studied world history at the college level have had instruction that is often presented through a lecture format with a heavy emphasis on factual information, a method not generally conducive to motivating secondary students.

Precollegiate history instruction has been the target of historians who are dissatisfied with the social studies in general. The concerns of critics tend to focus on the poor preparation of history teachers, the lack of organization and substance of the social studies curriculum including its emphasis on a child-centered orientation, and the poor quality of history textbooks. Teachers sometimes are accused of being poorly prepared to teach history in the schools. Elementary teachers in particular often are singled out as being ill prepared in terms of their academic training, while secondary teachers occasionally are assigned to teach history courses when they are really trained to teach other subjects or are primarily interested in some aspects of coaching. State credentialing requirements are frequently far too lax in setting the number of units or courses necessary for licensing. Individuals with minors in history and social science are frequently unprepared to teach those subjects and should not be credentialed to do so. The social studies curriculum also has been criticized as being poorly organized, attempting to accomplish too many things, and ending up by doing nothing well.

Commenting on the reaction of students to instruction in history, Robinson and Kirman (1986) have identified the following generalizations:

- Over the past 50 years students' tendency to dislike instruction in history has remained rather constant.
- The overall history curriculum has been rather steadily simplified to respond to a perceived decline in students' abilities.
- Not a great deal of attention has been paid to adaptations of the history curriculum to suit different subgroups of students. (p. 23)

In addition, some critics claim that history courses at the secondary level lack depth. This is especially true of the attempt to teach world history, often in the tenth grade, in a single year. Students have frequently reported that this is their least liked course. For suggestions on how to avoid this negative reaction to history, see Richard E. Gross, "World History: What Shall It Be?" *Social Education,* March, 1982, pp. 178–181. In essence, the critics have continued to complain that the teaching of history lacks the academic quality needed for the education of the nation's children (Gross & Dynneson, 1983). The social studies critics of history during the early decades of the twentieth century claimed that history placed too much emphasis on intellectualism and on individualism, whereas these critics would emphasize more of an applied knowledge of history that focused on social problems and cooperative social learning, social responsibility, and social efficiency related to citizenship education (Jenness, 1990).

History Instruction

As for the actual teaching of the subject, critics and students suggest that history instruction also seems to suffer from an over-reliance on a limited number of methods of instruction. Common complaints, like this one from Leinwand (1978), focus on lecture and an over-reliance on factual information.

> History teachers should listen to the historian who warns against making history simply an immense aggregate of particular facts. (p. 12)

Also students complain that their history teachers often follow an instructional pattern that requires them to routinely read a section (or a chapter) of the textbook and to answer a set of textbook questions, followed by a quiz or a test. In another common approach, students report that their history teachers use lecture and recitation instructional methods that require students to listen and to recall an endless series of names, dates, and events. It is evident that seriously considered selectivity is essential in organizing history courses and that the depth of the content covered is far more desirable than superficial survey-type classes that serve little educational purpose. Organizing classes that are more limited in scope but more thorough in treating subject matter calls for serious pre-planning. Such planning should consider which material is most basic and functional, current societal issues and needs, and student concerns and motivation along with the aims and objectives of history courses. Designers may well examine topics, themes, concepts, and problems among at least eight other ways to approach history classes besides the traditional chronological organization. Combining these approaches with a semi-chronological design may well spur student interest and learning and at the same time avoid what the renowned historian Arnold Toynbee called "that one damn thing after another approach" (Gross, 1982, p. 179).

In spite of the litany of criticisms leveled against history, it remains the most important single subject within the social studies. The strength of history lies in its utilitarian use as a means of preparing students for democratic citizenship. Kerry J. Kennedy (1991) described the role of history in developing "civic intelligence."

> History allows students to focus on the way in which other people in other times have come together to exercise their civic intelligence. It provides images of how the process of thinking together has created both inclusive and exclusive communities, just and unjust societies, and good and bad public practices. These can all be understood and evaluated in the context of the times that produced them and as part of the drama and excitement that makes historical study unique. (p. 78)

The teaching of history is often structured around a certain number of disciplinary generalizations. Lead by California in the 1960s, other states, including Wisconsin, Florida, Colorado, and Connecticut, asked academic experts to identify the prime concepts and generalizations stemming from their field of study. These fundamentals were to serve as a base for organizing and selecting content in elementary and secondary school social studies curricula. In California, for example, economists listed sixteen major generalizations under headings such as economic ends and means, measure of economic achievement, income and allocation of resources, and distribution and standards of living as a means of suggesting the key inclusions and emphases of their field (State Curriculum Commission, 1962, pp. 98–100). During the 1960s, the Colorado Department of Education also sponsored the development of *A Guide for Concept Development in the Social Studies* (1967, pp. 23 through chart). This guide listed and described key concepts for each of the seven disciplines of the social studies, including important disciplinary generalizations from each subject. This work also was the result of subject field experts from Colorado who worked alone or in teams consisting of scholars and educators. These two efforts were seminal models that were developed by academicians rather than educators and are valued as basic to the selection of social studies concepts and generalizations for instructional purposes in history and the social sciences.

The *Social Studies Framework for the Public Schools of California* (State Curriculum Commission, 1962) contains several generalizations that may be appropriate for helping teachers design historical instruction, including those devoted to:

Chronology, Sequence, and Change in History

Space and Time for a framework within which all events can be placed.

Man's struggle for freedom and human dignity has occupied a relatively brief period of time, as compared with the total span of man's existence.

Is It Important to Avoid Gender Bias in Framing Recommendations for use in Official Documents?

Should documents, recommendations, and policy statements written for the social studies reflect both genders to avoid the impression of gender bias? How has the use or application of language changed since the 1962 *Social Studies Framework* was written?

The past influences the present, and the present cannot be adequately understood without knowledge of the past.

History contributes much to man's preparation for his social and political life.

Change has been a universal condition of human society.

History reveals a degree of homogeneity in mankind during all periods of recorded time.

Past and present civilizations represent our cultural heritage.

Interdependence has been a constant and important factor in human relationships everywhere.

The efforts of people, great material achievements, and important ideas are delineated, assessed, interpreted, and placed in perspective by historians.

History demonstrates that mankind has been motivated by morals and ideals and by material wants and needs. (pp. 93–94)

In the mid 1990s national attention to establishing standards of basic content of subjects in the school curriculum resulted from public, professional, and political criticism of pupil inadequacies. Standards developed for U.S. history at a national history center sought increased attention to the roles of women and minority groups and brought immediate protest and challenges. Critics claimed the recommendations tended to be negative about the nation's story and that they threatened reductions in necessary emphases on American heroes, critical events, and patriotic deeds. Once again an attempt to state and organize a balanced base from the vast background from our history ran afoul of strong divergent opinions within American society.

The Study of Geography

Geography provides an understanding of the physical or natural environment of the earth's surface, including the various landscapes, climates, and natural systems that bring about changes in the human condition. The patterns of human existence reflect the changing natural and human conditions over time, space, and place; therefore, the study of geography provides students with important insights into the interactions that take place among people, their culture, and the natural environment.

Herodotus made extensive use of geography by describing the lands of distant peoples. The ancient Greeks also were interested in the shape of the earth and the land forms that characterized it. Early Greek and Roman **cartographers** used a grid system in which lines of longitude and latitude were used as a reference system. Ptolemy, the greatest map maker of his time, made detailed maps through the application of mathematical methods. In addition, Ptolemy was able to advance the use of the grid system and to develop a system of coordinate references. Although some of his calculations were based on inaccurate computations of the earth's circumference, his studies made us aware of climatic differences that occur in different regions according to longitude and latitude.

During the Middle Ages, map making remained a crude science except in the Moslem world. Arab traders were skilled navigators, and Moslem scholars improved on the maps of Ptolemy. Based on the expanding knowledge of Arabic travelers, scholars compiled descriptive studies of peoples living in different geographic settings. Consequently, scholars began to compare the lives of people under different climates and different environmental conditions. European adventurers and travelers such as Marco Polo learned about distant peoples through Moslem sources. In time, this knowledge contributed to a desire to learn about the earth and its people, and in turn, this knowledge would lead to a new interest in map making.

During the Age of Discovery, geography became the quintessential science, but it was not until the seventeenth century that the great vastness of the earth became known. Advances in map making led to voyages that resulted in encounters with distant peoples. Geographic knowledge expanded with advances in both the physical sciences and in human sciences. In the twentieth century, satellite technology was used to refine map making into a precise and accurate science. At the same time, the problems of map projection and an attempt to portray the roundness of the earth on a flat surface continue. Also, the study of **human geography** attempts to keep up with the changes in land use and settlement brought about by a dynamically changing technology and the great drain of irreplaceable natural resources. The interdependence of all peoples and all countries is becoming an important geographic focus that challenges us as distances are becoming diminished by improvements in transportation and communication.

Modern geography is an inclusive science and social science that is dedicated to the study of the physical features of the earth's surface **(physical geography)** and the various human activities (human geography) that take place on the surface of the earth. According to the authors of *Social Studies Framework for the Public Schools of California* (1962), geography "seeks to define the earth's physical and cultural features, to show their distribution, to make them understandable by explaining the basic forces or factors that affect them, and to present the more fundamental of their interrelationship." Physical geography is "to describe and explain the distribution of surface features and to define natural regions that are caused by and continuously affected by forces and processes in nature," while cultural geography deals with the distribution of people and their activities on the earth's surface (pp. 91–92).

As a discipline, geography seems to fall somewhere between the sciences and history. In addition, geography tends to combine still other disciplines as well as their methodologies into an aggregate study of both the physical nature of the earth's surface and human attempts to interact with their natural environments and resources.

According to Jan O. M. Broek (1965), geography can be associated with several viewpoints including a humanistic perspective, a social-cultural perspective, a historical dimension, and the facets of location. The humanistic perspective is explained by a "keen interest in the individuality of places, treasures the aesthetic values of the landscape, and recognizes that there are more things between heaven and earth than can be safely entrusted to a computer" (p. 21). According to Broek (1965), the social-cultural perspective includes the idea that: "Even seemingly pure physical studies of climate and relief are, if geographical, related to human notions and values of light, heat, slope, and height. Thus one can say that geography is concerned with the earth as the home of man" (p. 23). He further notes that the historical dimension deals with geography of the past "in such terms as 'subsequent occupancy' and 'cross-sections through time'. . . . By analyzing what a place was like in each successive stage the geographer would present a sequence series of 'stills'" (p. 28). The facets of location, the reference points with maps and globes "all have to do with the placing of things on the earth's surface. To find where something is requires defining its spatial relationship to known points" (p. 30).

Geography also has close links to economics and other social sciences such as demography and political science. The growth, movement, and placement of peoples or the laws and regulations related to production and trade are but two examples of such interconnections. In observing geography classes in numerous schools both here and abroad, we have frequently noted that broad-field human geography courses were the offerings most representative of the concept of social studies.

As was true of history, the basic building blocks of geographic knowledge are facts. But facts cannot stand by themselves in isolation out of context. Factual information is meaningful only when presented within the broader frame-

EARTH SCIENCE OR SOCIAL SCIENCE: WHICH IS BETTER?

What are the major differences between conceiving geography as a physical science or as a cultural one? Which approach do you believe students prefer and why?

work of concepts and generalization. Phillip Bacon (1981) addressed this issue when he wrote:

> Some geographers delight in wowing their audiences—students or colleagues—by rattling off such unassorted miscellanea as the 1920 population of Pocatello and the number of tons of copper mined at Bingham Canyon since the first shovel bit into ore-laden Utah soil. (p. 53)

Bacon goes on to explain that while factual information is very important to the study of geography, its most important application is in the development of geographic concepts. Bacon believes that geographic facts are useful and promote student thinking when they are associated with the four fundamental key geographic skills: *"spatial distribution, aerial association, spatial interaction, and regionalization"* (1983, p. 53). These four concepts tend to appear over and over again in various publications dedicated to the teaching of geography. For example, *A Guide for Concept Development in the Social Studies* (1967) describes spatial distribution, aerial associations, and spatial interaction according to the following meanings:

> The collection of locations of a set of similar physical or cultural phenomena constitutes a spacial distribution.
>
> Understanding spatial distribution involves the correlation of these characteristics, including
> - *Positive and Negative Aerial Associations.* The relationship between spatial characteristics may be either positive or negative (e.g., factors that might attract or repel human populations).
> - *Movement and Connection.* Movements of people and goods, and communication between places are aspects of spatial interaction. (Colorado Department of Education, p. 16 through chart)

Phillip Bacon (1989) describes the concept of region (in reference to regionalization) in his popular secondary geography textbook according to the following statement:

A region may be interpreted as a "unit of the earth's surface" that has one or more characteristics that set it apart from other regions of the world. (p. 756)

In addition to the key concepts stated above, five additional related key concepts have been recommended to precollegiate geographic education by the Joint Committee on Geographic Education (1984). They include the following:

- *Location.* Position on the Earth's Surface including both absolute (a precise point) and relative location (knowledge of the characteristics of place).
- *Place.* Physical and human characteristics including both the physical and human characteristics that distinguish one place from another.
- *Relationship Within Places.* Humans and environments including the advantages or disadvantages of a place in terms of how it affects human settlement and human culture.
- *Movement.* Humans interacting on the Earth including the characteristics of settlements, transportation, communication, cultural exchanges, economic exchange, and interdependencies that are of social, political, or economic nature.
- *Regions.* How they form and change and the criteria or characteristics that define and delimit a region as a social, economic, or political entity. (pp. 3–8)

In addition to working with key geographic concepts, students should be encouraged to learn some basic geographic skills so that they can be applied to a variety of learning situations both inside and outside of the school. Geographical skills reflect the work of the geographer and are associated specifically with skills related to interpreting and applying information in the form of maps, globes, charts, and tables. Physical geography tends to focus on the relationships between the earth, moon, and other planets in our solar system. This scientific information also is applied to the study of climate and the physical features of the earth. With this background, students are encouraged to study human conditions and activities in response to the various environments of the earth.

These five themes similarly outlined by the Joint Committee on Geographic Education (1955) also included the basic types of skills that geographers use in

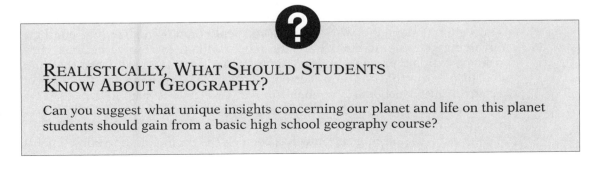

REALISTICALLY, WHAT SHOULD STUDENTS KNOW ABOUT GEOGRAPHY?

Can you suggest what unique insights concerning our planet and life on this planet students should gain from a basic high school geography course?

studying geographic questions and problems. These skills should be applied in all of the other related subjects of the social studies. Basic geographic skills include the ability to:

- Locate places over the surface of the earth.
- Describe the physical and human features of a place.
- Identify and describe both physical and human relationships within a place or between places.
- Recognize and describe human interactions that take place over the surface of the earth or within a region.
- Define a region in regard to specific physical features or human activities. (p. 3)

In addition to these key skills, students are encouraged to learn several basic geographic skills associated with maps, globes, charts, and tables. Student interest in geography often is heightened by activities associated with interpreting and constructing maps, charts, and tables. Older students should be encouraged to complete various projects associated with geographic research, especially as it pertains to the discovery of new physical relationships and human interactions.

To take full advantage of the instructional potential of geography, the teacher should supplement standard classroom textbook instruction with materials and resources from the National Geographic Society and from local and regional organizations that have recently been organized to promote geographic education. The materials of geography tend to be maps and globes. Flat maps have problems related to shape and the proportions of land and water areas. In the last few years, classroom teachers have been able to replace the more distorted Mercator maps with the less distorted Robinson maps, while recognizing that all flat maps are distorted in one way or another.

Students can study values issues through geographical instruction. For instance, an important geographic value issue is related to land use. History provides many examples of conflicts over acquiring or retaining territory. Many modern-day conflicts are fought over land disputes. Symbolically, the idea of the homeland is an idea that persuasively unites people in spite of many other differences. Geographic conflicts are currently taking place in most regions of the world. By studying the nature of these conflicts, students can better understand world affairs and will come to realize that conflicts involving geographic claims are the most difficult to resolve because they inflame extreme passions and reactions. In addition, they will learn that in a world of growing interconnections and increasing need for global and regional interdependence, nationalism and its elements such as tribalism, as evidenced particularly in Africa, remain as great obstacles to needed cooperative agreements and action.

As a school subject, geography has been on the decline in the public schools and in higher education. Over the past twenty years, many of the larger uni-

WHICH IS BETTER—A CONCEPTUAL OR SKILL APPROACH?

What would be the major differences between approaching geography as primarily a conceptual field of study or in offering the course with a major emphasis on skills?

versities have either eliminated or reduced their offerings in geography. As a result, most social studies teachers have had limited course work in geography. The current revitalization movement in precollegiate geography has forced school districts to provide workshops or short courses in the fundamentals of geography. In spite of the effort, quality teaching in geography is hindered by the teacher's lack of geographic knowledge and skills. This situation is particularly unfortunate because history occurs in geographic arenas, and many events in history cannot be explained or understood if separated from knowledge of the physical environment in which they occur.

Geography in the schools has gone through periods when it was considered an important instructional subject followed by periods when it almost disappeared from classroom instruction. Before the Civil War, geography textbooks reflected an emphasis on geography with a concern for the vastness of space, manifest destiny, and the influences of the frontier; after the Civil War, history became the dominant subject of the social studies curriculum. As American history settled into the curriculum in both the elementary and secondary grades, geography often came to be taught in connection with or in support of history. American history often focused on the growth of the nation from the Atlantic to the Pacific, and geography supported both the chronological and geographic march of events. Geography also came to support the teaching of world history as the geographic setting for places and people (Jenness, 1990). Unfortunately, much of the separate geography that continued to be taught was primarily physical in its emphasis.

The 1920s and 1930s witnessed a shift away from the dominance of physical geography and a movement toward social or human geography. During the 1930s geographic instruction tended to emphasize the study of people and places within the United States along with an understanding of the natural environment. Following World War II, geographic instruction shifted to world regions and the people and places of the world with a special emphasis on regional geography. At the same time, geography instruction often continued to emphasize "name and place" learning that tended to require students to memorize the names of capitals of states, nations, and endless lists of products.

IS HUMANKIND A PRODUCT OF ENVIRONMENT?

Explain several examples that you could use to help students understand the errors of geographical determinism. Explain why it is frequently recommended that geography should focus on societies and cultures in their crucial environmental settings. What basic human needs should be included in such studies?

As Chapin and Gross (1973) point out, there have been fundamental differences in the focus of precollegiate geography courses and college level geography courses.

> Professional geographers strongly disapprove of geographic content in the schools that unduly emphasizes importance of environment and neglects the concept that resources are culturally defined and that man makes choices in the use of his environment. Long after geographers rejected environmental determinism, the schools continued to teach this interpretation. (p. 105)

This fundamental difference between "school" and "college" geography was addressed in the 1960s by the High School Geography Project under the sponsorship of the Association of American Geographers, which attempted to reform the way geography was being taught in the schools. This project attempted to replace the emphasis on **environmental determinism,** places, and products with a better understanding of what geographers do and how they work (Winston, 1986).

Nevertheless, the importance of geographic instruction continued to fade until the 1980s when newspaper articles were reporting that students were becoming more ignorant about the names and location of places despite the fact that geography had been maintained in many school districts as a junior high subject and that in some cases it was offered as a high school course. Alarming media reports helped increase concerns of professional geographers over the condition of their discipline in the lower schools. Combined with support from the National Geographic Society, a new interest and support for geographic education appeared. At the present time, the teaching of basic geographic knowledge and information has become a more important part of elementary social studies. Nicholas Helburn (1991) has written that geography is important because:

> . . . students must *know* and understand it well enough to make intelligent decisions about society and the global environment. Further they must *feel* enough

WHAT DO YOUR STUDENTS NEED TO KNOW ABOUT CITIES?

In recent years, an emphasis on urban geography has proved popular. What do you view as being the prime geographical knowledge and skills for a geographical course oriented in this way?

concern to participate in finding and carrying out solutions to world wide problems. (p. 116)

Today geography is a basic subject within the social studies constellation of disciplines; however, it continues to retain its supportive role as a backdrop for historical events and as a basic skill area for the social sciences. This effort was supported by the belief that citizens need fundamental knowledge about their nation and the world. In the following statement, geographers (Joint Committee on Geographic Education, 1984) have successfully argued that:

We must strive to understand how the actions of our society influence other societies and how their actions affect us. A sound geographic education provides the perspectives, information, concepts and skills to understand ourselves, our relationship to the earth and our interdependence on the other peoples of the world. It reinforces and extends the processes of critical thinking and problem solving that are applicable to all parts of the curriculum. We must know *where* and *why* events are occurring if we hope to apply our intelligence and moral sensitivity toward improving the quality of human life on this planet. (pp. 1–2)

Barbara Winston (1986) outlined the following instructional concerns associated with geographic instruction:

- Geographic ideas often taught in the schools were judged as out of date.
- Geographic knowledge, as it is often taught in the schools, is a collection of unrelated facts to be memorized.
- Current emphasis on global education requires a revision of traditional regional geography. (pp. 50–52)

The new emphasis on geographic education in the schools has stimulated a renewed interest in the teaching of geography. This interest will hopefully bring about changes in the methods and materials that are used to instruct students in geography. Some of the current tests used to measure student competency in geography continue to emphasize place-name recognition over the understandings of important physical and human relationships, thus suggesting that there is a continuing need to improve geographic instruction in its current revitalized form. The *Social Studies Framework for the Public Schools of California* (State Curriculum Commission, 1962) contains several generalizations that may be appropriate for helping teachers design geographic instruction, including the following:

Physical Geography

Life on the earth is influenced by earth's (global) shape, its size, and its set of motions.

Earth movements of rotation and revolution are basic to understanding climate and time. . . .

Weather, climate, and earth crustal movements affect the surface of the earth and cause regional differences in land forms, minerals, drainage, soils, and natural vegetation.

Climate is determined by sunlight, temperature, humidity, precipitation, atmospheric pressure, winds, unequal rates of heating and cooling, and water surfaces. . . .

Soil, water, solar energy, and air are the natural resources most indispensable to man.

The physical elements of the earth are a unit, and no part can be understood fully except in terms of its relationship to the whole.

Cultural Geography

Man constantly seeks to satisfy his needs for food, clothing, shelter and his other wants; in so doing, he attempts to adapt, shape, utilize, and exploit the earth.

The significance of the physical features of the earth is determined by man living in his environment.

The extent of man's utilization of natural resources is related to his desires and to his level of technology.

The processes of production, exchange, distribution, and consumption of goods have a geographic orientation and vary in part with geographic influences.

The location of production is controlled by the factors of land (natural resources of the physical environment), labor, and capital.

The kinds of climate, soil, native vegetation and animals, and minerals influence the nature and extent of man's achievements within each region.

Competition for the acquisition of the earth's natural resources sometimes results in political strife, and even in war. (pp. 90–92)

SHOULD OR COULD GEOGRAPHY SERVE AS THE CORE OF THE SOCIAL STUDIES?

What arguments could you list for considering geography rather than history as the central core of the social studies program in both elementary and secondary grades? Explain your answer.

CONCLUSIONS

In the history section of this chapter, you learned that historians have consistently invested great amounts of time and energy in promoting the teaching of history in the schools. While the relationship between historians and social studies educators has, at times, been difficult, mutual support and cooperation best describe the history/social studies relationship. During the twentieth century, the discipline of history was influenced by several social and intellectual trends and movements. For example, during the Great Depression of the 1930s several influential historians became ardent social "reconstructionists" and accepted the idea that history could be used to reform American society. Several leading social studies educators accepted this same position and attempted to write social studies materials that emphasized a "reconstruction" theme. During the middle and late decades of the twentieth century, several historians were attracted to a Marxist interpretation of history. While these historians tended to interpret history as a form of class conflict that was driven by economic considerations, few social studies educators were willing to include a Marxist interpretation of history in textbooks or in presentations designed for school students.

In addition, you were presented with the idea that history teaching at the college level also has influenced the teaching of history in the schools. To some degree, the pedagogical practices that dominate college history departments also influence the pedagogical practices in the high school. In the 1890s, for example, history instruction emphasized a type of factual learning as did history instruction in the high school. In addition, history professors tended to transmit history knowledge through a lecture or a lecture and discussion format as did the high school history teachers. In recent years, history professors have attempted to extend their instructional practices by adopting new technologies such as the use of computers, simulations, student research, and project studies. High school teachers, while often more pedagogically flexible than college professors, tend to mirror many of these same practices.

According to the chapter section on geography, you should have acquired the idea that in the past, academic geographers have, as a whole, been somewhat distantly removed from the teaching of geography in the schools. Therefore, the teaching of geography in the schools tended to be quite different from the teaching of geography in academic institutions. For example, geography instruction in the schools has long required students to memorize long lists or what is often called "name/place" geography; in contrast, academic geography tends to focus on various problems associated with human culture and natural resources or the dynamics of relationships such as cause-and-effect relationships and time-and-place relationships. Geographers often have authored books and materials for school instruction according to the specifications of commercial textbook companies who are influenced by school teaching traditions.

Remember also, that geography as a higher education discipline does not command the influence that was characteristic of history. In fact, during the twentieth century, geography departments have been consolidated, merged, or eliminated. Therefore, you can safely conclude that in the past many social studies teachers did not take courses in geography, whereas almost every elementary and secondary social studies teacher has taken at least several courses in history. In spite of lack of support for geography at the college level, you should realize that since the mid-1980s geographers have played a major role in revitalizing the teaching of geography in the schools. Support for geography instruction at the college level actually has come as a result of a concern for geography instruction at the precollegiate level. In recent years, the public has become aware of the level of geographic ignorance that pervades public education because of the unfortunate deemphasis of the subject. Consequently, you can say that geography has become an "old" rising star in the social studies constellation of disciplines, due in part to the extensive support of influential sources such as the National Geographic Society and to the growing public understanding of the serious impact of global events on the United States.

REFERENCES

Bacon, P. (1981). Geographic and ecological basis of the social studies. In J. Allen (Ed.), *Education in the 80's: Social studies.* Washington, DC: National Education Association.

Bacon, P. (1989). *World geography: The earth and its people.* Orlando, FL: Harcourt Brace Jovanovich.

Broek, J. O. M. (1965). *Geography: Its scope and spirit.* Columbus, OH: Charles E. Merrill.

Chapin, J. R., & Gross, R. E. (1973). *Teaching social studies skills.* Boston: Little, Brown.

Colorado Department of Education (1967). *A guide for concept development in the social studies.* Denver, CO: Department of Education.

Commager, H. S. (1965). *The nature and the study of history*. Columbus, OH: Charles E. Merrill.

Downey, M. T. (1982). The new history and the classroom, in M. T. Downey (Ed.), *Teaching American history: New directions* (Bulletin 67, pp. 1–3). Washington, DC: National Council for the Social Studies.

Gross, R. E. (1982). World history: What shall it be? *Social Education, 46*, 178–181.

Gross, R. E., & Dynneson, T. L. (1983). *What should we be teaching in the social studies?* (Fastback #199). Bloomington, IN: Phi Delta Kappa Educational Foundation.

Gunter, M. A., Estes, T. H., & Schwab, J. H. (1990). *Instruction: A models approach*. Boston: Allyn & Bacon.

Helburn, N. (1991). The geographical perspective: Geography's role in citizenship education. In R. E. Gross & T. L. Dynneson (Eds.), *Social science perspectives on citizenship education* (pp. 116–140). New York: Teachers College Press.

Hogue, J. D., & Crump, C. (1988). *Teaching history in the elementary school*. Bloomington, IN: Indiana University Social Studies Development Center.

Jenness, D. (1990). *Making sense of social studies*. New York: Macmillan.

Johnson, H. (1940). *Teaching of history*. New York: Macmillan.

Joint Committee on Geographic Education. (1955). *K–6 geography: Themes, key ideas, and learning opportunities*. Washington, DC: Geographic Education National Implementation Project.

Joint Committee on Geographic Education. (1984). *Guidelines for geographic education: Elementary and secondary schools*. Washington, DC: Joint Committee on Geographic Education of the National Council for Geographic Education and the Association of American Geographers.

Kennedy, K. J. (1991). The historical perspective: The contribution of history to citizenship education. In R. E. Gross & T. L. Dynneson (Eds.), *Social science perspectives on citizenship education* (pp. 66–87). New York: Teachers College Press.

Leinwand, G. (1978). *Teaching of world history* (Bulletin 54). Washington, DC: National Council for the Social Studies.

Saxe, D. W. (1991). *Social studies in the schools: A history of the early years*. New York: State University of New York.

State Curriculum Commission. (1962). *Social studies framework for the public schools of California*. Sacramento, CA: State Department of Education.

Robinson, E. E. (1946). A new American history. *School and Society, 63*, 73–76.

Robinson, P., & Kirman, J. M. (1986). From monopoly to dominance. In S. P. Wronski & D. H. Bragaw (Eds.), *Social studies and social science: A fifty-year perspective* (Bulletin 78, pp. 15–27). Washington, DC: National Council for the Social Studies.

Schlesinger, A. M., Jr. (1992). *The disuniting of America: Reflections on a multicultural society*. New York: W. W. Norton.

Shotwell, J. T. (1939). *The history of history*. New York: Columbia University Press.

Winston, B. J. (1986). Teaching and learning in geography. In S. P. Wronski & D. H. Bragaw (Eds.), *Social studies and social sciences: A fifty-year perspective* (Bulletin 78, pp. 43–58). Washington, DC: National Council for the Social Studies.

Political Science and Economics: The Systems and Processes of Society

INTRODUCTION

In this chapter you will find that economics and political science share a common interest in explaining the institutional operations and processes of society. This shared interest is reflected in the term *political economy*, which suggests that economics and political science are critical co-aspects of a governing system. After reading this chapter, you should understand that the study of economics provides insights into the systems and the material culture that are designed to provide the sustenance, shelter, arraignments, and adornments essential to human well-being and existence. An individual alone may be able to provide some of his or her essential material needs; however, cooperative human interaction can generate a much richer and more varied material culture. Through the development of a cooperative economic system of production and exchange, individuals together can achieve the ultimate fulfillments of culture in religion, music, architecture, literature, philosophy, aesthetic expressions, and a higher technological achievement. You should also realize that the study of political science is dedicated to the study of politics and government with a special interest in the processes, policy-making goals, and procedures of government. The type of government that characterizes a society also reflects the relationship between individuals and rulers. In addition, the national government of a country reflects the values and the virtues that have come to dominate that society. These values and virtues are reflected in both simple and complex activities, including the selection of rulers, the nature of the decision-making processes, and the means that are used to resolve conflicts.

The Study of Political Science

Political science provides an understanding of the social relationships and political systems that are essential in regulating individual and group behavior within a society. The political systems protect, facilitate, and regulate society through processes and institutions that help to control both public and private behavior. At the same time, political systems differ from one society to the next. These differences influence the extent to which individuals can assert their own natural inclinations to achieve their goals and meet their own needs. Therefore, the nature of the political system determines the nature of citizenship that is at the heart of the **political culture.**

Political scientists study political systems, which operate through political and governmental institutions to express and enforce the will of those in power. In addition, institutions provide services to meet the needs of a particular society. The political system is also concerned with making decisions and resolving conflicts that arise from within and outside the society. Political processes are important procedural mechanisms of the political system; through these processes, laws and regulations are enacted as a means of ruling society. However, the primary function of the political system is to consider and develop government policies. The policy-making processes tend to reflect the values and attitudes underlying the political system. Policy may be thought of as political philosophy or the principle of the political will in action.

Political scientists use four perspectives when studying political systems (Sorauf, 1965). These perspectives include:

1. It studies the processes, behavior, and institutions of political systems in order to make systematic generalizations and explanations about the political.
2. It seeks generalizations about relations among political systems, especially the politics of nations in the international system.
3. It studies the end products, the public policies, of the political processes.
4. It studies, finally, ideas and doctrines about government and the political system, ideas such as the concepts of and justifications for democracy, justice, and equality. (p. 7)

The origins of the study of political science can be traced to the first appearance of urban centers along the fertile valleys where important ancient cities and empires emerged. Later, Plato and Aristotle would organize early foundations in which political thought emerged out of their concern for the nature of human societies. Law and the development of political institutions expanded under the Roman empire, especially in the development of the judiciary system in which civil laws were greatly refined. During the feudal ages, political relationships were agreed-to associations between members of noble families, while servile relationships existed between a noble lord and unfree peasants or serfs. In the Renaissance era, the feudal system was being replaced by emerg-

ARE YOU A POLITICAL PLAYER?

Do political systems exist in other organizations besides governmental ones? What about in high schools? If so, how could the political relationships be portrayed in a diagram?

ing nations and new systems of government. Eventually, the Age of Enlightenment would be characterized by new processes, and as a result of these processes a new age of democratic rule would appear.

By the first decade of the twentieth century in the United States, political science was becoming a separate and distinct field of study. Before the Civil War, Francis Lieber held a scholarly chair in political science at Columbia University as early as 1858. In 1903 a group of scholars organized the American Political Science Association.

As is the case with other disciplines, political science has more than one definition including this one by the State Curriculum Commission of California (1962):

> Political science is the study of government—of the theory and practice of man in organizing and controlling the power needed to formulate public policy and administer the public services. (p. 95)

David Easton (1967) defines political science as "the study of the authoritative allocation of values as it is influenced by the distribution and use of power" (p. 146), while Francis J. Sorauf (1965) states that political scientists define political science as "the study of political behavior, processes, and institutions, or as the study of political systems and the relationships among them" (p. 2). These varied definitions share certain themes related to the allocation of power, a concern for human behavior, and the identification of a shared ideology that determines the nature of political systems and institutions.

Political scientists tend to distinguish between the study of political science and government. The reason for this distinction is found in a fundamental debate over the boundaries of political science and the problem of limiting the concerns of the political scientist. According to Sorauf (1965), there are two important reasons for making this distinction.

> In the first place, it is only in certain political systems, most especially those of the Western democracies, that special institutions of government exist to perform only the political function. . . . Secondly, the institutions of government at best account for only part of the activity and part of the decisions in the political system. (p. 4)

PROVIDE REALISTIC LEARNING THROUGH
A POLLING EXPERIENCE

How can you help students understand the strengths and problems of political polling by carrying out such a study on a real issue in their school?

In other words, much of what interests the political scientist takes place outside the institutions of government, including the individual, social, and cultural behaviors that are outside the institutional setting of government.

Political science skills are specifically related to gathering information about political systems and predicting political behavior. Political systems and political behaviors are of great importance within democratic societies. Democratic societies provide their citizens with important rights and responsibilities that are beyond the rights and responsibilities of citizens living in totalitarian societies. In the United States, democratic rights and responsibilities are important components of government and are listed and described within a written constitution. The Constitution also specifies the powers and responsibilities of individuals as well as governmental institutions. Political scientists study and compare governmental systems and are particularly interested in the political means that are used to express the public will. In addition, they attempt to devise ways through which the public will can be expressed. The poll and the ballot are examples of the most common techniques of measuring the public will concerning social, political, and economic issues and concerns. Survey studies are also frequently conducted by political scientists, whose polling skills have been refined to such a great extent recently that they have been able to predict the winners of elections from small samplings within a very narrow margin of error. As in the case of the economist, political scientists depict political trends and information in diagrams, charts, tables, and graphs.

Political Science Instruction

Next to the study of American history, the study of American government is one of the most important components of the social studies curriculum. Civics and government courses are taught at all levels of the curriculum as a means of civic education. The study of government and civics in the schools includes the study of the origins, structures, and functions of government as well as the knowledge and competencies needed by citizens to participate effectively in the affairs of a democratic nation, state, and community. In addition, the California State Curriculum Commission (1962) notes that pupils should develop democratic procedural habits and skills.

> These include knowing how to read newspapers, speak in public, and conduct meetings; and how to be an action-minded participant in the affairs of the school, community, state, nation, and world. (p. 97)

Political science and government are important components of the social studies curriculum because civic education is needed to develop citizenship values consistent with democratic rule. The California State Curriculum Commission contends that citizenship and civic education are important elements of the social studies curriculum through which democratic citizenship is developed and enhanced. "To be a capable and conscientious citizen, the individual needs (1) to understand the structure and function of government; and (2) to develop citizenship skills" (p. 97).

The social studies includes political science components both in the elementary and secondary curricula. These components often are listed under the heading of "civic education." According to the authors of the *Civitas: A Framework for Civic Education* (Bahmueller, 1991),

> The aim of civic education is therefore not just any kind of participation by any kind of citizen; it is the participation of informed and responsible citizens, skilled in the arts of deliberation and effective action. (p. 1)

Civic education includes the study and the function of government, civic virtues pertaining to the citizens' commitment to the country and the republic, and a commitment to the fundamental values and principles of democratic rule. In addition, civic education is committed to civic action and community participation as important expressions of civic responsibility. Values issues within democratically ruled societies tend to focus on topics related to direct and representative forms of government. These issues also include the personal qualities of citizens, leaders, and officeholders and the positions of political parties and candidates on social, economic, and political issues. Other important issues include the effectiveness of governmental institutions and processes; the rights and responsibilities of citizens; justice, fairness, and equality within the political arena; the processes and means of change; the abuse of political power; and political corruption.

Citizenship education is an important aspect of civic education. According to Dynneson and Gross (1991), the social studies has been influenced by two instructional traditions that include "civic learning" and "socio/civic learning." Civic learning is an approach that promotes political education over social education. This approach emphasizes the study of the American political sys-

WHY DO STUDENTS SEEM TO PREFER CIVICS OVER GOVERNMENT?

In high schools, what are the differences between government and civics classes? Do these differences explain why some student surveys have rated civics courses as being more interesting and valuable than government courses?

tem including the concepts, skills, and values that are associated with that system. The socio/civic tradition is more vernacular in that it attempts to deal with government and civics according to the everyday experiences of common people. It is indirectly associated with political socialization and with many of the principles of progressive education. This approach takes into account the social and educational conditions that influence the education of children. Dynneson and Gross (1991) have recommended that the social studies attempt a new synthesis between the civic learning and the socio/civic approaches as a means of improving instruction in the study of government and civics. Because the overriding goal of the social studies is citizenship education, citizenship education has been perceived to include more than just the formal study of government. Citizenship education includes a socio/civic perspective that emphasizes active participation in the family, community, state, nation, and world; it also includes important social considerations related to social relationships, social responsibilities, and social involvement. Also at the heart of citizenship education are decision-making and critical thinking skills.

The instructional history of government and civics can be traced back to this country's beginning when the founders of the Republic felt a need to include civic elements in the school curriculum as a means of preparing children for democratic citizenship. In 1916 the NEA Commission on the Reorganization of Secondary education recommended that civics be taught in the ninth grade and that government be taught in the twelfth grade. The mission of citizenship education was based on the belief that democratic citizens were expected to participate in the affairs of the community, state, and nation. In addition, the study of government also was based on the need to teach students about the structure and functions of government. According to Shaver and Knight (1986), elements of progressive education led to the development of a "problems approach" to help students learn to study the social issues that arise in connection with governmental systems and policies (pp. 71–72).

At the beginning of the twentieth century, students were expected to study "civic government," which translated into the study of the constitutional tradition. The study of the Constitution included a detailed item-by-item study of both the English and the American constitutions (Jenness, 1990). The study of civics came to include the study of service occupations and the workings of local government similar to the current elementary study of "community helpers" (policemen, firemen, teachers, librarians, for example). In the upper elementary grades (junior high) the emphasis in civics was on the structure of government. During the 1920s and 1930s, government and civics textbooks tended to stress the values of the U.S. political system with an emphasis on citizenship, including traditional values of family, hard work, thrift, patriotism, and the virtues of the American way of life. This emphasis produced a somewhat mythical aura to these textbooks similar to that expressed by George Bancroft in his nineteenth century history textbooks or of the McGuffey readers of the same period. During the 1930s, government textbooks began to express more of a reconstructionist's perspective in which the role of government was to change from a laissez-faire orientation to a hands-on regulatory mission over the institutions of society.

A Problems of Democracy course was included in the high school curriculum in the early decades of the twentieth century. This course was designed for seniors as an issues course. From the 1920s to the 1960s, this course included a mixture of content from economics, sociology, government, and related subjects. Jenness (1990) suggests that this course was more of a reading course than an issues course. In effect, this course may have drawn students away from a "real" government instruction (p. 178). During the 1960s, the "new social studies" movement entered the curricular stream with a social science orientation that emphasized the concepts of political science and the ways that political scientists answer questions and solve problems. At this time, the Harvard Project created materials designed to help students learn about and study important social and political issues and to participate in political decision making (Shaver & Knight, 1986). Their problem-solving model became known as a "jurisprudential process" because it required the use and the weighing of evidence in the process of rendering a decision or in making a choice.

With the change in the voting age requirements from twenty-one to eighteen years of age, school districts began to replace the Problems course in the twelfth grade with an American government course. This course was justified on the grounds that students would soon exercise their right to vote, and the placement of a government course was deemed essential as a final form of readiness for students to prepare for meeting their adult citizenship responsibilities. Certain "traditionalists" also still disapproved of the emphasis on "problems" in government courses.

The study of government, especially American government, is an important aspect of civic education. Although government is related to the academic discipline of political science, courses in government attempt to help students gain a more general knowledge of the U.S. political system; the structure and organization of local, state, and federal governmental systems; and the civic nature of democracy, including the rights and responsibilities of U.S. citizens.

SHOULD STUDENTS STUDY NON-DEMOCRATIC SYSTEMS?

High school government courses often devote some time to non-democratic countries. Which foreign systems or nations do you believe deserve adequate comparative treatments? Explain why.

Also, the study of government is believed to provide students with certain essential citizenship values. It is hoped that students can learn to appreciate the nature and structure of the government by studying such values as the separation of power as a means of checking the excesses caused by the concentration of power as in the case of dictatorships. In addition, a knowledge of the structure and function of government helps students learn how the machinery of government operates and thus provides them with the means of accessing and *assessing* the system. Instructional design must deal with student attitudes toward government. Democratic citizenship can be advanced only under those conditions in which students are convinced that they are able to influence the actions and the directions of the ruling establishment.

In recent years, declining public confidence in government has lead to a high degree of political alienation, and this alienation is reflected in the attitudes of students. According to Woyach (1991), major elections find increasing numbers of young voters failing to exercise their franchise.

> The 1970s saw the average citizen become increasingly less interested in public life. Frequently less than half of the eligible voters vote. Opinion polls pointed to a decline both in people's faith in government and in their ability to influence government. In short, Americans were becoming increasingly alienated politically. (pp. 50–51)

The result of political alienation tends to be withdrawal and neglect of one's civic responsibilities. Social studies teachers have a responsibility to confront this problem by planning instruction around this important contemporary problem. Through various elements of instructional design, teachers can help revitalize the democratic ideals by emphasizing that the neglect of civic responsibility will ultimately lead to the loss of freedom.

One of the most valuable ways to instill these democratic ideals in classrooms and school, at all levels, is to grant students rights and responsibilities in the decision making and actions that characterize democratically organized and functioning systems. Students will "buy in" to programs and activities in which they find a personal part. One of the great errors of many elementary and secondary schools (and especially so in social studies classrooms) is the

CIVICS VERSUS CITIZENSHIP EDUCATION: WHICH IS WHICH?

In your opinion, what, if any, areas of emphasis should differentiate civics education from citizenship education? Would a teacher of math or biology have any responsibilities in either area? Explain.

failure to extend numerous participatory activities to pupils far beyond the typical voting on an issue or having a student council.

Civics and government courses in the social studies curriculum reflect several orientations for instruction. Shaver and Knight (1986) have described the disagreements and the confusion that surround this school subject. The range of civics and government instruction includes some of the following orientations: the study of the structure and organization of government (including national, state, and local descriptions), policy and decision making and the role of pressure groups, social criticism, comparative government, the intellectual-empirical study of political behavior from a social science perspective, and the study of the problems of democracy. While the study of the structure and organization is the approach taken by most government texts, civics courses tend to be more value oriented with an emphasis on the values of the American system and the American way of life.

During the 1970s, the American Political Science Association wrote a critical report on the teaching of civics in schools. This report suggests that teachers of government and civics in American schools present a naive and unrealistic picture of the U.S. political system and how it actually works with too much emphasis on historical events and too little emphasis on the study of issues and methods of scientific inquiry (Committee on Pre-Collegiate Education, 1971). There can be no question that "behind and under" the formalities of governmental structure emphasized in texts and courses is a complex of political and economic ties and arrangements that every citizen needs to understand.

Because civics and government have had a long history of being included in the social studies curriculum, ample materials are available for instruction. In addition, strategies for teaching this field have multiplied over the years. At the same time, some teachers are still relying on memorization and recitation of events, names, dates, articles, laws, and amendments. The abusive practice of having students memorize the articles and the amendments of state and national constitutions is beginning to be replaced by more meaningful experiences for students. Citizenship education relies on knowledge of the political and social systems and the development of cognitive skills needed to deal with

DO YOU AGREE THAT ALL POLITICS ARE LOCAL?

Government courses usually are centered on and give major attention to our federal government. What civic values can be developed if teachers allot more time and attention to state and especially to local government?

important societal issues. Currently, many teachers are using or developing a more hands-on involvement approach as a means of motivating student interest in the study of civics and government.

The *Social Studies Framework for the Public Schools of California* (State Curriculum Commission, 1962) contains several generalizations that may be appropriate for helping teachers design government and civic instruction, including the following:

- Throughout history, the peoples of the world have experimented with a wide variety of governmental forms.
- Two essential functions of government are to serve and to regulate in the public interest. The ultimate responsibilities of government are divided into five major categories: (a) external security; (b) internal order; (c) justice; (d) service essential to the general welfare; and, under democracy, (e) freedom.
- In a democracy, government is the servant of the people; people are not the servants of government.
- It is the business of government to do for the people what they cannot do or what they cannot do as well for themselves.
- When government is organized, it is essential that leaders be authorized to have power with which to act and that they be held responsible for its wise use.
- Democracy implies a way of life as well as a form of government.
- Democracy is based on certain fundamental assumptions. Among these are the integrity of man, the dignity of the individual, equality of opportunity, man's rationality, man's morality, man's practicality, and man's ability to govern himself and to solve his problems cooperatively.
- A chief goal of democracy is the preservation and extension of human freedoms.
- Civil liberty—freedom of thought, speech, press, worship, petition, and association—constitutes the core of freedom.
- Certain factors are necessary for democracy to succeed and survive. These include (a) an educated citizenry; (b) a common concern for human freedom; (c) communication and mobility; (d) a degree of economic security; (e) a spirit of compromise and mutual trust; (f) respect for the rights of minority groups and the loyal opposition; (g) moral and spiritual values; and (h) participation by the citizen in governmental levels.
- The citizen has civic responsibilities as well as rights.

CAN AND SHOULD THE TEACHER CONTRIBUTE
TO STUDENTS' POLITICAL OUTLOOK?

List the key concepts of rights and responsibilities that exist in the domain of political democracy. Why are schools and classes seldom organized or taught in ways that promote these qualities?

The Study of Economics

Through the study of economics, students learn that human beings have material needs that cannot be entirely satisfied. All needs and demands cannot be met because material resources are relatively scarce in light of human desires. Modern economics tends to focus on one important problem and that problem, according to Cole (1969), is *The means to satisfy the wants of the human race, even in the most affluent societies, are scarce.* In a word, the economic problem is scarcity" (p. 3). This scarcity may be the result of insufficient supply or of the lack of purchasing power or both. To maximize the chances of meeting material needs, societies have organized various types of economic systems. An economic system consists of the processes that are used in making economic decisions about how material resources will be allocated or which human needs will be met and which will not.

These systems are based on the dominant and accepted cultural values, beliefs, and attitudes regarding an appropriate or ideal economic system, a system designed to facilitate the production and distribution of material goods. Because human wants and needs are insatiable and because resources are limited, economic values related to scarcity underlie the decision-making processes that are used to determine which goods will be produced and who will acquire them. In addition, accepted economic values help to direct the activities of economic institutions (policy-making bodies, financial institutions, tariff boards, for example) that are developed to support the economic system.

The origins of economic systems stem from cultural and political sources. Cultural sources include philosophical beliefs regarding the ideal society as perceived from the perspective of a material culture. An ideal material culture becomes an important goal of society because it prescribes and defines important material aims (home ownership, private property, for instance). For example, an important aim of the ideal material culture would include a respectable standard of living for all citizens that satisfies basic needs to build a dynamic and productive community. One politician stated the goals of our

IF THIS IS SCIENCE, WHY THE CRYSTAL BALL?

In light of greatly varied opinions held by leading economists and the fact that their economic predictions are often incorrect, is it proper to call economics a "science"? If so, what aspects of economics may be properly designated as scientific?

material culture when he called for "a chicken in every pot and a car in every garage" as a part of his campaign rhetoric.

By tradition and by legislation, most economic decisions in American society are made within a market setting—what is produced is determined by market demand and the ability of individuals to bid for what they want. The relationship between government and the economy system is determined by changing economic conditions, especially in light of abundant resources, a strong fiscal environment, efficient labor, and adequate demand for finished goods. While the economic system may be considered the supporter of the political system, government does not make things; instead, its main role is to help create conditions that are favorable to the economic system.

The science of economics can be traced back to the ancient Greeks. They coined the term *economics*, and its original applications suggested the mundane concerns of daily life. The word translated into "house rule or the way the house was to be ruled." From these origins, the science of economics evolved slowly into the study of economic matters of the community and the state. The science of economics would not begin until the eighteenth century, but in the sixteenth and seventeenth centuries mercantile trading systems helped to lay the foundation for the early development of economic theory.

Much of mercantile trade was aimed at giving certain nations trade advantages and to see to it that heads of state had an ever-increasing treasury. Money was used to provide for colonial expansion and to raise armies and navies as a defense against encroaching powers. Therefore, mercantilistic theory was a forerunner or primitive form of a planned economy in which emerging nations were ranked in terms of power according to the amount of precious metal that they could accumulate. State treasuries were used by heads of state to finance challenges and to defeat foreign competitors.

The first modern economic theorist was Adam Smith. In 1777 he wrote the first important treatise on economic theory. Smith's book, the *Wealth of Nations*, prescribed a relationship between heads of state and the new merchant class. This theory became known as *laissez-faire capitalism*, which emphasized a government "hands-off" economic policy. According to Adams, the economy should operate according to "natural law," or the law of supply

IF ENTERPRISE IS FREE, WHY ALL THE RULES?

In spite of continuing arguments over the virtues of laissez-faire capitalism, ask students to list in one column the elements that limit free enterprise. In a second column, have them list aspects that are clearly laissez-faire in principle and in practice. In a third column, list laissez-faire aspects that government promotes. What do they think should be the title of our present economic system?

and demand as determined by the marketplace. As a result of this policy, markets would reward efficient traders and merchants who thereby increase their wealth. At the core of Smith's contribution was the idea that the marketplace should be open to all citizens who looked to their own self-interests and, in so doing, enhanced the wealth of the nation. Not until after the middle of the eighteenth century did economic studies become significant for serious scholars. Henceforth, the theories for economic systems that would emerge would become an important means for the distribution of wealth as well as for creation of new social classes based on wealth.

Pessimistic scholars of the nineteenth century began to criticize and attack the economic status quo as the factory system and industrialization wreaked havoc on the lower and rural classes. In time, utopian socialists offered solutions to the social ills that were emerging. Karl Marx, working off of socialist doctrine, developed the most threatening doctrine to laissez-faire capitalism, and his theory became the focus of a heightened class conflict of the late nineteenth and early twentieth centuries. Marx expressed the belief that the capitalist classes and working classes would become locked in struggle that would eventually lead to the emergence of a new economic (utopian) society. This new society would be characterized as governmentless, classless, and communal living.

As time passed, economics was further refined by precise mathematical analytical tools that were used to study problems and to predict future economic changes. At the same time, more sophisticated economic models were used to study the effects of various influences on the economy. During the 1930s, John Maynard Keynes wrote his *General Theory* in which he advanced economic theory and economic policy making, especially concerning the role of government. As a result of Keynes' work, government gained new economic tools for formulating a fiscal policy that could be used to fine-tune the economy, plans that were designed to help governments gain some degree of control over "bust and boom" business cycles. Historically these cycles had caused a great deal of economic hardship and social unrest within industrialized nations.

At present, governments are required to play an expanded role in economic policy because the individual alone cannot resolve economic problems, nor is the individual capable of changing economic practices. *The economic system is considered to be the sum total of human action and behavior related to earning and living and acquiring material goods.* To live in a community is to be a part of any number of interdependent groups where every individual is involved with or affected by the actions of others. Economic policy becomes the formulated actions that attempt to modify or steer the economic system into constructive or beneficial directions. In addition, economic policy is designed to help deal with fundamental economic problems such as the problems of scarcity and the distribution of wealth.

As consumers, we are forced to choose between the goods and services that are available to us for a price. While human beings will never satisfy every want, they can learn to improve their economic conditions. Individuals who make unwise decisions are accountable for their economic choices and must live with the consequences of their actions. Students are often taught certain economic principles designed to help them make better decisions. These programs are often under the heading of "consumer economics." Because human beings are economically interdependent, every individual needs some knowledge about the nature and function of the economic system. This system is the focus of study of a great number of experts called "economists" who attempt to learn something of the nature, the rules or laws, the operations, and the directions of the economic system. In turn, this information becomes the basis for solving current economic problems and for formulating economic policy.

Economic skills are reflected in the work of professional economists. In the United States economic activities are directly related to the acquisition of raw materials, production, labor, technology and capital. In addition, the activities of the economist include planning and decision making concerning setting priorities, manufacturing products, marketing and distributing products, controlling the money supply, and raising of capital resources. Recall that economics is claimed as the science that attempts to deal with material scarcity as it relates to the human condition. This condition translates into the economists' concerns for production, distribution, and consumption, based on various decision-making models and schemes.

Professional economists work in a variety of settings including universities, corporations, government, banks, and investment houses. An important aspect of their work is related to the study of the economy and current and future economic trends. Because of the problems that economists are called on to solve, they require great quantities of accurate information on a variety of subjects including the availability of goods, the number of employed people, the number of units of production that factories complete over a given period of time, the amount of money saved by consumers, and the amount of new capital being invested for research and development. Problem solving for economists often begins with the development of models that can be used to make decisions and predict future trends. The forecasts that result from predictive models often are used to make important economic decisions. Therefore, the reputation of an economist rests in large part on the accuracy of the prediction, and the quality of the prediction rests on the efficacy of the model and the adequacy of the information that goes into the forecast.

Economists often are called on to illustrate changes in economic behavior by preparing tables, charts, graphs, and other illustrative presentations that depict past, current, and future trends. Therefore, economists are called to illustrate information to help others understand the nature of the economic condition. For example, indexing is an important skill that is used to explain the cost of goods in terms of actual values; for example, pork chops cost only 25 cents a pound in the 1930s. Without realizing that the value of the 1930s dollar was much greater than today's dollar, students might conclude that the 1930s were the "good old days." By indexing, economists are able to provide a realistic understanding of the prices of goods in regard to the purchasing power of the dollar.

In the United States, the material culture is based on the ideal of economic "plenty" or the idea that in addition to basic needs, surplus goods will be available to all. Therefore, important economic values focus on the notion of a high standard of living. The economic system is designed to achieve the economy of plenty based on such free enterprise values as individual initiative, competition, and the free exchange of goods. According to these values, most economic decisions would be made in a marketplace in which every individual is a free economic agent who acts on his or her own behalf. Historically, the government played a role in the economic affairs of citizens; however, since the Great Depression, the role of government has changed. Although the actions and underlying values including individual initiative, competition, and marketplace decision making continued, the excesses of the marketplace were to be regulated. Consequently, the economic system was modified to include an expanded government role. This modification has led to disagreements and conflicts over the nature of the economy and the role of the government in the economy, including the limitations that have been placed on the activities of private business and on the marketplace.

The American economy tends to be a mixture of systems and values. For example, the marketplace still represents laissez-faire values, values that are checked by government regulations. As a result, an adversarial relationship has emerged between free enterprise and government. In the United States, government agencies attempt to regulate damaging and unfair economic behavior, while at the same time attempting to encourage commerce, standardize measures, and protect the consumer and the environment. In addition, the government attempts to secure international markets and trade and to develop monetary policy related to the regulation of banks and the supply of money. Business and government leaders have proven that they can cooperate on behalf of the common good of society. In recent years government officials and business leaders have worked together to formulate policies that will create jobs, promote American products, and improve educational opportunities.

How Do Systems Label Influence Perceptions?

Students need to understand the relationships, as well as the differences, between socialistic, fascist or dictatorial, and democratic societies. In the realm of economics, why is it sometimes difficult to separate practices shared in these systems?

The desire for an improved educational system is an example of a common ground that exists between government and business. In reaching agreement on private and public options and contributions to educational improvement or in promoting the health of citizens, however, serious areas of controversy prove difficult to resolve.

In some European countries, the government owns or controls basic industries that are operated for the general welfare of its citizens. These types of government are termed "socialistic" as opposed to "capitalistic." In most capitalistic countries, such as the United States, basic industries are owned by private groups and individuals. In most European countries, some form of socialistic system has dominated governments for many years. For seventy-five years the now-defunct Soviet Union was the most pronounced socialistic nation. According to these systems, sometimes called "communist," everyone is more or less considered equal in an economic sense and there is less competition and less individual initiative. The planned economic system is controlled by central planners rather than by the marketplace choices. According to this system, community values supersede those of the individual.

Japan is an example of strong governmental support of private business. In Japan, private enterprise has acted in partnership with government to promote Japanese products and control international markets. According to the Japanese system, cooperation is a means of competing in an emerging global economy.

Ethics and moral issues are related to economic conduct, and these issues change from one historic period to another and as new conditions emerge. In the past, the relationship between company owners and their employees was at times a source of social unrest and conflict. Working people often felt that they were treated unfairly by owners, and as a result, they organized labor movements that would represent their interests. Today, companies are being held accountable for the products that they produce, especially regarding the claims that are made in connection with consumer products. In addition, companies are being held responsible not only for the welfare of workers, but also for the effects that their activities have on the environment. The idea of "good citizenship" has been extended to corporations and to all aspects of their operations. The morality and the ethics of "good corporate citizenship" is becoming the standard for government regulation as a new way of doing business in the United States. To put the matter another way, new material culture is a product of the socio/civic culture that has been evolving since the beginning of the twentieth century.

Today, economic concerns are at the forefront of international relationships. In recent years, the competition between political systems, characteristic of the "cold war," has taken a back seat to economic trade and the competition between nations over market shares and improving trade balances. As a result, governments are playing a greater role in the affairs of their nations' economy, especially in terms of the issues of free and just trading and international finance. In a recent international trip, the President of the United States was accompanied by business leaders to pressure another trading nation to open their domestic markets to U.S. goods. Undoubtedly, the future relationships between business and government will become even more entangled because of changing conditions that advance the development of a global economy.

Economic Instruction

The study of economics slowly became a part of the social studies curriculum. At first it was taught as a course in a few school districts, and in 1916 the NEA Commission on the Reorganization of Secondary Education recommended that economics be included as a part of a twelfth grade course entitled "Problems of Democracy." In time, The American Economic Association advanced the teaching of economics in the schools (Armento, 1986). During the 1930s, there was a growing perception that school children needed instruction in economic matters as they pertained to the national economy and to their own personal affairs. In 1938 "economic efficiency" became a goal of the progressive-oriented curriculum. During the 1960s, separate instructional courses in economic education multiplied including programs for elementary students. For example, Professor Lawrence Senesh (1971) proposed that economics serve as the core of the K–6 social studies curriculum entitled Our Working World. The junior high school and the high school witnessed the greatest expansion of economic instruction in recent decades.

The curricular issues surrounding the teaching of economics in the schools tend to focus on a balance between consumer and personal economics and societal or institutional economics. Some authors have described this issue as a balance between "personal economics" versus "citizenship economics." The debate over the nature and the content of economic education has been discussed over the past fifty years with no final solution in sight. Some economists have held their subject to be too difficult for offerings at the elementary and secondary school levels. Certain leaders of the American Economic Association have held that, in an overcrowded social studies curriculum in the schools, economic understandings would be best integrated into the established courses of history, government, and geography. Others, however, have attempted to find ways to offer separate economic courses and units in the schools. In some instances, this has become a simplified "consumer economics." Unfortunately, because of factors discussed below, for many pupils economics has retained its unhappy title as the "dismal science."

According to Beverly Armento (Jenness, 1990), economics was taught in 40 percent of high schools by the mid-1920s with a relatively small enrollment of about 5 percent of the student body electing to take these courses. During the 1930s and through the 1950s, the emphasis was on economic education in the form of studying economics through concrete life situations rather than on the study of the abstractions of the economic system. Included in this approach was an emphasis on the free-enterprise system, intelligent use of income, occupational concerns, and current economic issues. By the late 1940s, there was a growing movement to emphasize the study of the American economic system and the institutions that supported the economic system. In 1949 the Joint Council on Economic Education was formed for this purpose. It sponsored many institutes for teachers and produced valuable teaching materials.

During the 1950s, the growing interest in developing instructional materials promoted the application of cognitive thinking skills to current economic issues. The "new social studies" movement of the 1960s promoted the teaching of economics as a social science in the curriculum with a greater emphasis on problem solving. The economists' methods of problem solving were incorporated into this approach as were the conceptual structures of the discipline. At the present time, economic education continues to be promoted as an important aspect of social studies instruction. This effort is supported by The National Association of Economic Educators, and a viable economic education program is promoted through Councils and Centers. School districts also participate in the development of economic education through the Developmental Economic Education Program (DEEP), which is designed to improve economic education through grades K–12 (Armento, 1986). Some states require high school students to take a course in "free enterprise" as a graduation requirement. In some states, economics is taught in connection with a global perspective. High schools with large college preparation enrollments tend to offer more in-depth economics electives, and while economics has made inroads into the social studies curriculum, its enrollments are relatively low (Jenness, 1990). Throughout the country, economics as an aspect of citizenship education has broad support with the business community in backing this aspect of social studies education.

The development of an appropriate economic education program for the schools has been hampered by some important concerns. The subject-matter content of economics is generally considered difficult and too abstract for most school children.

Is It a Case of Dreary Is as Dreary Does?

Economics has been called "the dismal science." To what extent is this charge related to the content of the subject and to what extent to economic instruction?

The complexities, for example, of the banking system and function of the Federal Reserve Bank are not easily presented. The response to this concern was to teach economic concepts and principles through a consumer or applied form of economics that is encountered in everyday transactions of life. While this approach was and still is popular in the lower grades, the critics of this type of economic instruction complain that students are not being prepared to understand the nature and complexities of the economic system. Consequently, students are charged with being economically illiterate and thereby unable to fulfill their responsibilities and the decision making that arise in connection with the political economy. Economic education programs designed to instruct students in the basics of the economic system often are considered too unrealistic to the life experiences of students.

A long-range problem associated with economic education focuses on teacher education. Despite the efforts of many individuals and groups, economic instruction within the social studies is limited by three critical factors that have thus far limited the effectiveness of economic instruction. Ronald A. Banaszak (1991) identified these issues in the following statement:

> The first is the ambivalent attitude most Americans have toward our economy. The second is the lack of popularity of economics in the school curriculum, due to its manner of instruction. Third is the widespread erroneous understanding of the economy by citizens. (p. 102)

Most social studies teachers have not had a single college course in economics. As a result, teachers are poorly prepared to instruct students in the concepts and the methodologies of economics. While this problem has been addressed by various attempts to train or retrain teachers in workshops and in-service programs, the problem remains. History teachers may find it difficult to teach students about economic issues that arise during various historical periods without some course work in economics. Banaszak (1991) lays much of the blame for the poor results of economic instruction in history and government courses on the twin problems of poor teacher preparation and the poor quality of instructional materials: ". . .many teachers have little training in economics, but it is also due to the poor quality of economic content in . . . social studies textbooks. . ." (p. 106).

How Might Consumer Economics Make Theoretical Economics Real?

In what ways can a teacher draw on the content and concepts of Consumer Economics to personalize and increase student interest and involvement in the subject matter?

Instructional materials for economics instruction have steadily improved and these materials are becoming grade-level appropriate. Before the 1960s, instructional materials were limited and often not field-tested in the classroom. Also, innovative teaching strategies have helped to improve economic instruction. In spite of these advances in materials and strategies, economics is still considered a very difficult subject to teach and to learn. While complicated, some of the skills of the economist can be learned and applied by students in a social studies class. Elementary students can learn to interpret and to construct simple charts and graphs that depict various items such as people, cars, or agricultural items for comparative purposes. Secondary students can learn more sophisticated skills: developing models, gathering information, illustrating charts and tables, drawing conclusions, and predicting future conditions.

Education can help individuals make the most of their economic predicament through an understanding of the economic system that is used to produce and distribute goods and services. In addition, students can learn to make sound decisions regarding their personal and family choices in the marketplace. Finally, students can learn to manage their own finances to maximize their potential for improving their standard of living. In democratic societies, the public can influence economic policy and decision making; therefore, the current economic system is considered a political economy. As citizens, students are expected to be economically literate and to contribute to the material well-being of the society as a whole.

Through the creative use of instructional design, the issue of the popularity of economic instruction in the schools can be addressed and remedied. Once accomplished, future generations of U.S. citizens should become more informed about the economic system, which has such a profound influence on the conditions of economic and social well-being. Economic understanding is important to the development of a good and just society. Furthermore, citizens must possess a basic level of economic knowledge in order to participate in most political decisions, thus making economic education an important part of citizenship education. Therefore, instructional design should include essential economic elements related to the personal and the public lives of democratic citizens.

WHICH APPROACH DO YOU PREFER?

Do you believe student economic understandings are best built via separate courses in economics, or when basic aspects of economics are woven into historical, governmental, and geographic issues in integrated social studies offerings? Explain.

Educational programs for precollegiate students attempt to provide students with a basic understanding of the current economic system. The *Social Studies Framework for the Public Schools of California* (State Curriculum Commission, 1962) contains several generalizations that may be appropriate for helping teachers design economic instruction, including the following:

- Economic welfare is a goal in most, if not all, modern societies.
- Productive resources are scarce, and human wants are unlimited.
- The full use of productive facilities directly influences economic welfare.
- Government can contribute to the maintenance of high-level production and employment, rapid economic growth and progress, and the stability of the dollar by proper use of its authority through sound fiscal and debt-management policies.
- High per-capita income is the result of high productivity of labor.
- In a competitive, private-enterprise system, prices indicate the relative value of goods and services.
- A market price system works best when both buyers and sellers are highly competitive, well informed, and able and disposed to act in accordance with the information available.
- There are many ways to organize economic activity.
- In a competitive market, each productive agent tends to receive as income a sum equal to the value of his productive contribution to society.
- Imperfections in competition create important public problems.
- The way to improve the standard of living for all the people is to increase productivity.

CONCLUSIONS

In the section of this chapter on political science, you learned that this discipline is represented in the school curriculum by government and civics courses and that these programs are considered an important component of social studies curriculum. The importance of government and civic instruction is found in connection with the desire to educate students for citizenship. While the entire school shares in the burden of educating students for citizenship, the social studies has been assigned the task of instructing students in civic education (political education as in the study of government) as well as citizenship (the acquisition of knowledge, skills, and values related to American society, including the traditions, values, and practices that are related to democratic living). Social studies educators have been divided over the extent to which civic education (political education) should be emphasized as compared with the broader aspects of citizenship education (socio/civic understandings).

In addition, you realize that many political scientists seem to prefer a civic education approach over a citizenship education approach and they often express an uneasiness over the nature of government and civics courses. However, they express a stronger discomfort over various citizenship education approaches that are used by the schools for the purpose of socializing children for adult living (for example, awarding signs of merit [stars] after student names for having tattled on their classmates and calling this the "good citizenship" deed of the week). As a result of this uneasiness, political scientists tend to view various citizenship education programs as naive, simplistic, and unrealistic. Consequently, political scientists, through the efforts of their professional organization, have attempted to promote a more academic type of instruction in order to deal with the realities of American political life.

At the same time, you should note that political scientists have acknowledged that political socialization is a reality and that the family and the school play an important role in this process. These studies have generated a great deal of information about the "civic culture" in U.S. society, information that could be applied to citizenship education courses in the schools. By incorporating the findings of political socialization within citizenship education instruction, social studies education could help resolve the current dilemma in the social studies curriculum and, in the process, help to make citizenship education a more acceptable approach to political scientists. For example, citizenship education could benefit from political socialization studies aimed at "the development of the political self," "methods of political learning," "discontinuities" in citizenship development, and the influence of the "agents" of political learning (including the family, school, and peers). See, for example, R. D. Hess and J. V. Torney, "The development of political attitudes of children," in Greenberg (1970).

Having read the section of this chapter on economics, you should realize that economic education has gained the influence and support of important outside agencies. At the same time, you should understand that while economists tend to support economic instruction in the schools, they tend to prefer economic instruction that focuses on the concepts, principles, processes, and practices associated with the economic system. Economists would tend to argue that as future voters, students are required to judge the merits of various economic proposals in light of their effects on the economic health of the nation and the community. Educators on the other hand, have attempted to develop more general economic education programs, which include the study of economics from the consumer's perspective. Consumer economics, including various aspects of personal economics, tends to focus on the need to help students develop an adequate economic literacy that may be useful to them in surviving the pitfalls and temptations of a marketplace economy. In addition, educators have encouraged students to study various aspects of the free-enterprise system and global interdependence from an economic perspective, perspectives that tend to emphasize societal concerns and certain value perspectives. As a consequence of differing goals, the social studies curriculum contains a variety of economic instructional programs that serve different purposes. Some economists would regard consumer economics, personal economics, free-enterprise economics, and related programs in global interdependence with a degree of disdain, while educators view the study of economic theories as too complex for most precollegiate students. These differences have lead to the development of a variety of economic education programs in which a wide range of instructional materials cover the full range of economic education concerns.

REFERENCES

Armento, B. J. (1986). Promoting economic literacy. In S. P. Wronski & D. H. Bragaw (Eds.), *Social studies and social science: A fifty-year perspective* (Bulletin 78, pp. 97–110). Washington, DC: National Council for the Social Studies.

Bahmueller, C. F. (Ed.). (1991). *Civitas: A framework for civic education. A Collaborative Project of the Center for Civic Education and the Council for the Advancement of Citizenship* (NCSS Bulletin 86). Calabasas, CA: Center for Civic Education.

Banaszak, R. A. (1991). The economic perspective: Economic literacy and citizenship education. In R. E. Gross & T. L. Dynneson (Eds.), *Social science perspectives on citizenship education* (pp. 88–115) New York: Teachers College Press.

Cole, C. L. (1969). *The economic fabric of society.* New York: Harcourt, Brace & World.

Committee on Pre-Collegiate Education (PS4, Summer 1971). *Political education in the public schools: The challenge for political science.* Washington, DC: American Political Science Association.

Dynneson T. L., & Gross, R. E. (1991). The educational perspective: Citizenship education in American society. In R. E. Gross & T. L. Dynneson (Eds.), *Social science perspectives on citizenship education* (pp. 1–42). New York: Teachers College Press.

Easton, D. (1967). *The political system: An inquiry into the state of political science.* New York: Alfred A. Knopf.

Greenberg, E. S. (Ed.). (1970). *Political socialization.* New York: Atherton Press.

Jenness, D. (1990). *Making sense of social studies*. New York: Macmillan.

Senesh, L. (1971). Orchestrating of social science in the curriculum. In I. Morrissett & W. W. Stevens, Jr. (Eds.), *Social science in the schools: A search for rationale* (pp. 125–135). New York: Holt, Rinehart & Winston.

Shaver, J. P., & Knight, R. S. (1986). Civics and government in citizenship education. In S. P. Wronski & D. H. Bragaw (Eds.), *Social studies and social science: A fifty-year perspective* (Bulletin 78). Washington, DC: National Council for the Social Studies.

Sorauf, F. J. (1965). *Political Science: An informal overview* (also under the title *Perspectives on political science, Social Science Series*. T. H. Mussig & V. R. Rogers, Eds.) Columbus, OH: Charles E. Merrill.

State Curriculum Commission. (1962). *Social Studies Framework for the Public Schools of California*. Sacramento, CA: State Department of Education.

Woyach, R. B. (1991). The political perspective: Civic participation and the public good. In R. E. Gross & T. L. Dynneson (Eds.), *Social science perspectives on citizenship education* (pp. 43–65). New York: Teachers College Press.

The Behavioral Sciences: Sociology, Psychology, and Anthropology

INTRODUCTION

In this chapter you will learn that the behavioral sciences consist of three important disciplines that are dedicated to the study of human behavior. Sociology, psychology, and anthropology are distinguished by their traditions, orientations, approaches, and methodologies, which are aimed at gaining insights into the subtle sociological, cultural, and psychological influences that shape and direct human behavior. Within each discipline are distinct schools of thought which often result in specialties that study specific types of human questions and problems. At the same time, you will find that the peripheral areas that separate these disciplines are broad; therefore, these disciplines tend to overlap to a greater extent than do many of the other social science disciplines. For example, the discipline of sociology shares many topics, generalizations, and concepts with anthropology and psychology. Sociologists and cultural anthropologists study the same types of questions using many of the same theories and techniques. (Overlaps also occur with specific areas of study or separate disciplines, some of which have grown out of sociology, such as criminology, demography, and social work.)

The Study of Sociology

Sociology provides an understanding of group relationships that influence and determine individual and group behavior within social settings. Social settings tend to dictate the standards of what is and what is not appropriate behavior, standards of behavior that include such areas as dress, etiquette, demeanor, deference, rhetoric, and acknowledgment of shared values, for example. Social relationships within each social setting span a wide range of interests that change over time. These attitudes and behaviors change in accordance with group characteristics such as age, gender, education, occupation, wealth, experiences, and influence.

The origin of sociological study is recorded in the earliest chronicles of civilization, especially social influences that were based on kinship relationships. At that time, one's place in society was considered fixed by the laws of birth. Each individual inherited his or her social position and in turn passed on this same position to his or her children. Later, the advancing urban age brought radical changes as kinship patterns gave way to new patterns based on social relationships. Social relationships were based on trade, reciprocity, and specialization. As a result of these changes, new study areas began to emerge as a means of examining human relationships and behavior. During the nineteenth century, scholars established new disciplines that focused exclusively on the study of human behavior from a scientific perspective. The work of the French scholar Auguste Comte led to the first scientific study of society. Comte completed a six-volume study entitled *Positive Philosophy* that established a new scholarly standard for an emerging sociology. Comte used the methods of "positivism," which combined scientific observation techniques with experimentation. Through the application of these techniques, Comte believed that the whole of society could be studied, described, and understood (Hebding & Glick, 1976). Later Herbert Spencer identified and explored the subareas of sociology including religion, stratification, social control, and politics. In addition, Spencer interpreted society in "organismic" terms, as he was greatly influenced by the writings of Charles Darwin. Spencer believed that a society is the product of the forces of "natural selection" and the "survival of the fittest." According to these principles, society is the product of both social and natural influences and the struggle to survive in an aggressive and hostile world. While others disagree with Spencer's interpretation of Darwin's work, sociologists became interested in the idea of social change and social progress.

Emile Durkheim, considered to be the father of modern sociology, emphasized the idea that society was a total entity or an entire system of interrelated parts. The interactions between components of society produced societal similarities and differences. As a result of this belief, sociologists attempted to identify and explain the overall design and organization of society as an integrated whole. For Durkheim, groups served to restrain the behavior of individuals; therefore, in a complex social setting, the influence of groups can be used

WHY DO YOUTH NEED SOCIOLOGICAL UNDERSTANDINGS?

In terms of the purposes of sociology stated earlier, what modern conditions in American society underscore the increased importance of sociological understandings on the part of young citizens?

to explain individual behavior, including abnormal behavior. He notes that, "When people get together in groups or institutions, something happens that differs from what happens to lone individuals" (Eshleman, 1986, p. 111).

In addition, Durkheim believed that relationships between individuals strongly influence human behavior. According to this belief, when two individuals interact, each person modifies the behavior of the other (Eshleman, 1986). Max Weber further refined sociological thinking by focusing his study of human behavior within the social environment. Weber concluded that human action can be understood in terms of the expectations of social groups or society. According to Weber, individual human behavior can be understood through a study of the internal or subjective meanings that each person applies to his or her actions: "Once values, motives and intentions were identified, Weber contended, sociologists could treat them objectively and scientifically" (Eshleman, 1986, p. 113).

Karl Marx dealt with human behavior from a position called "historical materialism." According to Marx, social change occurs because of economic influences. Economic influences are seen as sources of human conflict that lead to important societal changes. For Marx, "social conflict was at the core of society and the source of all social change" (Eshleman, 1986, p. 113). He further concluded that revolution was an essential means of bringing about social change.

Modern sociology has been defined as the study *of human social life, groups, and societies* (Giddens, 1991); or, as *"the scientific study of human interactions and products of such interactions"* (Hebding & Glick, 1976, p. 31). Giddens (1991) acknowledges the large scope of sociology:

> The scope of sociology is extremely wide, ranging from the analysis of passing encounters between individuals in the street up to the investigation of global social processes. (p. 2)

According to Alpert (1963), sociologists tend to be concerned with the logical explanation of ordinary and exceptional social phenomena by seeking to fit them into a general sociological framework of structure in order to:

WHICH SOCIOLOGISTS, OTHER THAN MARX, OFFER A WELL-REASONED EXPLANATION FOR SOCIAL CHANGE?

Describe a historical event in which the insights of a sociologist might more satisfactorily or completely explain its cause than a conventional historical account. Explain your answer.

> discover the principles of cohesion and of order within the social structure, the ways in which it roots and grows within an environment, the moving equilibrium of changing structure and changing environment, the main trends of this incessant change and the forces which determine its direction at any time, the harmonies and conflicts, the adjustments and maladjustments within the structure as they are revealed in the light of human desires, and thus the practical application of means to ends in the creative activities of social man." (p. 53)

Explanations related to social structure are worked out in the form of **social theory.** Once developed, a social theory may help to direct research activities that will establish, modify, or nullify theory. Several social theories may be developed to explain the same social condition. Therefore, "social theories offer explanations of the social world—why people marry, attend sporting events or behave differently in different social situations" (Eshleman, 1986, p. 114).

California's State Curriculum Commission (1962) just described the interests and concerns of sociologists as including the processes through which groups are formed, why they persist, and why they break up, including the study of the interworkings of groups and the relationships that are formed and the behaviors that result.

> Social interaction and communication are the general processes through which more specialized processes evolve. These include association, dissociation, and stratification; cooperation and accommodation; competition and conflict; and assimilation. (p. 107)

Individuals are born and live within a relatively large number of group settings, and in each of these settings different processes, rules, patterns of organization, and expectations are applied. Group values tend to become generalized values that are imposed on the individual through various group processes. Throughout one's life, individuals join formal and informal social groups. Each group provides a social setting from which each person gains a sense of identity and belonging. Groups develop out of many social considerations including age, class, gender, ethnicity and race, and recreational interests. Values related to what is worth knowing, believing, and doing help to form and maintain group membership. These values are imposed on the members through group interactions and processes. The dissociation of groups occurs when unifying values weaken or change or the conditions that led to the formation of the group are no longer considered important.

A focus of sociological study is social organization or the identification and analysis of organizational patterns. It identifies patterns within groups and societies and the social forces that bring stability and order to the social setting. According to Eshleman (1986), it "focuses on how the various parts of society fit together to maintain the equilibrium of the whole" (p. 115). Another important aspect of sociological study is related to the unique human application and interpretation of symbols and signs within the social setting. Every person reared in a particular social setting learns a relatively large number of symbolic expressions. These expressions range from facial expressions to concrete symbols in the form of letters, numbers, and pictographs (crosses, crests, flags). For example, in early Christian times, a simple fish drawn with just two lines marked the person or place of a believer. Symbols are a part of the processes of human interactions and communication. When symbols are expressed in a particular way, social messages are sent to those within the group or society. Persons who are outside the group or society will not fully understand the meaning of the message. Eshleman (1986) further notes that the social interaction view of sociology is based on the belief that "humans are unique among all forms of life in their capacity to symbolically represent themselves, ideas, and objects" (p. 118). Therefore, symbolic understandings allow human beings to communicate meaning across the culture in the form of written and oral language.

> Because humans can agree on and share the meaning of symbols (words, gestures, stop signs), they can communicate effectively. Since these meanings are learned in interaction with others and are not instinctive or strictly personal or psychological creations, they are necessarily social. (Eshleman, 1986, pp. 118–119)

The sociologist's methods of working are specifically concerned with learning about human groups and societies through the application of observational skills. The sociologist specifically studies human behaviors that develop as a result of human interaction, behaviors that are learned and practiced within the social setting of the groups. Group interaction tends to produce both social harmony and cohesion and conflict and dissociation. In studying the social dynamics of a group, the sociologist attempts to detect and assess the extent to which group cohesion is challenged by the forces of dissociation. According to Weber, sociologists can address important social problems only by getting close to the social situation in which the act or action is taking place.

WHAT ARE THE INFLUENCES OF GROUP SETTINGS ON INDIVIDUAL STUDENT LEARNING?

Educators are very interested in how group or cooperative learning settings contribute to pupil motivation and learning. Identify the elements in such situations that tend to promote these positive conditions.

> To gain *Verstehen* (understanding) the sociologist might get involved personally in the activities, might observe them without personal participation, might talk to the participants or engage in any activity that enables him or her to be in the 'shoes of the actor.' (Eshleman, 1986, p. 113)

By observing both the formal and informal interactions of social relationships, the sociologist is able to formulate and study all types of questions and problems related to groups. When studying a particular group, the sociologist ultimately will learn how and why the group was formed, its historical origins, its original purposes, and if the group ceases to exist, the reasons for its disintegration. As a part of this study, sociologists would observe and possibly participate in group meetings to gain insights into the more subtle influences at work.

Because sociological study rests on research methodology techniques that are suited to the gathering of information about groups and societies, sociologists focus on the social behaviors related to areas such as marriage, religion, occupation, political rule, recreation, reciprocity, and child rearing. Therefore, they have developed appropriate study techniques or tools that can be applied within the social setting. The main research tools of sociologists include techniques for (1) gathering information, (2) doing direct observation, and (3) analyzing various forms of social behavior. The tools and techniques of the sociologist include experiments, role playing, sampling, tape recordings, questionnaires, interviews, and sociometric measures. Of particular interest to teachers is a clear understanding of pupil preferences for associates and subgroup relationships in their classrooms. The teacher can use the techniques of *sociometry* to gather and tabulate these revealing interhuman preferences (Gross & Zeleny, 1958, pp. 497–512).

Social studies students would benefit from the study of sociology as a means of understanding social relationships and interactions within group settings. By focusing on various sociological topics, social studies teachers could help their students understand the nature of the society in which they live. This understanding can be advanced by clarifying the purpose of important social, economic, and political groups and institutions. Society is organized around groups and the society functions according to institutional practices; therefore, to understand the nature of society, students need to study the role that groups play in forming, maintaining, and destroying groups and institu-

SHOULD THE FOCUS OF SOCIAL STUDIES BE PRIMARILY ON SOCIAL PROCESSES?

Proponents claim that the entire social studies program from kindergarten through twelfth grade should be organized and taught in terms of basic social processes, that is, how American society is organized and functions according to social, economic, and political groups and institutions. (See, for example, the argument by Marshall and Goetz [1936], one of the original proposals for this approach.) Do you believe there is now more potential for such a reformulated curriculum of social education? Why or why not?

tions. The study of social groups would include family, church, school, club, and various other types of community groups and institutions. At the same time, the study of social systems is an important aspect of the social studies curriculum beginning in the elementary school with the study of family, neighborhood, and community, and extending through the secondary curriculum with the study of social groups in U.S. history and separate courses as civics and government related to American society. For years, high school students have had the opportunity to study various courses on family relationships.

In spite of the potential of sociology as a social studies subject, very little from the formal discipline of sociology usually is taught in the curriculum programs of the schools. This condition is explained by Thomas J. Switzer (1968):

> First, the structure of the curriculum in U.S. schools generally does not include sociology as a course of study. . . .A second major factor accounting for so little sociology being taught in grades K–12 has been a general disinterest in precollegiate education by professionals in the field of sociology. (p. 124)

Also, most social studies teachers have had little or no training in sociology. In addition to other works on the field cited in this chapter, two helpful and nontechnical introductions to sociology have been offered by Peter Berger (1963) and C. Wright Mills (1961).

Sociological Instruction

The coincidental role of sociology in the social studies curriculum includes the study of communities in the elementary school and the growing interest in the teaching of a social history during the Progressive Era. From 1910 to 1920, Rolla Tryon reported that the number of electives courses in sociology increased, but the demand for electives would not sustain this growth (Jenness, 1990). In addition, aspects of sociology are expressed in the study of Community Civics, and sociological issues were often an important element of the Problems of Democracy course offered in the twelfth grade beginning in the 1920s. Jenness (1990) also notes that in the 1930s during the era of the "New Deal," the scientific techniques of sociologists were considered compatible with the goals of social reconstruction, and sociological electives were appearing in high schools. The relationship between sociology and the goals of the social studies often was indirect or disconnected, thus having the effect of reducing the instructional importance of sociology. The "new" social studies movement witnessed the development of sociology projects such as the American Sociological Association-sponsored project entitled Sociological Resources for the Social Studies (SRSS). SRSS emphasized the processes of socialization, institutions, social stratification, and social change. Jenness (1990) points out that this approach had the advantage of making these materials attractive to courses other than separate classes in sociology. For example, Robert Fox and his colleagues in Michigan in the 1960s and 1970s developed social science laboratory experiences for elementary children. During this time, the number of students taking elective courses in sociology continued to grow, due in part to the disappearance of Problems of Democracy courses in the high school. Currently, many larger high schools offer an elective in sociology.

Today, in some programs, students are also given the opportunity to study societal problems in separate courses, but this usually is not a part of the required curriculum. Social studies teachers can incorporate some of the primary skills of the sociologist into their programs and courses, including techniques and processes associated with information gathering and analysis in interactive situations. In addition, the social studies curriculum is designed to help students understand something about the nature, structure, and operation of groups that have existed or currently exist in the United States. The *Social Studies Framework for the Public Schools of California* (State Curriculum Commission, 1962) contains several generalizations that may be appropriate for helping teachers design instruction, including the following:

- The work of society is performed through organized groups.
- Communication is basic to the existence of culture and groups.
- The expressions of man's biological drives are influenced by his social environment.
- Socialization results from the methods of child training and the experiences of childhood.
- An established society, association, or social group gradually develops patterns of learned behavior accepted by and common to its members.
- Within any large and complex society, sub-societies with varying cultures exist.

- People with a common culture sometimes become grouped as social classes and think of themselves as having (a) status or position; and (b) roles or functions quite distinct from those of other classes.
- Culture tends to standardize human behavior and to stabilize societies by developing many interrelated and elaborate institutions.
- National migration develops cultural diversity within groups and cultural diffusion among groups.
- Individuals generally function as members of communities.
- Cooperation is illustrated by the way in which members of families and other more intimately related social groups tend to work together in performing functions of community living and in attaining common goals.
- Societies require a system of social control to survive.
- Some of the techniques of social control that are used by groups on individuals to secure conformity are shunning, ostracism, gossip, jeering, praise, approval, and acceptance.
- Social control, particularly in complex societies, is also partially secured by formal, codified rules of behavior (laws), infractions of which result in formal penalties. (pp. 106–108)

The Study of Psychology

Psychology provides an understanding of both animal and human behavior and usually the focus is on individuals rather than groups. At the core of psychological interests is the acquisition of behavior and behavioral change. Psychology assumes that behavior is not fixed, but is primarily the product of the environmental conditions and circumstances. Environmental changes can lead to changes in individual behavior; therefore, each person is involved in the constant process of change. Psychologists tend to believe that individuals will modify their behavior to meet the requirements of life. Depending on societal standards, human behavior can be classified as normal or abnormal. At the same time, psychologists recognize that certain abnormal behavior is the result of maladies that are unrelated to the environmental conditions or to the norms of society.

Early Greek scholars were interested in the physical and mental nature of human beings. Philosophers described this nature as dualistic and recommended that students be educated according to both their physical and mental natures. An interest in the nature of objects (trees, rocks, etc.) helped to generate a new perspective in which the laws of nature might be understood through the techniques of observation. In time, these techniques were applied to the study of human behavior. During the Renaissance a new emphasis on science lead to the scientific study of human behavior. These studies were assisted by the inductive and more powerful scientific method. The new age of science eventually lead to an experimental psychology that was greatly expanded in the nineteenth and twentieth centuries.

During these same centuries, the experimental methodology lead to the organization of the first laboratory facility as a by-product of German science. Soon afterward, the new methodology was practiced at John Hopkins University. This new methodology was characterized by the use of random samples and experimental and control groups that were given a treatment and a placebo (false treatment). The effects of the treatment were measured and compared to determine their influence on the experimental group. These experiments were replicated again and again to validate the results.

In the United States, the study of psychology was divided into schools of thought including structuralism and behaviorism. **Structuralism,** the school of psychology that sought to determine the structure of the mind, grew out of the experimental movement, but it continued to be influenced by the ideal of the dual nature of human beings. As a consequence, early studies using a structural orientation used *introspection* as the means of describing experiences. This approach was opposed by scholars who preferred to think of psychology as a means of studying the relationship between mind and behavior. In time, this approach lead to the establishment of **behavioral psychology,** which studied the interaction between mind and behavior and emphasized the learning process. In time, John B. Watson convinced psychologists that the proper study of psychology was the study of behavior because he believed that the mind could not be operationally observed.

In the twentieth century, another school of psychology emerged in Germany known as **field,** or **Gestalt, psychology.** Field theorists believe that the "whole is greater than the sum of its parts." Gestalt psychologists believe that patterns or the organization of phenomena, the configuration of an idea, are more important than all of its parts. The behaviorists and the gestaltists differ over the issue of nature/nurture controversy (**nature** being the influence of natural or biological determinism and **nurture** being the influence of culture or the social environment). The behaviorists tend to interpret behavior in terms of

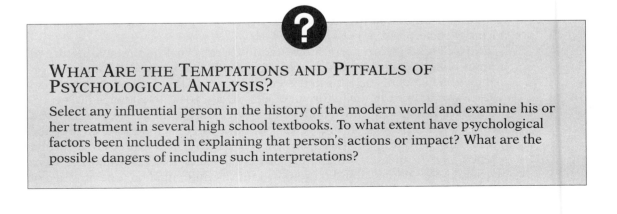

WHAT ARE THE TEMPTATIONS AND PITFALLS OF PSYCHOLOGICAL ANALYSIS?

Select any influential person in the history of the modern world and examine his or her treatment in several high school textbooks. To what extent have psychological factors been included in explaining that person's actions or impact? What are the possible dangers of including such interpretations?

Just Give Me the Facts!

Psychological contributions have proved an important element in the test and measurement movement, particularly on aspects of objective assessment. (See Chapter 12 of this text.) What arguments can be made to justify the extensive use of such items (such as multiple-choice, true and false, matching, and completion questions) on numerous social studies tests, both teacher-made and commercial? Why do some teachers reject this emphasis?

environmental and cultural influences, whereas the gestaltists believe that inherited influences determine the perception that individuals are capable of developing (Morgan, 1974). Most American psychologists are attracted to behaviorism. They support the idea that individuals are flexible and are not predetermined by the conditions of birth; however, current biologically oriented studies underscore the importance of genetic factors.

Psychoanalytic theory, Sigmund Freud's theory that the origin of personality lies in the balance between three components of the mind, was an outgrowth of medicine, and it has influenced clinical psychology. To treat his patients' personality disorders, Freud used **psychoanalysis,** a method in which he used dream analysis to get patients to resolve their unconscious conflicts between the components of the mind. While there are many differences between psychoanalytic theory and other schools of psychology, psychoanalysis is less controversial today than it was in the past (Wertheimer et al., 1986).

During World War I, psychological testing emerged out of a need to determine whether or not military recruits were suited for military life. Later, more refined testing techniques were designed to help place military personnel into specific job categories. Morgan (1974) explains how widespread psychological testing has become as a standard means of evaluating individual attributes in schools, businesses, and government.

> During the last 50 years, psychological tests have pervaded the United States to such an extent that major steps in the course of most individuals' educational and professional careers are typically preceded, and not infrequently altered, by standardized psychological tests. (p. 173)

Because human behavior is varied and complex, the focus of psychology is varied and complex. This complexity is reflected in specializations that have emerged within the discipline. The study of psychology in higher education has been classified according to (1) general psychology, which tends to focus on the nature and methods of psychology that are of a philosophical and technical nature; (2) psychology as a natural science, which is associated with three types of problems related to measurement, learning, and speed of reaction; (3) psychology as a social science, which tends to focus on the study of personal relationships; and (4) interdisciplinary psychology, which may explore areas such as culture, politics, and history (Walker, 1970).

Clifford Morgan (1974) listed over twelve psychological subfields or specialties. Among these areas are clinical psychology, which is interested in the diagnosis of emotional disorders; counseling psychology, which tends to focus on milder forms of emotional disorders; school and educational psychology, which tends to provide testing and guidance services within the school setting; personality and social psychology, which tends to focus on the personality problems of individuals that are of a nondeviant nature; developmental psychology, which focuses on changes that occur as a result of the life cycle; psychometric psychology, which focuses on measuring and evaluating various traits and characteristics; industrial psychology, which focuses on the selection and placement of individuals within a business or school setting; and experimental psychology, which focuses on the study or exploration of fundamental behavioral principles. Wertheimer (1986), too, has commented on the complexities of the field of psychology:

> Psychology, then, is a sprawling, fragmented field that encompasses a wide variety of problems, issues, trends, aims and methods. Its foci are so varied that different sub-fields may have very little in common with one another. There are tens of thousands of psychologists, some of whom do research with the methods of the natural sciences, others of whom do research with the methods of the social sciences, and most of whom try to apply psychological knowledge to solving the problems of industry, the classroom, the military, intergroup tension, and the clinic. (pp. 176–177)

In spite of the complexities of psychology, its aim is to understand and to predict behavior (California State Curriculum Commission, 1962). Some common definitions of psychology include, "the science of human and animal behavior" (Morgan, 1974, p. 2); "The science of mental activity" (Hilgard, 1963, p. 39); and the scientific study of the activities of human beings as they interact with their environment (Walker, 1970, p. 1). The common thread that unites modern psychology is the use of empirical evidence as the only acceptable means for making claims or drawing conclusions. Wertheimer (1986) further reinforces the importance of this evidence:

> Almost all psychologists see their field as a research-oriented discipline that bases its conclusions (and all conclusions are viewed as tentative) upon empirical evidence; that is, that uses the methods of the natural sciences and of other social sciences to study a broad range of problems of human (and animal) behavior. (p. 165)

Psychological skills are specifically related to the study of the mind and behavior. The methodological techniques of the psychologist include observa-

TO EMPHASIZE OR TO BALANCE: WHICH IS BETTER?

If you were offering a separate high school class in psychology, would you try to treat and equally balance the subfields of the discipline? What arguments would you give for concentrating on the dual area of social psychology?

tional means that are used to record subject reaction on various types of tests and experiments. According to Wertheimer (1986), one of the tools available to psychologists is statistics:

> Characteristic of all areas of psychology is a high level of sophistication about inferential statistics, a set of mathematical tools that are used for drawing inferences about populations of people or animals from data on samples which have been systematically selected from those populations for close observation or experiment. (p. 167)

Psychology also has been combined with sociology into a relatively new and attractive subfield known as social psychology. The focus of social psychology is on examining human behavior within social context. According to Stephan and Stephan (1990):

> Social psychology is concerned with how people, and the social forces that impinge on them, affect one another's thoughts, feeling, and behavior. (p. 2)

It is particularly valuable in studying and providing evidence of the impact of the media in influencing individual and public opinion.

The strength of social psychology is that it draws on the somewhat different content, theories, methodologies, and perspectives of two fields in the study of human behavior. While sociology tends to focus on group behavior, psychology tends to focus on individual behavior; therefore, a combined approach provides a more balanced view by reconciling individual behavior as a result of human interaction within a broader social environment.

Another important and related subarea of psychology is human growth and development. Although individuals grow and mature at varying rates of development, certain patterns of development are shared by all human beings. Cognitive development is an example. The development of cognitive abilities in children is particularly important in instructional design. Psychologist Jean Piaget was able to identify important differences between the cognitive development of children and that of adults (Piaget, 1950). He identified four developmental stages that children pass through as they age and mature. This development is considered a biological process rather than a cultural process; therefore, it is held that educational intervention cannot accelerate or advance the progress of this development. Piaget encouraged teachers to learn about the mental abilities of students according to his stages of development and to attempt to provide instruction that is appropriate according to the characteristics of each stage. Piaget's theory is based on the assumption that the child's mind is not an adult's mind. The child's mind is in the process of *becoming* an adult mind. Psychologists also have developed a number of theories related to the nature of learning including the means of motivating learning, lower and higher levels of learning, intuitive learning, creativity learning, and problem solving.

Psychological studies focus a great deal of attention on the processes of the mind and human intelligence. The study of mental processes includes the input of information, the processes of organizing information, recall, and the application of knowledge. Experiments with laboratory animals as well as human volunteers are the source of knowledge about the processes of the brain. Intelligence is studied through various scales or measurements of intelligence. Tests are norm-referenced to allow psychologists to compare individual scores with a standard or representative score norms. Over the years hundreds of studies related to IQ have suggested that the frequent blanket acceptance and use of test results alone should be avoided.

Professionally trained psychologists are skilled in several types of studies associated with growth, learning, and behavioral problems of the individual. These studies include (1) scientific observations of individual behavior (observations are not considered to be as scientifically sound unless exact techniques are used to allow for precise measurements; therefore, scientific observations take place under controlled conditions that follow precise processes according to specific schedules); (2) interview techniques, which are used to prepare case studies on specific behavioral problems (in clinical group situations, psychologists may witness and record observations of specific types of social interactions); and (3) experimental designs, which are based on a hypothesis, control and experimental groups, and measures related to the independent and dependent variables to measure the effect on the independent variable when the dependent variable is treated or manipulated.

Values are recognized as important influences on human behavior as they appear to influence human emotion, motivation, and personality. Individual differences often are explained, in part, by the values and attitudes that develop as a result of experience. In the 1960s, Lawrence Kohlberg (1966) organized a moral development theory related to the growth of moral reasoning. According to this theory, there are three levels of moral development which include six stages. Kohlberg based this theory on the assumption that the rate of moral development varies among individuals, with some individuals arriving at a relatively high level of moral reasoning early in life. Regardless of the rate of moral development, the stages are considered sequential and fixed according to cultural universalities (all cultures being the same in this regard) (Kohlberg, 1973). Kohlberg argued that instruction accelerates the

HOW MIGHT A MORAL EDUCATION PROGRAM BE SUCCESSFULLY DEFENDED?

In recent years, emphasis on values education grew out of certain psychological studies and research. Widely practiced initially, this emphasis came under attack for value neutrality, and currently, moral education instruction tends to have more of a philosophical and social base. Can you list some possible forces and events that led to this strong public reaction? (Back, 1972)

rate of moral development by exposing students to moral dilemma episodes. Values also play an important role in the formation of an individual's self-concept, which is an important aspect of personality. Throughout life, individuals associate their identity with their values. These values help to define individual character, and values also perform a function in helping individuals make decisions and choices.

Psychology Instruction

Psychology has been included in the social studies curriculum as an elective course for many years. The placement of psychology within the curriculum has been associated with both the social studies and the sciences. In some schools psychology has been taught in connection with courses related to biology or to health. During the 1920s and the 1930s, psychology often was associated with life-adjustment programs that were aimed at helping students deal with social and emotional development. In the 1960s, curriculum projects in psychology emphasized the study of human behavior. One such course is discussed in Bare (1986):

> Mosher and Sprinthall describe their curriculum as a course in individual and human development to be taught to high school juniors and seniors. The core of the course, intended for all students, is essentially cognitive and presents materials from the discipline pertinent to understanding individuals and human development. (p. 184)

Psychological projects emphasized the academic or social science study of human behavior. Bare (1986) reports that, by the 1980s, psychology courses were included in the curriculum of over half of the nation's high schools. In addition to these projects, Bare notes that the American Psychological Association provides precollegiate teachers with a newsletter entitled the "High School Psychology Teacher," lectures named for S. Stanley Hall, workshops, and awards for outstanding teaching.

Over the years, psychology instruction has tended to reflect two different approaches in the teaching of psychology. In the elementary and secondary schools, a form of "humanistic psychology" has been taught to help students better understand and appreciate themselves and others. For example, students in the lower elementary grades focus on the study of self, especially self-appreciation. In the larger high schools, students often are offered electives in the form of "general psychology," in which they learn many of the principles and concepts of the "science of psychology" and elements of social psychology minus the heavy emphasis on experimentation and statistical analysis.

Elements of psychology are included in history and government courses as an aspect of personality analysis and the study of individual behavior under various social, economic, and political circumstances. An important indirect goal of the social studies is to encourage students to develop a positive self-identity and to be able to work cooperatively with others in a group setting. These goals tend to emphasize an indirect application of psychology by emphasizing the unique attributes of each student as well as a generalized respect for other individuals. Consequently, the social studies may influence the development of personal values as students study the psychological nature of important persons in history and current affairs.

Allan Brandhorst (1991), while discussing social psychology, addresses the instructional role of psychology and its possible application to instructional design. The potential of social psychology as a subject area for the social studies is based on its unique synthesis of psychology and sociology.

> Social psychology as a discipline has traditionally focused its attention on analysis of social behavior. Like sociology, the analytic perspective of social psychology incorporates a concern for patterns of organization of society; like psychology, social psychology is concerned with the study of individual behavior. (p. 161)

In spite of the interest in psychology as an elective school subject, it remains a peripheral discipline within the social studies constellation of disciplines because psychology does not tend to support some of the important goals of the social studies. For example, psychology usually is not considered a subject that would be related to citizenship education. In addition, psychology often is considered to be related more to the sciences, and in the past, the synthetic nature of psychology has allowed it to be used in a variety of programs other than the social studies. Some of the more controversial aspects of psychology, such as the study of deviate behavior, render the subject matter inappropriate for precollegiate instruction in the minds of some educators. Additionally, psychology is typically presented as a highly objective field of study while important elements of social studies education in the lower schools are much more subjective in design and instruction.

The *Social Studies Framework for the Public Schools of California* (State Curriculum Commission, 1962) contains several generalizations that may be appropriate for helping teachers design instruction, including the following:

- Behavior is caused and is not its own cause.

- Human behavior is purposive and goal-directed.

- Behavior results from the interactions of genetic and environmental factors.

- As a biologic organism, the individual possesses at birth certain physiological needs, but the methods of satisfying these needs and their subsequent development are to a great extent socially determined by his particular cultural unit.

- Through the interaction of genetic and social and physical environmental factors, the individual develops a pattern of personality characteristics.

- Individuals differ from one another in personal values, attitudes, personalities, and roles; yet, at the same time, the members of a group must possess certain common values and characteristics.

- Each of the social groups to which an individual belongs helps shape his behavior.

- Socialization processes, such as methods of child training, differ markedly in different social classes, groups and societies.

- The satisfaction of social needs is a strong motivating force in the determination of individual behavior.

The Study of Anthropology

Culture serves as the focus for wide-ranging subfields of anthropology. The most notable characteristic of anthropology is its synthesis of natural and social sciences, whereby anthropologists study various non-Western cultures from naturalists' and culturalists' perspectives. Thus, the study of anthropology is focused on the study of culture, and the task of the anthropologist is to describe and compare cultures and cultural change over time. Pelto (1965) has defined **anthropology** as *"the study of man and his works"* (p. 1), while Douglas L. Oliver (1964) prefers to define it by specifying *"what it is that those people called anthropologists actually do"* (p. ix). Clyde Kluckhohn (1949) suggests that anthropology "provides a scientific basis for dealing with the crucial dilemma of the world today; how can peoples of different appearance, mutually unintelligible languages, and dissimilar ways of life get along peaceably

ANTHROPOLOGY, PSYCHOLOGY, AND SOCIOLOGY: WHICH IS WHICH?

As you understand it, how does anthropology differ from sociology and psychology? Then write a statement that justifies the study of anthropology as the embodiment of a true social studies approach?

together?" (p. 1). Anthropology is sometimes referred to as the "science of humankind" and the focus of anthropological studies is "culture." **Culture** may be considered the body of human knowledge and experience that is expressed by a community of people in the form of traditions, customs, rituals, technical practice, artistic practice, political practice, and economic practice, or the integrated "whole" that distinguishes one culture from another. The unique holistic and naturalistic nature of anthropological studies was described by John Chilcott (1991) when he wrote:

> Anthropology is unique among the social sciences in that its holistic, naturalistic study of the human condition provides a broad-based perspective on reality. The traditional comparative analysis of anthropology, wherein a similar social phenomenon or social process is examined across cultures, provides an objective description or "mirror" with which one can better understand one's own culture. (p. 184)

Ancient Greek scholars were the first to apply a systematic approach to the study of peoples and cultures. Herodotus described the social systems and customs of peoples that he had observed in his travels (Pelto, 1965). During the height of the Roman empire, scholars became interested in distant lands and peoples, and they compared the social practices of the Roman people with the social practices of other peoples, especially regarding family and marriage customs. During the late Middle Ages, European explorers and traders began to travel to unknown regions of the world and developed an interest in newly discovered indigenous peoples.

The scientific study of anthropology paralleled advances in the physical sciences and in the growing body of physical evidence that suggested that human life was much older than had been believed. This evidence was in the form of stone tools and skeletal remains that appeared to have "primitive" features, such as the ones found in the Neander Valley of Germany in 1857. Charles Darwin, in 1859, published *The Origin of Species* in which he put forth his famous theory of natural selection. As a consequence of new discoveries, Darwin's anthropological theory challenged the perception that species were fixed or unchanging. In 1851 Lewis Henry Morgan published an ethnographic study of the Iroquois Indians in which he devised various stages of cultural development that range from savagery to civilization. Morgan's work contained a brilliant and systematic study of kinship relationships which helped form the basis for cultural and social anthropology.

American anthropology was greatly influenced by the work and the teaching of Franz Boas. Boas trained the first generation of American anthropologists, and the students of Boaz distinguished themselves in new anthropological specialties that helped to establish the boundaries of American anthropology (Owen, 1986). In 1902 the American Anthropological Association was organized, and anthropology departments spread throughout the nation (Leaf, 1974). Anthropology departments, commonly found in major universities, reflect the specialties of anthropology, including cultural and social anthropology, archaeology, physical anthropology, ethnology, and linguistics.

The formation of the discipline reflected a somewhat awkward attempt to place several different and highly specialized areas of study under one discipline. Each distinct branch of anthropology had its own focus of interest and its own unique field techniques. At the same time, the uniting influence that brought the specialties together was an interest in the study of culture, the ways and means of survival in the natural and social world. Some of the pioneers of anthropology envisioned a discipline that would rescue the record of vanishing cultures for posterity; however, social and cultural changes were taking place so rapidly that such an ambitious goal proved impossible. Modernism and the spread of industrialized technologies were simply overwhelming and changing traditional cultures, and anthropological studies could only salvage some of the fragments of traditional cultures.

Anthropologists worked according to the traditions and methodologies of their specialty, and out of their efforts a more complete picture of the natural history of humankind eventually emerged. Margaret Mead (1964) expressed the diverse specialties of the branches of anthropology when she wrote:

> I think it is still fair to treat anthropology as a field science, whose members work with fresh field material, studying living speakers of living languages, excavating the earth where archaeological remains are still in situ, observing the behavior of real mothers' brothers to real sisters' sons, taking down folklore from the lips of those who heard the tale from other men's lips, measuring the bodies and sampling the blood of men who live in their own lands—lands to which we have to travel in order to study the people. (p. 5)

Historically, cultural anthropologists, in Europe known as **ethnologists,** studied non-European cultures in order to describe these cultures prior to changes brought about by contact with Europeans. Cultural anthropologists applied a field study process called participation-observation as a means of observing and describing cultures. The process of participation-observation includes living among the people under study, interviewing informants (native

WHAT IS AN APPROPRIATE ANTHROPOLOGICAL TOPIC OF STUDY?

Would it be possible for high school students to mount an ethnological study of their school? What elements in such an ethnographic setting might prove antagonistic, controversial, or difficult to examine?

experts) regarding aspects of the culture, gathering and recording information (including tape-recording and photographing activities), organizing and summarizing field notes, and writing a final report. The final report or ethnography describes the notable features of the culture. These anthropologists are trained to study the rules and the systems that characterize and produce the patterns of culture. By studying and comparing cultures, social and cultural anthropologists hope to be able to come to a better understanding of human nature and the ways and means of cultural development and cultural history. Ethnology, like cultural anthropology, focuses on the systematic comparison and analysis of cultural characteristics of ethnic groups. Ethnography reports attempt to address the characteristics of the culture as a whole, including the social, political, and economic systems that are used within the culture. According to Owen (1986), the primary task of ethnographers is

> to attempt intellectually to enter behind the eyes and into the minds of their hosts and thus look out with them and share their vision of the universe. By this means ethnographers hope not only to discover the cultural directives to which their informants customarily respond, but also to lower or eliminate their own cultural biases. (p. 142)

Physical anthropologists are interested in the characteristics of human populations and the environmental forces that contribute to the development of these physical human characteristics. Trained in the techniques of science, physical anthropologists study the physical characteristics of a people including such features as height, skin tones, and blood type. As a general aim, physical anthropologists are interested in explaining the process of human evolution and the mechanics of this process, including the study of genes and the process of natural selection; therefore, physical anthropologists might spend a great deal of time in measuring various physical features of a people in order to identify the dominant features of a human population. According to Owen (1986),

> Physical anthropology poses two basic research questions: (1) What has been the course of human evolution? (2) What is the nature and significance of human physical variation? (p. 141)

Physical anthropologists have now, for example, produced evidence that human ancestors existed on this planet over hundreds of thousands of years.

Archeology, an older science, evolved into a systematic means of investigating past civilizations from the artifacts that have survived antiquity. While archeology is sometimes classified as a subfield of cultural anthropology, it is unique in terms of its focus and its methodologies. With its interest in the evolution of civilization, archeology attempts to reconstruct the chronology of events and technologies that have contributed to the advancement of civilization. Owen (1986) explains the importance of this study:

> Today it is widely known that archaeologists excavate in the ground to uncover remains of past cultures. By this means, they attempt to obtain a record for the past million or more years of the world's non-literate cultures. Archaeologists, thus, are responsible for telling the human story for over 99 percent of its duration and also form most of its tangled global route. (p. 142)

Archaeologists study the remains of a historic culture and attempt to reconstruct the characteristics of that culture by excavating, reassembling, and dating artifacts according to material, design, and chronological pattern. The archaeologist is interested in the evolution of civilization and the technical development of culture as observed through the architecture and the artifacts that were excavated from past and present occupational sites. Ultimately, the archaeologist is attempting to reconstruct a historic record of the past that does not exist in a complete form, especially in a written form; therefore, the archaeologist attempts to reconstruct the time line of civilization. Because field work requires the use of several specializations, field teams often consist of botanists, chemists, geologists, museum specialists, and other professionals who work under the direction of a chief field archaeologist. The main divisions of archeology have been organized according to geographic areas of the world such as New World archeology and Old World prehistory. New World archeology focused on the subareas of North, Central, and South America and developed such specialties as the Southwest and Mesoamerican archeology. Old World prehistory developed specialties that focused on Europe and the ancient Mediterranean civilizations, Asia, and Africa.

Linguistic anthropologists are interested in language, especially among traditional peoples. Linguistic systems provide valuable information about cultures and their ancient internal and external relationships. Because unique human languages were often developed in geographic isolation, these languages are in danger of being lost because of cultural contact with other more technically advanced cultures. Besides studying the structure of language, the linguist is interested in recording and preserving these endangered languages. The linguist uses various means to translate the oral language into written forms, in addition to an analysis of the language according to various geographic relationships. Therefore, according to Owen (1986), the focus of anthropological linguistics includes the descriptive linguistics and historic linguistics. Descriptive linguists record speech by using an international phonetic alphabet that permits any spoken sound to be given a written symbol such as ⊘ for "no." As Owens (1986) notes,

> Historical linguistics examines the genetic relationship of described languages in order to study the history and change in language clusters. (p. 143)

Anthropological skills also reflect the four subfields of the discipline as a means of studying human behavior in cultures. While specialized, all subfield skills attempt to focus on culture, but from different perspectives including:

- the historic development of culture and civilization
- organizational patterns, structure and function of culture (the way it operates, changes, and survives)
- social mechanisms through which culture is expressed including social practices, language, and artistic expressions and the interactions between cultures (the results of cultural contact)
- survival adaptations to the environment (for example, tools and technologies, food, clothing, shelter)
- various forms of social living including marriage and family life
- geographic domain of culture
- various beliefs and practices related to the natural and the spiritual world as a cultural perception

The broad categories of anthropological skills include participation-observation, excavation, biological measurement, and various linguistic skills. As a consequence of the complexities of these specialties, it is very difficult for an anthropologist to be a generalist because anthropology field work requires an in-depth application of skills from the humanities, social sciences, and natural sciences (Owen, 1986). Nevertheless, because of its spread of interests in humankind, some hold anthropology to be the broadest in scope of all the social sciences.

Because culture is an expression of values in society, the anthropologist is interested in cultural values and their effects on past and present cultures. The acquisition of cultural values helps the individual develop a sense of identity that serves as the source of loyalty as well as an awareness of what is appropriate behavior within groups and in individual conduct. Owen (1986) describes anthropology as

> a humane science: its goal is to understand human development without reference to preconceived moral, ethical, aesthetic, or ideological convictions so as to enable humankind to reach its full potential, whatever that may be. (p. 149)

The ethics of anthropology require that anthropologists not be judgmental in describing different human practices and cultural values as expressed in the

LET'S "DIG" UP THE PAST!

High school students become intensely involved when social studies teachers organize a mock archeological "dig." Cite an example of a specific dig (related to an ancient culture such as Mayan, Egyptian, or Greek, for example) and list artifacts to be included that would accurately reveal certain key aspects of a given society or culture. Explain your choices.

traditions, customs, and rituals of the culture. Instead, the anthropologist must keep an open and objective mind about what is culturally worth knowing, doing, possessing, and believing.

Cultural values that are characteristic of a culture are often expressed in symbolic form. Symbols have values attached or assigned to them, and for the outsider to understand them, the anthropologist must learn about the meaning of the symbol and the ideas with which they are associated. Symbolic meanings tend to be understood by cultural members who have associated the symbol with an idea or the belief. Prior to initiation of youth into the ritual life of the culture, they are expected to learn the cultural meanings and use of various symbols as a part of the process of socialization.

Anthropology Instruction

Anthropological content is a part of the social studies curriculum, and anthropology subject matter is contained within a variety of standard courses; but this subject is seldom taught as a separate course in either the elementary or secondary school. (One contemporary anthropologist told the writers that researchers in his field were immersed from top to bottom in the entire "garbage can" of humanity. Such a broad and general claim nominates anthropology as a central core for social education.) In the late 1940s, a few teachers organized and taught anthropology courses as innovative electives. These courses were developed out of a perceived need to help students learn about non-Western cultures, peoples, and nations (Dynneson, 1986). As early as 1939, Jules Henry proposed that courses and supplemental approaches be prepared to advance anthropology instruction in the schools. By the 1950s, a few teachers were actively teaching anthropology in the secondary schools.

The first elementary course appeared in 1957 as an experiment to try to discover the extent of student interest. During the "new" social studies movement, several projects developed courses and units for the K–12 social studies curriculum (Dynneson, 1986). At the height of the "new" social studies movement, several curriculum projects focused in part or entirely on anthropological instruction. For example, the Anthropology Curriculum Study Project (Dynneson, 1975) generated an excellent set of high school materials that was designed as a supplement to world history. The most notable of these projects was *Man: A Course of Study*. While this program was more than anthropological, its rise and decline represents the type of controversial troubles that can accompany the behavioral sciences, especially when suggested at the elementary level of instruction.

By 1957, federal and private financing for the development of experimental curriculum programs was disappearing, and the attempts to make anthropology a separate course within the social studies curriculum disappeared for all practical purposes. At the same time, anthropology content became a supplemental aspect of regular courses in world history, cultural studies, area studies, and global studies. At present, the teaching of anthropology within the social studies is restricted to a few urban high schools, although survey studies indicated that between 1965 and 1975 aspects of anthropology often became a regular component of social studies instruction (Dynneson, 1986).

Like the other behavioral sciences, anthropology is seen as containing such controversial topics and issues that some educators, as well as certain public critics, favor the elimination of this discipline as a separate subject within the curriculum. Students and teachers, on the other hand, seem to find the subject matter of anthropology to be extremely interesting and, as a consequence, anthropological content is finding a growing supportive role in the social studies.

According to *A Guide for Concept Development in the Social Studies* (The Colorado Advisory Committee on the Social Studies, 1967), anthropology is concerned with the following generalizations:

HELPING YOUR STUDENTS MAKE CROSS-CULTURAL COMPARISONS

To help students recognize the contributions of anthropological studies, have them select two different societies of interest to them and to then draw comparisons and contrasts of cultural characteristics, such as customs, traditions, rituals, and key social practices that mark each group.

- As an animal, man occupies a unique place among living things
- The family is the basic unit of society in the transmission of culture
- Culture is tools
- Culture is language
- Culture is the means for curing illness
- Culture is the means for quieting fears
- Culture is the means of adjusting to and changing the environment
- Culture is acquiring food, shelter, and clothing
- Culture is social control (pp. 8–chart)

CONCLUSIONS

In this chapter you learned that psychology and sociology have been included as elective courses in the high school, and while the enrollments in these courses are relatively small, students seem to find behavioral sciences to be of great interest. In addition, you learned that anthropology, the least taught behavioral science, has always played a contributing role in the social studies curriculum, especially in connection with world history, American history, cultural studies, and area studies. Since the 1960s, behavioral science content has been used to broaden the students' understanding of social influences and to help them realize that individual and group behavior is a product of one's social environment. At the same time, the behavioral sciences are important to the study of social institutions including the family, the school, and the community. In recent years, the behavioral sciences have helped students better understand current national and global trends, including changing social systems, human conflicts, and cultural differences.

In spite of the growing acceptance of the behavioral sciences in the schools, you should realize that behavioral scientists hold certain reservations about including their disciplines within the social studies curriculum. For instance, behavioral scholars are concerned that the schools are not equipped to present their disciplines according to the standards that they feel must be established to present sensitive social issues in the classroom. Also, many of these same scholars have suggested that precollegiate students may not possess the maturity needed to explore various aspects of human conduct from a nonjudgmental perspective. Furthermore, many disciplinary scholars believe that the typical elementary or secondary social studies teacher is not qualified or prepared to teach the behavioral science disciplines. Consequently, academic scholars often have criticized precollegiate instruction on the bases of the materials used, teachers' qualifications, and the concerns associated with the operation of institutional schools. For example, commentators have expressed

SOCIAL SCIENCE VERSUS BEHAVIORAL SCIENCE: WHICH IS WHICH?

Do you believe it is correct to classify sociology, psychology, and anthropology as "The Behavioral Sciences"? Why or why not?

the concern that the schools have had to purge instructional content in order to make it acceptable to the various special interest groups who monitor the schools. As a result, the schools have been required to develop noncontroversial curricula.

You can safely conclude that critics of the schools believe that teachers' academic freedom should be limited; that is, they favor restricting teachers' freedom to determine what they will teach. Consequently, behavioral scientists often are reluctant to promote the teaching of their disciplines in the schools because they fear that their subject matter would be stripped of much of its intellectual substance. Nevertheless, behavioral science organizations and behavioral scholars have cooperated in developing instructional materials for the schools. This was demonstrated in the 1960s when educators and behavioral scholars were able to develop substantive disciplinary programs for the schools. In spite of these occasional cooperative efforts, however, most experimentally developed curriculum programs have failed to reach their intended audiences.

Recall that the social studies is often considered the means through which the academic disciplines of history, geography, political science, economics, sociology, psychology, and anthropology are transmitted to students in the precollegiate schools. Those who prefer the disciplinary approach tend to see the educational mission of the schools narrowly focused on the transmission of content knowledge. In opposition to this position, social studies educators have tended to prefer a broader mission for the schools in which the necessity to transmit content knowledge is balanced with the desire to help meet the social needs of the student, family, and society. For much of the twentieth century, most social studies educators interpreted the mission of the schools as primarily a social/educational mission. Historically, however, the pendulum of instructional development has moved between these two positions depending on the extent to which societal influences (social movements, political mandate, and economic conditions) focused on the educational enterprise.

The question of whether the schools are to be assigned an educational mission or a social/educational mission is important because this issue determines the direction and the nature of instructional programs for the social studies.

Presently, most social studies instructional programs transmit content knowledge and prepare students to deal with various social concerns related to their citizenship. According to conditions, social studies educators are required to:

1. address the future needs of its citizens and fulfill various academic requirements related to history and the social sciences.
2. provide a structural means through which different disciplines can be presented in various patterns of organization.
3. develop unique and effective instructional programs for youth, especially concerning the changing psychological and social needs of students.
4. develop materials that require students to confront those difficult and persisting social, economic, and political problems that are ingrained within the fabric of American society and increasingly on a global level.

Finally keep in mind that history and the social science disciplines provide the social studies with the knowledge base and certain methodological processes that are the basis for social studies instruction. At the same time, this knowledge base and these methodological processes must be modified to be grade-appropriate for students at the precollegiate level. Social studies educators must be able to design instruction that helps students develop a knowledge base on which more complex understanding can be built. It must be realized that the social studies are *not* the social sciences and that content modification will take place, including the addition of prime social values for instructional purposes. Consequently, the social studies educator should possess an in-depth knowledge of the seven disciplines associated with the social studies. They also need skills for shaping the content and processes of these disciplines into instructional experiences that are meaningful to youth, as well as supportive of community desires for civic education.

REFERENCES

Alpert, H. (1963). Sociology: Its present interests. In B. Berelson (Ed.), *The behavioral sciences today* (pp. 52–64). New York: Basic Books.

Back, K. (1972). *Beyond words: The story of sensitivity training and the encounter movement.* New York: Russell Sage Foundation.

Bare, J. (1986). Teaching psychology in high school. In S. P. Wronski & D. H. Bragaw (Eds.), *Social studies and social science: A fifty-year perspective* (pp. 179–188). Washington, DC: National Council for the Social Studies.

Berger, P. L. (1963). *Invitation to sociology: A humanistic perspective.* New York: Doubleday.

Brandhorst, A. (1991). The social psychological perspective: Social content, process, and civil ideologies. In R. E. Gross & T. L. Dynneson (Eds.), *Social science perspectives on citizenship education* (pp. 161–183). New York: Teachers College Press.

Chilcott, J. H. (1991). The anthropological perspective: Anthropological insights for civic education. In R. E. Gross & T. L. Dynneson (Eds.), *Social science perspectives on citizenship education* (pp. 184–194). New York: Teachers College Press.

Colorado Advisory Committee on the Social Studies. (1967). *A Guide for concept development in the social studies.* Denver, CO: Colorado Department of Education.

Dynneson, T. L. (1986). Trends in precollegiate anthropology. In S. P. Wronski & D. H. Bragaw (Eds.), *Social studies and social science: A fifty-year perspective* (pp. 153–164). Washington, DC: National Council for the Social Studies.

Dynneson, T. L. (1975). *Pre-collegiate anthropology: Trends and materials.* Athens, GA: Anthropology Curriculum Project.

Eshleman, J. R. (1986). Sociology theory to social action. In S. P. Wronski & D. H. Bragaw (Eds.), *Social studies and social science: A fifty-year perspective* (pp. 111–123). Washington, DC: National Council for the Social Studies.

Giddens, A. (1991). *Introduction to sociology.* New York: W. W. Norton.

Gillen, J. (Ed.). (1954). *For a science of social man: Convergences in anthropology, psychology, and sociology.* New York: Macmillan.

Gross, R. E., & Zeleny, L. D. (1958). *Educating citizens for democracy.* New York: Oxford University Press.

Hebding, D., & Glick, L. (1976). *Introduction to sociology.* Reading, MA: Addison-Wesley.

Hilgard, E. R. (1963). Psychology: Its present interests. In B. Berelson (Ed.), *The behavioral sciences today* (pp. 38–51).

Jenness, D. (1990). *Making sense of social studies.* New York: Macmillan.

Kluckhohn, C. (1949). *Mirror for man: The relationship of anthropology to modern life.* New York: McGraw-Hill.

Kohlberg, L. (1966). Moral education in the schools: A developmental view. *School Review, 74,* 1–30.

Kohlberg, L. (1973). Moral development and the new social studies. *Social Education, 37,* 369–375.

Leaf, M. J. (1974). *Frontiers of anthropology.* New York: D. Van Nostrand.

Marshall, L., & Goetz, R. (1936). *Curriculum making in the social studies: A social process approach.* Part 13, Report of the Commission on the Social Studies. New York: Scribners.

Mead, M. (1964). *Anthropology: A human science.* Princeton, NJ: D. Van Nostrand.

Mills, C. W. (1961). *The sociological imagination.* New York: Oxford University Press.

Morgan, C. T. (1974). *A brief introduction to psychology.* New York: McGraw-Hill.

Oliver, D. L. (1964). *Invitation to anthropology: A guide to basic concepts.* Washington, DC: The American Museum of Natural History Press.

Owen, R. C. (1986). Coming of age in anthropology. In S. P. Wronski & D. H. Bragaw (Eds.), *Social studies and social science: A fifty-year perspective* (pp. 139–152). Washington, DC: National Council for the Social Studies.

Pelto, P. J. (1965). *The nature of anthropology.* Columbus. OH: Charles E. Merrill.

Piaget, J. (1950). *The psychology of intelligence.* New York: Harcourt.

State Curriculum Commission. (1962). *Social Studies Framework for the Public Schools of California.* Sacramento, CA: State Department of Education.

Stephan, C. W., & Stephan, W. G. (1990). *Two social psychologies.* Belmont, CA: Wadsworth.

Switzer, T. J. (1968). Teaching sociology in K–12 classrooms. In S. P. Wronski & D. H. Bragaw (Eds.), *Social studies and social science: A fifty-year perspective* (pp. 124–138). Washington, DC: National Council for the Social Studies.

Walker, E. L. (1970). *Psychology as natural and social science* (Basic Concepts in Psychology Series). Belmont, CA: Brooks/Cole.

Wertheimer, M., et al. (1986). Psychology: Social science, natural science and profession. In S. P. Wronski & D. H. Bragaw (Eds.), *Social studies and social science: A fifty-year perspective* (pp. 165–188). Washington, DC: National Council for the Social Studies.

PART THREE

The Selection and Organization of Subject-Matter Elements:

DESIGNING INSTRUCTION ACCORDING TO CONCEPTS, SKILLS, AND VALUES

What understandings and background knowledge do teachers need in order to organize and present social studies concepts, skills, and values in the most appropriate ways?

In Part Three you will learn that the elements of content include lists of selected concepts, skills, and values that are organized for emphasis within an instructional program. These content elements have been selected and organized to address the specific learning goals that are commonly outlined in instructional objectives. Moreover, concepts, skills, and values serve as the focus of instruction in the day-by-day development of lessons, units, courses, and the curriculum. For example, a course in geography would include selected concepts related to physical and human geography as well as certain skills related to the interpretation of maps, globes, and charts and the values that are to be promoted in connection with land use.

Therefore, you will learn that the elements of content are the basic building blocks of instruction programs. Frequently, these elements are highlighted and repeatedly addressed throughout the program of instruction. Typically, textbooks include:

- lists of vocabulary terms (for example, concepts, events, and places) that will be described according to their distinguishing features or characteristics
- lists of skills (for instance, locating, writing, analyzing, sequencing, accessing, interpreting, illustrating, problem solving, decision making, computing) that will be learned as processes for dealing with various forms of content information
- lists of values (for example, idealized qualities of an individual, benefits of a political system, an examination of human conduct, an emphasis on democratic principles) that will be described in regard to their influence on human behavior and events

Once identified, these elements can serve as the foci or emphasis of instruction; therefore, a common practice for commercial textbook publishers is to list the elements of content at the beginning of a chapter and to highlight these terms when they appear in the narrative of the text with either bold or italic print.

Earlier in Parts One and Two of this text, you learned that the components of content were selected and organized according to certain design principles and patterns related to the "structure of the discipline." This approach was based on the belief that the structure of the discipline (concepts and methodologies) should be the sole source of content for the curriculum. This position was included in Jerome Bruner's recommendation that the selection and organization of content elements be based on the structure of a discipline (knowledge base, organization, and processes), which he justified with the argument that "early learning (of the elements of content) renders later performance more efficient through what is conveniently called nonspecific transfer or, more accurately, the transfer of principles and attitudes" (Bruner, 1963, p. 17). While this approach was popular in the 1950s and 1960s, it ran into problems when applied to the precollegiate level of instruction because of the nature and needs of the student (Tanner & Tanner, 1980).

You will find that these next chapters are rooted in the work of psychologists and curriculum experts. For example, both Bruner and Jean Piaget (1950), while taking different positions on the learning nature of the child, influenced content selection and organization in regard to the philosophical, psychological, and biological principles that pertain to the mental development of children. The work of Bruner and Piaget contributed to the development of the **"spiral" concept in curriculum design.** The "spiral" concept is based on the belief that the content elements of a discipline must be presented only when children are in a state of "readiness," that is, when children are able to relate subject-matter content according to their stage of mental maturity (past learning serving as the bases for future learning). Therefore, the "spiral" concept in curriculum design is based on the idea that students could profit from the study of the same ideas, skills, and values at different points in their mental development. As a consequence of their recommendations, several experimental curriculum frameworks were organized around the structure of the discipline and child growth and development principles in which the key concepts, target skills, and core values of a discipline or subject area were arranged in a repeated or "spiral" design (elements that proceed from a simple presentation to a complex presentation) (Taba, 1962).

The influence of Bruner and Piaget affected the selection and organization of important events, persons, places, processes, laws, and technologies that would be included in the study of history and social science subject matter. According to the "spiral" curriculum design, key subject-matter elements were selected for use as the organizational pattern for a course or for the entire school curriculum. Then the same set of content elements would be repeatedly taught or sequenced at a more sophisticated level as students advance from one grade level to the next. For example, the concept "taxation" might be introduced in the seventh grade and re-introduced in the eighth and ninth grade levels. Presently, certain states have adopted curriculum frameworks that emphasize history and geography concepts, skills, and values according to repeated patterns. According to Doll (1979),

> When this is done, even crudely, it is possible to build a "spiral curriculum" in which the same subject, but not the identical subject matter, is taught on several occasions during one's school experience. For example, selected portions of American history may profitably be taught in the fifth, eighth, and eleventh grades of a pupil's schooling. (p. 105)

In addition to the spiral concept of curriculum design promoted by Bruner and Piaget, there seems to be a growing emphasis on the organization of content elements according to the psychological approaches, including those of Benjamin Bloom and Robert Gagne (Dececco & Crawford, 1974; Gagne, 1977; Kemp, 1985). Their approaches tend to focus on developing the building blocks of content according to hierarchies and sequential patterns that are somewhat related to the structure-of-disciplines approach. Bloom, for example, analyzed knowledge according to the level of cognitive thinking (levels that ranged from recall to evaluation) required to learn and use subject-matter content, while Gagne used structured patterns of vocabulary development as preparation for more complex learning that is to follow.

Also, you will find that in recent years curriculum experts have had a considerable impact. For example, various diagramming and webbing processes have been used to select and organize the components of instruction. A **webbing** process is often used to sequence the order in which concepts, skills, and values are to be developed and presented to students. Also, the elements of content might be arranged according to a *deductive* scheme beginning with a generalization and proceeding to a particular fact (or set of facts). In other cases, the elements of content might be organized according to an *inductive* scheme beginning with a fact (or set of facts) and working toward a general idea, hypothesis, or relationship. In this way, the arrangement of content elements in a social studies program provides an orderly plan of instruction according to an organizational scheme that entails the principles of scope, sequence, continuity, and integration. Thus, curriculum designers and instructional planners employ various design schemes to develop the content elements for an instructional program, while teachers also often follow similar schemes when presenting the content elements to students.

The Elements
of Knowledge

INTRODUCTION

In this chapter you will learn that the ultimate aim of knowledge is to find truth and to form an accurate perception of reality and that knowledge and truth are at the heart of the educational process. According to John Dewey (1916), "knowledge furnishes the means of understanding or giving meaning to what is still going on and what is to be done" (p. 341). Daniel and Laurel Tanner (1980) describe the nature of knowledge as "not a mere end product of inquiry but a by-product and resource for solving problems and producing intelligent action" (p. 56). Knowledge can be acquired as a result of several influences including observations, experiences, and various learning processes. The school serves society by performing important services that are designed to pass on essential knowledge to youth. More technically advanced societies require an efficient educational system to sustain an expanding knowledge base and to guarantee continuation of cultural advancements and the development of new technologies.

The problems associated with knowledge acquisition have led scholars to develop knowledge systems (or disciplines) as a means of organizing subject-matter content so that knowledge could be presented to students in an orderly and logical fashion. The social science disciplines arose out of the attempts of nineteenth century scholars to develop knowledge systems that focused on scientific means applied to the study of social conditions. Accompanying the rise of new disciplines was an emerging inquiry system that attempted to apply new principles and processes to the acquisition of knowledge and the solution of problems.

New pedagogical approaches followed the development of disciplines and these pedagogical approaches included various schemes for organizing and presenting the content knowledge of disciplines. One such scheme focused on teaching students the "structure of knowledge" or rather the "structure of the discipline." This approach actually began in the 1920s as scholars sought guides and unifying organizations to overcome instructional particularism (that is, the isolated teaching of unrelated information, information presented without benefit of a framework). Gestalt psychologists also believed that students would gain a better grasp of the subject matter if they learned the structure of a discipline or subject matter, including its order, organization, and processes (Taba, 1962). Jerome Bruner and others advanced the idea of a structure of knowledge within a curriculum reform movement in the 1960s. According to Bruner (1960), students can make better use of knowledge when they have "an understanding of the fundamental structure of whatever subject we choose to teach." Bruner goes on to explain:

> Many things go into learning of this kind, not the least of which are supporting habits and skills that make possible the active use of the materials one has come to understand. If earlier learning is to render later learning easier, it must do so by providing a general picture in terms of which the relations between things encountered earlier and later are made as clear as possible. (p. 12)

According to Bruner, a more meaningful knowledge (a more understandable knowledge) comes from an awareness of the structural form or design of a discipline. Therefore, understandings begin when students begin to ask certain questions such as: What is the structure of the discipline (its key concepts and methodologies)? What purpose does the structure serve? What arguments were used in justifying a particular structural design? How is the structure employed? or Under typical conditions, how is the structure of the discipline used?

In a related, but somewhat different approach, Hilda Taba (1962) explored the teaching of content knowledge through an understanding of the basic elements of knowledge. The characteristics of subject matter lead to the clarification of the nature of knowledge by identifying and classifying the elements of knowledge (facts, concepts, generalizations, and processes) into several component parts. Once completed, the identification and clarification of the elements of knowledge could become the focus of instruction. While Taba was generally concerned with organizing curriculum design according to the application of key concepts, Roy Price and his colleagues (1965) applied the use of pre-identified key concepts in social studies instructional design.

Taba (1962) had made careful distinctions between "the levels of content and the differences in function that these levels may serve" (p. 175). Over the years, Taba settled on the idea that instruction can be improved by classifying knowledge according to four levels and focusing on these four levels of knowledge in planning and executing instruction. These levels included "specific facts and processes," "basic ideas," "concepts," and "thought systems." For instructional planning purposes many of these same elements were presented in the form of knowledge elements that can be related to the structure-of-a-discipline idea. In time, the building blocks of knowledge came to consist of factual information, concepts, generalizations, and the processes of knowledge (or the skills and processes that scholars use to answer questions or in solving problems). According to this approach, the focal point of instruction should

CAN YOU RECALL VARIOUS DISCIPLINARY ELEMENTS?

In previous chapters you have been introduced to the major elements of history and the social science disciplines. Select one discipline and develop a statement that satisfactorily explains the structure (content and processes) of that discipline.

help students acquire an adequate knowledge of key concepts, based on the belief that the best means of acquiring knowledge is within the contextual framework of a concept or an idea.

Facts, Concepts, and Generalizations

The acquisition of subject matter is an essential goal of most social studies instructional programs. The selection and the organization of subject matter can greatly influence the extent to which instruction will be successfully learned by students. Consequently, the way in which content is arranged within the instructional setting becomes an important consideration. Kemp (1985) has described the subject content as providing

> the substance of information for any topic. Information in turn leads to knowledge, which is the structure of relationships among factual detail. The ultimate result is intellectual thought and understanding. (p. 60)

Facts

Factual information plays an important role in helping students acquire essential knowledge related to any course, topic, or idea. A **fact** can be operationally defined as *the most basic element of knowledge which has meaning* *within a contextual setting.* In other words, factual information such as percepts, names, dates, statistics, and details are meaningful within a larger context of an idea or a concept.

Unfortunately, factual information often is used in inappropriate ways within the instructional setting. Teachers sometimes mistakenly focus on the acquisition of factual knowledge as isolated elements of knowledge that students are expected to recall and apply. Many educators agree that application of factual knowledge is a common and serious error, mainly because today's fact becomes tomorrow's fiction. Factual knowledge tends to have meaning only within context. For example, this morning's temperature reading has meaning only for an individual within the context of what clothing to wear to be comfortable for this day. Two weeks from today, most individuals will not find any value or meaning in recalling specific temperatures. At the same time, the temperature at which water boils may be of interest to those who cook. This information may be applied to a variety of occasions in which water must be boiled to help to prepare a dish. In another situation, this same information may be of interest to an automobile driver traveling across Death Valley on a hot summer's day without the benefit of an additional supply of water. Factual information is meaningful within a descriptive context because a certain amount of factual information must be acquired and retained in order for learning to advance. Unhappily, numerous teachers in their evaluation of student progress construct tests that do not go beyond the mere recitation of facts.

The search for the unifying means of organizing instruction leads one to believe that ideas should replace descriptive knowledge (facts) as the focus of instruction. At the same time, one is cautioned to remember that factual information within a conceptual context allows the student to gain specific knowledge, whereas concepts taught without the benefit of factual information allow the student to gain only a general understanding of the idea or concept. The acquisition of concepts can be strengthened when percepts and factual information are presented as aspects of an idea or a concept. (The term *percepts* is often used interchangeably with the term *facts;* psychological references often refer to percepts as inputs from sensory organs. See Wilson, Robeck, & Michael, 1969, p. 141). Immanuel Kant pointed out that concepts without sensory data percepts are empty and that percepts without concepts are blind.

Concepts

Taba (1962) defined concepts as "complex systems of highly abstracted ideas which can be built only by successive experiences in a variety of contexts" (p. 178). According to D. A. de Vaus (1986), concepts "are simply tools which fulfill a useful shorthand function: they are abstract summaries of a whole set of behaviours, attitudes and characteristics which we see as having something in common" (p. 40). And Kemp (1985) has described concepts within the instructional setting as *"the relating together of factual details, objects, or events that share common features and are assigned a single name"* (p. 61).

According to Leland H. Stott (1974), within the field of psychology and human development there are two schools of thought regarding how concepts are learned by children. These two schools include the *objectivistic* approach and the *cognitive* view.

The Objectivistic Approach

The **objectivistic** approach is associated with behavioral psychology and recommends that children learn to make word labels or object associations. Eventually the students learn about the attributes of the objects and learn to classify them according to specific categories. This approach may be very useful in helping elementary students develop a reservoir of content knowledge related to the content of the social studies. For example, when introducing a new idea to students, the teacher should first present the word label and then associate the word label with a picture or a description of the idea. The most important elements of factual knowledge are associated with vocabulary development.

It is important that students learn to associate word labels with the object that it identifies. The main defining feature of a concept is a descriptive characteristic or word label. Each concept is labeled, and these conceptual labels are learned in association with the concept. Once students learn to associate the label with the concept, it can be more easily recalled. Therefore, a word label provides the context around which factual information is organized to give clarification and meaning to a concept. Gary Borich (1992) applies the same principles described above to the concept of "frog":

> For example, to learn the concept of a frog involves learning the essential characteristics that make an organism a frog, as distinguished from closely similar animals (for example, a green chameleon). In other words, the learner needs to know not only the characteristics that all frogs have (green color, four legs, eats insects, amphibious) but also what characteristics distinguish frogs from other animals.

According to this approach, concepts should be introduced and taught as a unit in association with word labels. The teacher might begin by providing students with an example of the concept (picture, explanation, example), then examine the component parts of the concept, and then follow up with variations and applications of the concept to other related situations.

The Cognitive Approach

The **cognitive** approach emphasizes the internal resources of the individual; therefore, previous learning serves as a resource for learning new content. Because the acquisition of new knowledge rests on the ability of the learner to relate new information within the framework of already acquired knowledge; teachers are expected to strive to constantly prepare students for new knowledge by establishing those preliminary understandings whereby this knowledge can be received, retained, and applied. This approach relies on the buildup of experiences that prepare the students to learn new ideas or to expand their current base of conceptual knowledge. Consequently, an important responsibility of the teacher is to see to it that the students have an adequate knowledge base of experiences before introducing a new or more complicated concept. According to this approach, knowledge must be meaningful if students are to acquire, retain, and integrate it. The learner must understand what is being communicated, be able to relate it to a wider network of concepts, and recognize its psychological meaning or significance (Pratt, 1980). Words, labels, ideas, facts, or percepts evolve into concepts and eventual generalizations only over a long period of time, maturation, and varied experiences that enlarge the student's background of knowledge. For example, a preschooler may designate any body of water a "river." This is a word or percept by which young children may identify like aspects of their environment, whether it is a pond or the sea. Gradually the pupil comes to know that there are different types of bodies of water (brooks, lakes, oceans); that there are varying names or designations for rivers (streams, Amazon, the Blue Danube, Father of Waters); that there are different kinds of rivers (wide, dirty, fast-running, tributary); that there are varied uses for the word or for words that have similar meaning (river of blood, stream of credit, highway of commerce); and that rivers serve different roles and uses (source of drinking water, means for exploration, factor in irrigation, flood threats). Thus, over a considerable period of time, the learners build a rather full understanding of the percepts and concepts involved in their everyday environment. The word *river* now takes on many connotations and is used and understood abstractly. The word *river* has become a concept.

The Model Approach

Mary Alice Gunter, Thomas H. Estes, and Jan Hasbrouck Schwab (1990) have advanced a third approach for concept attainment. They explored the idea of concept attainment, and in this connection they have developed a **concept attainment model.** According to these authors,

> *Concept attainment* is the process of defining concepts by attending to those attributes that are absolutely essential to the meaning and disregarding those that are not; it also involves learning to discriminate between what is and is not an example of the concept. (p. 90)

Their model (Gunter et al., 1990) consists of the following eight steps, the first three being completed by the teacher prior to instruction:

1. Select a concept and write a definition.
2. Select the attributes.
3. Develop positive and negative examples.

What Is in a Name, Date, or Statistic?

In their expectations of student learning, why do you believe that so many teachers have failed to move beyond facts and word labels to the development of ideas, images, operations, understandings, and generalizations?

4. Introduce the process to the students.
5. Present the examples so the students can identify the essential attributes.
6. Have the students write their own concept definition.
7. Give additional examples.
8. Discuss the process with the class. (p. 91)

These authors further explain that in preparing to use the "concept attainment model" with students the teacher should identify the concept, its definition, related attributes, provide examples, and be prepared to explain its relationship to other concepts being studied.

Concepts include such abstract ideas as freedom, democracy, and equality. These complex ideas are important to the whole social studies curriculum, and they form the basic threads for developing instructional programs. "Democracy" is an example of an abstract concept in which certain conditions must be present for a government to qualify as such. These conditions include certain traits or characteristics such as the right of citizens to participate in electing a leader. At the same time, there are different types of democracies, such as republican forms and parliamentary forms. The defining characteristics of a democracy focus mainly on the nature of the relationship between the rulers and those who are ruled. Jean Piaget suggests that abstract concepts are inappropriate to students before the age of eleven. According to Piaget (1950), young students are unable to deal with abstract concepts and ideas; therefore, instruction in abstract concepts such as "democracy" might be better addressed after students enter upper elementary grades or junior high school (Wilson, Robeck, & Michael, 1969).

Generalizations

As children learn concepts, they begin to discover conceptual relationships called generalizations. Paul Hanna and John Lee (1962) defined a generalization as "a universally applicable statement at the highest level of abstraction relevant to all time or stated times about man's past and/or present, engaging in a basic human activity" (p. 73). Basically, **generalizations** are statements

IN LIGHT OF A HISTORICAL EVENT, IDENTIFY A RELATED CONCEPT(S)

Indicate a concept growing out of historical study and list the specific facts and experiences that a teacher could use to help students grasp the concept.

that relate the meaning of two or more concepts to express a general rule or principle (for example "poverty and illiteracy are common characteristics of the underprivileged"). Because generalizations are made up of concepts (concepts being made up of related facts), it is important that each component part of a generalization be taught with special attention paid to its parts and especially to the relationships.

Factual knowledge is deemed as having little functional value beyond an immediate time and as a step toward concept development, but generalizations are valuable understandings that help the students gain a broader perspective of systems, approaches, and practices within nature and society. Generalizations should be the product of instruction. Wesley and Wronski (1964) claimed that the "ability to generalize is the apex of the process of learning; it is the key to further and more expeditious learning" (p. 223).

Of particular importance to learning is the nature of generalizations which allows the individual to transfer what was learned in one situation to be applied to other similar situations. Generalizations that express social relationships are learned as a part of the experiences of life; when they are established incompletely or erroneously, they must be corrected. For example, an individual may have had an unsatisfactory experience with a person of a certain ethnic background and, as a result of this experience, transfer negative feelings to all other persons of that same ethnic background. In this case, an important task of the teacher is to identify and correct such erroneously formed generalizations.

The importance of helping students acquire and understand generalizations was further advanced when Paul Hanna and his students attempted to make a comprehensive list of generalizations from the social sciences that might be applied to social studies instruction. Over time, more than 3,500 generalizations were identified and classified according to disciplinary categories. An example of one such generalization taken from economics states: "People tend to move from areas of lesser to areas of greater economic opportunity" (Hanna & Lee, 1962, p. 68). The criteria used in identifying generalizations included that there be no known exceptions to the statement; that the statement not be bound by geographic place or time; that the factual data associated with the generalization not be generalizations; that the concepts associated with a generalization not be defined as generalizations; that the generalization not be based on opinion but based on scientific observation; and that the generalization be applicable to all human beings and not to individuals or within isolated communities (p. 73).

According to Michaelis (1988), there are three basic types of generalizations, which include descriptive, conditional, and prescriptive. *Descriptive generalizations* are limited to a time or place—for example, economic differences between the North and the South caused the Civil War. *Conditional generalizations* are limited by an "if-then" condition—for example, if the price of wheat goes up, then farmers will plant more wheat. *Prescriptive generalizations* depend on value preferences—for example, conflict should always be resolved by compromise and not violence.

Jerrold E. Kemp (1985) has suggested that students can be taught to analyze generalizations through several different processes, including a diagramming process similar to the process of diagramming sentences by breaking them into their component parts and examining each part separately. In addition, the generalization might be analyzed according to either a deductive method (starting with the principle or law and going to the details) or an inductive method (starting with the details and working to the principle, law, rule, or overall process). *Webbing* is a similar process that can be used to analyze the relationship between facts, concepts, and generalization. In addition, webbing can be used to identify and illustrate the instructional relationships between the elements of content (concepts, skills, and values). But more important still, the webbing processes can be used to design and plan instruction and to present instruction to students. In addition, students can learn to apply a webbing scheme to analyze an event, a process, or documents and to help them solve problems.

Generalizations serve an important role as guides to our thinking and behavior. As students mature and develop, they begin to form general statements, rules, and principles. As they grow to recognize the relationships

What "Rules" (or Standards) Should Students Follow When Formulating Generalizations?

If instructors present generalizations directly without introducing the percept or concept, students may memorize the principle without understanding it. Should teachers conclude all of their social studies lessons with an attempt to have students make generalizations about what they have learned? Why or why not? Under what conditions can a teacher initiate a study with a generalization? What are the dangers in having students make too many generalizations about history lessons?

between several concepts, students' insights develop into generalizations (statements that are usually or generally true). Therefore, for example, as they come to realize that rivers are frequently avenues of easy transportation so that trading centers often have developed at the convolution of rivers and other bodies of water or accessible land forms, they may generalize: "Towns frequently arose at favorable bodies of water or at water and land connections." Each day, continually, as students read, discuss, and study, they are constructing generalizations.

Organizing Knowledge for Instruction

Instructional materials contain factual data, concepts, and generalizations that are organized and presented to enhance and encourage student learning. In addition, the teacher uses facts, concepts, and generalizations in all types of presentations and interactions with students. Effective instructional design requires that the elements of knowledge be organized and presented according to an appropriate relationship or within a correct design pattern. Instructional design should follow these guidelines: (1) factual information and percepts (inputs from sensory organs) should support the development of concepts and should be presented within a conceptual context; (2) concepts should be considered the most important focus of instruction and the basis for the development of important generalizations; and (3) generalizations should be considered the outcome or result of instruction and not the beginning of instruction.

The following terms are provided as examples of the types of concepts that are commonly associated with the study of history and the social sciences within the social studies:

• *History:* frontier, colonialism, manifest destiny, blockade, Copperhead, loyalists, muckrakers, mugwump, scalawag, sharecropper, suffragist, utopian, epoch, dynasty, origins, causes, consequence, documentation, medieval, civilization, emancipation, rebellion, empire, Holocaust, New Deal, Underground Railroad, open-door policy, Reformation, primary source

• *Geography:* altitude, climate, conservation, ecology, space, interaction, environment, location, mesa, plateau, ocean, continent, space, region, resources, soil, urban, rural, plain, alpine, aquifer, arable land, archipelago, atmosphere, atoll, axis, basin, range, boreal, cultivate, elevation, erosion, estuary, fall line, fjord, flood plain, glacier, glen, globe, greenhouse effect, moraine, parallel, permafrost, savanna, steppe, tributary, tropics, tundra, urbanization

• *Political science:* citizenship, constitution, politics, taxation, sovereignty, treaties, diplomacy, ballot, assembly, autocracy, bipartisan, bureaucracy, canvass, caucus, confederation, conservative, liberal, filibuster, injunction, municipality, plurality, republic, writ, rule, law, hat-in-the-ring, pork barrels, gerry-mander, impeachment, lobbyist

• *Economics:* bankruptcy, marketplace, principle, bond, business cycle, profit, depreciation, dividends, credit, fiscal policy, expenses, liquidity, mortgage, premium, price-earnings ratio, taxation, recession, retail, securities, services, demand and supply, stock, surplus, unemployment, price, yield

• *Sociology:* status, assimilation, caste system, collective behavior, collectivism, conjugal family, cooperation, crime, crowd, demography, discrimination, divorce, ethnic group, fad, family, gender, ghetto, group, incest, institution, population, primary group, ritual, role, social class, social mobility, social pattern, society, status, subculture, urban

• *Psychology:* adolescence, aggression, anxiety, attitude, behavior, brainstorming, conditioning, drive, ego, emotion, perception, personality, heredity, imprinting, instinct, intelligence, learning, mind, motivation, norm, stimulus, sublimation, concept, dysfunction, empathy, homeostasis, insight, internalize, range, receptor

• *Anthropology:* aborigine, acculturation, adaptation, culture, enculturation, ethnocentric, ethnography, ethnology, evolution, kinship, matrilineage, mores, folkways, patrilineage, race, artifacts, band, blade tools, caste, civilization, classic, culture patterns, culture trait, dialect, diffusion, descent, dowry, elites, lineage, magic, moiety, mutation, myths, peasants, primates, ritual, species, symbols, taboo, tribe, witchcraft

In 1965 the Social Studies Curriculum Center at Syracuse University identified thirty-four concepts fundamental in the social studies curriculum. According to the center authors, Price, Hickman, and Smith, the concepts selected for the social studies were acquired from history and the social sciences based on the following criteria:

> The difficult choice of concepts to be developed and concepts to be deferred was based on (1) scope and (2) uniqueness. If a concept could be developed to include the concepts or sub-concepts recommended by several disciplines it was given priority over some important concepts limited to a single discipline. No concept was chosen merely because it was different. If there was good reason to believe the student would probably never in any other way be exposed to a particularly important concept of a single discipline, uniqueness determined which of the several such concepts should be chosen. (pp. 7–35)

Based on these criteria, the following concepts were included and listed as "substantive concepts":

> Sovereignty of the Nation-State in the Community of Nations
> Conflict—Its Origins, Expressions, and Resolution
> The Industrialization-Urbanization Syndrome
> Secularization

Compromise and Adjustment
Comparative Advantage
Power
Morality and Choice
Scarcity
Input and Output
Saving
The Modified Market
Habitat and Its Significance
Culture
Institution
Social Control
Social Change
Interaction

Five concepts were classified as "value concepts" and included the following:

Dignity of Man
Empathy
Loyalty
Government by Consent of the Governed
Freedom and Equality

Three concepts were included under the heading "concepts of method" or methodological concepts and included the following:

Historical Method and Point of View
The Geographical Approach
Causation

Finally, the authors listed "techniques and aspects of methods" that are designed to complete the methodological means of teaching concepts. They include:

Observation, Classification, and Measurement
Analysis and Synthesis
Questions and Answers
Objectivity
Skepticism
Interpretation
Evaluation
Evidence

The methodological means of dealing with the cognitive aspects of knowledge acquisition was further advanced by the work of Benjamin S. Bloom (1956). According to Bloom and his colleagues, there are six levels in the cog-

Can You Suggest Some Changes?

What are your reactions to the list of key concepts as program guides organized by the Syracuse Social Studies Center? What alterations or additions would you make and why?

nitive domain. These cognitive levels have been used to identify and classify various instructional objectives. By using Bloom's taxonomy, it is commonly believed that the teacher can select which cognitive level (thinking level) that students will use in achieving an instructional objective. The six levels are listed according to a hierarchy that ranges between lower (the knowledge level) and higher (the evaluation level) levels of thinking or cognitive processing. The six levels include:

- Knowledge level, which requires students to recall or repeat factual information

- Comprehension level, which requires students to describe an event or give an example of how a process works

- Application level, which requires students to use information in solving a problem

- Analysis level, which requires students to examine each component or aspect of an event in order to examine the influences that were present and may have influenced the outcome of the event

- Synthesis level, which requires students to combine features or elements in order to create a new understanding

- Evaluation level, which requires students to judge the behavior of a group or an individual or to judge the outcome of an event in terms of its positive or negative effects on future events

For the purpose of organizing a unit or lesson, it is suggested that the teacher begin designing and planning instruction by identifying the concepts to be taught and generalizations to be reached. Once this task has been completed, instructors should match each concept with an appropriate cognitive process(es) (for example, recall, description, explanation, examination, or rating). By making an appropriate match between concepts and processes, the teacher should be better able to design an effective means of instruction. A more detailed explanation will be presented later under such topics as "instructional strategies" (Chapter 11) and "designing instruction" (Chapter 15).

CONCLUSIONS

In reading this chapter, you learned that knowledge acquisition is a prime goal of education and for many educators the single most important instructional task in social studies education. Much of the criticism directed at the schools centers on the extent to which students are able to demonstrate their knowledge of subject matter on various tests. Unfortunately, glaring headlines report that students seem to know very little about the subject-matter content of the social studies. In addition, the public has become concerned by an alarming student drop-out rate indicating that many students believe that education is of little value to their future welfare. Teachers, on the other hand, sometimes complain that to maintain current enrollments, instructional programs have been reduced to a level of mediocrity seldom experienced before.

We can safely conclude that much of the problem points to a lack of concept development within current instructional programs. Therefore, to help students improve their knowledge of the social studies, your instructional programs should focus greater attention on those selected concepts that will serve as the foundation of the student's base of knowledge. Subsequently, as a teacher you will come to appreciate that concept development must begin in the lower grades and continue to develop as long as the individual is in the school. In addition, you have learned that you must continually monitor students' conceptual resources for those errors that have been established in the past and are expressed in the form of misconceptions. Many misconceptions are caused by factual errors that can hinder the pupil's ability to form generalizations. Moreover, misconceptions in connection with social studies information can lead to misunderstandings of the great historical events that have shaped the nation as well as misunderstandings of the nature of the institutions and systems that regulate daily life in the United States. There can be little question that along with identifying prime content the teacher must institute a related program of skill development that will enable students to grasp concepts and to be able to make generalizations.

REFERENCES

Bloom, B. S. (Ed.) (1956). *Taxonomy of educational objectives. Handbook I: The cognitive domain.* New York: David McKay.

Borich, G. D. (1992). *Effective teaching methods* (2nd ed.). New York: Macmillan.

Bruner, J. S. (1960). *The process of education.* New York: Vintage Books.

DeCecco, J., & Crawford, W. (1974). *The psychology of learning and instruction* (2nd ed.). Englewood Cliffs, NJ: Prentice-Hall.

de Vaus, D. A. (1986). *Survey in social research.* London: George, Allen & Unwin.

Dewey, J. (1916). *Democracy and education.* New York: Macmillan.

Doll, R. C. (1979). *Curriculum improvement: Decision-making and process* (2nd ed.). Boston: Allyn & Bacon.

Gagne, R. (1977). *The conditions of learning* (3rd ed.). New York: Holt, Rinehart & Winston.

Gunter, M. A., Estes, T. H., & Schwab, J. H. (1990). *Instruction: A models approach.* Boston: Allyn & Bacon.

Hanna, P. R., & Lee, J. R. (1962). *Content in the social studies* (Section one: Generalizations from the social sciences). In J. U. Michaelis (Ed.), *Social studies in elementary schools* (Thirty-second Yearbook of the National Council for the Social Studies, pp. 62–98). Washington, DC: National Council for the Social Studies.

Kemp, J. E. (1985). *The instructional design process.* New York: Harper & Row.

Michaelis, J. U. (1988). *Social studies for children: A guide to basic instruction* (9th ed.). Englewood Cliffs, NJ: Prentice-Hall.

Piaget, J. (1950). *The psychology of intelligence.* New York: Harcourt, Brace, Jovanovich.

Pratt, D. (1980). *Curriculum: Design and development.* San Diego: Harcourt, Brace, Jovanovich.

Price, R., Hickman, W., & Smith, G. (1965). *Major concepts for social studies.* Syracuse, NY: Social Studies Curriculum Center.

Stott, L. H. (1974). *The psychology of human development.* New York: Holt, Rinehart & Winston.

Taba, H. (1962). *Curriculum development: Theory and practice.* New York: Harcourt, Brace & World.

Tanner, D., & Tanner L. N. (1980). *Curriculum development: Theory and practice* (2nd ed.). New York: Macmillan.

Wesley, E. B., & Wronski, S. P. (1964). *Teaching social studies in high school* (5th ed.). Lexington, MA: D.C. Heath.

Wilson, J. A. R., Robeck, M. C., & Michael, W. B. (1969). *Psychological foundations of learning and teaching.* New York: McGraw-Hill.

Psychomotor, Basic, and Complex Skills

INTRODUCTION

In reading this chapter you will learn that skills are an important aspect of content knowledge because they provide the means through which individuals can gain access to or expand their knowledge. According to Webster's *Ninth New Collegiate Dictionary*, the word *skill* is defined as "the ability to use one's knowledge effectively and readily in execution or performance (or) a learned power of doing something competently" (p. 1104). Through the acquisition and practice of skills, a student is able to continue to learn independently. In addition, skills enable persons to gain a degree of control over their environment through interaction and experiences with various aspects of knowledge that can be used to synthesize or create unique solutions and answers to contemporary questions and problems. Norris M. Sanders (1966) states that skills have the following characteristics:

1. A skill is a physical, emotional, and/or intellectual process.
2. A skill requires knowledge, but knowledge alone does not insure proficiency.
3. A skill can be used in a variety of situations.
4. A skill can be improved through practice.
5. A skill is often made up of a number of sub skills that can be identified and practiced separately. (pp. 10–11)

In studying about instructional skills, you will learn that as a general rule, skills should accompany and be compatible with the acquisition of knowledge because skills are important instructional devices that, when used properly, allow students to become efficient learners. Daniel and Laurel Tanner (1980) have stated that "skills are recognized not as ends in themselves but as instrumental to the development of the ability to think reflectively" (p. 158). Skill development should have a higher priority within the instructional setting because most students do not retain content knowledge, especially when such knowledge is not applied at the time when it is taught. As Chapin and Gross point out,

> Studies show that even college students forget about three-fourths of the content in their courses; younger students probably forget more. Thus, merely acquiring social studies content has limited value as a major objective. (p. 2)

Consequently, skills are functional elements of learning and performance; therefore, skill acquisition is important because it allows individuals to learn new information and to apply that knowledge. Certain **basic skills,** such as reading, observing, and listening skills are used to acquire new knowledge (or for learning), whereas **applied skills,** such as measuring, illustrating, and problem solving skills, are aimed at performance. These skills are often termed **entry level skills.** Dick and Carey (1978) note importance of identifying entry level skills:

> If specific skills are required to perform the instructional goal, they will be required for all persons. The varying factor among the groups would be the skills they possess when they enter the instruction. Their skill level would determine which skills would be considered entry behaviors and which would be included in the instruction. (p. 56)

Instructional skills, or target skills, provide a means for students to learn concepts and ideas in activities that include their participation. The interrelated nature of skills has been described by Chapin & Gross (1973):

> For clarity, skills have been assumed to be discrete entities; however, they cannot be considered to be isolated from the rest of the educational process. Skills are interrelated with understandings and attitudes, they depend on knowledge, and they have values attached to them. (p. 7)

How Important Is Instruction in Skill Acquisition?

Teachers frequently are charged with overlooking skill development or with believing that skills grow only out of related content learning. Can you explain this instructional misunderstanding?

In the social studies, most skills to be developed are in the complex intellectual category of thinking. Students can learn many of these in well-structured group work and through teacher-directed classroom discussions and questioning.

Skill Development

Skills are often acquired through practice, refinement, and reinforcement. Like memory work, skills may also be acquired through memorization without regard for understandings, insights, or meanings; therefore, skills can be acquired as habits. For example, psychologists have been very successful in training animals to perform certain functions on cue; students can be trained in the same manner. This type of training can be help prepare students for various tasks. In reaction to these practices, some educators have insisted that skill development be taught within the context of purpose and in association with specific understandings. John Dewey (1966) especially opposed the development of habitual skills that are outside the context of thought.

> Any skill obtained apart from thinking is not connected with any sense of the purposes for which it is to be used. It consequently leaves a man at the mercy of his routine habits and of the authoritative control of others, who know what they are about and who are not especially scrupulous as to their means of achievement. (pp. 152–153)

Skill development requires practice in the amount determined by the complexity of the skill as well as by student abilities and needs. According to David Pratt (1980),

> Three main stages in skills learning are cognitive, fixation, and automation. Practice is not essential at the first stage, when the learner gains a cognitive understanding of the skill. Practice is necessary at the second stage, when variable and awkward performance gradually becomes consistent, accurate, and precise. At the third stage a high degree of speed and coordination are achieved. (p. 312)

Because of inexperience, some students will require more practice than will others; also, more complex skills require more practice. Once a skill has been demonstrated, students must practice under supervision. Through positive feedback, students are encouraged to make changes and corrections to improve their performance with ample opportunity to repeat and practice.

Target skills are taught because they are deemed essential to the development of further learning. Once identified, these skills should be taught and practiced according to a pre-established process in which the skill is broken down into essential elements and organized into sequential patterns or steps. For example, students are assigned the task of locating Lisbon, Portugal, on a flat map according to its coordinates by following directions such as these:

1. Your task is to locate Lisbon, Portugal, on your desk map.
2. Locate the gazetteer in the back of your geography textbook.
3. Locate Lisbon, Portugal, under the letter *L* in the gazetteer.
4. Write down the coordinates for Lisbon, Portugal.
5. Locate the latitudinal line for Lisbon, Portugal.
6. Locate the longitudinal line for Lisbon, Portugal.
7. Pinpoint the intersection between the latitudinal line and the longitudinal line and place a dot at this point.
8. Go to the wall map of Europe and compare the "dot" on your map with the wall map location.
9. If the two maps indicate the same location for Lisbon, Portugal, label your map. If the two maps indicate different locations, repeat the previous steps.
10. Following the same process, locate Buenos Aires, Argentina.

These steps should be performed according to a certain sequence in which each step would be taught independently or separately from the other steps. Each step thereby provides the information or the behaviors that are needed to complete the task or that will serve as the basis of the remaining steps. The first step in the skill development process is a skill demonstration to help students focus on the process. In the second step and following steps, students are encouraged to perform and practice the skill. When planning skill instruction, teachers should try to motivate their students to want to learn and apply new skills. In addition, a well-planned skills program should include diagnostic measures that estimate the extent to which each student has learned the target skill. (As a word of caution, remember that it is unwise to assume that students are skilled or proficient in the skills needed to complete a new assignment or task. Therefore, it is important that teachers identify all related skills that are needed to complete a specific task or assignment and make sure that their students already possess these skills.) Students may regularly have difficulties in meeting the teacher's requirements because they have not acquired all of the skills contained within an assignment or task.

The context in which a skill is learned should represent a reasonable facsimile of situations in which it is most likely to be used outside of the class-

WHICH STEPS IN WHAT ORDER?

Select a prime skill from a high school social studies course you will be teaching. List the specific steps you would follow in teaching the skill to students.

room. In other words, the teacher should attempt to create an environment or replicate the conditions under which the skill would most likely be applied. For instance, in teaching the skill of locating information in a library, it would be better to take the students to the library rather than to have the librarian come to the classroom. Immediately after the teacher and librarian have described to students how to locate a resource, they should give them an opportunity to practice locating other resources. The same principle could be applied in developing map skills. Students could learn to use a map by constructing their own maps of the classroom, school, or neighborhood. A field trip for observation, for example, is a valuable preskill activity prior to constructing maps of an area. In another exercise, students could learn to locate objects in the classroom by drawing a map of the room with reference lines in the form of a labeled grid. They could then call out the object once reference points had been identified.

Skill instruction in the classroom should be based, in part, on the students' learning styles and on the requirements of the instructional program (course, unit, or lesson). Individual learning styles may be a factor in the selection of skill development activities. While some students might benefit from step-by-step instruction that is meticulously followed, other students might benefit from a trial-and-error process in which the skill process is practiced and refined.

The timing of skill instruction is also an important concern as students should have the mental maturity to understand the processes that they are learning. In planning skill lessons, teachers need to find out the extent to which their students are prepared to learn a new skill. Skill attainment may be mandated by the goals of instruction. Students often are taught to read, write, and compute numbers in the primary grades because these skills are designated to be taught early in the educational program. For example, students are taught directions (north, south, east, and west) in the early grades so that these skills can be applied to a variety of tasks at a relatively early age.

Skill complexity or the level of skill difficulty is one of the most important factors in determining when a skill should be taught. The level of skill difficulty is related to the number of subskills associated with the target skill and the degree of proficiency that is required to acquire the skill. Complex skills tend to include more subskills than do simple skills. In addition, complex skills often require sophisticated cognitive processes.

The expected level of skill proficiency also determines the extent to which students will have difficulty in learning a skill in order to meet instructional requirements. Most teachers expect that their students already possess an adequate level of skill development to learn and apply what is taught in the classroom. But this assumption is often misleading because basic skills take years to develop and to refine. In reality, over half of the students in elementary and secondary schools possess only minimal skills and need continuous instruction to develop basic and complex skills.

When planning a skill lesson, teachers should be able to state the expected level of proficiency before they assume that students have adequately attained the target skill. Skills proficiency generally requires practice under a variety of conditions. In most classroom situations, skills taught at the beginning of the year will be lost by the end of the year unless they are used continually. Important social studies skills such as reading, writing, communicating, problem solving, and map interpretation must be applied continuously if they are to be mastered over time.

Skill Categories

Skills can be classified according to (1) simple skills that are learned at a relatively early age and are fundamental to later learning—such as the identification of colors, numbers, and letters; labeling objects; simple associations; and various types of psychomotor skills such as throwing a ball; (2) basic skills that are necessary to acquire knowledge or to access knowledge—basic skills in the social studies include abilities such as reading, writing, listening, communicating, social skills, and study skills; and (3) complex skills that are applied skills (doing and thinking) in association with complex processes and intellectual applications including abilities such as locating information, researching, illustrating information, giving oral reports, problem solving, decision making, and critical and creative thinking.

Psychomotor and Simple Skills

Within the social studies, **simple skills** tend to be acquired through experiences that help students form associations. These include activities such as alphabetizing, matching names to faces, measuring, and engaging in various motor skills. Simple skills include motor skills that are learned and developed to some extent in childhood, skills that require a coordinated physical ability related to the manipulation of arms, legs, eyes, and fingers in maneuvering physical objects. According to Pratt (1980),

> *Motor skills* relate to control of physical movement primarily through muscular operation and range from the manipulative use of fingers to gross motor skills such as running or swimming. (p. 175)

Social studies instruction often requires the use of various motor skills in activities such as illustrating and constructing projects. The development of simple skills often takes on the form of mental habits, habits that require little in the way of intellectual thought. Simple skills are usually developed through repeated practice without regard to the wide-ranging conditions under which they will likely be applied in activities (for example, cutting and pasting might be used to illustrate an idea or a concept).

Basic Skills

Basic skills consist of processes that human beings acquire in order to access knowledge. In school these processes are often associated with language arts skills such as listening, speaking, reading, and writing. Morse and McCune (1964) describe basic skills that also may be grounded in the development of simple skills—skills that are developed through repeated practice or skills that take on a mechanical characteristic.

> Some manipulations are more obviously on the mechanical side and may be reduced almost to the point of automatic responses. Such are the so-called basic skills of writing, word recognition, ciphering, and simple place location. (p. 26)

Teachers often complain that many of their students lack the basic ability to read the classroom textbook even when the text is grade-level appropriate. According to Chapin and Gross (1973),

> . . .teachers face students who have a wide range of reading abilities. Moreover, it is estimated conservatively that by the end of the sixth grade approximately 10 percent to 25 percent of all students are 'seriously' below grade level in reading—typically defined as two grade levels below normal. By other estimates, one-third of the elementary school children and one-fourth to one-third of the high school students are handicapped readers. Below-grade reading achievement for the disadvantaged is well documented. (p. 21)

In addition to the ability to decipher words and sentences, reading appears to be rooted in various thinking skills. Reading in the social studies requires certain intellectual skills associated with critical thinking, problem solving, and various validating, clarifying, and evaluating skills, as well as a body of social studies (history and social science) information. Reading also requires various ancillary skills associated with vocabulary development and research skills such as information gathering and library use. Vocabulary development by itself may not resolve the reading problem because reading problems are best addressed through a combination of cognitive and skill approaches. According to this approach, the social studies teacher would encourage oral reading along with activities that are designed to help students gain better insights into the meanings of words and sentences. Preston (1969) observes that

> . . . knowledge of social studies vocabulary of typical pupils is vague and inaccurate and that the direct teaching of vocabulary, when relied upon alone, has proved disappointing. Data and insights from the field of linguistics . . . suggest that oral reading, writing, and dramatization, if closely tied to the pupil's reading, will enable him consciously to supply elements of spoken language in his reading which are missing in the printed sentence. (p. 32)

Based on this finding, vocabulary development should be connected to comprehension-enriched experiences and activities. Thus, reading comprehension appears to be related to vocabulary development and the intellectual ability to understand the ideas and the concepts that are embedded within a written message or passage. It also appears that good readers are constantly reading while poor readers tend to avoid reading. In reporting on his observations of thirty-two teachers of above average, average, and below average students in social studies classrooms, Herman (1969) reported that

> During these observations, it was common to observe a teacher telling his children to read several pages in the social studies textbook and then see him saunter aimlessly around the classroom. What did many of the pupils do while they were supposed to be reading? They read a few sentences or paragraphs and then gave up. They pretended to be reading until another activity began. If a child thought that he was not being watched, he might fondle a toy in his desk, doodle, look around the room, tie and retie a shoe lace, or interact with a friend—anything, except read. (p. 5)

Teachers can demonstrate orally, as pupils follow in their texts, various aspects of good reading. Also, teachers can have each class member read aloud a section of text as the other students follow the print in their books and listen. While oral reading differs from silent reading, the instructor can gain valuable clues from such exercises about particular reading needs of students in the class.

Social studies teachers can help students improve their writing abilities by using a well-planned social studies writing program. Writing programs should include both individual and group settings. Group activities can be used to teach a variety of writing skills such as locating resources, selecting information, and organizing reports according to various formats—for example, introduction, body, conclusion, references, and citations. Also, writing centers might be used to help students develop their writing skills using the step-by-step process approach.

Because writing consists of several subskills, some of which must be learned in preparation for writing (speech and letter sounds, for example), some of which are learned through writing activities (such as vocabulary, syntax rules, punctuation, outlining), and some of which are learned over time with practice (editing, argumentation, and creative thought, for instance). Writing requires compliance with standard grammatical conventions. In addition, because writing requires cognitive abilities, it might be said that writing is thinking on paper; therefore, writing is not easily mastered, and most writers must continue to strive to improve their abilities if they are to become "good" writers. Chapin and Gross (1973) point out some of the differences between written and spoken language that make the mastery of written language difficult:

> Writing should be far more precise and exact than speaking because written language is in a symbolic format and can be more easily misinterpreted. . . .Writing also has its own structures and conventions (spelling and punctuation) that often differ markedly from the spoken language. (p. 83)

Therefore, students should be encouraged to improve their writing skills by continually striving to make refinements through revising and editing and by expanding their semantic understandings. In describing the necessity of practicing precise word choices as a part of acquiring good writing skills, Todd (1963) reinforces the importance of making choices between alternative words that have similar meanings:

> The ability to "say it," to express on(e)self [sic] with clarity and precision, is not, unfortunately, an inherited talent. It has to be learned, and the learning process involves the mastery of a number of skills. Since skill can be acquired only through practice, the way to learn to write is to write. . . .(Todd, p. 121)

Writing can be used to promote learning in the social studies as it can be used to explore subject-matter content. By working with newspapers, magazines, journals, and books, students can learn by exploring and investigating. By writing editorials, developing their ideas on paper, and writing essays on contemporary problems, students can learn to interpret issues and events. By writing reports and essays that argue in favor of one policy or program over another or in writing letters to newspapers, students can learn to present their ideas in a reasoned and logical way.

Because writing tends to be a personal process, students should be encouraged to express their differences (personality, experiences, beliefs, outlooks) in their written works. Unfortunately, the desire to write is often hampered by various standard teaching practices related to the evaluation of written work. Many

To Assign or Not to Assign: What Are the Determining Factors?

Some social studies teachers assign very few writing assignments and lessons. Why do you think this is so? What type of writing experiences are most important in social studies skill development?

teachers tend to grade written work on general or superficial standards rather than on individual standards. Syntax, grammar, and punctuation errors are relatively easy to detect and usually lead to the conclusion that the student is a poor writer (Chapin & Gross); consequently, students are encouraged to comply with these standards rather than experiment with their creative abilities.

Observing is an important learning skill in the social studies that is often associated with the study of human behavior and social relationships. Psychologists, sociologists, and anthropologists consider observation to be an important scientific means for gathering information. Scholars within these disciplines are trained to apply observational techniques to a variety of social problems and questions as a means of obtaining new information. According to Chapin and Gross (1973),

> *Observation*. . . goes beyond viewing and stresses respectful adherence to a scientific model. It is more concentrated and is often used to measure quantitatively. . . . (p. 74)

Social studies students can learn and practice a basic type of systematic observation to gain new insights into various classroom activities. This systematic observation should be based on certain guidelines or rules that are established for the classroom and are appropriate to the types of activities used for instructional purposes. For example, students might be taught to make scheduled observations of weather or traffic over a period of time (hours, days, weeks, or even months). In addition, students might be encouraged to identify and describe the characteristics of the behavior prior to the observation activity. Trained observers are sensitive to the various subtle reactions when observing social relationships. For instance, students might observe nonverbal clues such as facial expressions and body language as an indication of nonverbally expressed feelings and attitudes. At the same time, they would be cautioned not to interpret such expressions in terms of specific meanings. Preston and Herman (1978) suggest that students learn the processes of observation by adhering to some of the following recommendations:

(1) having several observers instead of one and (2) asking observers to pay close attention. . . .(3) having the observers take notes or snapshots and (4) trying not to take sides if the observed event is a sports contest or an argument. (pp. 216–217)

Observational skills can be taught through various classroom activities. But first, it is recommended that the teacher demonstrate the specific observation skills that the students are to learn. For instance, the teacher might select a group of students to stage an event while other students are instructed to record their observations related to specific behaviors. Following this activity, students should be encouraged to describe the event in terms of their observations as a part of essential class feedback discussion.

Listening is one of the most important fundamental means of learning in the social studies in which verbal sounds (symbols) are used to transmit information (Jacobs, 1963):

In listening, the individual hears familiar sound combinations to which, in terms of his experience, he brings meaning and from which he also simultaneously takes meaning, and acquires, thereby, sources for reaction, interpretation, and knowledge. (p. 141)

Most students have difficulty in separating important information and ancillary information; therefore, the teacher's task is to provide the cues that students need to direct their attention and to focus on essential ideas. By training young children in set procedures for listening (including the cues and signals that are designed to catch their attention), they can improve their listening skills as they mature and advance into adolescence.

Listening to learn is an acquired skill that is associated with active participation in a directed flow of information. According to Jacobs (1963), to be effective listeners, students must be able to relate to the oral message and to cognitively sort, classify, and evaluate the information into various mental frameworks: "Students need to be taught that, at its best, listening is active. A person hears, comprehends, reacts, and retains when he listens" (p. 142).

Social studies students can be taught to listen and to respond to verbal instruction called **exploratory listening.** Exploratory listening requires that the students apply new information immediately following a teacher's oral presentation. For example, a teacher might explain the judicial procedure used to determine the guilt or innocence of an accused defendant. Following the explanation, the teacher could give students role cards and ask them to try the accused in a mock trial. Evaluation would be based on the teacher's looking for specific instructional elements related to the directions given to the students.

The ability to speak before a group is also an important social studies skill. Individuals often are judged according to their ability to express their ideas or to share and exchange information coherently and intelligently. An important

WHY DO COMBINATION SKILLS LEAD TO MORE EFFECTIVE INSTRUCTION?

Suggest an activity for a social studies class that contains learning experiences related to both observation and listening.

goal of the social studies should be to help students develop their public speaking skills; therefore the teacher should he!p students acquire some the fundamental skills related to oral communication. Oral communication skills are developed by teachers who provide ample classroom opportunities for students. Oral communication should take place in a variety of settings and situations. In addition, oral communication skills may be enhanced through a variety of activities related to individual oral reports, group discussions, and various forms of oral group reports (panel presentations, debates, or round table discussions, for example) (Chapin & Gross, 1973).

When involving students in oral communication activities, teachers should remember that students often become anxious and are sometimes reluctant to speak formally before others. In light of this concern, students might be encouraged to participate in group presentations beginning with more simple formats such as oral group book reports where four or five students cooperate in an oral presentation. Later, more complex tasks might follow in which students present a group report according to shared subtasks (introductions, holding illustrations, explaining a point, summarizing, and asking for questions, for example). As confidence builds, students might be encouraged to participate in role-playing activities, debate, or dialogues. Finally, each student should be encouraged to make a five-minute solo presentation before the entire class. Depending on the individual student and the situation, an outline or notes may be used as long as the student does not read them. The entire class should be encouraged to receive oral reports with interest and to express their appreciation in a courteous and enthusiastic expression (applause, for instance). Continuous class discussion helps to motivate the desire to speak in class, and this activity is enhanced when students are encouraged to prepare for discussion through various study and research activities.

An important goal of social studies education is to help students acquire certain basic social skills related to group work, participation in cooperative projects, and the development of social relationships. The development of social skills begins within the family and extends to the neighborhood as the child develops social relationships outside of the family. When most children enter school, they possess some basic social skills such as a knowledge of the rules of etiquette (salutations, sharing, waiting turns, requesting, and thanking); however, some students do not possess even rudimentary social skills. Elementary teachers typically spend a great deal of time and effort in helping their students develop basic social skills within the school and classroom setting. Most social skills associated with the social studies involve the development of group skills. **Group skills** usually are aimed at helping individual students to work cooperatively toward a common goal or to perform a shared task. Students are encouraged to share the responsibilities for performing the task, resolving a problem, or completing an assignment as a requirement of group work. In addition, group work requires that students learn to support their fellow group members who are serving in a leadership capacity, and in turn each student is encouraged to take on the responsibilities of leadership should the need arise.

The development of study habits is an important aspect of skill development in the social studies. To a large extent, effective instruction rests on the willingness of students to prepare themselves for learning; therefore, the teacher should be able to expect students to spend time reading, reviewing, and studying in preparation for instruction. Class time set aside for instructional preparation is well spent when teachers have trained their students in certain study skills. For example, supervised social studies reading might follow a process in which a textbook chapter or passage is read according to a procedure that is aimed at improving reading comprehension. This process might follow certain steps in which a passage is read several times for purposes ranging from an attempt to grasp an initial awareness of certain ideas to developing an in-depth understanding of specific concepts. In addition, students might be taught study skills to prepare them to take tests. Because testing skills vary according to test type, different study skills should be taught. For example, essay tests require study skills different from those involved in multiple-choice tests. Essay tests require, among other skills, an ability to organize information into logical patterns and to persuasively attack or defend one's position on an issue, whereas multiple-choice tests require the elimination of various incorrect choices in search of the correct answer.

Complex Skills

Complex skills are intellectual skills as well as applied skills (thinking and performance). These skills are often called complex skills because they entail complex processes (skills that are associated with the methodologies of history and the social sciences) and various intellectual processes (procedures associated with problem solving, decision making, and critical and creative thinking). Consequently, complex skills are closely tied to content knowledge and should not be taught in isolation apart from content instruction. As was the case with basic skills, teachers should list the subskills (related skills or prerequisite skills) to be sure that students possess the prerequisites needed to learn the new skill. Each of the disciplines associated with the social studies uses special disciplinary processes or methodologies to advance subject-matter knowledge, answer questions, or solve problems. For example, geographers may employ various skills and techniques associated with maps, tables, and charts to resolve certain questions about an area or a place, while the political scientist may employ surveys, questionnaires, or polls to resolve questions about future political behavior.

In other words, each discipline has developed a set of specialized inquiry tools, some of which are shared and some of which are specific to the discipline, in order to perform the scholarly function of advancing their knowledge. Many of these same techniques may be employed as instructional skills in the social studies classroom. At the same time, many of these skills are complex procedures that cannot be fully mastered at the precollegiate level of instruction. In spite of this limitation, these skills can help students gain a more sophisticated insight in the study of human affairs. Therefore, an important goal of the social studies is to help students acquire and apply some of the disciplinary skills associated with history and the social sciences. In the following two examples, the disciplines of history and geography are used to illustrate two characteristic processes used within specific disciplines to acquire new knowledge:

Historians are skilled in organizing important events chronologically. Associated with this skill is the ability to detect cause-and-effect relationships between events and their consequences. Social studies teachers may decide that students should learn to detect cause-and-effect relationships by developing a time line. In this process, students organize the central events of a period (ten years, for example) along a segmented base line. After the events are listed in sequence on the time line, students try to trace the influences of earlier events on later events in order to detect various possible relationships and consequences. Items and events related to an entry on the base line may be placed on a second line below (as well as pictures, charts, and symbols) and linked by dotted lines to the main event directly above.

Geographers are skilled in detecting specialized regions that may exist over an expanse of territory. Regions often are identified by recording certain characteristic features, by studying maps, and by locating information on a map. For example, a geographer may wish to identify the region of a country that specializes in growing pecans. Pecan trees require certain climatic conditions including a relatively long growing season. The geographer gathers year-by-year production results about the pecan market and then plots the information on a map. As a result, the geographer is able to draw a boundary line around the area that is characteristically pecan country. Thus, the geographer has identified a specialized region. Social studies teachers may decide that students should be able to recognize the special regional features of their state. Teachers could then provide students with an outline map of the state and a data sheet indicating county-by-county agricultural productions. Teachers instruct the students to use a symbol system to indicate the extent to which each county produces various crops and to draw a boundary around the counties that excel in various crops.

Another important goal of the social studies is to help students acquire and apply certain cognitive (thinking) skills that are based on various learned procedures. According to Pratt (1980),

> *Cognitive skills* include such abilities as recognition, discrimination, analysis, and problem solving. This category includes both rational/logical skills and creative/intuitive skills. (p. 175)

Some experts have developed the idea of hierarchical skills based on the complexity of the cognitive process. Benjamin Bloom (1956) developed a taxonomy in which he associated basic skills with five (or six — see page 143) levels of knowledge (Wilson, Robeck, & Michael, 1969). Each level of knowledge requires a higher order of cognition or thinking. In the social studies, complex skills include intellectual skills as well as specific skill processes characteristic of history and the social sciences. Complex skills require complex thinking and the use of advanced cognitive processes. For example, decision making is an important complex skill that is commonly classified as a cognitive skill. Complex skills are different from other skills as they require a form of meticulous checking and double checking in order to satisfy certain requirements. For example, in a problem-solving exercise, students learn to follow and execute a series of steps that make up the problem-solving procedure. Once the exercise has been completed and a tentative conclusion reached, students should recheck their work to see that they considered every possibility at each step of the procedure. Morse and McCune (1964) describe complex skills as complex mental processes:

> . . . skills which involve higher mental processes and are more closely interwoven with acquired knowledge. Such are skills of critical-mindedness and related abilities of refraining from jumping to conclusions, evaluation of given sources of information, analysis or related parts of a problem, and retention of an open mind. Within the range are other skills or abilities such as those of proper use of reference material, interpretation of social data presented in tabular or graphic form, and making an adequate summary. (p. 26)

In an applied form, problem solving is taught in the social studies as a process skill that helps students reach a conclusion based on the exploration of an unresolved issue. The process is often presented in the form of a step-by-step deductive procedure beginning as a statement of the problem. Once the problem has been defined, students are encouraged to develop a hypothesis or a possible solution to the process. The hypothesis is tested (explored under many conditions) to determine whether it will hold up under a variety of conditions or settings. Finally the hypothesis is accepted, rejected, or modified depending on the results of the assessments performed. When a modified hypothesis is formulated, further examination will follow to determine whether this proposed solution seems valid. For example, students are asked to propose a solution to a conflict over a herd of cattle on an open range claimed by two different ranchers with virtually equal claims. The cattle were not branded, and the ranchers were not aware that their neighbor held grazing rights to the same range. Rancher A claimed he had approximately 300 cattle, mainly pregnant cows. Rancher B claimed he had approximately 500 cattle, a mixed herd with many pregnant cows. Once the range herd was rounded up, 900 cattle were located containing 300 yearlings cattle. The students were assigned the task of satisfying both claims in the most equitable manner. Two student teams were organized to represent the interests of rancher A and rancher B, and they had the authority to reject offers that were not in their interests.

Decision making is an intellectual process that requires students to select the "best" alternative choice based on a set of conditions or circumstances. This process requires that the students review and describe the issue or the problem to be resolved and identify the various alternatives that could be used to resolve the issue, problem, or question. They study the effects and consequences of each possible alternative choice. After each possible selection has been compared according to the same set of characteristics, the final selection is presented with a list of reasons for selecting this choice over the other alternatives. For example, students are assigned the task of deciding between several alternative overland routes between St. Louis, Missouri, and San Francisco, California. According to this exercise, it is May 15, 1846, and the reason for traveling is to search for gold. The Plains Indians are becoming increasingly hostile, and in the southwest there are hostile exchanges between the Apache and the Comanche Indians. *The Farmer's Almanac* suggests that the coming winter will be severe. Several possible routes are traced on the students' desk maps, including (1) the southern Santa Fe Trail (requiring extensive northern travel) which would connect with or continue along the Old Spanish Trial; (2) the more northern route along the Oregon Trail, which then

What Can Students Learn from Wrong Decisions and Wrong Solutions?

What particular skills of significant importance are built through problem-solving and decision-making learning activities? Indicate several specific issues most pertinent for such analysis in a particular course.

swings south along the California Trail; and (3) several possible alternative routes or cutoffs that follow either the southern or northern routes and then strike due west over various possible "gaps" in the Sierra Nevada Mountains and then head straight west to the coast. The students are asked to consider possible hostilities along the trail; the distance that must be covered, the travel time, which is limited to twenty miles per day (mountain travel five miles per day); travel difficulties because of elevation, obstacles, lack of supplies, animal feed, and protection; and the cool summer and approaching winter. Student decisions should be based on a process of elimination and on their justification for the decisions made. Following this exercise, the teacher will assign a reading from the 1846 Donner party experience.

Mastering Skills

Although students can begin to master a skill under the supervision of their teacher, mastering a skill requires a great deal of individual experience and practice. For example, a person may learn to write a term paper in school; at the same time, an elementary or secondary level of writing would not be good enough to have the paper published in a weekly journal. In other words, skill mastery is measured in degrees of attainment and refinement. Skill mastery is a quest for excellence or perfection, standards that few students will fully attain. When a skill is to be taught, the teacher needs to remember that some students will master the skill better than other students; therefore, the teacher needs to consider the level of attainment (level of proficiency) that is to be established in order to consider the skill established. At the same time, the teacher should provide ample opportunities for students to apply the target skills throughout the school year. Ultimately, the success of skill development in the social studies rests on the ability of the students to solve a problem by selecting and applying those skills that they believe are best suited in their quest for solutions. In other words, the overall goal of skill development is to help students develop a range of skills that they can apply to their particular needs and circumstances both within and outside the classroom.

Most skills consist of a variety of subskills, some of which are obvious and some of which are not. For example, locating a place on a map involves a variety of related skills including the ability to use the grid system, interpret map symbols, and use scale. According to Jarolimek (1963), the assessment of skill acquisition is an important element of the skill acquisition process and might be based on the following criterion: "To be skillful means that one is able to do something with proficiency in repeated performances" (p. 19).

STATE THE SKILL AND GIVE THE STEPS

To accurately assess a student's grasp of a particular skill (which you indicate), what are the procedural steps that you should plan and follow in building student competency? It should be noted here that specific examples for the development of skills identified in this chapter, such as those of group work or problem solving, are further explained with suggested uses and applications in subsequent chapters. See particularly Chapter 11, devoted to instructional strategies and activities.

Skill Assessment

Skill assessment in the social studies can take many forms ranging from pencil-and-paper tests to class and individual observations by the teacher; however, skill acquisition and development rely on student performance. Therefore, it is recommended that skill assessment in the social studies be based on performance more than on pencil-and-paper tests. In other words, the teacher should measure skill development based on the extent to which each student has mastered the skill by being able to perform when called upon to do so. For example, map skills should be assessed according to how well the student can demonstrate specified map skills by performing these skills on a map. The same would be true of intellectual skills such as problem solving, decision making, and analyzing and critiquing a report, for example. (Remember that typical lesson and activity assignments provide continuing opportunities to assess progress of the competencies.) The development of these complex skills should be assessed according to how well each student can actually perform the skill to meet the requirements of a lesson.

CONCLUSIONS

In this chapter, you learned that a well-balanced instructional program for the social studies can be measured in part according to the skills that are selected to help prepare students for successful living in the present and in the future. In short, skill development in the social studies should focus on those psychomotor, basic, and complex skills that are needed by individuals to preserve the best elements of our current civilization while allowing for its expansion in constructive directions. The acquisition of social studies skills, as a goal of instruction, is in some respects more important than the acquisition of social studies knowledge because skills enable students to access and apply information, which is an essential part of any learning.

The application of knowledge is largely determined by the norms of society that regulate the social, economic, and political behaviors of groups and individuals. U.S. citizens must be aware of these norms and be able to skillfully apply them in a society that values enterprise and self-reliance as much as cooperation and collaboration. More often than not, individuals should be prepared to work toward shared goals by cooperatively participating in joint efforts aimed at improving the well-being of their communities. Over time, skills should help to liberate individuals by allowing them to become independent learners who are free to pursue their own interests.

In particular, you should realize that social studies skills are aimed at helping pupils deal with change that is being driven by an ever-accelerating explosion of knowledge. As a consequence, no individual or group is capable of keeping abreast of more than one or two segments or threads of knowledge. Most technical books are out of date before they reach the book store, and students who graduated from college yesterday may soon be out of touch with their evolving specialties. Because of the rapid nature of technological change, students must be equipped to deal with a dynamic and changing society that requires constant learning, decision making, and measured actions. Therefore, to live a successful life, the individual must constantly keep abreast of changing times. To put the matter another way, knowledge is power, and knowledge in today's terms can be mastered only by those who can access and apply it in a proper and constructive manner. Consequently, students must be skilled in the processes of accessing and sifting through volumes of information to select and apply those essential ideas that strengthen their knowledge base and enable further learning.

REFERENCES

Bloom, B. S. (Ed.). (1956). *Taxonomy of educational objectives. Handbook I: The cognitive domain.* New York: David McKay.

Chapin J. R., & Gross, R. E. (1973). *Teaching social studies skills.* Boston: Little, Brown.

Dewey, J. (1966). *Democracy and education.* New York: The Free Press.

Dick, W., & Carey, L. (1978). *The systematic design of instruction.* Glenview, IL: Scott, Foresman.

Herman, W. L. (1969). Reading and other language arts in social studies instruction: Persistent problems. In R. C. Preston (Ed.), *A new look at reading in the social studies* (pp. 1–20). Newark, DE: International Reading Association.

Jacobs, L. B. (1963). Speaking and listening. In H. M. Carpenter (Ed.), *Skill development in social studies* (Thirty-third Yearbook, pp. 131–147). Washington, DC: National Council for the Social Studies.

Jarolimek, J. (1963). The psychology of skill development. In H. M. Carpenter (Ed.), *Skill development in social studies* (Thirty-third Yearbook, pp. 17–34). Washington, DC: National Council for the Social Studies.

Morse, H. T., & McCune, G. H. (1964). *Selecting items for the testing of study skills and critical thinking* (Bulletin 15). Washington, DC: National Council for the Social Studies.

Pratt, D. (1980). *Curriculum: Design and development.* New York: Harcourt, Brace, Jovanovich.

Preston, R. C. (1969). Newer approaches to handling the vocabulary problem. In R. C. Preston (Ed.), *A new look at reading in the social studies* (pp. 21–33). Newark, DE: International Reading Association.

Preston, R. C., & Herman, W. L., Jr. (1978). *Teaching social studies in the elementary school* (4th ed.). New York: Holt, Rinehart & Winston.

Sanders, N. M. (1966). *Classroom questions: What kinds?* New York: Harper & Row.

Tanner, D., & Tanner L. N. (1980). *Curriculum development: Theory and practice* (2nd ed.). New York: Macmillan.

Todd, L. P. (1963). Writing. In H. M. Carpenter (Ed.), *Skill development in social studies* (Thirty-third Yearbook, pp. 115–130). Washington, DC: National Council for the Social Studies.

Webster's Ninth New Collegiate Dictionary (1991). Springfield, MA: Merriam-Webster.

Wilson, J. A. R., Robeck, M. C., & Michael, W. B. (1969). *Psychological foundations of learning and teaching.* New York: McGraw-Hill.

Education for Values

INTRODUCTION

In this chapter you will learn that values are associated with behaviors and attitudes that are symbolic of a unified social group or a people, especially regarding certain ways of thinking, acting, and doing. Values evolve over time as a result of changes in society's standards and in patterns of social contact. Because values are so influential in human behavior, it is important to understand the nature of values, how they are acquired, and the role that they play in individual, group, and societal decisions.

The term *value* pervades our writings and conversations. Yet, when we are asked to define *values* or to describe the nature of values, difficulties arise. According to Armstrong (1980), "The term *value* is a slippery one that demands definition before a productive discussion can proceed" (p. 257). These difficulties are associated with the ambiguous understandings that most individuals hold about the nature of values. According to John Dewey (1966),

> To value means primarily to prize, to esteem; but secondarily it means to apprize, to estimate. It means, that is, the act of cherishing something, holding it dear, and also the act of passing judgment upon the nature and amount of its value as compared with something else. (p. 238)

While values may be stated orally or in written form, students should be encouraged to recognize, analyze, or interpret values as an aspect of their social education. The disciplines that especially focus on human values (sociology, psychology, and anthropology) tend to emphasize the importance of a systematic observation and analysis of behavior. As a result of the work of behavioral scientists, it has been recognized that individuals, groups, and societies may have stated values that are seldom practiced; therefore, students should recognize that when it comes to a study of values, actions do speak louder than words. Even so, values and related moral and ethical issues are encountered in every aspect of human activity, making it necessary for individuals to

WHAT IS YOUR ETHICAL IMPACT?

In educating for values, would you accept the statement that an instructor's strongest source of ethical impact is in the classroom model that he or she provides? Why or why not?

be able to distinguish between values that are consistently practiced and those that are not. The learner needs to understand the factors and forces responsible for such dichotomies.

Value-Related Terms

While values often are classified according to personal, group, and societal values, several value-related terms are applied within the instructional setting, including virtues, beliefs, attitudes, aesthetics, ethics and morals, and cultural values. These terms are briefly described in the following paragraphs:

• **Virtues** are normally accepted as a high standard of moral excellence. According to Mortimer J. Adler (1984): "Whether or not we are morally virtuous, persons of good character, would appear to be wholly within our power—a result of exercising our freedom of choice" (p. 89). While some may disagree with Adler's strong statement, philosophers believe that each individual may select from among moral and intellectual virtues. Moral virtues are related to moral conduct and include such elements as honesty, temperance, courage, and justice, all of which are related to the notion of prudent behavior. Intellectual virtues involve decision making through the process of judging and making decisions about one's moral conduct.

• **Beliefs** are convictions regarding the truth of a statement, event, or idea. Most individuals hold a certain level of confidence regarding the nature of objects, individuals, and ideas, thus allowing them to predict future behaviors, outcomes, and events. Beliefs may represent open or closed values: open values are not closely held or defended and, like attitudes, are open to question, whereas closed values are not open to discussion and debate. For example, religious beliefs are often well established and not open to discussion or change; such closed values are termed *dogmas* (rigid beliefs that are not to be questioned).

- **Attitudes** can be described as a predisposition to behave in certain ways toward certain phenomena (other human beings and physical objects). Thus, attitudes may be acquired through various forms of direct influence such as classroom instruction or as the result of parental suggestion. Overall, it might be said that attitudes are more specific than values. The strength of one's feelings can be described according to an affective scale that ranges between the extremes of love and hate or joy and anger. Extreme negative feelings can result in strong expressions and actions. Banks (1986) describes these differences between attitudes and values:

> Values, unlike attitudes and other beliefs, are not related to any specific things, persons, or groups, but are very general and influence a person's behavior toward a large class of objects or persons. (p. 407)

- **Aesthetic values** are those that are assigned to cultural characteristics such as objects, persons, designs, and other artistic expressions. They are a measure of beauty, grace, and preferences (or taste). Individuals often attempt to acquire "beautiful" objects that tend to enhance their image or social status within the community. Aesthetic values change over time as new fashions replace old ones or as new art forms replace old ones. Standards of aesthetic beauty tend to persist over time and come to represent a recognized cultural characteristic. These characteristics can become emblematic of a society, culture, or civilization. Ancient Greek civilization, for example, is represented by certain aesthetic forms, monuments, pottery, dress, and architectural features.

- **Ethics and morals** consist of judgments associated with standards of good conduct; therefore, ethics are a standard for assessing human conduct. Societies tend to impose an ethical obligation or moral duty on its members. For example, a society might hold that adults are obligated to care for their children, that teachers are obligated to serve as moral models for their students, that lawyers are obligated to serve the best interests of their clients, and that doctors are obligated to render care unto their patients. Morals are what we consider to be right and wrong within a society. Education is often used to teach students how to know the difference between right and wrong expressions and actions. However in most societies, families are expected to teach their children "good" behavior so that they will be able to make "good" decisions and to resist "wrong" decisions or actions.

- Mores, folkways, customs, and traditions are expressions of **cultural values**. *Mores* consist of the basic habits, practices, and beliefs of a cultural group, whereas *folkways* include a unified way of thinking and behaving. *Customs* are shared practices of a cultural group; traditions consist of customs that are handed down from one generation to the next. Mores, folkways, customs, and traditions are expressions of a way of thinking, believing, and acting; when taken as a whole, they represent a certain cultural life-style.

Personal, Group, and Societal Values

Values influence most aspects of human existence and tend to operate at different levels within every social structure. At a most basic level, values help to determine individual behavior and at their most complex level, values help to determine institutional practice. Except for a few rare isolated individuals, most people live in a social environment that requires certain compromises to accommodate a stable and orderly society. From the point of birth, individual values are shaped to accommodate group and societal needs through a process called *socialization* (Giddens, 1991). Socialization is a learned process in which child rearing and education play a major role. At the same time, each individual is quite different from other individuals in the same society or culture. These variations are due, in part, to individual, family or group differences. Individuals tend to experience somewhat different value-building experiences, depending on their social and economic conditions, which can affect their perceptions and expectations regarding the whole of society.

Personal Values

It generally is believed that individuals are *not* born with values, but values are acquired from birth and are an aspect of personality. **Personal values** associated with human traits are often expressed through behavior (individual conduct) or patterns of behavior that tend to characterize an individual. Personal values are:

1. Normally freely chosen by the individual in the face of other alternatives
2. Highly prized by the individual and usually are freely and firmly acknowledged in public as well as privately
3. Standards for assessing conduct and for choosing between alternatives

4. Expressed in conduct and affect the beliefs and life-styles that individuals hold regarding the nature of reality, the good life, and the good society

Once acquired, values are continued, strengthened, modified, or sometimes abandoned in favor of other values over the course of one's lifetime. The nature or character of an individual is often described in terms of his or her physical, emotional, or intellectual nature as well as his or her behavior. According to Lewis (1990),

> Although the term *value* is often used loosely, it should be synonymous with personal beliefs about the "good" the "just" and the "beautiful," personal beliefs that propel us to action, to a particular kind of behavior and life. (p. 7)

But more important still, values contribute to a person's perceived moral character, and ultimately a person's values are used to describe or to define that person within a specific social sphere. Thus, *personal values contribute to those behaviors that articulate an individual's perspectives about what is right, appropriate, and worth knowing, believing, and doing, and these expressions and actions come to characterize each person as an individual.*

Group Values

Group values, sometimes referred to as collective values, are acquired as a result of group affiliation or group membership. Almost all individuals hold membership in several groups, including the family, church, school, social organization, occupational field, club, or lodge. Individuals are greatly influenced by the shared values of associated group members. For example, family members are influenced by those who make up the family unit, members of a group of friends are influenced by other group members, and workers are influenced by their workplace group or by their fellow workers.

WHEN THE LINE IS CROSSED, WHAT'S NEXT?

When a student's values conflict with the group's values and behavior expected in the classroom and school, how should this variance be handled by the teacher and the administration?

It appears that group values result from an accord that group members establish. Consequently, no two groups (families, churches, clubs) are exactly alike. In spite of these differences, group values are important because they affect individual behavior. Group values are used to (1) determine priorities and goals within a defined social setting (family, classroom, workplace, community, or society); (2) establish standards of appropriate conduct in selected social settings; (3) develop a sense of self-identity in the individual; and (4) serve as the basis for group decision making. Thus, *group values are shared values that are expressed when individuals come together and function as a group, and these same values are an important aspect of individual behavior even when away from the group.*

Societal Values

Societal values represent a general agreement among the various social groups that make up a broader social unit called a society (community, nation, or corporation of people). Members of a society share common traditions, values, and institutions, which are expressed in certain characteristic interests, behaviors, and activities. Within the societal setting, values consist of shared beliefs that help to unify a diverse people. Moreover, Barth (1990) asserts that societal values tend to focus on stated principles or beliefs that are "The results of judgments made by an individual or the society as a whole which determine the relative importance or worth of a thing, idea, practice, or belief" (p. 370).

In addition, all societies vary according to certain cultural characteristics such as technology, language, environmental setting, historical experiences, religion, custom, tradition, life-style, and worldly outlook. For example, most traditional societies are united by biological similarities and similar cultural practices, whereas complex pluralistic cultures are united by ideological elements related to the economic and political systems that characterize the institutional organization or structure of society. In the United States, for instance, most individuals share a common belief in a democratic political system and a free-market exchange system. Also, American society tends to value teamwork on the one hand and self-achievement on the other. In addition, most individuals value a nonauthoritarian government that tends to encourage a high standard of living for its citizens. Therefore, *societal values are shared by various groups and by most individuals in society; consequently, societal values serve as a social "glue" that promotes unity or at least attempts to prevent social fragmentation.*

Once established, values help to direct behavior and choices. The importance, or relative strength of the value, may be measured to the extent that the individual, group, or society is willing to support and defend a stated value. Therefore, a scale might be constructed to determine whether a given value is

HOW CAN WE HOLD THE PIECES TOGETHER?

Some current social observers claim that traditional American values are deteriorating, a serious challenge to the preservation of the society itself. Give an example of such a change evident in our educational settings. Then state your opinion as to what this change implies for social studies curriculum and instruction.

a value in fact and practice or merely just a stated one. The range of this scale might begin with speaking out in favor of a value and end with a willingness to make "real" contributions to preserving and strengthening the value. For example, a value scale would attempt to measure the extent to which individuals, groups, or societies are willing to sacrifice (privileges, property, or life) in defense of values. While individuals may be willing to make great sacrifices for family, this same level of sacrifice may not hold for an institutional ideal or for some aspect of the social system. Therefore, the strength of a value is determined by the extent to which the individual, group, or society is willing to go or to sacrifice to achieve or maintain that value. An example of the strength of a personal value (liberty) was demonstrated during the early days of the American Revolution when political activists could be jailed or executed for their beliefs, and yet, Patrick Henry publicly exclaimed: "Give me liberty or give me death." This statement, along with other revolutionary activities, actually could have cost revolutionary leaders their lives if the British had won the war.

Value Sources

Values are acquired within a social context or as the result of social interaction or experience. According to some writers, values emerge out of physical, social, intellectual, or emotional systems that are used to regulate human behavior within a social setting. Hunter Lewis (1990) described six different value systems considered to be the source of personal, group, and societal values. The systems described by Lewis include the following:

1. Authority that instructs the individual in what to believe, such as the crown or the church

2. Logic or the use of some form of reason in making value judgments, such as assessing the worth of a process or product or in making choices

3. Sensory experiences or the use of sensory organs in directing value judgments, such as the use of sight, hearing, smelling, tasting or touching in making selections

4. Emotion or the use of feelings, such as the use of positive or negative feelings in choosing between two alternatives

5. Intuition (adult abstract thinking) or an unreasoned mental insight or a certain familiar feeling, such as an unexpected feeling that this is the correct answer to an unresolved problem

6. Science as the bases of developing a value system or the application of a specific process, such as following a formula or process in order to accept or reject a new idea. (pp. 23–131)

Some elements of each of these sources are present within the educational setting. Pratt (1980) contends that four techniques can be used to help students acquire values: "Four techniques have greater potential, particularly if used in combination: information, reinforcement, modeling, and involvement" (p. 317).

Subsequently, it may be possible to indicate means by which particular values can be attained; therefore, values education rests on the assumption that certain educational practices can help students to build or modify certain values or their value systems. The following are some possible examples of the instructional means that may be used to develop student values.

- Active involvement in problem study and resolutions concerning issues that are important for the learner

- Presentation of examples or endorsements provided by persons whom the learner may respect or love (parents, peers, teachers, sports heroes, for example)

- An emotional experience or description of vivid events that greatly influenced, changed, or redirected a person's life

VALUE MODIFICATION: HOW MIGHT IT WORK?

Outline a plan for a specific set of lessons or a particular unit in which you present the sources of values involved and teach students ways they might alter or change related attitudes. Do you think that such a plan will actually result in changed values among the students? If not, what further steps are implied?

- Rational appeals for the application of reason and logic in order to correct a perceived social injustice
- Cooperative issues-settling activities that involve capable individuals from varied racial and ethnic backgrounds
- The exercise of strong group pressure for the acceptance of a position regarding a standard for appropriate behavior
- Enforcement of a long-time group, societal, or cultural custom
- Participation in role-playing and socio-drama activities aimed at revealing a social predicament such as poverty, prejudice, exploitation, and other unfavorable human conditions
- Modeling of the value being sought

Values Education

The American public has always held education accountable for teaching moral values and character education. Despite this long-standing notion, some scholars claim that values have been so abstractly described and defined that they cannot be systematically taught in the classroom. Instead, they feel that students should make their own decisions and learn to think critically about important social concerns. Social studies teachers, on the other hand, are required to deal with human values in explaining the influences that have shaped social, economic, and political systems and events. Consequently, the teaching of values is at the center of a long-running debate regarding the nature and role of values in instruction.

One recent argument pertaining to this debate states that, for society to advance, core values and beliefs should be discarded or disregarded. This argument was based on the idea that truth could be derived only from empirical findings that could be certified by continual empirical verification. Those who take this position argue that empirical evidence should be the sole basis of truth and that the scientific method is the only legitimate source of truth. Ironically, this point of view has to some extent become dominant in the American university in the twentieth century. This position, however, is opposed by the critics of empiricism who advocate the presentation and advancement of certain central moral values and life-styles in order to strengthen the moral foundations of American society. Moreover, according to this point of view, the truth can be arrived at through reasoned argument in which inferences are explored along logical pathways. This means that ideas can be tested and accepted or rejected according to their soundness when compared to the consequences of past human experience. But even more important, the testing of ideas according to this approach can be used to help prevent the politicizing of education institutions and individuals by special interest groups with hidden value agendas. In addition, this approach is aimed at helping prevent the acceptance of ideas and life-styles that may damage the stability, social health, or well-being of society.

Traditionally, values education has been based on the idea that a hierarchy of societal values emerges out of human experience which must be examined, tested, sustained, or modified by each succeeding generation. As a consequence, values education has become and remains an important responsibility of the entire school as well as an important responsibility of the social studies teacher. Gross et al. (1978) acknowledge that

> Our failure to maintain ethical, value-oriented emphases in the social studies where youth may come to understand why they hold certain beliefs inviolate, how to work to extend them, as well as gain the strength to stick by them when need be, may, indeed, be our greatest challenge in creating a viable curriculum for social education that will serve well the coming generation and the future of our nation. (p. 8)

Overall, values education is considered a limited social studies responsibility that is usually associated with the development of societal values, whereas personal values are often considered a school-wide responsibility and are indirectly acquired in the school setting through various social and instructional experiences. Values education in the social studies is defended as an important aspect of social studies instruction because it is an important element of human experience and an essential factor of human existence.

At the same time, it is not easy for teachers to provide concrete value lessons because of certain technical problems related to the abstract nature of values. As abstractions, values cannot be directly observed or measured; consequently, it is difficult to plan or to present a value lesson. For example, it is difficult for teachers to (1) convert an aspect of value instruction into a specific behavioral objective, (2) explain an event from a value perspective, (3) provide concrete examples of specific values (for example, "justice"), and (4) assess value instruction.

In spite of these difficulties, the social studies teacher cannot avoid values education mainly because of the nature of social studies content and because of the responsibilities associated with citizenship education. As Taba (1962) points out,

> Values are implicit in the very functioning of the culture, from the use of technical devices to the requirements of jobs and civic participation. They are implicit also in institutional dynamics and the forms into which education is cast, from grouping to counseling. This means also that education for values is all-pervasive and largely unconscious. The task of education is to make this process conscious,

rationally defensible, and, as far as the role of the curriculum is concerned, more effective. (p. 69)

The most often cited essential purposes or goals for including values education in the social studies curriculum are to address the following needs:

- To develop a set of values that can be used to help students think reflectively in order to fulfill their responsibilities as members of their community and as citizens of a democratic republic
- To help students develop various analytical skills that can be applied to various events, issues, and conflicts that arise within a social setting
- To promote the development of worthy personal values that will help them chose a constructive life-style
- To clarify the role of values in human affairs as illustrated in events and issues, past and present, which help to explain contrary values and why differences can lead to conflicts and clashes as well as to solutions
- To make inferences regarding the role of values in past events and in the contemporary affairs of humankind
- To enable students to interpret, explain, and predict human behavior through the identification and application of societal values
- To teach a systematic means to identify and clarify the practices and habits that exist in a culture, especially regarding those behaviors that are contradictory or irrational

In spite of the recognized importance assigned to the goals of values education, the social studies is, to some extent, caught up in a dilemma in which many educators have come to believe that it is wrong to impose values on students, and yet the failure to promote certain moral, political, social, and economic values may diminish the survivability of American society. Hence, the question: *"Can social studies teachers help students study and acquire values and at the same time encourage them to acquire the intellectual integrity that is so necessary for living in a complex scientific society dedicated to the survival of a democratic way of life?"*

This dilemma is compounded by the fact that teachers, administrators, parents, and students may not share the same values, and as a result of these differences, values education can lead to controversies in the school. As Taba (1962) suggests, at the core of controversy is the issue of whose values should be adopted.

In a culture such as ours, with many contradictions and ambiguities, individuals need systematic aid in clarifying the contradictions and in making conscious the many emotional habits which the culture implants on an irrational and unconscious level. (p. 69)

Nevertheless, social studies teachers soon learn that values issues cannot be avoided and that some controversy will arise as a result of teaching social studies content. Therefore, it makes good sense to meet the education of values responsibility head-on by providing a systematic approach and programs for values instruction.

Values Education Approaches

Social studies literature contains a variety of values approaches and programs that have been developed to address a perceived student need (Kirschenbaum, 1992). The following approaches are sometimes described in various social studies methods textbooks, and some of these approaches have been featured in certain instructional programs with rather specific educational aims. An examination of these instructional values approaches shows that they might be classified according to one of two categories, including (1) values acquisition approaches and (2) values reflection approaches.

Values Acquisition Approaches

Values acquisition approaches are aimed at helping students acquire, maintain, or advance toward specified value goals. The central and shared characteristic of these approaches is their focus on the acquisition of specified values or behavioral traits that have been sanctioned as correct and proper according to certain social norms or standards.

Inculcation

Modeling is just one process that is commonly used in the classroom to help build or modify certain specific values. More specifically, modeling influences the values of students by emphasizing "desirable" societal values. This process is associated with attempts to **inculcate,** or to indoctrinate, socially acceptable values through a process of planned instruction. Modeling also refers to the approaches and behavior of the instructor in the classroom. The manner in which the teacher conducts the learning experiences, the environmental atmosphere, and the very personality of the teacher can promote many values. This approach often is sanctioned by educational authorities as a means of promoting positive social values associated with citizenship or the "American way of life" and in stopping social behavior that is deemed harmful or destructive. For example, through much of educational history, *character* has been a commonly used term to describe the use of educational means to help students acquire personal values. These values would be used to help guide the student to appropriate or proper actions within the family, school, and community. According to Taba (1962),

> Probably the most frequently used approach to values education in the elementary and junior high school is the indoctrination of values considered correct by adults. Such values as justice, truth, freedom, honesty, and equality are taught along with legendary heroes, stories, rituals, and patriotic songs. (p. 409)

Techniques such as modeling generally are based on the use of positive and negative reinforcements to help shape student values. For example, a teacher might dismiss student's comments that are contrary to the intended and desired value and behavior. Consequently, the most characteristic feature of modeling is its preference or bias that favors an affirmed value. Therefore, inculcation approaches are considered to be subtle forms of indoctrination in which certain values, either directly or indirectly, tend to be imposed on the students. As Barr, Barth, and Shermis (1977) report, to some extent, indoctrination has been associated with the general tenor of social studies as well as much of education. They claim that:

> By far the most important issue in the social studies has been the question of indoctrination. No other single issue has so dominated the discussions and debates in the field. The social studies grew out of the obvious and clearly stated goal of the educators of a new nation to create unity and patriotism. . . . A survey of textbooks over the last 200 years and a concurrent study of research of classroom practices lead to the conclusion that the most consistent characteristic of social studies education in the United States has been efforts at indoctrination. . . . Regardless of what the scholars believed, the culture as a whole has looked to the social studies as an important means of indoctrinating national loyalties. (pp. 16–17)

At the same time, indoctrination in one form or another seems to meet public and parental approval. It appears that many parents are especially concerned about the self-centered and antisocial behavior evidenced by some of today's youth. As a result, there is a growing emphasis on positive value change, including forwarding traditional values that have characterized the American spirit. (self-reliance, hard work, obeying authority, neighborly cooperation, prudent conduct, thrift, charity, and patriotism). At the same time, it must be acknowledged that there is strong opposition to inculcation and indoctrination within educational circles. Critics of inculcation challenge this approach by attacking the idea of imposing values on students, especially students who are living under a democratic form of government.

Nevertheless, most social studies educators recognize a core of values that are fundamental to American society. Few would argue against pupils' experiencing such principles as:

SHOULD PARENTAL VALUES BE REFLECTED IN THE SCHOOL?

Schools frequently are criticized for their failures in values education. Should teachers attempt to support the ethical concerns of parents and social groups in the community? If so, what guidelines should teachers follow to incorporate these values in their lesson plans?

- Inviolability of human rights—no matter race, ethnicity, or creed
- Equality of opportunity for all men and women
- Belief in the rule of law within a constitutional government
- Majority rule with the protection of minorities and their views as well as for the opportunity for these to become majority positions
- The right of free association and free speech
- The need for universal education
- The acceptance of personal and civic responsibilities that balance our freedoms

Also, few people would reject moral standards such as honesty and integrity, empathy for the welfare of others (particularly the underprivileged and handicapped) justice and fairness, and cooperative service in the resolution of community problems. Such values, including the Golden Rule and similar attitudes, have been confirmed in many studies, even in some other cultures, as being commonly accepted qualities of ethical and civic character. It would seem, therefore, that the challenge is to use such principles in organizing curricular and instructional imperatives, designing approaches and experiences that may advance these qualities in students.

Moral Reasoning

Moral reasoning is based on the belief that each child develops an ability to determine the difference between what is "right" and "wrong" within a social context. Reflecting the work of Jean Piaget, Lawrence Kohlberg (1975) developed a theory of moral reasoning based on three levels of moral development with six basic moral stages (*Level I Stages:* the punishment-and-obedience orientation, the instrumental-relativist orientation; *Level II Stages:* the interpersonal concordance, the rule of law orientation; *Level III Stages:* the social contract and legalistic orientation, the universal-ethical principle orientation).

(See Banks, 1986, p. 412, for a good overview of Kohlberg's theory.) During each stage the child evolves a concept of what is "just and fair" under a given set of circumstances. During the early stages of moral development, the children tend to base their concepts of justice or what is right and wrong on direct notions of the consequences of their behavior such as "Mother will scold if you talk during nap time." As children advance in their moral maturity, some pass through each of the stages until they reach the age of reason in which behavior is based on their analytical moral reasoning of a situation (Kohlberg, 1975).

The aim of moral reasoning is to help students acquire a higher level of moral cognition and behavior through appropriate instructional experiences that are keyed to the student's level of development. At the most advanced and final stage of moral reasoning, the individual is able to apply universal ethical principles that are based on justice, reciprocity, equality of human rights, and respect for the rights and dignity of every person. Because the stages of moral reasoning are influenced by the social context, teachers are able to help students advance in their ability to reason morally by providing them with certain moral dilemmas, sometimes in the form of a story in which they must use logic to resolve a conflict or situation. An assessment of the logic used by students in resolving a moral dilemma helps the teacher determine their moral reasoning level of maturity. Once this is determined, the teacher can devise an instructional program that will help advance the student to the next level of moral reasoning.

Action Activities

The purpose of this acquisition approach is to provide students with opportunities to participate in school and community activities and projects that are important and of interest to them. These projects and activities help demonstrate that students can exercise a certain degree of influence over the circumstances in their lives. At the same time, participatory experiences help students clarify their values and recognize the need to be able to work cooperatively with others in order to achieve certain worthwhile goals.

For many years rules for classroom government and school students council approaches have been used to engender civic values. In many situations, however, these situations limit important student rights and responsibilities and make few contributions to the building of positive democratic values. We contend that extended opportunities in the school and classroom for student discussion, resolution, and action would make significant contributions to values development. Much research and many publications have reported on the efficacy of student involvement in educational affairs. Here the goals and objectives of a free society are reached because the aims have been accepted by children and youth as real, important, and *as their own*. Readers seeking representative examples of value building via pupil action programs could well profit from the now-historic programs of the Citizenship Education Project of Teachers College, Columbia University, or from striking examples pro-

How Will You Help Students Deal with the Shortfall Between Idealistic Rhetoric and Limited Adult Performance?

Many American youth have become negative and depressed over the moral education that they encounter in school and the community because they have experienced the failures of adult society to live up to ethical principles; they are led to believe that our social and political systems are hypocritical. What specific actions should teachers and officials take to counter this serious threat to good citizenship on the part of youth?

vided by the national study of the civic education project team of the National Council for the Social Studies over a quarter of a century ago (see, for example, Vincent et al., 1958, and Robinson et al., 1967).

At the core of action approaches is the notion of empowering students to become effective participants in the affairs of the school and community. The main assumption of this approach is based on the belief that the level of an individual's participation in community, state, and national affairs is hindered by personal attitudes and bureaucratic barriers that discourage participation and foster alienation of youth toward the institutions of society. According to Fred M. Newmann (1975):

> Despite familiar rhetoric about ideals of self-determination and consent of the governed being the keystones of democracy, there is a suspicion, among youth and adults, that these rights do not, and perhaps never did, exist in America, and there is a growing sense of powerlessness, alienation, and pessimism about the future. (p. 1)

By providing students with community action projects, educators can help students acquire the abilities necessary for participating in and influencing the social, economic, and political forces that impact their lives. Therefore, as a result of participatory experiences based on the interests of students, new attitudes and skills can be acquired that will enhance citizenship participation in the affairs of society.

Multiculturalism

In the 1950s Hunt and Metcalf pioneered an instructional model to help students deal with problems that were connected with American culture. Their approach was aimed at certain social problems and conflicts that arose because of religion, social class, morality, racial differences, and other issues.

According to the Hunt and Metcalf model (1968), students were expected to analyze cultural problems by identifying and defining value concepts, projecting and appraising the consequences according to a set of criteria, and attempting to justify the criteria used in assessing the consequences.

Starting in the 1960s, multicultural value studies were developed to help provide a more balanced perspective for students regarding the role of minority groups in influencing the affairs and development of American society. In addition, multicultural approaches were justified as a means of helping students to acquire the following values:

- Certain values related to the equality of all groups
- A respect for various cultural points of view
- An understanding of the ways that cultural elements often become shared elements that help to develop a new and unique culture
- An appreciation for one's racial and ethnic heritage
- An empathetic attitude toward others to help mend racial strife

Consequently, social studies programs have come to emphasize multicultural values that aim to provide students with a diversity of perspectives associated with varied subcultures in American society, such as African-American studies, Asian-American studies, Mexican-American studies, and Native American studies. In the social studies these programs often are presented in contrast to classes that present a European-American or "mainstream" perspective (Banks, 1986). Controversy exists over the balance, emphases, and appropriate relationships of multicultural elements to traditional curricular organization.

In some cases, these studies encourage minority students to value their cultures and to maintain their cultural values (including their native language as in the case of bilingual education). Some state social studies frameworks

?

HOW CAN YOU AVOID ETHNO-NATIONALISM AND STILL TEACH DIVERSITY?

In some instances, lessons or courses designated as featuring a multicultural or ethnic emphasis have tended to isolate the pupils and even hindered multicultural goals because of the heavy emphasis on a particular minority group, its values, and way of life. Under what circumstances can multicultural social studies offerings be justified and the foregoing problems be avoided?

require the teaching of a multicultural approach with a special focus on the minority groups living within the local community or region. In the social studies, the emphasis on multicultural values has, to some extent, replaced a more traditional emphasis aimed at integrating students into a mainstream American way of life, a perspective that was strongly emphasized during the early decades of the twentieth century. In addition, a multicultural perspective seems to have become institutionalized in the public schools as indicated by its strong emphasis in social studies textbooks.

Values Reflection Approaches

Values reflection approaches try to help students make inferences and analyze, clarify, or resolve various value issues and predicaments. The central and shared characteristic of these approaches is their focus on developing reflective intellectual skills related to the study of values and the resolution of value predicaments. Most values reflection approaches share similar characteristics such as a process approach that emphasizes the necessary consideration of resolution means. In general, these processes require defining and clarifying terms, identifying underlying assumptions, assessing the extent to which actions or decisions were reasonable and justified, considering personal impact, and assessing the overall results of actions on future events. In addition, values reflection approaches are used to help students achieve a balanced or unbiased perspective regarding various social issues, thus encouraging students to (1) avoid making quick decisions based on emotional appeals, (2) research or study an issue by tracing its roots and evolution, (3) examine all sides of an issue in light of the accepted norms and values of the times in which it was a concern, (4) examine all sides of an issue and to weigh the positions against evidence that has been verified, (5) consider the effects of a decision in light of each student's accepted personal, group, and societal values, and (6) to estimate the future impact of the decision on subsequent events.

Inferential Reasoning

Social studies subject matter contains ample resources that can serve as the basis for teacher-developed values education programs that can help students think reflectively about values. An important goal of these activities is to help students develop value reasoning skills that they can apply to contemporary and historic conditions and events. Historical subject matter, for example, contains descriptions of incidents in which individuals were required to make decisions that involved important underlying value considerations. To a certain extent, the study of history is the study of human values that were tested under difficult and trying circumstances. History is also full of situations in which individuals acted or reacted to social, economic, or political pressures and temptations in order to overcome self-interest in favor of the well-being of others. When applied to past or historic events, an inferential approach helps students to reconstruct the nature of the social environment(s) that helped to shape the times. According to inferential reasoning, students would be encouraged to reconstruct these events from a values perspective that *might* have been present at the time that an event occurred. Similar opportunities for such reflection exist in the content of all of the disciplines contributing to social education.

Inferential reasoning is used by historians and social scientists in reconstructing events, societal conditions, and cultures. For example, anthropologists use inferential reasoning to reconstruct past cultures from the remaining artifacts that have been excavated at a particular site or corresponding region. These artifacts are located, recorded, and organized or classified according to a reconstructed chronology in which relationships are explored and debated. The final task of the anthropologist or archeologist is to make inferences about the people from the material or evidence. The inferential reasoning process is aimed at reconstructing the social conditions that dominated the times and especially the values that helped to shape and guide human activities. This is an inductive process that works from a specific event to a general value or set of values; therefore, it is a process that begins with an event, piece of evidence, or artifact in order to identify an underlying value(s). Thus, the process begins with events or phenomena that flowed from inferred values. We have developed a procedure called an *inferential value reasoning process* formed largely on the work of anthropologists and archaeologists. This process might be based on the following steps:

An Inferential Value Reasoning Process

Step 1:   Locate, assemble, and review evidence.

Step 2:   Organize and classify evidence.

Step 3:   List the inferred values that may have been used by those making decisions or taking actions.

Step 4:   Evaluate each inferred value as a means of eliminating weak value contenders.

Step 5:   Consider each remaining asserted value in light of its effects and outcomes.

Thus social science subject-matter content can be used to explore values through an inferential reasoning approach. For example, geographer and author Phillip Bacon (1989) includes the following statement in his geography textbook:

> Each group of people leaves a distinct imprint on its human habitat or the place where that group lives. The imprint, or effect, is known as the cultural landscape. Examples of cultural landscapes include the fields people clear and farm, the

crops and livestock they raise, and the style and distribution of the villages and cities they build.

The skyscrapers of New York City's cultural landscape, for example, show how humans there have changed the environment. (p. 26)

While Bacon does not directly address values, Bacon's statement could be used as the basis for a value inference activity regarding past and present "cultural landscapes."

In a similar vein, subject-matter content from government textbooks contains many topics and descriptions of events that suggest that certain unstated or underlying values helped to direct important decisions or helped to generate important public policies. For example, decisions that lead to the allocation of resources, the collection and distribution of taxes, and policies regarding national defense are all based on value positions that could be explored through an inferential reasoning process.

Values tend to underlie all aspects of human activity, including the legal system and the jurisprudence processes. Each of these human activities can be explored through an inferential values approach in which students attempt to reflectively identify and reconstruct the values that contributed to human actions.

Analysis

Value analysis is an approach that encourages students to study various individual, group, and societal values that may have contributed to historical or contemporary events, decisions, and public controversies. This process encourages students to use rational thought processes to analyze a value issue. During the 1960s and 1970s, Oliver and Shaver (1966) and Newmann (1970) developed an educational approach for helping students use policy-making and value strategies to analyze decision-making processes in issue-settling settings. Currently these student materials are in the process of being revised.

Analysis and decision strategies tended to require a careful examination of an event and the evidence that was used to settle an issue. This approach is similar to the rational processes and the use of evidence found in courtrooms; thus, the term *jurisprudential approach* is sometimes used to describe this type of analysis. More importantly still, students are encouraged to learn to weigh and evaluate evidence and to assess the logic of arguments in light of the evidence. Therefore, students are encouraged to deal with different types of evidence and to assess its reliability as a means of testing the soundness of a decision. Subsequently, an important aspect of students' classroom work may focus on identifying and analyzing issues and events according to logical thinking processes and scientific investigation. As a first step, students might attempt to identify the evidence that contributed to a decision. Next, students can examine the reliability of the evidence that was used in making a decision.

At this point, students would try to determine whether or not the evidence warranted the decision. Finally, students might attempt to assess the decision's effectiveness in regard to outcomes and in light of other possible options.

Clarification

In recent years significant attention has been given to helping students consider and make judgments on value issues by first enabling them to understand their own values. *Value clarification* approaches are designed to help students examine their values and build a system of values that are based on a process of rational adaptation. This process grew out of John Dewey's writings as interpreted by Louis Rath, Merrill Harmin, and Simon Sidney (1966). Rath and his colleagues developed an approach to help students deal with values, including such categories as prizing beliefs and behaviors, choosing beliefs and behaviors, and acting on beliefs (Rath & Kirschenbaum, 1972, p. 19). They conclude that

> the value-clarification approach does not aim to instill any particular set of values. Rather the goal of the value-clarification approach is to help students utilize the . . . process of valuing in their own lives; to apply these valuing processes to already formed beliefs and behavior patterns and to those still emerging. (p. 20)

In addition to the process identified by Rath, other value clarification processes have been more specifically applied within the social studies. For example, James Banks (1986) developed a model for helping students identify and clarify their values. Banks' Value-Inquiry model includes the following steps:

1. Defining and Recognizing Value Problems: Observing-Discrimination
2. Describing Value-Relevant Behaviors: Description-Discrimination
3. Naming Values Exemplified by Behavior Described: Identification-Description, Hypothesizing
4. Determining Conflicting Values in Behavior Described: Identification-Analysis
5. Hypothesizing about the Sources of Values Analyzed: Hypothesizing
6. Naming Alternative Values to Those Exemplified by Behavior Observed: Recalling
7. Hypothesizing about the Possible Consequences of Values Analyzed, Predicting, Comparing, and Contrasting
8. Declaring Value Preferences: Choosing
9. Stating Reasons, Sources, and Possible Consequences of Value Choices: Justifying, Hypothesizing, and Predicting (pp. 416–421)

During the 1970s value clarification was introduced in the schools with mixed results. While many educators promoted and praised this approach, parent groups in some communities opposed this approach, which frequently concerned controversial personal and social issues, on the grounds that values

Can One Avoid Moving from Preference to Bias?

Do each of the value reflection approaches described previously promise to avoid inculcation? In educational situations is it really possible to avoid indoctrination? Explain.

and value clarification should be left to parents and religious leaders. Critics also charged the movement with a subjectivity that could promote "dangerous" values or fail to strengthen traditional social values.

Conflict Resolution

In the social studies, **conflict resolution** is generally addressed in studies that help students deal with social conflicts within and between societies. Social scientists have long recognized that conflicts are a common aspect of human relationships. **Conflict theory,** for example, describes conflicts and tensions within society that help to bring about change or, if carried to an extreme, possibly destroy the state, society, or culture or lead to warfare between groups, tribes, or states. In stable societies, conflicts are kept under control by positive social contrivances such as various forms of cooperation, social integration, institutionalized concern for the welfare of others, mediations, and disinterested resolution panels or designated individuals such as arbitrators or ombudsmen. According to Lenski (1973),

> Both (cooperation and conflict) contain elements of truth. Cooperation is certainly a pervasive feature of all human life and so, too, is conflict. (p. 41)

Conflict resolution approaches have been developed as an instructional means for analyzing the resolutions and outcomes of historical and contemporary conflicts. For example, in 1975 Dynneson developed a Social Conflict Analysis System (SCAS) for analyzing various conflicts by identifying the underlying causes and values that contributed to the conflict.

> Our concern with social conflicts ranges from violence on the school grounds to wars between states. The reality of the times is that our children not only face the interpersonal social difficulties that occur in peer relationships, but they also share the adult's concern for national and world conditions. (pp. 267–269)

According to this approach, before solutions to social conflicts can be formulated, the underlying individual, group, or societal values must be identi-

HOW CAN SCHOOLS OFFICIALS KEEP THE SCHOOLS OUT OF VALUE CONFLICTS AND STILL EDUCATE?

When several constituencies in the school district or community are in conflict over a particular value issue, should the school take some action to try to resolve the matter? Select an issue related to social education and explain your answer.

fied and addressed. Frequently compromise needs to be attained. Therefore, to resolve a conflict, the people involved must try to change existing perceptions of virtues, beliefs, attitudes, aesthetics, ethics and morals, mores, folkways, customs, or traditions that may have caused the conflict. Various related or similar guides and approaches that are aimed at helping students resolve conflicts by analyzing value issues have been published such as Nelson (1974) and Superka (1974).

Continuing challenges to the principles of a democratic society are conflicts such as those between individual rights and social needs or personal freedom versus social responsibilities. Daily, the media provide examples of serious arguments, struggles, and violence over seemingly unresolvable problems. These problems often lead to lawsuits or arbitrary governmental decisions unsatisfactory to the contestants. An entire social education program could be organized around conflict resolution between individuals and groups and the values issues involved. At one time, the typical twelfth grade capstone course in social studies, called "Problems of Democracy" or "Senior Problems," was so focused. The real need is to infuse such studies in appropriate units and lessons throughout the social studies curriculum.

CONCLUSIONS

Regardless of the subject they teach, teachers are involved in both direct and indirect efforts to socialize students according to the values that are characteristic of American society. According to their socialization role, teachers are expected to help students acquire the knowledge, skills, and values that are necessary for a useful adult life. Therefore, teachers attempt to help their students acquire personal, group, and societal values that are considered appropriate and characteristic of an idealized model of living. Values education, however, is more than just a school responsibility; it is a joint responsibility shared by the family, school, and community. The teacher cannot educate students for value development or the development of moral and ethical behavior without the support of parents.

Once informed, most parents will support a school policy of freedom for pupils to learn and for teachers to teach. Occasionally, controversial topics can prove seriously divisive, no matter how carefully they are introduced and how wisely they are handled. In such instances it may be necessary to postpone immediate treatment or to approach the issue by using similar historical examples or by examining the problem in the context of other regions, nations, or societies.

Nevertheless, it is unfortunate that surveys, especially at the elementary school level, have shown that both pupils and teachers indicate that such units or lessons, even brief discussions of current controversial affairs, should not be included in the class offerings. More distressing is the fact that numerous teachers have reported avoiding controversial issues even when brought up by pupils in the classroom.

If we are truly concerned about value development and moral and ethical behavior, the study of value conflicts is one of the most important and motivational factors in the education of young people. Values are commitments to action that need to be examined and used in problem resolution in a free society. Students not only need to understand their own values, but they should be open-minded and willing to listen to others. In certain troublesome situations, students need to learn to be able to compromise, to accept counterproposals, and in our complex world with its newly emerging situations and difficulties, even to learn, hoping for later solutions, how to live with the unresolvable.

It is also necessary for teachers to realize that no matter how well they organize and handle certain lessons devoted to crucial issues and to value conflict situations, a portion of their pupils may well not become involved or accept the standards being sought. Values that are not evident or possible in their own lives and environments mean little to damaged personalities, to physically and mentally deprived children, to those from homeless families— to victims of our society and economy, a host of alienated citizens whom Simpson (1971) referred to as "democracy's stepchildren." In her book, Simpson well identified the basic needs in the development of democratic personalities and values.

The school can and should try to make whatever possible contributions to the betterment, growth, and progress of these children and youth. But many of these goals will be attained only through organizations and institutions beyond the school or through cooperative programs with these other social agencies in the community.

REFERENCES

Adler, M. J. (1984). *A vision of the future.* New York: Macmillan.

Armstrong, D. G. (1980). *Social studies in secondary education.* New York: Macmillan.

Bacon, P. (1989). *World geography: The earth and its people.* Orlando, FL: Harcourt, Brace, Jovanovich.

Banks, J. (1986). *Teaching strategies for the social studies* (3rd ed.). New York: Longman.

Barr, R. D., Barth J. L., & Shermis, S. S. (1977). *Defining the social studies* (Bulletin 51). Washington, DC: The National Council for the Social Studies.

Barth, J. L. (1990). *Methods of instruction in social studies education.* Lanham, MD: University Press of America.

Dewey, J. (1966). *Democracy and education.* New York: The Free Press.

Dynneson, T. L. (1975). Preparing today's students for tomorrow's social conflicts. *The Social Studies, 66,* 267–269.

Giddons, A. (1991). *Introduction to sociology.* New York: W. W. Norton.

Gross, R. E., et al. (1978). *Social studies for our times.* New York: John Wiley & Sons.

Hunt, M. P., & Metcalf, L. E. (1968). *Teaching high school social studies* (2nd ed.). New York: Harper & Row.

Kirschenbaum, H. (1992). A comprehensive model for values education and moral education. *Phi Delta Kappan, 73,* 771–776.

Kohlberg, L. (1975). The cognitive-developmental approach to moral education. *Phi Delta Kappan, 57:* 670–677.

Lenski, G. (1973). The nature of society. In W. J. Chambliss (Ed.), *Sociological readings in the conflict perspective* (pp. 40–43). Reading, MA: Addison-Wesley.

Lewis, H. (1990). *The question of values: Six ways we make personal choices that shape our lives.* San Francisco, CA: Harper & Row.

Nelson, J. L. (1974). *Introduction to value inquiry.* Rochelle Park, NJ: Hayden.

Newmann, F. M. (1975). *Education for citizenship action.* Berkeley, CA: McCutchan.

Newmann, F. M. (with the assistance of Donald W. Oliver). (1970). *Clarifying public controversy: An approach to teaching social studies.* Boston: Little, Brown.

Oliver, D. W., & Shaver, J. P. (1966). *Teaching public issues in the high school.* Boston: Houghton Mifflin.

Pratt, D. (1980). *Curriculum design and development.* San Diego, CA: Harcourt, Brace, Jovanovich.

Rath, L., & Kirschenbaum, L. W. H. (1972). *Value Clarification.* New York: Hart.

Rath, L., Harmin, M.H., & Sidney, S. (1966). *Values and teaching.* Columbus, OH: Charles E. Merrill.

Robinson, D. W., et al. (1967). *Promising practices in civic education.* Washington, DC: National Council for the Social Studies.

Simpson, E. L. (1971). *Democracy's stepchildren.* San Francisco: Jossey-Bass.

Superka, D. (1974). *Approaches to value education* (Newsletter #20). Boulder, CO: Social Science Education Consortium.

Taba, H. (1962). *Curriculum development: Theory and practice.* New York: Harcourt, Brace & World.

Vincent, W. S., et al. (1958). *Building Better Programs in Citizenship.* New York: Citizenship Education Project, Teachers College, Columbia University.

PART FOUR

The Selection and Organization of Instructional Components

OBJECTIVES, MOTIVATION, STRATEGIES, ACTIVITIES, AND EVALUATION

What planning and organizational skills does the

social studies teacher need to design the components

of an effective instructional program for students?

In Part Four you will learn that the selection and organization of instruction is directly related to the choice of instructional components used to implement an overall plan of instruction. The components of instruction include the experiences, behaviors, and capabilities that students need to access, understand, and use subject-matter knowledge. While subject-matter knowledge is important, its success depends not so much on *what* is studied as *how* that study is conducted and how it affects the students' capacities, attitudes, and self-confidence in their ability to learn and act outside of the classroom.

As you acquire and develop your planning skills, you will come to understand why a program of instruction should contain a diverse range of objectives, each serving a specific purpose in regard to subject-matter content and each addressing the physical, social, and mental needs of students. In a design sense, instructional objectives are important because they help guide and direct various teaching and learning tasks, including both those tasks that the teacher performs and the tasks for which the students are responsible. In addition, the objectives are directly related to the other components of instruction. As rule of thumb, each evaluation item should specifically indicate the extent to which a certain objective has been achieved. In addition, motivational items as well as strategies and activities are directly tied to instructional objectives.

From your own school experiences, you are already aware that learning cannot take place unless there is a need and a desire to learn; therefore, as a student you realize that motivation is an important component of instruction that must be included as a part of the instructional setting. According to Taba (1962),

> If there is no wish to learn, there is no learning, even though the environment may be rich in stimulation. Learning sets cannot be developed in a motivation vacuum, and a rich learning environment is not an actual learning environment for those who will not or cannot take advantage of it. (p. 102)

Consequently, when planning and executing a program of instruction you must plan certain activities that will create or enhance your students' desire to learn the subject matter.

Strategies are the means of presentation by which you will convey subject-matter content to students. For example, subject-matter content may be taught to students in lectures, directed discussions, films or other media, research projects, guest speakers, field trips, or other means. Subsequently, the teacher must be able to choose the most appropriate strategy(ies) for a specific instructional purpose. Also, for students to gain firsthand experience with subject-matter content, the teacher must select and organize learning activities that will be effective in giving students practical knowledge about the topic.

Evaluation is the means by which you will measure how much students have changed (grown in the learning sense) their behavior in desired ways as a result of instruction. The type of evaluation used may be determined by the nature and purpose of instruction. For example, a program of instruction may be based on the extent to which the objectives of instruction were attained. Teachers also tend to emphasize knowledge acquisition as a means for determining grades. When instruction is based on objectives, most teachers tend to use a criterion-referenced plan of assessment. A norm-referenced approach, on the other hand, is based on the extent to which one student's achievement is measured against the achievement of other students. Therefore, you must consider your purpose for instruction and your expected outcome when organizing an evaluation plan. All in all, you will have a wide range of assessment types and items to choose from when developing a plan of evaluation.

Instructional success tends to rest on your ability to choose and to integrate content with planned learning experiences. This integration usually results in a teaching-learning plan that is designed and followed as a way to structure (or order) the components of instruction according to certain learning principles such as those identified by Taba (1962) in regard to scope, sequence, continuity, and integration (See Chapter 15 of this text for a more detailed explanation).

The Identification
and Formulation
of Instructional
Objectives

INTRODUCTION

In this chapter you will learn that the ultimate source of instructional objectives seems to be textbooks, curricula, and the policies of the educational establishment. However, instructional objectives are reflections of values that were ultimately derived from the culture and society. Therefore, instructional objectives are really values regarding what should be taught in the social studies as well as values pertaining to how the social studies should be presented to students. This idea is summarized by Borich (1992):

> Texts, curricula, and policies are interpretations of these values shared at the
> broader national level and translated into practice through goals and objectives.
> Texts, curriculum guides, and school district policies can no more create objec-
> tives than they can create values. (p. 133)

Therefore, you will come to realize that instructional objectives are the applied and practical means through which societal values and theory are expressed in the classroom. At the same time, the initial source of aims or goals, the ultimate specificity and implementation, rests with you, the classroom teacher.

On the practical side, the application of behavioral objectives in instructional planning is helpful because it enables you to specify the desired outcomes of instruction. In addition, objectives are the basis for selecting instructional resources and activities. Also, by stating your objectives prior to instruction, you will be able to measure the extent to which the objectives were achieved. Moreover, with the use of instructional objectives, you as well as your pupils will be aware of the purpose of instruction and what is required as an indication of successful learning. According to Kemp (1985),

> By knowing what is expected from the stated learning objectives, learners can better structure the study procedures and prepare for examinations. Also their self-confidence to proceed with the forthcoming learning activities will be improved. (p. 78)

Finally, the use of instructional objectives helps to make the teacher more cognizant of the changes that should take place in student behavior that signal successful instruction and learning.

A behavioral objective is a statement about what your students will be able to do following instruction. Therefore, behavioral objectives direct students toward the acquisition of specific behaviors. According to Langdon (1973),

> In simple terms, objectives are necessary so that you know *where* you are headed in designing; *how* you will get there and through *what* means; *how* you will provide for the students to get there; *how* the students will know when they have learned; and finally, *how* you can check to see that all such planning and actual design did achieve what it set out to do. (p. 6)

According to Gagne, Briggs, and Wager (1992), objectives (behavioral objectives, learning objectives, or performance objectives) are defined as

> a precise statement of a capability that, if possessed by the learner, can be observed as a performance. . . (and answers the questions) . . . "What will these learners be able to do after the instruction, that they couldn't (didn't) do before?" or "How will the learner be different after the instruction?" (p. 125)

The use of behavioral objectives helps the teacher to:

- Identify and select important learning goals for students
- Teach more effectively toward those goals
- Measure student learning regarding the fulfillment of those goals

It then should follow that instructional objectives are statements about specific student behaviors that must be, in some observable and measurable way, witnessed by the teacher as an indication that learning has taken place.

At the same time, when involved in developing goals and aims for specific units and lessons, it remains essential that you keep in mind the fundamental purposes of social studies education. These purposes focus on helping shape young citizens who can capitalize on their talents, understand their rights and responsibilities, and recognize the art of living among other and different peoples, coupled with a strong social concern for the problems facing society. In addition, the purpose of social studies education is to help youth focus on individuals who exemplify good character and to help them understand how to accept and adapt to perpetual change. Gross (1976) explains that an important goal of the social studies is to help students learn how to direct that change in ways that their values tell them are right. In other words, there are ultimate social studies goals toward which instructional objectives should be directed, and we dare not overlook them in the development of specific objectives.

Identifying Behavioral Objectives

Identifying behavioral objectives is not simple even though there are many sources of objectives such as the curriculum framework, course study guides, the teachers' edition of the textbook and related materials, and the elements of content (concepts, skills, and values). When developing course and unit objectives, you should examine the content materials that are to be taught, the theme of instruction, the instructional outline, and student projects and activities. After you complete an instructional plan, you may wish to have other interested teachers review course and unit objectives. Curriculum objectives developed for a state or school district should be checked by outside design experts.

Because the teacher is the ultimate arbiter and selector of instructional goals, the problem is to develop a clear and realistic idea of what students are to learn and do. In actual practice, teachers often identify objectives and write test items following instruction rather than prior to instruction. To some extent, teaching is a process of discovering meaning and direction as a result of instruction; however, when behavioral objectives are to be used, teachers are expected to have a clear understanding of their expectations, priorities, and outcomes ahead of time.

In reality, even when a behavioral objective approach is used, specific expectations and outcomes may not be made clear until relatively late in the planning phases of program development. This is so because objectives are often derived from the instructional materials, and until these materials have been reviewed and the various learning activities have been developed, objectives cannot be clearly stated.

In addition, objectives cannot be forwarded until the teacher has evaluated the students' capabilities to get a reasonable idea of their abilities in light of the teacher's instructional expectations (Kemp, 1985). The characteristics of the learning task and the learner's characteristics and capabilities must be considered when writing objectives. Successful classroom instruction rests, to some extent, on local factors related to the knowledge of the students who will be receiving instruction. In every school setting, there are student differences related to abilities and interests. Gagne, Briggs, and Wagner (1992) point out the importance of these differences:

> Relations between characteristics of the learner and the ease and effectiveness of learning have a number of implications for the practical task of instructional design. The designer needs to take account of the outcomes of learning . . . and be cognizant of how these different outcomes may be brought about in different learners. (p. 118)

While most individuals share certain characteristics such as sensory capabilities, they are different in areas such as intelligence, styles of learning, motivation, gender and ethnic backgrounds, prior learning, language, and basic skill development (Smith & Ragan, 1993). Therefore, behavioral objectives must accommodate both the instructional program and the students. As a result, the attributes of students should be reflected in the instructional objectives, especially in the verbs and the objects that are selected, but also in the situation or setting in which the learning task will be experienced and in the performance criteria that will determine whether or not learning has taken place.

Formulating Objectives

Behavioral objectives contain a variety of components, the most important of which are the *behavior* (verb), the *object of the behavior*, and the *conditions* under which students are to perform the task. The verb specifies the behavior to be observed when the student has mastered the objective. The object is the content, skill, or value that the student will encounter, apply, or manipulate in connection with the behavior. The working conditions establish the setting, time frame, or conditions in which the student will be placed or the resources the student will be supplied when attempting to achieve the instructional objective. In addition, the teacher may wish to establish a *standard of acceptable performance* in determining whether or not students have mastered the objective. The length of the behavioral objective statement is determined by the need for clarity. A clearly identified objective is preferred over an unclear

Whence Cometh Your Objectives?

Develop a specific list of all the sources for the objectives you might develop for a particular unit that you identify for a civics or government class.

objective. In some cases the objective may require longer statements than shorter ones. At the same time, the instructional designer should avoid unneeded or unnecessary statements such as "after instruction has been completed. . . ." A pitfall for beginning teachers is to agonize over semantics. This was demonstrated when a beginning teacher developed a card file of definitions of behavioral terms such as "name," "list," "describe," and the like because she was so concerned about semantic use. This hair-splitting process is not necessary. Instead, the teacher should simply analyze the content of the lesson and ask the question: *What should students be able to do to indicate that they have mastered this topic, skill, or value?*

While all instructional objectives tend to follow the same format, there are differences. Course objectives tend to be broader and more general than are unit or lesson objectives. This difference is due to the amount of content to be covered and the length of time that it takes to learn the content. Typically, a course covers a large number of units and chapters and course objectives take anywhere from four to nine months of instructional time to achieve. Units typically include from one to four or five chapters and take from two to six weeks to complete; thus the instructional objectives are more specific and can be achieved in a relatively short period of time. Daily objectives cover very specific elements of content and take one lesson or class period to present. Gunter, Estes, and Schwab (1990) point out these differences:

> Learning objectives are written at different levels of specificity. Objectives for a course are stated in more general terms than objectives for a lesson to be completed in a class period. But whatever the level of generality, objectives provide the framework and a guide for the specific instructional decisions that follow. (p. 19)

Writing an Objective

To clearly communicate a learning objective to students, the teacher must be able to formulate and communicate a precise idea of what is expected. According to Gunter et al. (1990),

There is no magic formula for writing out objectives. But when instructional objectives are clear, it is possible to select effective strategies to bring about the learning desired. In addition, clear objectives make the process of evaluation easier. (p. 21)

Over the past twenty years, various authors have helped to specify basic components that should be used in describing the learning task. According to Gagne et al. (1990), five components should be included in an instructional objective: *situation; learned capability verb; object; action verb;* and *tools, constraints,* and *special conditions.*

situation: this is the condition under which the learning task takes place, such as in a small group, in a learning center, or in whole-class discussion. The situation is often specified in the objective and serves to stimulate or motivate learning. In some objectives the situation may not be specified as it is not important or critical to the learning situation.

learned capability verb: this is a special verb that helps to clarify "the learning outcome the demonstrated behavior actually represents." Gagne and his colleagues have identified nine standard verbs that are used to describe human capabilities and related intellectual skills. They include five categories:

a. Intellectual Skills—*discriminate, identify* (concrete concepts), *classify* (defined concept), *demonstrate* (rule), *generate* (higher-order rule and problem solving)

b. Cognitive Strategy—*adopts*

c. Verbal Information—*states*

d. Motor Skill—*executes*

e. Attitude—*chose*

[Note: *learned capability verbs are **never** used as action verbs but are used to support action verbs.*]

object: the content of the student's performance (or the object of the learned capability verb). For example, the students might be asked to locate something on a map. The object is the thing that is to be "located," "named," "listed," "constructed," etc. such as cities, landmarks, historical sites, etc.

action verb: this component is used to explain how the performance or behavior is to be completed, thus specifying what the teacher can expect to witness when the student correctly performs the task. Numerous action verbs can be selected for this purpose, all sharing the common feature of being observable or measurable.

tools and constraints, or *special conditions:* these are the special tools, equipment, or materials that the teacher may wish to specify in con-

READY OR NOT, LET'S DESIGN YOUR FIRST OBJECTIVES

Draft three instructional objectives for a social studies unit that you will be teaching. Incorporate the five components recommended by Gagne.

nection with the learning task. In addition, the teacher may wish to specify that an acceptable performance be based on certain performance criteria such as three correct selections out of five possibilities. (pp. 127–129)

Sample Objective:

special condition:	Working in small groups
situation:	with an outline map of the United States,
learned capability verb:	students will state
objective:	the five largest inland ports along the Mississippi River
action verb:	by labeling each city's location.

Alternative Components

Within the school setting, objectives are sometimes written in a simplified or less detailed manner than the one shown above. According to this abbreviated form, only two components are essential: the verb (behavior) and the object of the verb. In addition, the teacher may wish to state the situation or task condition (for example, the setting) in which the learning task will be performed. Also, the teacher may wish to state the performance criteria that will be used to indicate a satisfactory level of performance. Table 9-1 shows an example of two such simplified objectives.

Remember that regardless of the format or pattern used in writing an objective, most experts agree that the objective should contain a *verb* or observable learning outcome and an *object* of the action. In addition, the conditions under which the behavior is to be performed and the performance criteria that will specify satisfactory completion may also be obligatory. Also, other components may be needed to help make clear the outcomes of instruction. As a rule of thumb, the objective should be as concise or as brief as possible.

Table 9-1.   Sample Objectives

Behavior (verb)	Object	Task Condition	Performance Criteria
To locate	the five largest cities along the Mississippi River	on a classroom atlas	with at least three correct placements
To label	the five largest cities along the Mississippi River	on an outline map	with at least three cities placed and labeled correctly

Action Verbs and the Elements of Content

Since instructional objectives are the mechanical means used to advance instructional programs, they tend to focus on the subject-matter content that is emphasized in textbooks and the essential elements that are contained in study guides. More specifically, instructional objects tend to focus on themes, concepts (vocabulary, events, descriptions, and data), skills (processes that are to be acquired, practiced, and applied) and values (that are to be analyzed or acquired) that form the organizational structure of content knowledge. Therefore, most objectives are classified into three basic categories: *cognitive domain* (knowledge elements), *psychomotor domain* (skill elements), and *affective domain* (value elements) (Borich, 1992).

Cognitive Verbs

When identifying cognitive (knowledge) objectives, the teacher also may need to plan instruction that channels students into higher levels of thought. Benjamin Bloom and his colleagues (Bloom et al., 1956; Krathwohl et al., 1964) have developed a taxonomy of educational objectives that has been used to affect the intellectual development of students. Bloom's cognitive hierarchy contains the following categories:

- Knowledge—the recall level of thinking
- Comprehension—the descriptive level of thinking
- Application—the utilizing level of thinking
- Analysis—the disassembling level of thinking
- Synthesis—the combining or mixing level of thinking
- Evaluation—the judgmental level of thinking

In selecting a cognitive action verb, the teacher may decide to select the level of thinking that it evokes (either recall, application, comprehension, analysis, synthesis, or evaluation) by selecting a verb from one of the categories described in Table 9-2.

Affective Verbs

In addition to the cognitive domain, Bloom and his colleagues devised categories that corresponded to their scheme for helping students deal with values and attitudes (Krathwohl et al., 1964). According to their structure, the affective domain consists of five levels of affective complexity ranging from the receiving level (least complex) to the characterization level (most complex). As individuals move from one level of value commitment to the next, Bloom believed that they rely more on their own independent feelings, attitudes, beliefs, and values and less on outside influences. For example, at the *receiving*

Table 9-2. Cognitive Action Verbs According to Bloom's Cognitive Domain

Knowledge behaviors (gathering information):	recall list name recite label define	match relate repeat draw write select	order memorize recognize reproduce arrange duplicate
Comprehension behaviors (confirming information)	describe illustrate explain summarize interpret rewrite compute change defend	match classify identify report select convert transform restate	compare extend distinguish display discuss express locate review
Application behaviors (using information)	describe apply solve model modify report prepare solve	illustrate dramatize act out draw choose interpret practice use	demonstrate make reconstruct produce classify collect measure

Table 9-2, *continued*

Analysis behaviors (breaking down or taking apart)	analyze explore separate examine categorize subdivide verify	appraise contrast compare question criticize experiment	differentiate distinguish take apart research check out calculate
Synthesis behaviors (combining or putting together)	combine create mix incorporate formulate produce collect	construct organize reorganize develop arrange compose plan	write prepare generalize relate design assemble
Evaluation behaviors (assessing or judging results)	compare critique decide evaluate support defend estimate	judge appraise predict value attack score	assess recommend select choose rate prioritize argue

level, the individual is merely aware of the value or attitude in question. At the *responding* level, individuals may comply with values they feel are expected of them by others. At the *valuing* level, they display the behavior that is consistent with the value they hold. Individuals advance to the *organization* level, where they make appropriate choices based on the values they hold. Finally, at the *characterization* level, individuals consistently behave in ways that are compatible with their values.

You Can Easily Convert Your Objectives. Try It!

State a major goal for a social studies course you identify. Then write the goal in terms of each of the five levels of attainment suggested in Table 9-3.

Table 9-3. Affective Action Verbs According to Bloom's Affective Domain

Receiving level (aware of and passively attending to certain values, attitudes, and beliefs)	attend awareness control listen look to be aware	notice point out share to take in encounter
Responding level (attending to or complying with certain value expectations by giving an appro- priate or expected response)	comply obey participate follow perform	practice react reply answer
Valuing level (displaying behaviors that are appropri- ate and consistent with values, beliefs, and attitudes)	display express argue debate prefer insist	accept reject esteem regard desire
Organization level (commitment to one's values or set of values based on reason and choice)	select compare reason formulate hypothesize	decide assert order prioritize demonstrate
Characterization level (consistent display of behaviors that are compatible with one's stated values)	display defend determine re-examine persist	insist internalize resist personalize demonstrate

Psychomotor Verbs

Skill objectives are of two types: intellectual skills related to cognitive processes, such as those associated with problem solving, decision making, or discovery, and psychomotor skills related to refined motor skills needed for the manipulation of objects and materials. Psychomotor skill development tends to be a process of practice and refinement that may continue over a relatively long period of time until a certain level of proficiency is achieved. For example, sports players tend to practice and refine certain sets of skills that may help to improve their game. In the social studies, students are involved in skills such as reading, writing, communicating, illustrating, and interpreting—skills that require certain psychomotor skills. Therefore, certain sets of action verbs may be employed to help students learn certain psychomotor skills that can be used in connection with social studies content. In 1969, Anita J. Harrow and Gary Borich identified a taxonomy of psychomotor levels that students achieve before they can master a neuromuscular skill. Each level of the psychomotor taxonomy has to be correlated with certain verbs that may be used in writing instructional objectives. Harrow and Borich labeled the entry level of skill development as the *imitation* level and the most complex level the *naturalization* level. A full description of these levels is shown in Table 9-4.

Verbs and Assessing Outcomes

As a rule of thumb, instructional objectives should be observable and measurable; therefore, they should be concrete rather than abstract. A common pitfall for beginning teachers is to use verbs that cannot be observed or measured. For example, it is not uncommon to find abstract verbs such as *learn, know,* and *appreciate* in lesson plans or in sets of published materials. These verbs are not appropriate because the verb selected must also indicate how the

Table 9-4.   Psychomotor Verbs According to Harrow and Borich's Psychomotor Domain

Imitation level (the psychomotor action or physical process is observed or modeled and then attempted by the novice)	repeat copy imitate grasp duplicate	attend watch sense practice
Manipulation level (the psychomotor action is performed according to written or oral direction with no visual assistance)	read follow listen attempt	experiment change modify
Precision level (the psychomotor action is performed without any type of assistance)	correctly independently precisely accurately	replicate refine
Articulation level (the psychomotor action is performed in sequence with accuracy and speed)	integrate coordinate confidently	quickly accurately adeptly reproduce
Naturalization level (the psychomotor action is performed as a routine behavior without hesitation or error)	automatically speedily expertly	naturally spontaneously easily

WHAT ARE SOME CREATIVE TECHNIQUES TO REMIND STUDENTS OF THE UNIT OBJECTIVES?

Review the goals of a social studies unit you have just completed with your class. Describe how you might explain these goals to students at the beginning of the unit the next time you teach this material. Give several examples.

extent to which the behavior has been established will be measured. Thus the verb *know* does not specify how the teacher will be able to observe or measure whether the student knows some specific item of information or can correctly perform a certain process or function.

In recent years most social studies courses, units, and lessons have been based on the identification and use of verbs that can be correlated with assessment items. As a general rule, each action verb will generate test question items or specific types of observable behaviors that indicate that the specified objective has been achieved.

Criticism of Behavioral Objectives

For many years educators have engaged in an ongoing controversy over the value and use of behavioral objectives. The names Tyler, Mager, Gagne, Bloom, and Krathwohl are frequently cited in these arguments. (For a good discussion of these different points of view, see Mager, 1962, and Eisner, 1967.) Gradually most of these researchers have accepted views that recognize both the values of behaviorally stated objectives and their limitations, especially in terms of overall and highly general statements of goals. Some of these views include the following:

• It has been claimed, at times, that the classification of the elements of content (knowledge, skills, and values) has lead to a type of pedagogical particularism—a mechanical form of instruction that presents content elements in an isolated form or without making connections to other related content elements. Most curriculum experts agree that in its natural form, content knowledge is integrated with direct interrelationships between content elements. The problem of isolated elements can be avoided by integrating the elements from the three planning categories into the same presentation during classroom instruction. In other words, some form of particularism is required during design and program development to systematically account for all of the important content elements that are a part of an event. At the same time, teachers must be able to re-integrate these elements into some type of organic or instructional whole for classroom presentation purposes. This re-integration is important so that students can make connections between the elements of content that are present in a phenomena or event. For example, an idea such as *taxation* (cognitive content element) tends to be associated with certain skills such as *calculating* (skill content element) a sales tax, which in turn may evoke certain feelings such as *anger* (affective content element) over having to pay an increased payment. Indeed, cognitive, affective, and psychomotor elements are often considered different facets of the same phenomena; also, thinking can lead to certain interrelated actions and behaviors such as writing a letter of protest.

• A common misconception associated with the use of behavioral objectives is the perception that less complex behaviors are easier to establish than more complex behaviors. According to design experts such as Borich (1992), some of the so-called simple behaviors require more resources and more time to establish.

> The ease with which a behavior can be taught is not synonymous with the level of the behavior in the taxonomy (i.e., lower or higher). These designations refer to the *actions required of the student and not the complexity of the activities required of the teacher to produce the behavior.* (p. 132)

For example, students may be taught a process for analyzing a case study in one class, whereas it may take several days for them to be able to recall the sequence of events that lead up to the Civil War. This misunderstanding can be addressed by recognizing that basic knowledge and skills lay the foundation for more complex levels of cognitive operations and thereby take a longer period of time to develop, but once in place they can more quickly facilitate complex operations. Also related to this misunderstanding is the idea that lower-level (simpler) cognitive behaviors are less desirable than higher-level behaviors. For instance, greater value is often placed on activities that involve higher cognitive knowledge and skills including the various forms of inquiry (such as problem solving and decision making). But it is only through the acquisition of the so-called simpler elements of gaining basic (factual) knowledge and skills that hypotheses and generalizations can be built. Therefore, higher-level social studies knowledge and skills rest on an essential foundation of simpler elements of knowledge and skill. Some of the criticism associated with behavioral objectives aimed at the recall level of knowledge is the result of the tendency for teachers to overly rely on "recall" action verbs that are more easily used in specifying measurable behaviors. For example, most teachers tend to rely on verbs such as *to name* or *to list* rather than such action verbs as *to interpret, to solve,* or *to defend.* Teachers can avoid this problem by carefully reviewing available action verbs from categories other than those designated as recall level (according to Bloom's taxonomy) of verbs. In this way, the teacher can help to determine the level of thinking that students will use or participate in when working on a specific learning task.

- It often is claimed that teachers who have not had extensive experience with writing behavioral objectives tend to make them too complex, especially by making student performances unnecessarily awkward and involved. For example, when asking students to label an outline map, the inexperienced teacher might state: "The students will open their box of colored pencils, select a red, blue, and green pencil and use the red color to indicate cities of over 100,000 population, blue to indicate cities of less than 50,000, and green to indicate cities of less than 10,000. On completion of these tasks, the students will return the colored pencils to their boxes." Such an involved statement is unnecessary. A simple statement about labeling cities is all that is required based on the understanding that the teacher need not write out every detail of instruction. In other words, objectives are not instructional directions, but they are goal statements that specify learning outcomes. Therefore, objectives should be simple and straightforward statements of what students will be able to do following instruction.

- It is sometimes charged that teachers occasionally become overly concerned with a specific task related to course content to the point that they fail to consider the effects that subject matter may have on students. From a motivational perspective, objectives that do not contain a consideration of the needs and interests of students are bound to be less effective than objectives that do. Also, objectives may contain unrealistic conditions that are less effective than more realistic objectives. For example, it is more realistic to visit an actual courtroom than it is to attempt to create a courtroom in the classroom.

- Finally, critics assert that behavioral objectives often are inflexible and tend to be less effective than objectives that allow for a variety of appropriate responses. For example, an objective that requires a specific student response or a single "right" answer such as "naming" the date that Columbus set sail to the Americas is less desirable than an objective that allows for multiple (even experimental and creative) responses such as "describing" the personal reasons Columbus sought to explore new lands. This problem is solved once teachers realize that behaviors need not be limited to one specific act or outcome. In other words, as teachers gain experience in writing objectives, they are able to overcome some of the more rigid self-imposed limitations associated with dealing with the mechanics of writing behavioral objectives. Some cautions should be observed about goals: that persons are more important than goals, so that goals should not overshadow the centrality of people; therefore, do not let a desired outcome stifle creativity. In addition, the means or strategies used to implement a goal are as important as the goal itself. It is

What Is the Best Reason for *not* Writing Instructional Objectives?

Even though stating objectives behaviorally is favored by many educational experts, frequently both formal printed lists of aims or objectives stated by teachers are not formulated in behavioral terms. Which of the arguments discussed above have you encountered before to justify *not* providing behavioral objectives? Do you believe that any of these arguments are reasonable? Explain.

also important to avoid trivial objectives developed for purposes of ease of assessment.

CONCLUSIONS

The idea of basing instruction on objectives has its origins in the scientific age of the late nineteenth and early twentieth century when the development of the scientific process also was used to help clarify and streamline educational processes. During the early years of the twentieth century, John Dewey played an important role in developing both the scientific process (the identification of a problem, formulation of a hypothesis, collection and analysis of data, and conclusion) and the systematic steps in planning educational programs (Tanner & Tanner, 1980). Since that time, the scientific movement in education has been advanced by the work of behavioral psychologists and others, which in turn has lead to a discrete curriculum field called "instructional design." According to Smith and Ragan (1993),

> The term **instructional design** refers to the systematic process of translating principles of learning and instruction into plans for instructional materials and activities. An instructional designer is somewhat like an engineer. Both plan their works based upon principles that have been successful in the past—the engineer on the laws of physics, and the designer on basic principles of instruction and learning. . . .
> Through this systematic process both the engineer and the instructional designer plan out what the finished product will be like. (p. 2)

In this chapter you learned that behavioral objectives have become a key planning tool for instructional designers and allow you to chart a course of instruction. In this way, instruction becomes directional and purposeful with little

HOW CAN SUPPLEMENTAL RESOURCES MAKE OR BREAK YOUR UNIT?

Aims for a course, unit, or lesson can be either advanced or limited by the availability of instructional and learning resources. Indicate a unit for a particular course and list five specific sources related to objectives that would affect the design and enrich the presentation of your unit.

wasted classroom time. Thus, instructional objectives permit you to become more effective and more efficient and therefore to become more productive.

Instructional objectives are also used to address some of the social concerns of American society that have emerged out of diversity. In this way, the application of objectives has come a long way in less than a century. At one time objectives were seen as the tool of narrow-minded educators who would limit the options of the teacher and lock-step students into a rigid educational straitjacket. This is no longer the case. The use of objectives is now seen as a means for planning a rational diversity or "a scientific calculated way of meeting and dealing with heterogeneity of individual talents and social backgrounds" (Taba, 1962, p. 4). In other words, the modern use of instructional objectives is helping you to establish diverse goals and directions in your quest to meet the individual needs of students. Therefore, seen in its proper role, instructional objectives are liberating and directional management planning tools that can promote learning according to the desires of the teacher and the needs of students and society.

REFERENCES

Bloom, B., Englehart, M., Hill, W., Furst, E., & Krathwohl, D. (1956). *Taxonomy of educational objectives: The classification of educational goals. Handbook I: Cognitive domain.* New York: Longman Green.

Borich, G. D. (1992). *Effective teaching methods* (2nd ed.). New York: Merrill/Macmillan.

Eisner, E., et al. (1967, Autumn). Educational objectives: Help or hindrance? *The School Review*, 250–282.

Gagne, R. M., Briggs, L. J., & Wagner, W. W. (1992). *Principles of instructional design.* Fort Worth, TX: Harcourt, Brace, Jovanovich.

Gross, R. E. (1976). The social studies teacher: Agent of change. *The Social Studies* (July/Aug.), 67:147–151.

Gunter, M. A., Estes, T. H., & Schwab, J. H. (1990). *Instruction: A models approach.* Boston: Allyn & Bacon.

Harrow, A. J. (1969). *A taxonomy of the psychomotor domain: A guide for developing behavioral objectives.* New York: David McKay.

Kemp, J. E. (1985). *The instructional design process.* New York: Harper & Row.

Krathwohl, D., Bloom, B., & Masia, B. (1964). *Taxonomy of educational objectives. The classification of educational goals. Handbook II: Affective domain.* New York: David McKay.

Langdon, D. G. (1973). *Interactive instructional designs for individualized learning.* Englewood Cliffs, NJ: Educational Technology Publications.

Mager, R. F. (1962). *Preparing instructional objectives.* Palo Alto, CA: Fearon Publishers.

Smith, P., & Ragan, T. J. (1993). *Instructional design.* New York: Merrill/Macmillan.

Taba, H. (1962). *Curriculum development: Theory and practice.* New York: Harcourt, Brace & World.

Tanner, D., & Tanner, L. (1980). *Curriculum development: Theory and practice* (2nd ed.). New York: Macmillan.

10

Motivating Student Learning

INTRODUCTION

The well-worn adage, "You can lead a horse to water, but you can't make it drink," has a certain ring of truth to it when applied to learning. Many teachers have long complained that their students are ill prepared for instruction, and worst of all, many simply are not interested. As a result, educators have searched almost every aspect of instructional design for promising practices and materials that might arouse student interest in the subject matter. Underlying the search for promising practices and materials is the assumption that within every student is a hidden biological or psychological switch that controls human motivation. Therefore, teachers are constantly seeking new ways of presenting information to students in the hope that they can somehow access this switch and trigger the students' desire to learn.

In this chapter you will learn that motivation is commonly defined as a combination of intrinsic and external or extrinsic influences. Thus, motivation is multidimensional, stimulating individuals to thought, investigation, discovery, and conclusion. Such activities, as Russell (1971) points out, energize for action and determine its directions.

Motivation within a school setting has been characterized according to the following statement by Borich (1992):

> Motivators are those things that influence learners to choose one activity over another (e.g., homework vs. baseball, a love note vs. paying attention, fighting vs. studying). (p. 344)

Like other human characteristics, motivation is an aspect of an individual's natural tendencies and the accumulated experiences acquired within a complex social environment.

Internal and External Influences

The internal origins of motivation are often associated with an individual's physiological makeup or those genetic traits that are passed on by one's parents. At the same time, most experts suggest that motivation is the result of learning to prefer and to avoid certain conditions that they have experienced in the past. According to Wlodkowski (1978),

> There is good evidence that many learning activities that involve manipulation, exploration, and information processing provide satisfaction in and of themselves. (p. 153)

Motivational influences also appear to be the result of social interactions, although individual behaviors can be independent of or in accord with others within a specific social setting. In addition, it appears that usually before an individual can become motivated, both internal and external motivational forces must be synchronized or in harmony. According to Borich (1992),

> Motivators can be *internal*, coming from within the individual, such as a tendency to be aggressive. Motivators also are *external* coming from the environment, such as the social pressure to be "tough" in the eyes of one's peers. Behavior often is the complex blending of these two sources of motivation. When both internal and external sources motivate in the same direction, they powerfully influence a learner's behavior both in and outside the classroom. (p. 344)

Internal Influences

Human emotions are an important natural and internal aspect of behavior that can be aroused by external influences. Emotions are associated with certain kinds of experiences; therefore, while emotions are biological in origin, they are shaped and channeled by social experiences. In recent years, psychologists have investigated the role of negative and positive emotions associated with learning conditions, such as punishment and the accompanying emotions of fear and anxiety within the instructional setting. The use of punishment often has been used in connection with education. The nineteenth century schoolmaster, American and British, was often depicted as an absolute tyrant who regularly used fear and intimidation to motivate students. In rural America, the subtle fear of the wood shed or the cane was well established in the minds of children before they entered school. Until recent years, it was not uncommon to hear that the "board of education" awaits those who regularly violate school or classroom rules. In reaction to this image, many individuals and parents

WHAT IS THE RULE OF AVOIDANCE?

Several centuries ago in developing their plan for education, the Jesuits stated that teachers should never punish with a religious task. Why do you think this rule was established? Give an example of a similar principle that should characterize efforts to maintain motivation in public schooling today.

have opposed the use of physical punishment in the school, while others continue to support it. The question remains, Does or should punishment, imagined or real, play a motivational role in education? With few exceptions, psychologists would suggest that punishment or negative reinforcement should not be used because it may lead to undetermined results (Russell, 1971).

At the same time, a state of mild anxiety may heighten student motivation and enhance learning. Because of boredom and the conditions of a secure environment, individuals may become complacent. Many educators are convinced that students become disinterested in learning because they are not expected to participate in the instructional setting beyond listening, watching, or taking notes. Therefore, any method of heightening student participation also heightens motivation. In addition, students who are "appropriately challenged" seem to become more energized and motivated than those who are not challenged. In other words, learning that contains some element of *risk* seems to inspire learning, whereas risk-free instruction does not seem to motivate learning. The risk factor seems to elevate students to a mild state of anxiety that stimulates excitement, which in turn heightens the desire to learn. Thus, learning activities that are somewhat emotionally charged, challenging, and competitive tend to generate more energy than do passive activities such as a lecture (Russell, 1971).

Overwhelming risk, however, may threaten the individual and trigger an avoidance reaction. For some students, standing before their peers to deliver a report may create so much anxiety that it produces a state of panic. However, certain activities can awaken the natural tendency to be curious about new and different ideas; realia and other objects have been used to heighten student interest and to motivate the desire to learn more about a subject.

In recent years, scholars have also delved into various aspects of achievement theory. Achievement theory is based on the assumption that individuals will attempt to keep up a certain standard or level of performance in order to maintain their status within the group and their sense of self-worth. Russell (1971) observes that

School achievement, although it is only one aspect of the larger achievement domain, certainly occupies a significant place in the active life of most individuals. Academic learning in school is an activity to which a standard of excellence has traditionally been applied, and success and failure have been strongly associated with school. (p. 40)

According to this theory, once students have experienced success, they tend to maintain or to extend it as best they can; therefore, students who encounter early success in the classroom are more likely to attempt to carry that success forward throughout other instructional experiences. Thus success does breed the desire for continued success.

External Influences

Behavioral scientists acknowledge the importance of social and physical environments as influences on human behavior. The environment includes the actual physical setting of the school and classroom as well as the teacher and other students that are together during the school year. The social environment of the classroom is a product of the personalities and the social relationships that develop between the teacher and his or her students as well as inter-student relationships. Social relationships are considered important factors that strongly influence student motivation because human beings tend to exert a profound social influence on each other. According to Kroeber (1948),

The environmental factors are themselves a composite of geographical influences and of the economic, emotional, and other social influences that human beings exert upon each other. (p. 190)

The learning environment associated with social influences is determined by many factors, some of which are beyond the control of teachers; therefore, teachers should work to maximize their influence over controllable factors in order to create the "best" learning environment. Schools and classrooms represent microcosmic societies in which students encounter a variety of social conditions that they may not face outside of school. At the same time, no two schools are exactly the same, and these differences profoundly influence individual students. The environment of the instructional setting helps to determine the degree to which students will become motivated to learn (Dynneson & Gross, 1991, pp. 18–19). In other words, the environment of the school includes more than bricks, mortar, furniture, instructional materials, and bulletin boards. More than any other external factor, the human factor contains great potential for influencing motivation (Russell, p. 54).

DO OLDER STUDENTS NATURALLY LOSE INTEREST
OR IS IT SIMPLY REDIRECTED?

The natural impulse to learn that usually characterizes children in the elementary grades often seems to be lost in the junior and senior high school years. To what extent is this due to inherent or genetic factors? What are several steps that secondary school teachers could take to help avoid this condition?

The Teacher's Role in Motivation

Educators have long debated the extent to which teachers can directly motivate their students. Some have argued that teachers have little control or influence over student interest in the subject matter. For example, Raymond Wlodkowski (1978) suggests that the myth that teachers motivate students is not true.

> Teachers do not motivate students. In fact, no one motivates anyone. We can make things attractive and stimulating. We can provide opportunities and incentives. We can allow for the development of competence and match student interest with learning activities, but we cannot directly motivate students. . . . Between what we do as teachers and what students do as learners are the students' perceptions, values, personalities, and judgments. These elements decide the final outcome of student motivation. (p. 14)

Other educators, however, argue that teachers can motivate learning by creating the "right" conditions. For instance, Ivan Russell (1971) states:

> The role of the teacher is viewed as that of stimulator of student behavior which constitutes the learning experience. Motivation for school learning is a learning in itself. As such, it can be created out of the proper experiences. In turn, teachers can nurture and cause to grow stronger the desire to learn. (p. 5)

Russell supports the widely held position that even though students come to school with a strong set of motivational tendencies, the teacher has a reasonable chance of modifying and redirecting those motivations so that learning can take place. For example, if learning can be made rewarding for its own sake, it can also become self-perpetuating, while learning that becomes threatening and punitive is usually avoided. Assuming that teachers can influence student motivation, they may be able to detect and treat the effects of low learning motivation.

Observing Motives

Teachers must learn to carefully observe students' behaviors within a systematic process, a process based on principles that are appropriate within the instructional setting and are germane to the natural and social characteristics of students. Don Dinkmeyer and Rudolf Dreikurs (1963) have suggested that the following principles make observations in the classroom helpful in dealing with motivational problems:

> Observation of behavior can be an extremely profitable technique if a frame of reference and a set of principles are chosen that make observation dynamically meaningful. Usually, observation is used for descriptive rather than diagnostic purposes. It can provide vital information if the observer:
>
> 1. Knows the subjective field in which the behavior takes place. This requires seeing the situation through the eyes of the child rather than in terms just of the educator's values and experiences.
> 2. Knows what to look for. Instead of observing what the child does and how he does it, one must see his purpose, the goals of his actions.
> 3. Records and observes all pertinent behavior, characteristic and routine as well as unusual, since every movement of the child has meaning.
> 4. Recognizes that behavior is not merely a response to outside simulation, but a creative act of the child in trying to find a place for himself.
> 5. Is aware of the analytic frame of reference to be used in the interpretation of the observed behavior.
> 6. Looks for recurring patterns.
> 7. Is aware of the child's stage of development. . . .
>
> To obtain the greatest value in all observation, one needs to be aware of the meaning of behavior. *To understand a child properly, one must realize that his every act is purposive and expresses his attitudes, his goals, and his expectations.* (pp. 39–40).

Establishing Relationships

Next, the teacher can create positive social relationships with students and promote the development of a positive learning environment in the classroom. To a large extent, the teacher determines the degree to which learning is rewarding or punishing. There exists a great body of literature that recommends that teachers adapt a positive rather than a negative position when exhorting students to learn. Unfortunately, as Wlodkowski (1978) points out, threats and punishment are often used as a means of motivating students to learn.

There is no doubt that many students can be forced to learn or at least be coerced into doing learning tasks. By punishing them, threatening them, and holding back desired activities and objects, we can scare and intimidate students into performing learning-directed behavior. We often do this under the rationale that, "learning to read and write is more important than waiting for students to want to learn." But is it? (p. 16)

According to William Glasser (1969):

The schools assume built-in motivation, but when it does not occur, they attempt to motivate children with methods analogous to using a gun. Although guns have never worked, the schools, struggling to solve their problems, resort to using bigger and bigger guns—more restrictions and rules, more threats and punishments. Reality Therapy says that teachers and students must become involved; that when students are involved with responsible teachers, people who themselves have a success identity and can fulfill their needs, the students are then in a position to fulfill their own needs. (p. 22)

Encouraging Motivation

Educational authors and psychologists alike tend to support the idea that positive encouragement is the best means of enhancing learning motivation. In the 1960s, Dinkmeyer and Dreikurs (1963) laid the foundation for "encouragement theory" as a means of overcoming the negative side of evaluation. They claim that by establishing positive teacher/student relationships, teachers will be more likely to present learning tasks that are appropriate. Thus, students will respond by recognizing that the results of their work, regardless of its merits, will not be punished. In other words, many of these authors would like to shift the environment of the classroom from a negative one to a supportive one.

Dealing with the Unmotivated

The unmotivated student who is often the less able student requires more care and attention than do other students. The development of basic concepts skills and special teaching techniques is particularly important, thus requiring the development of supplemental materials and arrangements. According to Chapin and Gross (1973),

Two basic issues in designing social studies materials for slow learners (or poor readers or the "hard-to-motivate") are: (1) the amount of attention given to vocabulary development and a reading skills approach, and (2) the selection of techniques used to motivate or reward the slow learner to read the materials. (p. 34)

In recent years, educators have been concerned about unmotivated and underachieving students because they have a high potential for becoming "students at-risk" or potential dropouts. Many school districts have developed separate programs for these students with individual tracking and special counseling programs. Some experts suggest that to help these students, teachers need to challenge them while providing them with a maximum level of encouragement and support. In addition, some educators have suggested that *criterion-based* evaluation tends to help these students overcome the negative effects of *norm-referenced* evaluation (for a more detailed explanation see Chapter 12) in addition to providing a positive learning environment and the development of a positive teacher/student relationship.

In recent times, psychologists and educators have studied motivation in instruction to help students improve their learning capabilities. In this regard, John Keller (1983) developed his ARCS Model, which was an attempt to influence the motivation of students toward their learning tasks. According to Smith and Ragan (1993):

> ARCS is an acronym containing four major conditions for motivation: Attention, Relevance, Confidence, and Satisfaction. (p. 310)

According to Keller, these four conditions are needed for students to become interested in instruction, which is assumed to be a necessary factor in learning. According to this model:

- *Attention* relates to the need to call students' attention to the material or content.

- *Relevance* relates to the need for students to assign value to the content or material.

- *Confidence* relates to the need for students to realize that they can successfully learn the content or material.

WHY MIGHT COOPERATIVE PLANNING GIVE NEW MEANING AND ENERGY TO CLASSROOM INSTRUCTION?

Why, for both motivated and non-motivated students, is it wise to incorporate teacher/pupil planning into numerous aspects of the content and assignments of a unit? Select a three-week social studies unit and indicate specific examples where you could include student input.

- *Satisfaction* relates to the need for students to gain a sense of gratification or reward as a consequence of learning the content or material.

In recent years, this process has been designed into an instructional presentation to motivate student interest. Thus motivation is becoming a standard component of instruction along with behavioral objectives, strategies, activities, and evaluation.

Designing Instruction for Motivation

In addition to the ARCS elements, other motivational elements could include the following: developing learning objectives, pacing instruction, varying instructional experiences and methods, and providing specific motivational activities. By establishing clear and vital learning objectives, the teacher can take the first step in assuring learning success; however, stimulating the desire to learn is more complex than writing objectives. Instructional objectives that are stated according to specific student performances are observable and measurable, thus enabling the teacher to recognize how well students are able to acquire or to meet instructional goals.

While less carefully crafted goals are acceptable, there is a concern that when the teacher is not able to precisely state a goal in performance terms, students have only a vague idea of what they are to do or learn. The result of vaguely stated goals is a lack of focus, a mounting sense of insecurity about what is expected, and confusion about how to proceed. Consequently, student motivation is diminished as students consult with each other over what to do and end up following undesignated student leaders.

But even precisely stated goals that are clearly understood by students may be ignored and avoided because students may lack the knowledge or skills to perform the learning task. For example, students may clearly understand that the teacher has assigned a writing task in which they are to compare the two sides of a political argument. Because students have never been taught the techniques of making a comparison, they may become frustrated and discouraged. As a result, students respond by turning in copied or poorly crafted papers, while some conveniently forget to do the assignment or copy the work of their friends.

Most educators agree that students are more interested in instruction when they are direct participants in the learning/teaching process. Direct participation is more than discussing issues or completing worksheets. It includes such activities as cooperative learning, tutoring dyads, participation in games, and simulations in which decision making and problem solving are emphasized. Learning contracts, one-on-one teacher/student interactions, the use of historical fiction, individualized learning measures such as bar graphs, and activities that are associated with student interests and learning styles are further examples. In addition, learning activities that are based on patterns of instructional organization that evolve and lead from their present level of experience to new levels of experience help to promote student interest. Therefore, instructional preparation should take account of the motivational levels of different students, because instructional planning for highly motivated students would differ from instructional planning for unmotivated students.

In 1987, we (Dynneson, Gross, & Nickel) conducted a four-state survey regarding student preferences of instructional practices as a means of improving instructional effectiveness related to citizenship education. The survey results included the following findings (Dynneson, 1992):

> According to our analysis of survey data, respondents strongly preferred citizenship activities based upon current events and activities related to individual needs and interests. (p. 198)

While student responses to this item were not surprising, we also learned that, according to these same students, teachers seldom seem to use student interests when planning and executing instruction (Dynneson et al., 1987). While student perceptions may be incorrect, it suggests that students are often unmotivated because of teachers' failure to know or to include student interests when planning and executing instruction. If true, an important motivational design element often is overlooked or ignored by teachers, thus limiting instructional effectiveness.

Pacing is an important motivational consideration that indirectly affects both the efficiency and effectiveness of classroom instruction. Effective instruction tends to develop its own pattern and rhythm that can be used to maintain momentum and thereby affect student motivation. The momentum of instruction requires that students keep pace with the instructor, thus motivating them to listen, clarify, meet task requirements, stay alert, and anticipate future directions. The lack of momentum or the breakdown in momentum encourages loss of interest, distraction, the waste of instructional time, and preoccupation with other matters of an instructional or personal nature. Consequently, it is important that pacing and momentum become a part of instructional design for courses, units, and lessons. In planning lessons, for example, the teacher should designate and estimate time segments for each aspect of the lesson and attempt to meet this pre-established schedule. At the same time, the teacher should be willing to violate the pacing schedule for "good" reasons such as appropriate questions or related examples, while avoiding the pitfalls of frivolous distractions or attempts to "de-rail" the instructional task at hand.

Instructional variation is an important indirect means of maintaining and increasing student interest in instruction. Young children, adolescents, and adults all tend to lose interest and become distracted unless they experience a change of pace, rhythm, topic, presentation, activity, and media. Even changes in seating arrangement and instructional location can be temporarily motivating. In the 1920s and 1930s, the Hawthorne studies suggested that the social conditions within a setting have an important influence on human behavior and motivation. While elements of these studies were later rejected, they are interesting from an instructional perspective. To some extent, the social environment may cause individuals to become more productive or less productive. According to these studies, individuals who share things in common and are amicable tend to be more productive, whereas in another situation, these same elements may retard productivity because they reduce competition for the sake of the group as a whole (Tausky, 1970).

The ability to plan and execute instruction requires a great deal of knowledge and experience not often acquired within the typical teacher training program of many colleges and universities. Study after study suggests that social studies teachers use only a limited number of methods when presenting instruction to students (Morrissett, Hawke, & Superka, 1980). Most notably, social studies instruction is dominated by teacher presentations or the lecture method, with textbook-based discussion or recitation as the next most used instructional method. From a motivational perspective, many other instructional methods (such as cooperative learning, socio-drama, simulations, and problem solving) can promote better student participation and thereby increase student interest in instruction. These methods are all detailed in the next chapter.

In most well-designed courses, units, and lessons, motivational activities can usually be directly planned and executed in several places. For example, within a typical unit of instruction, there are three or more points of motivation—at the beginning of a unit when the teacher should be enthusiastic about the topic's importance and relate it to past learnings, in the middle when the teacher relates the subject to the interests and lives of the students, at the end when the teacher gives examples or calls attention to the value of what the students have learned in the daily lives of people, and finally when the teacher attempts to transfer what was learned into other settings or situations.

Courses, units, and lessons should begin with direct motivational activities that are designed to arouse student interest in the topic or subject matter. To

WHEN TEAMS COMPETE, CAN EVERYONE WIN?

Identify the important principles involved in each of the following aspects of unit planning and teaching: provide a variety of learning experiences, elements of group work, individual assignment options, and opportunities for healthy competition.

select an appropriate motivating activity, the teacher must know the subject matter and the interests of her/his students. Ideally, the opening motivating activity will link subject matter with student interest and experiences, thus helping them relate what is to be learned with what they are interested in and what they have already experienced. The actual motivating activity may be a guest speaker, demonstration, game, picture, or display. The main criterion for determining the activity is the extent to which the activity will arouse student interest. (See Harmin for examples of motivation strategies, pp. 23–86.)

Each lesson should contain direct motivational items such as warm-up questions or response items such as "what if" questions. Students tend to respond positively to activities that encourage their participation in various aspects of a topic such as making maps or activities that depict the location or place where an event took place. In addition, students tend to enjoy and are stimulated by various forms of illustrations ranging from drawings and cartoons to graphs and chart work. The study of social problems and problem-solving and decision-making activities helps energize student interest in almost any topic. By developing related exercises, the teacher is able to encourage students to share their experiences with a similar or related idea, process, or situation. Students tend to become more interested and involved in most topics if the teacher is interested.

Courses, units, and lessons should close in a way that directly emphasizes the important concepts, skills, and values that were presented during instruction. Therefore, closure should review and reinforce the main points of instruction. Closure activities are often in the form of participatory activities that end instruction on a high note and bring all of the instructional elements together to help students grasp the overall meaning of the unit or course. As a result of the culminating activity, students will hopefully have an opportunity to review, clarify, correct, and reinforce what was taught. In other words, course, unit, and lesson culminations should instill a degree of confidence in students and thereby enhance their desire to want to learn more.

Is There a Difference Between the Barracks and the Classroom?

The following principle has been used in military training: If the pupil hasn't learned, the teacher hasn't taught. Do you accept this statement? Why or why not?

CONCLUSIONS

This chapter has provided an explanation of the importance of motivation in instructional settings. Motivation has been an important focus of the behavioral sciences as psychologists, sociologists, and anthropologists have developed and investigated theories as to whether motivation is the product of both biological and cultural influences. Psychologists have asked: Do certain inherited and learned traits dispose some individuals to a high state of interest in learning, while other inherited and learned traits dispose others to be disinterested? Sociologists have asked: Do some families and groups dispose their members toward learning, while other families and groups discourage learning? Anthropologists have asked: Do some cultures prize learning and others devalue it? The results of these investigations suggest that motivation is a complex human trait that operates according to complex biological, sociological, and cultural conditions that cannot be totally controlled, especially within an educational setting.

In every society parents tend to play an important role in developing their children's values, beliefs, and attitudes regarding learning within the society and especially within the school. In the 1980s, Dynneson, Gross, and Nickel explored the role of parents in the community and the school in developing citizenship in American schools (Dynneson, 1991). The results of these studies showed that the family was the single most important influence in the lives of students. According to Dynneson and Gross (1991),

> The environment, the home, and family are constant factors that seem to affect citizenship development during the entire formative years of life. The home environment is established by the parents in order to provide children with basic needs, including shelter, food, and clothing. The personality of the parents and the nature of their relationship, including their values and attitudes toward children and child rearing, greatly affect children's experiences. (pp. 16–17)

Thus, we learned that during the formative years the child is greatly influenced by parental values and attitudes toward life, society, and learning. Moreover, family living seems to influence the child in many subtle ways, some of which are intended and some unintended. For example, the child's status within the family, the parents' expectations for the child, and the extent to which the child is supported in meeting family expectations are all factors that can affect the child's desire to learn. Of these factors, perhaps the most critical factor is the extent to which parents read, study, explore, seek out new experiences, and respect learning as a worthwhile goal.

Next to the family, we learned that a student's close personal friends have an important influence on the extent to which learning is valued as a worthwhile pursuit (Dynneson, 1991). Most personal friendships are formed within the community and at school. The results of sociological studies generally support that middle-class and upper middle-class communities tend to value learning, whereas lower middle-class and poverty-level communities tend to value education less. Students from core inner-city neighborhoods often express less interest in learning than do students from suburban communities; however, students of the working classes and students in poverty can overcome community influences if they are supported at home and in school and if their close personal friends value learning as a worthwhile goal. It is also essential that they are helped to perceive the import of learning activities for themselves.

Our studies (Dynneson, 1991) also found that teachers have an important influence in the lives of students, especially when the student/teacher relationship is positive. In addition, teachers are almost exclusively in charge of the learning environment of the classroom. Thus, as a teacher you can help to determine the nature of social relationships within the classroom. Also, you will determine the extent to which the classroom presents a positive learning environment. Most of all, you will determine the extent to which instruction will be presented in interesting ways, ways that foster the students' desire to learn. Subsequently, motivating learning in the classroom requires specifically planned activities aimed at promoting interest in aspects of course, unit, and lesson development.

In some instances the links between motivation and learning remain obscure; but certainly an unmotivated student tends to learn far less than an interested pupil. It is important that you recognize the need for continuing motivation with most students. Mentors should always consider: What is the most interesting and intriguing aspect of the content I wish to teach? How can I inject realistic human nature into the lesson? Can I promote kinesthetic activities as part of the assignment? Are there special talents among the class (including myself) that can enrich the unit or lesson? Such motivational factors are clearly prime keys to sustained learning.

REFERENCES

Borich, G. D. (1992). *Effective teaching methods.* New York: Merrill/Macmillan.

Chapin, J., & Gross, R. E. (1973). *Teaching social studies skills.* Boston: Little, Brown.

Dinkmeyer, D., & Dreikurs, R. (1963). *Encouraging children to learn: The encouragement process.* Englewood Cliffs, NJ: Prentice-Hall.

Dynneson, T. L., Gross, R. E., & Nickel, J. A. (1987). An Exploratory Survey of Four Groups of 1987 Graduating Seniors' Perceptions Pertaining to (4) Student Preferred Citizenship Approaches, (5) Teacher Preferred Citizenship Approaches, (6) Citizenship Approaches and Elementary Students, and (7) Citizenship Approaches and Secondary Students, Unpublished research report.

Dynneson, T. L., & Gross, R. E. (1991). The educational perspective: Citizenship education in

American society. In R. E. Gross & T. L. Dynneson (Eds.), *Social science perspectives on citizenship education* (pp. 1–42). New York: Teachers College Press.

Dynneson, T. L. (1991). Citizenship development: The role of the family, the school and the community. *Educational Horizons, 69,* 200–205.

Dynneson, T. L. (1992) What's hot and what's not in effective citizenship instruction. *The Social Studies, 83,* 197–200.

Glasser, W. (1969). *Schools without failure.* New York: Harper & Row.

Harmin, M. (1994). *Inspiring active learning.* Alexandria, VA: Association for Supervision and Curriculum Development.

Keller, J. M. (1983). Motivational design of instruction. In C. M. Reigeluth (Ed.), *Instructional design theories and models.* Hillsdale, NJ: Lawrence Erlbaum.

Kroeber, A. L. (1948). *Anthropology.* New York: Harcourt, Brace & World.

Morrissett, I., Hawke, S., & Superka, D. P. (1980). Six problems for social studies in the 1980s. *Social Education, 44,* 561–569.

Russell, I. L. (1971). *Motivation (Issues and innovations in education series).* Dubuque, IA: Wm. C. Brown.

Smith, P., & Ragan, T. J. (1993). *Instructional design.* Merrill/Macmillan.

Tausky, C. (1970). *Work organization: Major theoretical perspectives.* Itasca, IL: F. E. Peacock.

Wlodkowski, R. J. (1978). *Motivation and teaching: A practical guide.* Washington, DC: National Education Association.

Instructional Strategies and Activities

INTRODUCTION

This chapter explains the nature of social studies strategies in light of social studies content and describes various ways to plan strategies for instructional purposes. David Pratt (1980) acknowledges the importance of varying instructional strategies:

> Research on human learning has found that learning is highly idiosyncratic. Different people learn best in different ways; an instructional strategy that helps one student may have little value for another. (p. 299)

In time you will realize that the difference between creative and uninspired teaching is determined by the strategies teachers use in presenting content, skills, and values to students. Unfortunately, most teachers rely on a limited number of strategies (methodological techniques) that are applied repeatedly regardless of the content to be taught. Creative teachers, on the other hand, are aware of and employ a large number of instructional strategies. Instructional effectiveness is also improved when teachers make a "good" match between the content to be taught and the instructional strategy used to present the content.

Social studies content has unique characteristics that influence the application of instructional strategies. History and some social science content are commonly presented to students in the form of a narrative that requires reading and reading comprehension skills. In 1896, for example, the Committee of Seven recommended a list of six basic methods to be used in teaching history. Professor Saxe (1991) lists these as basic teaching strategies for history in the following statement:

To accomplish the most modest aims of history, the conferees suggested six basic methods: use of textbooks, collateral readings, written work, written recitation or tests, student notebooks, and extensive map-geography work, as a supplement to historical exposition. (p. 69)

While this list echoes a rather "old-fashioned" idea of how to teach history, it is interesting as a point of reference in comparing "modern" instructional strategies with the older ideas of lecture and recitation. Today most modern social studies methods textbooks recommend a greater variety of resources and approaches including the use of pictures, maps, charts, other illustrative media, group discussions, and projects that require analytical skills. Students are also expected to acquire a variety of social and individual skills that can be applied to social studies content.

The Nature of Instructional Strategies

Strategies are the means (techniques, processes, and procedures) to be used in presenting content to students in an instructional setting. According to Barth (1990), strategies have been defined as ways of "sequencing or organizing a given selection of techniques, i. e., during one class period the strategy was to use the following techniques: lecture, discussion, and workbooks" (p. 370).
For our purposes, we will use the following definition of strategies:

A teaching (or instructional) strategy is the technique that the teacher employs to help students learn the content of the course, unit, or lesson.

In other words, a teaching strategy is a delivery system aimed at establishing, clarifying, and expanding the student's ability to understand and to interact with the content of the subject. The subject matter is not merely "presented." Rather, the teacher should choose strategies that provide for the active *involvement* of the student in the learning process.

Strategies and the Elements of Instruction

In planning, teachers need to keep in mind that the strategies they employ to present the content to students are often determined materially by the nature of the subject matter. This includes the elements of content (knowledge—facts, concepts, generalizations, skills, and values) to be taught. In addition, teachers should consider the activities that will provide students with optimum experiences related to learning subject matter in the selected instructional setting. The teacher is responsible for designing effective learning experiences that meet pupil needs as well as instructional goals. At the center of effective instruction, therefore, are the settings and the means by which content is presented or addressed. The instructional strategy will vary according to the following elements:

1. *The teaching of an element of knowledge* (fact, concept, or generalization). Examples of strategies (teaching techniques) related to the development of knowledge might include vocabulary development, word/label/picture association, webbing demonstrations, synonyms and antonyms, displays and classification by category(ies), cause-and-effect studies, and written and oral reports.

2. *The teaching of a skill* (the acquisition, practice, and/or refinement). Examples of strategies related to the development of skills might include demonstrations, guided practice, transfer examples, illustrative films, guest experts, library research, production of charts and graphs, and interviewing techniques.

3. *The study or acquisition of an attitude or value.* Examples of strategies related to the development of value study and acquisition might include demonstrations of the following: objective thinking in the analysis of a statement, decision making based on a set of criteria, simulations of an event in which the outcome is measured on the basis of a moral or ethical standard, and modeling a desired behavior.

The strategy to be employed by the teacher determines the nature of instructional relationships during the teaching-learning process. For example, during a "teacher presentation" (lecture), the teacher may present the content orally while students listen, take notes, or ask questions of clarification. In a "discussion" the teacher usually asks a question and invites students to respond and interact with other students as a means of exploring the subject.

Setting and Characteristic Strategies

The instructional setting describes both the physical and social setting that will be used to facilitate learning through the instructional strategy. The setting or learning environment in which learning experiences are presented tends to influence cognition or the mental images and understandings that students come to associate with objects, processes, and preferences. According to Marsh (1977),

> Let's be realistic. It is unlikely that local community studies will foster marked student advances in the growth of citizenship responsibilities, the growth of behaviors appropriate within a framework of community expectations and tolerances, and so on. Nevertheless, they can provide students with an exciting and stimulating range of real-life situations. "A cow looks and certainly smells differently [sic] in the flesh than from in the dictionary. A common council or a legislature in action is a much more human institution than the textbook descriptions may suggest." In their long experiences at school students have very few opportunities actually to witness at firsthand people, objects, and processes other than those within the school confines. (p. 207)

The settings and techniques described in the following sections are typically associated with social studies instruction. The techniques mentioned in each instance are representative approaches that normally "reach" students as they work to meet instructional goals. References are included that give detailed information on key procedures.

Whole-Group Settings

A **whole-group setting** is one in which the teacher presents content to the entire class at the same time. Whole-group strategies tend to reflect a type of teacher-to-student interaction that is teacher-centered. The teacher or presenter tends to serve as a resource that interprets various forms of printed material or provides additional information connected with the textbook or other instructional materials. Typical presentation types include lecture, teacher-led discussion, media presentations (including films, slides, filmstrips, pictures, posters, and transparencies), guest speakers, small-group presentations, or oral reports to a class. Questioning by the teacher occurs in many settings; it is also a common element in large-group instruction.

Lecture Techniques

Many teachers who understand children and the weaknesses of extended lectures use a short lecture style interposed with questioning and pupil discussion. With typical high school students, a forty- or fifty-minute lecture is a most unfortunate strategy. Even a gifted lecturer or a long lecture on a most immediate or exciting topic will cause the attention of many students to wander. Research evidence suggests that even a highly motivated lecturer may teach far less using this method than supposed. A combination of a short and effective lecture combined with several other strategies related to interesting content is the most satisfactory approach here and should be but one of a

What Are the "Whys" and "Whens" of Lecture?

Under what circumstances should a teacher use lectures? In high school, how should a teacher construct presentations that differ from typical college lectures?

series of teaching encounters of different kinds, often within a single class hour. Occasionally, a teacher may have reason to lecture at some length but it should not be a common practice. Instead, the teacher might combine lecture with, for example, a lesson to teach note taking and an outline of the lecture on the chalkboard. Short ten- to fifteen-minute introductions, overviews, explanations, and summaries are frequently appropriate. Research also suggests that verbal reception may be more effective with older students who are relatively serious and open-minded than with junior high or elementary school pupils. Generally, therefore, teacher "talks" are to be preferred over formal lectures.

Questioning Techniques

After lectures or shorter talks, the most frequent whole-group approach is questioning techniques. Here again, most teachers interpose class discussion with questions and opportunities for students to raise questions. Student queries may be answered, often preferably, by other class members instead of the teacher. Aiming to improve thinking skills, the instructor will frequently avoid answering a student query directly by posing a thought-provoking question to the questioner or to the class for further consideration.

Generally, it is best to state a query and then call on a specific student. Research shows that a few seconds of wait-time are very helpful in giving students an opportunity to think the matter through rather than having them fumble for immediate answers (Rowe, 1986). Another approach, borrowed from ancient Socratic questioning, is asking one student a series of questions, including asking the student to explain the reasons for the answer and having the student consider alternative answers to the initial positions taken. Even if the teacher moves from student to student during a questioning session, it is wise to plan ahead with clusters of related queries. For example, a teacher might move from "what" to "why" and eventually to conclusions and their potential impact.

Some levels and kinds of questioning reach from a question of knowledge and comprehension to more complex analytical, interpretive, and synthesizing answers. Some studies have concluded that the cognitive level of questioning

When Does Waiting Get Results?

Research has revealed that teachers often move immediately to another student when the first pupil queried cannot answer. What do you believe might happen if the instructor would wait a few seconds before rephrasing or moving on to a second student? How might the teacher wait for an answer without creating a threat to the student?

by many teachers is often too simple and involves seeking mere factual information. As with any other strategy, the teacher should give time and thought to the best procedures and the kinds of queries to employ, depending on purpose. For example, it is important to teach pupils how to question. This calls for exercises, activities, and discussion so that meaningful and precise queries may be advanced that are not only clear but that also stimulate class curiosity. This, of course, is also a challenge to the teacher in designing questioning techniques. Clearly, though, as the teacher plans and perfects questioning strategies, the growth in student knowledge and competency is multiplied. Helpful detailed articles and entire books have been written with specific examples related to a number of questioning techniques. Concerned readers may wish to consult Sanders (1966) or Hunkins (1972).

Discussion Techniques

In one form or another, discussion should be the most frequently observed activity in social studies classrooms. In the ideal classroom the teacher is not a dispenser of information but a facilitator of a basic learning process. Discussion is a way of presenting and clarifying content by means of oral interactions between teachers and students. It is even more important as a means of promoting the exchange of information and ideas between students, resulting in many cases in extended knowledge, mutual understandings, and recognition of other points of view by individual students. In addition, discussion takes various forms, ranging from a chapter review or exchanges of opinions concerning a current event to the more formally planned discussion that originates with a subject described in the textbook. Discussion should follow the return of tests to the students and may relate to specifics of homework and classroom behavior, suggesting that there are daily opportunities for classroom discussion.

When discussion is used to explore the content of an instructional program, considerable preparation is required on the part of both the teacher and the students. Formally planned discussions require certain prerequisites that include a study of subject matter prior to the class meeting as well as the preparation of discussion queries that will initiate the oral interactions.

What Do Teachers Actually Mean by Discussion?

Teachers frequently report that they are using class discussion, but observers of these classes notice that most of the period is devoted to questions and comments, usually offered by the teacher. What steps should instructors take to ensure true discussion in their classes?

The quality of a classroom discussion rests on student preparation and the ability of the teacher to direct or manage teacher-to-student interactions and student-to-student interactions. The way discussion topics are stated will determine the quality of students' responses. Numerous classroom observational studies support the conclusion that about 80 percent of the time in a classroom someone is speaking and that within 80 percent of that time it is the teacher. In optimum social studies situations, both percentages, especially the second should be reduced. The key goal in discussion is to practice cooperative deliberation and group thinking toward problem resolution or best possible answers. To prepare students to participate effectively, class guidelines should be established including the following elements: to think before speaking; to be able to state reasons, examples, and sources for their comments and views; to accept criticism and contrary opinions in a responsible way; to be open-minded; and above all to listen.

Listening

Compared with other elements of successful discussion, listening is a skill that is seldom explored by the teacher, and little is written about the skills of listening. But one-half of satisfactory discussion is attentive listening. Again, the teacher is responsible for building listening competencies. In the frequent controversy that marks discussion in social studies classes, the social studies mentor should not depend on what may or may not have been taught about listening in English or other classes. Initially, especially at the beginning of the year, a class enumeration of blockages to effective listening would be in order. This can be followed by discussion of conscious efforts and practice necessary to overcome listening problems. These problems may include wandering minds, hearing problems, uninteresting speakers, and the climate and temperature of a classroom. (The rules of attentive listening will hold not only for reactions to guest speakers or to student oral reports, but also to the comments forwarded by class members during heated discussions.) Eventually teacher and class can develop procedures for facilitating attentive listening. These solutions can include improving the students' ability to carefully grasp and consider main points, learning new words and terms, identifying propaganda, and differentiating between fact and opinion (See Chapin and Gross, 1973, Chapter 3, or Taylor, 1969).

Playing the Devil's Advocate

In addition to preparing related questions, teachers can use a variety of other techniques associated with discussion strategy. The teacher may play the "devil's advocate" by presenting the least acceptable or a "temperature raising" solution to an important problem or issue and thereby prompt the students to challenge the solution and to consider and offer alternative solutions. At times the teacher may ask open-ended questions for which there is no obvious answer. Open-ended discussion requires students to seek possible outcomes. When exploring textbook content, the teacher may begin with questions that lead to descriptive answers but then use these answers as the basis for student interpretation or evaluation of the issue as well as of the textbook presentation. Students should also consider the influence of the passage on themselves and why they react as they do.

Small-Group Settings

An important and traditional social studies method of helping students to learn cooperatively is to use small-group settings. Students tend to vary in their ability to work effectively with others. Such task-oriented associations provide a preparatory challenge for teachers. In small-group work in social studies, students are usually required to contribute to the efforts of the group regardless of their preferences. Additionally, the bases for associations and interaction are commonly determined by factors related to the subject-matter topic and assignments. In some of these activities, pupils select their associates. More frequently, depending on the learning goals and the teacher's knowledge of class members, the teacher selects the committee and may even designate roles such as chairperson or recorder. This approach is most frequent with long-term cooperative learning assignments such as for the entire period of a unit. In short-term situations, for example, the instructor may merely have the class count off from one to four or five and then have all members of each number comprise a group.

The purposes and virtues of small-group organization are many and should be considered when designing instruction. Many capable teachers regularly conduct committee-centered classrooms. Committees can do much more than mere housekeeping or having bulletin board responsibilities. As indicated previously, small groups are a most valuable way to involve students in key elements of social studies content, from building skills of cooperative planning to contributing to evaluation and grading. The abilities to investigate objectively, to analyze and reach some conclusions, as well as numerous other social studies skills should be a regular part of both long- and short-term committee assignments. Teachers need to remember that in the small group the individual often has far more opportunities to contribute and to become truly involved than in many alternative total-class learning situations. Thus, small-group organization and activities through direct involvement of the individual student leads to personal motivation and learning because the students come to perceive the study as related to their personal needs and goals.

The small group or committee is used by some teachers to divide the work over a unit when a great deal of content is to be covered. Each class member will be expected to read text accounts or other common class materials; but small groups of students concentrate in depth on certain portions of the topic. After extensive preparation on their subtopics, they share their aspect of the study with the entire class. An American history teacher, for example, might assign small groups to investigate the different causes often listed for the Civil War. After several days of reading, library research, and discussion, each committee will report its findings and conclusions to the entire class, which will then attempt to separate underlying causes from immediate ones and try to establish a hierarchy of basic causes.

Committees and Cooperative Groups

Committee selection and organization is an important consideration for these studies. A variety of criteria are called for as a means of student selection for various assignments. Among these guidelines are abilities, interests, compatibility, experience, and leadership. Students need to recognize these criteria when making their own selections, and ideally, as a class, they should be involved in their development. It is important that these bases for selection are rotated to give students a wide range of group organization experiences in connection with social studies learnings. Small-group or committee studies attempt to help students learn how to develop the supportive and the leadership roles necessary to achieve specific goals. While the goals of small-group work are important to classroom instruction in terms of a particular lesson, the ability to work cooperatively is a central goal of small-group assignments and activities.

The attitudes required of successful committee work include the development of friendly relationships, a willingness to contribute to the committee goals, a desire to contribute ideas, and a willingness to provide leadership when required. Because most committee studies require research and reporting abilities, each student should have some training and experience in these areas. The teacher is expected to help each pupil develop the skills associated with needed research techniques (especially those associated with library work), communication, and reporting skills—all important elements of much small-group work.

Cooperative efforts require social interaction skills, and these skills call for careful planning by the social studies teacher. Students should be taught to set goals and to systematically work out the tasks designed to achieve these goals.

WHAT GUIDELINES WOULD YOU FOLLOW IN SCHEDULING SMALL-GROUP WORK?

Prepare an outline of a three-week social studies unit. Indicate where and what kind of small-group learning activities will be included.

Social studies instruction can provide a great variety of opportunities to employ one or another of small-group approaches. At one time these were typically called *committee work* as we have used the term. In more recent years *cooperative learning* and *group processes* are the favored labels. No matter the name, it is a crucial approach. Research indicates that when you organize a group of more than ten to fifteen students on a project, much of the verbal exchanges, interplay, and common learning activities is lost because the group is too large and individuals fail to find the opportunity or ways to participate effectively.

Buzz Groups and Dyads

Frequently teachers break whole groups into small sets (three to seven members) for short-term discussion. After a few minutes the class reassembles and the subgroups report on the results of their conversations. These informal arrangements are called *buzz groups*. Buzz groups are particularly effective for motivation, to get students to state initial opinions, to select or narrow a topic, and to share brief reactions. They can also be one element of teacher-pupil planning in shaping learning activities and time schedules for the lesson or the week ahead. Some teachers use the smallest group of all—the dyad. Here pairs of students are assigned a topic or problem. Students are expected to share their views, to listen carefully to one another, to settle a program of investigation, and to come up, if possible, with a joint conclusion. Depending on the topic, the dyad may only briefly share opinions with one another or may spend an extensive amount of time, spreading over several days, on their paired activities. Frequently such pairs will share their findings or conclusions with the entire class.

Panel Groups

Committee organization and reports can take different forms, the most common being panels. Round tables and debates are often employed. Debates, once very popular in school programs, have been replaced in numerous schools by town meetings or forum formats. While debates have proved to be excellent means for developing quick thinkers and effective arguers, they have lost favor since some hold that the process tends to encourage "victory" on one side and the use of certain unfair means to attain the winning decision. Such group work in numerous instances comes to include individual oral reports. To do well in the individual portions of committee reports, students need training in organizing their portions and in setting time limits. Many need help in effective oral communication and in building personal competence before a class. In all cases the students speaking should be encouraged to use outlines and notes but never be allowed to read their statements. Oral reports by committees and individuals usually call for follow-up queries by class members and teachers. A final discussion and evaluation of both the content presented and the effectiveness of the presentation are in order. Young people benefit personally and gain self-confidence from these speaking opportunities, which should be regular elements of most teaching units.

Students seem most comfortable with panel presentations where a group of three to six individuals share the reporting of a topic. In these instances, teachers need to discuss procedures with the class and to establish any necessary rules. In initiating group work, the teacher may prepare a written outline of responsibilities for the group and its individual members toward attaining successful presentations. As indicated previously, panels tend to end up as separate individual reports although sometimes a chairperson may deliver a unified statement. Separate subreports are to be expected since many topics contain different parts or subareas. Panelists should be encouraged to seek questions and reactions either during or after their presentations. Summaries or overview conclusions are often necessary on the part of the teacher.

When panels move toward a round table format, they become more of a discussion group and less separate factual presentations by individual members. In most instances, it is necessary to choose a chairperson who has special qualities to help forward the group investigation and to organize the discussion. Such individuals, especially moderators in panel reports or forums, are crucial to the success of the enterprise. A forum tends to take the structure of a town meeting with a full class or large audience. They normally provide for participation from the floor in the form of questions and statements. The aim is to ensure that students express a wide range of viewpoints that deserve careful considerations by everyone involved.

DESCRIBE THE MOST EFFECTIVE ARRANGEMENT

In committee and panel reports, what elements should you include that provide optimal learning for the participants, the listening class, and yourself as teacher?

The social studies classroom with its subgroupings is an ideal training ground for building the competencies and the student attitudes that reflect basic democratic qualities of fair problem solutions. Helpful free guides for these types of programs are provided by some organizations devoted to effective public involvement in civic affairs. Many books and articles that detail the guidelines for success in teaching with small groups are also available (Cohen, 1986; Margolis, et al., 1990; Schmuck & Schmuck, 1975; Slavin, 1983).

Individual Settings

Individual settings are those in which content is provided to or by a single student. Included are tasks and materials that are designed for or by each student according to some pre-established criteria (remedial, advanced, personal need, or self-interest, for example). Even individually oriented lessons and activities that may be listed as remedial are not necessarily so in the "catch-up" sense. Considering maturity, genetic, experiential, and other personal variations, such as family or cultural background, in any class there are actually far more differences between members than likenesses. Thus, there is continual need for a variety of individualized approaches.

Individual strategies tend to reflect a type of teacher-to-student interaction in which the teacher has assessed the special needs of each student and has prescribed instruction according to those needs and/or interests. Individualized instruction is characterized by direct interaction between the materials or content selected to meet particular needs and interests. Typical types of teacher-to-student or student-to-material interaction would include contract studies, self-paced instruction, modules of study, data base activities, computer-assisted instruction, poster activities, creative projects, interviewing, pupil research, independent study, and writing assignments.

Organizing Notebooks

Pupils benefit particularly from regular opportunities for writing in their social studies work assignments. Notebooks, for example, are frequently required. They may contain unit and lesson grade sheets, lists of aims, assignments, copies of all pieces of written work, notes, outlines, homework questions, and even personal essays or other writing related to the topic being studied. Such notebooks provide a helpful record for assessment and review for pupils and teachers as well as for concerned parents. Some instructors have students keep their class notes, content outlines, and other materials on the left page and on the opposite right page of their notebook students are asked for related free expressions or reactions. Student comments and reactions provide valuable insights for teachers who wish to understand their charges and assess the impact of a lesson.

Student Research

Well-stocked classroom reference shelves are important in providing pupils with sources for research and writing assignments. The school library is a richer source of information for student research and reports. Pupils at all levels benefit from instruction in library use. Frequently the school librarian will help instruct social studies classes meeting in the library with hands-on assignments and exercises devoted to finding and using available books and materials. Most teachers expect far more research into a problem than the employment of a single encyclopedic entry. It is typical to expect as a minimum from three to five supportive references from different sources. Similar source references, as well as written notes or outlines, should always be expected to accompany oral reports.

Teachers can also incorporate a valuable variety of pupil research and study into the construction of imaginary diaries. These can consist of mock personal experiences during some event or period in history or may take the form of a detailed daily exposition of travel experiences as the class moves through the study of a foreign country or of a particular region or culture area of the world.

Tutoring Sessions

Other opportunities for individual work occur when the teacher schedules conference times during class sessions to meet with students. Personal review of notebooks, faulty homework, and private questioning on assignments can prove most worthwhile. Why must all students, for example, give oral book reports to the entire class? In some cases this may be a helpful experience; but in other instances a private oral book review with the teacher may be more valuable and satisfactory for both teacher and pupil. This can be a time-saver for the entire class. In some situations when the teacher discovers that the pupil has valuable information to share with fellow students, the pupil can be encouraged and scheduled to share it. Many teachers allow approximately one class hour a week to be devoted to independent individual activities. At this time some class members may be reading assignments or related materials in the room or in the school library, while others may be involved in notebook assignments or planning small-group reports or projects. During the hour the teacher confers with several students; one may need help with missed class work, one may be reporting on independent study progress, and another may be discussing an element of the course reading that she may not understand.

Today few teachers use formal contract agreements with students on assignments or studies to be completed and on established grades; but with a variety of settings and approaches to meet individual needs some teachers establish checklists of learning activities. Checklists may include a point system with different credits in terms of time involved and the difficulty of the work. Students can then anticipate what grade they may receive if the "package" is well completed.

Technical Settings

Technical settings are those in which the teacher presents or provides content to students through a mechanical medium, including projectors, computers and their software, audiovisual equipment, communication apparatus, and self-teaching programs in the form of printed manuals and computer software. A characteristic trait of these strategies is the student-to-machine interaction. Technical instruction often includes diagnostic and achievement assessments which the student completes in order to advance to the next topic or level of instruction.

Film Media

Long before the appearance of the modern computer, teachers recognized the value of pictorial learning. Films, properly introduced and thoughtfully followed with class discussion, became a standby over a half-century ago. As Hollywood produced colorful and more dramatic movies, commercially prepared school films found it difficult to emulate their attraction, and typical school schedules made it very difficult to use uncut films. For a number of years, a committee of the National Council for the Social Studies had a contract with Hollywood producers allowing them to cut many movies, especially historical ones, so they could be shown in a single class hour. Unfortunately this helpful arrangement was not continued into more recent years. Today edited film videos have prompted a return of commercial movies to enriching classroom instruction. Numerous filmstrips are available commercially for use in lessons and units. Social studies departments and school libraries often have catalogued collections of filmstrips and sets of slides that have been built up over a number of years. An up-to-date filmstrip has a particular advantage in providing numerous instances for temporary halts as teachers raise or answer queries, point out important elements of a frame, or even engage the class in a brief discussion.

Television

The advent of television brought a dramatic increase in media programs useful in school learning, and eventually a number of projects were developed to bring motivating and valuable content to children in many small and isolated school situations. Some school districts built TV production facilities and or installed televisions in many classrooms. Unfortunately another great opportunity for educational impact and improvement did not work out. Problems from local school scheduling to teachers' resistance to modifying their approaches, as well as the growing incompatibility of many nationally televised offerings with school objectives and programs, contributed to disuse. Although public TV continues to serve valuable educational purposes, often these programs are not carried during school time and learners become involved only at odd hours in their own home. The use of videotapes now

How Can Community Resources Be Incorporated into the Classroom?

Which nonschool resources can regularly be referred to and used in planning social studies units and lessons? Provide some examples of various technological assistance that can be of value in enriching your instructional design.

promises numerous opportunities to bring the excitement and knowledge in the outer world to pupils in the schoolroom. Their potential impact and use is still to be ascertained, but it can be significant.

Computer-Based Instruction

Many of the early social studies programs for computers were overly drill or game oriented, and pupils became more interested in gaining points or in winning than in learning the history or geography that a particular game or program was to promote. However, in recent years sophisticated and motivational learning packages for many social studies topics have become available. A great virtue of the computer program at this stage of development includes their interactive features and the fact that teachers can find a variety of ways to link these to individual needs and rates of progress of their students. With the great increase in available video and TV learning packages and the reduction in price of media projectors, the modern social studies classroom will be linked increasingly to an audiovisual lab or a computer center, thus tremendously enlarging the library potential of the school and greatly expanding the options for assignments and individually oriented learnings.

Projected Images and Transparencies

The total educational value of technical media is still undetermined, but it is clear that by themselves the machines and their programs cannot adequately replace able and responsible mentors. The professional classroom educator must be available and remain alert to numerous opportunities to move beyond technical media presentations and to adjust their use to individual and class needs. Regular opportunities exist, for example, to use items or programs developed largely for individual study with the entire class. Depending on lesson aims and availability, teachers will frequently use more prosaic technical aids such as the opaque projector. This is a valuable instrument for enlarging or portraying book pages, pictures, small maps, and other materials directly on the classroom wall without having to produce transparencies or copies.

Even more common today is the overhead viewer. Teachers find them particularly valuable in presenting materials to a class and in being able to face the class at the same time. As their facility with using the overhead viewer has increased, many teachers have come to use the viewer instead of the traditional chalkboard. One may not consider chalkboards as prime examples of the use of media, but without a doubt whether it is an old chalkboard or a new overhead viewer, this is a prime and almost daily source of learning in all schoolrooms.

Creative and Project Settings

Creative settings are those in which the teacher and/or students present content in a form designed to generate a new student expression or product in response to an event, content, stimuli, predicament, or emotional condition. Creative strategies are characterized by a student-to-stimuli interaction in which the pupils are required to express their reaction in unique and creative ways. Student expressions would be in the form of a product that attempts to communicate their individual reactions. Typical types of these expressions of feelings would include writing creative stories or poems, drawings and paintings, musical expressions or dance, murals, collages, cartoons, and models. Frequently such approaches are designated as projects. These student-executed items may include the creation of a product or a replica or involve notebook reports or class presentations.

Student-Produced Presentations

In settings discussed previously, some of the illustrative strategies suggested, such as diaries of imaginary trips, certainly have a creative element. Many opportunities exist for creative activities with video cameras. Pupils are also able to produce slide presentations on topics of concern. With a 35-mm camera, flash attachment, and close-up lenses, students can photograph actual scenes including examples of architecture, living conditions of citizens, and

WHY MIGHT STILL FRAMES OFFER MORE LEARNING POTENTIAL?

List several examples of why filmstrips may prove a more effective instructional device than a movie on the same topic?

other sources in the community relating to an educational topic. Beyond this, photographs of pictures in books, maps and charts, or shots taken in museums can combine to provide highly instructional possibilities for an entire class, let alone the small group responsible for the slide show production.

Artifacts, Realia, and Art

Lessons regarding objects or realia enable students to be particularly creative in classroom presentations. Many items from newspapers, posters, pictures, stamps, and dig findings to old guns, clothing, and former household items provide opportunities for motivational learning. Pupils need help in preparing the oral portions of such presentations, but they often prove to be the highlights of the experiences in a particular unit. The artistic abilities of some students should not be overlooked. Some students can produce wonderful drawings and pictures for bulletin boards and lessons, and promoting such activities—for example, for illustrations in a unit—can provide students with these qualities with helpful recognition and credit.

Cartoons

For history and government classes, cartoons are particularly valuable in gaining pupil understanding of conflicting public opinions about events and in building their insights into propaganda techniques. Even more valuable than having them analyze dramatic cartoons reproduced in book collections or from current news sources is the student-produced cartoon. In a particular unit, teachers may ask each student to produce a cartoon related to an event or issue in the period or topic the class is studying. This will often lead to extensive reading on the students' parts and to valuable classroom discussion when the cartoons are viewed and evaluated by their classmates.

Dramatic Presentations

Students with dramatic inclinations will often seize the opportunity to present a skit or a dramatic episode. Dramatic episodes can be produced entirely by a group of students or they may wish to dramatize portions of an actual play about an event in history. For example, these events may include a scene from a colonial witchcraft trial or a scene in which arguments are given in developing an AIDS prevention policy. It is not necessary in most instances to include appropriate clothing, props, or makeup. These skits can be organized as radio plays or broadcasts or can be taped for either audio or audiovisual presentation.

Projects

The idea of the project is sometimes credited to Professor William H. Kilpatrick of Teachers College, Columbia University, who in his dynamic teaching and writing played a major role with thousands of teachers in implementing Dewey's ideas of hands-on pupil involvement in learning activities. Projects became increasingly popular in the 1920s and 1930s, particularly at the elementary school level. They frequently included construction activities of one

kind or another, especially of models, but could include anything from bringing and studying live animals in classes to neighborhood cleanup work. Projects can involve individual pupils, small groups, or an entire class. As the unit
method of organization developed, projects often became one of the learning
experiences or options therein. High school instructors adopted the term for
such learning activities. Here again, in social studies, a project can include a
variety of pupil-selected assignments or creations where they may prepare bulletin board displays, interview business proprietors, carve a model Tahitian
war canoe, produce an ethnic area map of their community, or prepare a dio-
rama featuring battlefield trench arrangement. The key to the successful
employment of creativity in the classroom is an alert and open-minded mentor
who recognizes the possibilities of these options.

Contemporary Settings

Contemporary settings are those in which the teacher presents contemporary
events to students to enhance their awareness and concerns over current
issues and problems. Contemporary strategies are characterized by student-to-
current affairs interactions in which students are expected to become
informed participants in the affairs of the community, state, nation, and world.
Good citizenship requires the development of a certain level of concern and
involvement in contemporary affairs regardless of the course of study or grade
level. Typical types of student-to-contemporary affairs interactive strategies
include news reporting, current events bulletin boards, student newspapers
and news programs, news story scrapbooks, library research, news discussions and analysis, panel reports, news films or videos, and news quizzes.

Current Events

Current events help students to understand the importance of contemporary
issues and events that influence their future. Students are aware of the current
events that occur in their neighborhoods and school, but frequently are not
aware of local, state, national, or world events. Therefore, the social studies
teacher has a direct responsibility in connection with current events. This
responsibility is a routine one in that it should become a regular part of the
curriculum program.

Most social studies teachers feel that current events are an important part
of their students' regular work because of the need to encourage students to
become informed and participatory citizens. Because these students are
becoming citizens of a democracy, they are expected to make intelligent decisions regarding the nation's social, economic, and political affairs. The basis
for this intelligent decision making is knowledge and information. Pertinent
information and knowledge can be acquired through a daily routine of reading
newspapers and from radio and televisions broadcasts. Many families, how-

ever, take no newspapers or news magazines and pupils seldom listen to or watch news broadcasts on their own initiative.

The classroom, therefore, should become a center for promoting interest in the news and news analysis. Interest in the news can be built in several ways so that students will be encouraged to participate in news analysis and discussion. Current events information and news analysis are ideal means for both concept and skill development. A teacher, for example, can provide a current events bulletin board where individual students or committees place and then report on important news items. Special attention is given to events that relate to the current unit or topic of class study. Local, state, national, and world maps can be used to locate and describe the sites and areas named in current events stories. Excellent large bulletin board size maps of regions in the current news are often provided regularly by the companies who produce weekly pupil-oriented newspapers or magazines for use in the schoolroom.

Daily, Weekly, or Individual Lesson Approaches

Use of these specially prepared weekly sources of information that are written in terms of student interest and reading levels is held by some teachers as the prime way to introduce pupils to the need and value of keeping up with current events. Other teachers, however, prefer to use regular daily papers and news magazines as sources the students will continue to use when finished with their schooling.

What options exist for curricular approaches to the study of contemporary issues? Surveys of teacher strategy find that the majority of instructors prefer to devote one class period each week to current events. Most of these teachers have a set day, but others vary the day depending on other elements of the week's work. Some teachers favor a short, almost daily, reporting of current developments by class members at the beginning of the class hour. Other teachers discount this approach as being too brief to allow proper depth and analysis or, on the other hand, dislike the tendency of these reports and discussions to stretch out too long into the class hour, thereby taking time needed for the regular curriculum study. This brief daily approach is, however, favored by some of these instructors in keeping up with crisis developments such as an outbreak of war or a serious natural disaster such as a hurricane. A third variation in approach to current events is to provide blocs of several days to catch up on news between the ending and beginning of course units. Student assignments include library research, reading in depth on news backgrounds, cartoon analysis, classroom debate, and the use of guest speakers. Teachers using this approach believe that it best helps pupils to gain skills and the depth of understanding they need for related class discussions and decision making related to conclusions about current affairs.

Course-Based Current Events

Two other approaches to current events instruction deserve consideration. The first is the regular and natural reference to these developments by teachers and students as they proceed through their normal course studies. Most teachers indicate that they try to incorporate such references to the established class work with the frequent opportunities that exist for this treatment. A geography or history teacher, for example, covering the Middle East has such opportunities on a near daily basis. A geography teacher involved in the study of weather and climate will find numerous contemporary events to tie to the course topic. With regular front-page developments, the civics teacher may find almost too many such opportunities. Teachers of economics dealing with inflation, international trade, or gross domestic product (GDP) have numerous opportunities to integrate current developments into the unit of study. If, however, instructors are not alert to these relationships and opportunities or if they are overly dedicated to covering the course materials in their disciplinary intent, unfortunately they will do little with the constant availability of current events in the real world that can be linked to the course subject matter with motivational results.

Current Events-Focused Instruction

The strategy of extemporaneously designing curriculum and basing instruction primarily on current events is found infrequently and has been known to have been abused by ill-prepared and lazy instructors. However, certain dedicated teachers instead of trying to fit current events into the regular curriculum use appropriate contemporary affairs and issues as an approach into the prescribed course of study. Thus, a contemporary event becomes the initial focus for a unit or topic pertinent for the social studies course being offered. Daily, world events provide numerous developments that link to social studies courses. This linking strategy can be somewhat difficult to tie to typically organized chronological history courses; however, in government, geography, and economic classes this approach can be used easily. In such a program, all elements of the normal semester or year's curriculum may not be followed or experienced in the logical order of curriculum guide requirements; but a large majority of called-for content can be reached by a knowledgeable and creative

What Are Your "Druthers"?

In what manner would you prefer to organize and handle contemporary affairs in a social studies course you are teaching? Explain your answer. Will the development of national subject-matter standards hinder or promote such organization? Why or why not?

instructor. Mentors who shape their instruction using contemporary events can adequately and motivationally incorporate the required subject-matter content into units and lessons that are very purposeful for the students. For some theorists and practitioners this approach is the ultimate current events setting; contemporary affairs would be central and not supplemental in the program. This approach is not practical in certain situations in which highly programmed lists of essential elements and their related achievement tests dominate the instructional setting.

Disciplinary Settings

A *disciplinary setting* is one in which the teacher presents subject-matter content through a historical or a social science methodological technique. Disciplinary settings are characterized by a student-to-disciplinary methodological interaction in which methodological approaches are used to gather or organize information within the classroom, school, or local community. Typical types of student-to-disciplinary interactive strategies unfortunately are often lacking in classes not featuring the methodological *means* (processes) of the discipline.

Methodological Activities Approach

Numerous courses merely depend on exposition as the major technique for teaching the discipline. Appropriate methodological strategies might include the analysis of documents, interpretation of diaries, interviews with eyewitnesses, polls, surveys, map construction and interpretation, development of indexes, charts, and tables, systematic observations, shaping and use of questionnaires, attitude and opinion measurements, planning and executing laboratory experiments, excavations, and graphic representations of economic data or of land forms and soil areas. Some of the foregoing examples are parts of assignments in various disciplinary settings; but too typically, for example, in a history course, student interactions with subject-matter skills may be limited to producing time lines and copying maps.

Chapters 3, 4, and 5 in Part Two of this text contain numerous examples of disciplinary settings and their possible strategies, some of which are listed above. Frequently approaches and methods that can be employed in one disciplinary setting are also applicable in courses of other related academic fields. Interviewing, for example, is a strategy that may be employed in government or sociology courses, as well as in other disciplinary settings. Without an accompanying variety of valuable strategies and opportunities for multidisciplinary arrangements, a narrow disciplinary organization coupled with an expository approach to subject matter remains unsatisfactory for most elementary and secondary school students. Undoubtedly, this accounts for the low and negative ratings pupils continue to report for many of their social studies courses.

Structure Approach (Generalizations and Methodologies)

If a course is being offered in the name of history or any one of the social sciences, it should adequately reflect the unique or prime elements that help characterize that discipline as a separate field of social study. This characterization of a field is frequently designated as its structure. As explained previously, the structure of a discipline includes two elements. These special contributions of any of the social disciplines need to be clearly identified and practiced by students of those subject-matter areas. The first element is the **fundamental generalizations,** based on supporting facts found in research and evidenced in major publications of the discipline. The second element is the particularly **unique and essential research techniques and study skills** that are the marks of scholarship in that discipline. Thus, in presenting content under the label of a particular discipline, any teacher should first involve the students in developing the competencies that mark a professional in the field. Only then will the student be able to correctly generalize and draw sound conclusions as to the findings presented in subject-matter narrative.

Far too many instructors fail to properly introduce their students to the basic methodological skills in their discipline. Many history students, for example, even in their early college courses, have little or no experience with the fundamental competencies of historical research and analysis. Instead these skills have been presented only in expository fashion with what certain historians claim to have happened. At the same time, some teachers use source accounts and class assignments to get students to draw historical conclusions from primary and secondary sources; although long advocated, relatively few high school classes have had the advantage of such experiences (for an excellent presentation, see Johnson, Chapter 15).

Also in too many social studies classes, the approach is primarily fact centered. The important applicable generalizations that should arise from social studies courses are not identified or may be presented only as a conclusion at some point without the needed content background. Some years ago a structured social studies framework based on generalizations was developed mutually by subject-matter academicians and educators in the states of California and Colorado (State Curriculum Commission, 1962; Colorado Advisory Committee on the Social Studies, 1967). In these studies, the key generalizations were identified by specialists in history and each of the social science disciplines. These documents were quite influential, being reflected in a number of other state guides that were produced subsequently. In California, detailed units built on the state framework were to be developed in district, county, or local school courses of study. Generally, however, these entities did not build an adequate base of skills and supporting facts so that students would ultimately be really enabled to generalize on the most important learnings accruing from each disciplinary area; nor did the state-approved texts have the content or organization that properly paralleled the key generalizations. Recent interest in establishing standards for each disciplinary field tends to reflect the foregoing movement; but precise standards linked to state assessment may prove even more retrogressive if they reduce teacher creativity with strategies and end with pupil memorization of standards.

Community Settings

A *community setting* is one in which the teacher presents or reinforces subject-matter content by exposing students to community resources and facilities. Community setting strategies are characterized by an interaction in which local resources are brought into the classroom or where students go into the community to gain firsthand experiences with class topics. Typical types of student-to-community interactive strategies include field trips, guest speakers, participation in community projects, community mapping, local history study, research projects in the area, interviews, part-time work experience, and cooperative ventures with local businesses, service clubs, and other public and private organizations.

Almost a century ago, John Dewey opened the doors of his laboratory school at the University of Chicago to community sources. The children were to bring their social studies and other subjects into the community and the school was open to a variety of community contributions. The full realization of this concept on any significant scale has never evolved. Most schools have stood as isolated castles from the multiple learning opportunities in the locality by a moat of indifference and ignorance of the rich mutual resources.

Community-Centered Approach

A number of striking but significant examples of true community-centered schools have existed in this country and abroad. But as personnel change and communities evolve and as educational views are altered both in schools and in the locality, a new and changing community with different needs appears, and these experimental lighthouses have tended to disappear with such developments. Recent public concern, however, over the quality of education has brought a renewed interest in the local schools from parents and concerned citizens, which has led to some increased contacts between schools and communities. This renewed interest has been characterized in numerous situations by enlarged public involvement and gains in control over many aspects of education that previously were handled primarily by school boards and school administrators. In these situations, many opportunities exist for schools and community to work together in education; but too often these situations seem to be rather one-way streets of civic involvement in educational matters.

The ideal concept of community-centered education assumed a broad two-way avenue between school and locality. Parents would use the school facilities; they would contribute by serving as teachers aides, visiting speakers, informal counselors, and mentors for remedial and reference work as well as having some administrative responsibilities. Pupils would conduct a variety of learning activities and studies in the locality. Parents and teachers would work together on projects in and out of school. Students would participate officially as members or as observers in local government agencies. Social studies classes would sponsor vocational fairs as valuable career days with guests from businesses and organizations in the town.

Field Trips

The most conventional community interaction for pupils has been the field trip. Valuable information and insights are gained by students from planned and well-organized field trips. Some are long-distance as trips to the state capitol, to Washington, D.C., or increasingly even to foreign countries. Rewards in learning relate directly to teacher and student pre-planning and preparation, as well as to necessary debriefing and follow-up. For local visits, such as to the county court, a meat packing plant, or a large recycling operation, pupils gain an amazing amount of new and extended information. Despite logistical problems, teachers should not overlook these community resources, which are highly rated by students in course evaluations. Instructors also should not take for granted that their pupils have even visited well-known, historical, or other nearby cultural sites. Recently, a junior high teacher in a school some twenty-five miles from San Francisco was presenting a unit on China. She was inclined to reject a student's request for a class visit to San Francisco's Chinatown. She inquired of the class and surprisingly discovered that over half of the pupils had never made a trip there with their families or friends. Even if pupils have made such visits, a thorough and carefully pre-arranged school field trip will motivate a number of new learnings.

Community Observations

Often community studies begin with the use of local, city, or county maps followed by a tour or class walks. This is a useful strategy in geography, for example. As the class comes to understand districts and zones (official and "cultural"), economic and sociological insights grow into some of the key differences and problems in the community and its surroundings. On-site experiences from observing areas with homes of the wealthy to viewing depressed sections with evidence of homelessness and decay provide necessary, realistic understandings. Links to the rest of the nation and to international contacts can grow from identifying commercial signs and corporate and product names found throughout the country to observing thousands of foreign cars waiting in delivery yards or foreign sources of food.

Community Surveys

Some community-centered school programs in social studies include continuing surveys of the community. Results may be published from year to year, records

Can You Design a Community-Focused Unit?

Select a topic appropriate for a community study in a social studies class. Draft a unit plan for it that contains appropriate learning activities drawn from those suggested in this chapter.

may be extended, and findings may be shared at meetings with community leaders and citizens. Class studies may amass information on the following aspects of local life: "The history of our community," "Food costs and quality in our town," "The employed and the unemployed," "Experiencing the welfare system," "Housing in our locality," "Strengthening public security and protection," "Waste disposal and environmental problems and issues in our area," and "Improving community functions and facilities." It is easy to envision how certain governmental agencies, local businesses, and private organizations might prefer not to have students questioning, examining, and making suggestions in certain of these study areas. Nevertheless, in some instances where school classes have carried out such research and analysis, public and private action has followed to improve conditions identified by the students. The results of such a learning strategy are particularly valuable for the students in having experienced elements of democracy in action rather than having only read about such issues and met only the ideally functioning system often described in textbooks.

Simulated Settings

A *simulated setting* is one in which the teacher presents content through a game or simulation in which historical or social science events, issues, or problems are enacted in the classroom. Simulated setting strategies are characterized by a student-to-situation interaction in which commercially or teacher-prepared situations are organized around hypothetical or actual events and conditions. Students are expected to become absorbed by the situation and are asked to role-play, make decisions, and resolve predicaments. Simulation and game strategies incorporate many aspects of other strategies such as problem solving, decision making, critical thinking, and socio-dramas applied to a particular set of circumstances. In addition to simulations, typical types of student-to-situation interactive strategies include board, class, and computer games, role playing, pantomime, dramatizations, historical reconstructions, reenactments, and study and discussion of problem cases.

CAN YOU PROMOTE TEACHER/STUDENT COOPERATIVE PLANNING?

Considerable evidence shows that active student involvement in the learning process helps increase motivation and ensures the attainment of course and unit objectives. Select an example of a simulation or a case study and detail how you would provide for pupil involvement.

Case Studies

By giving students actual or fictional case studies but not providing them with the concluding accounts of the situation, teachers can pose analytical dilemmas to students to be resolved. After reading and discussion, they may try to complete the case and reach resolution individually or as a group. If conclusions cannot be reached, students conclude with alternatives or may declare the problem a dilemma. The case study is a valuable strategy for skill building, particularly in strengthening critical thinking abilities. Case studies have been used primarily at collegiate levels, and high school teachers may not be applying the strategy because of the relative lack of commercial products. Most instructors who use case studies develop the materials themselves (Christensen, 1987; Wassermann, 1992).

Dramatics

Formal dramatics finds minimal use in social studies courses, but some teachers, especially in history classes, may conclude a unit or end a semester's work with a large-scale overview simulation that may even involve several classes or in a few cases the entire student body. Essentially, this strategy involves students in reading and preparing to become involved for an evening or a day or two in a major enactment. In American history, for example, they might participate in a formal tea dance of the 1920s or a Charleston Party—minus the cigarettes and the alcohol! Generally, in histo-dramas there are no memorized parts; but all students are prepared in as authentic garb as possible and with authentic music or props to provide a representative and experience in typical roles and situations of the era (Sutro & Gross, 1983).

Role Playing and Socio-drama

Most role playing, often extemporaneous and for rather short periods of time, includes involvement of several class members in a real or imaginary episode. It could be a cabinet meeting of President Washington and Jefferson, Hamilton, Randolph, and Knox discussing some issue facing the new U.S. government; a group of union leaders deciding whether to strike; a daughter and her parents arguing about a family rule; or a simulated meeting of class officers with the school principal concerning the prom. Practitioners have found that on occasion students have developed surprising changes in attitudes and understandings as a result of role playing. This is particularly true when students are assigned controversial roles in which they must portray a point of view that they disagree with or doubt. When students role-play political, economic, or social issues, teachers gain valuable insights into pupil knowledge and belief, which can be helpful in shaping details of lessons on moral values or ethical implications.

In more extended simulated situations, usually related to a social issue, teachers give students assignments before the actual role playing and provide them with opportunities to study, discuss, and prepare for their roles. Such simulations move the approach into what is usually referred to as socio-drama. In this strategy, role playing also does not include scripts or rehearsals, but the group involved is usually expected to conclude with some resolution of the issue.

In some cases, the teacher may play a role in the simulation. In others, the teacher may intervene to raise an important query or to contribute some information that may help keep the event on a realistic path. In addition to the necessary class preparation for a simulation, it is very important to have a class discussion following the presentation. Frequently a role play or a socio-drama may be repeated, sometimes with new personnel, to see how different or similar conclusions might be reached.

Once a class is familiar with this approach, students come to enjoy the experience, which they recognize is valuable in helping them to understand other people's attitudes and why individuals hold their beliefs. Socio-drama emerged from psychological approaches to adult problems. Modified, they eventually had considerable acceptance, more as playlets at the elementary level. High school pupils can, however, learn and benefit personally from these experiences. A number of volumes teach the skill of role playing and contain sample problem stories (Shaftel & Shaftel, 1982).

WHAT ARE THE PROFITS AND THE PITFALLS OF CLASSROOM SOCIO-DRAMA?

Socio-drama and role playing have proved valuable in helping students understand the opinions of those who hold different viewpoints. What potential dangers exist in employing these techniques? How can they be avoided?

Pictures, Photos, and Drawings

Motivated and revealing class discussion can occur from the use of projected pictures (Muessig, 1958). Projected pictures can be photos or drawings shown to the entire class on a screen or paper copies that can be spread about classroom tables. This strategy involves small groups of three to five students in analysis and decision making. Sets of such pictures have been commercially produced for classes in sociology and psychology, but teachers can find numerous question-raising pictures in daily papers and magazines. Here again we have valuable interactions between media and students and between the students themselves. Depending on the photograph selected and the topic of study, the teacher may ask students to try to identify, for example, whatever they can about the individuals in the pictures, what they are involved in and why, as well as possible results. Role plays and socio-dramas easily follow such class discussions.

When teachers are concerned about value development and character education, strategies presented in simulated settings offer significant avenues of instruction that have great appeal to students and provide valuable experiences in solving problems, clarifying values, making decisions, and resolving conflicts.

Problem Settings

A *problem setting* is one in which the teacher presents content to students in the form of predicaments that require inquiry, issue analysis, and decision making. Students must try to resolve problems by applying various processes and procedures to gather information, seek possible solutions, draw and test conclusions, and defend results based on reasonable evidence and logical reasoning. Cognitive development strategies are characterized by student-to-predicament interactions in which the student is required to solve or resolve the issue or problem by choosing between alternatives, drawing conclusions, or providing a solution. Typical types of student-to-predicament strategies include questioning techniques, problem resolution, discovery activities, critical thinking, creative thinking, analysis and problem clarification techniques, deductive and inductive reasoning activities, and decision making. According to Gilliom (1977),

> Inquiry-oriented teaching involves creating a setting within which students feel compelled to pursue solutions to problems that are meaningful to them. It falls largely on you, the teacher, to launch inquiry by surfacing and giving immediacy to the problem to be pursued, and to nurture the process by supporting and assisting the students in their search for warranted answers. (p. 3)

Inquiry strategies include several approaches that teachers may use to involve students directly in finding outcomes, solutions, resolutions, and associations with social phenomena. Inquiry methods were derived from scientific techniques, which have in recent years been applied increasingly to social content. Originally known as "scientific thinking," this approach was introduced to the educational setting at the turn of the twentieth century by scholars including John Dewey. They had become convinced that students would benefit from learning processes that could be applied to finding solutions to all kinds of problems. One of the most attractive attributes of this strategy focuses on the immediate involvement of students in the teaching/learning process. Generally, this approach shifts the role of the teacher from an expository one to the role of guide and resource person, and it shifts the role of students from being passive recipients of information to that of active, direct problem solvers.

Because of its contribution in developing essential skills and promoting worthy values for individuals living in democratic societies, many leaders in the field of social education have held issue-centered instruction as the centrally important setting for both the elementary and secondary school social studies curriculum. Proponents of this instruction include those who would organize the entire program in terms of vital and continuing issues (including the terms *themes*, *topics*, and *problems*) to those who accept disciplinary settings of subject matter, but who advocate using a problems approach to most of the units and lessons being taught. (Aspects of this approach are also discussed under "Intellectual Skills" in Chapter 6.) Teachers using other settings do employ aspects of inquiry and problem resolution strategies, but in far too limited and incomplete fashion to satisfy proponents of the problem approach. (Some representative publications that have forwarded the problems approach over the past quarter century include Hunt & Metcalf, 1955; Massialas & Cox, 1966; Engle & Ochoa, 1988.)

Problem Solving

This approach to learning begins when students are taught to recognize problems and to apply a step-by-step examination of the problem. The scientific process of forming a hypothesis, gathering evidence, testing the hypothesis, and developing a conclusion is commonly used with problem solving. Teachers employ from four to eight or ten guiding steps and substeps. (Numerous publications on inquiry and problem resolution present these lists or formulas; one of the best is still found in Beyer, 1973.) Before inquiry experiences can be presented successfully, students must have learned the problem-solving steps and processes associated with inquiry. In addition, the teacher should be able to challenge student conclusions so that the defense of the inquiry approach rests on the weight of evidence.

Problem-solving processes are applied to open-ended predicaments in which deductive and inductive forms of reasoning may suggest a solution. In a deductive process students are required to identify (describe and clarify) a problem by framing it precisely, propose possible solutions to the problem (a hypothesis), gather information or apply the hypothesis to a variety of condi-

"Teacher, Do We Have to Do Inquiry Today? Please Just Tell Us!"

Issue-oriented social studies curricula and the related emphases on the skills of problem resolution and wise decision making have been held by proponents as the very heart of true social studies. Can you explain why this theory and its practices, although praised by some theorists and researchers, have not gained major acceptance by social studies teachers?

tions, and to conclude whether or not the hypothetical solution is a valid solution or whether the hypothetical solution should be modified or even rejected. Suppose for example, that before taking a field trip students are asked to list (a form of a hypothesis) what they expect to see and experience while on the field trip. The next day they will review the pre-field trip list and compare it with their experiences. They must then modify certain assumptions and draw conclusions. As a check on students' work, the teacher is expected to review the lists or the components of the process and, at times, to challenge student conclusions. The selection of an appropriate problem-solving topic should be guided by the following concerns: community views and traditions; pupil maturity, background and interest; teacher preparation and attitudes; relationship to school program and aims of the course; available time and the urgency of the issue; materials and facilities available; social significance and possible contribution to student learning; and chance for consensus, resolution, and pupil action.

Decision Making

While competency in all steps of the problem-resolution process is necessary, pupils need particular help with the decision-making aspects of the procedure. Decision making is a process that is best applied to questions that can be narrowed to choices between alternative possibilities. Through a process of speculation, examination, and prediction (students are asked to speculate about the short- and long-range effects of each choice) various alternative choices are eliminated until a final choice is selected. Decision-making activities can be applied to historical events in which decisions were made and the consequences are known. In the study of historic situations, students should be encouraged to reconsider all optional choices that might have been made, especially those that might have led to a more constructive outcome. Current events can be studied through a similar decision-making process. When students are involved in issues such as euthanasia or the death penalty, motivation for learning is generally high.

Discovery

When students are asked to uncover associations and relationships, a discovery process can be used in which the student identifies relationships involved in a query. Students try the validity of a relationship by applying the associations to a variety of conditions. An important part of discovery is to eliminate plausible causes and to zero in on the most likely cause (basic or immediate) of a specific event such as the cause or causes of the Intifada or the resignation of President Nixon or problems such as divorce, child neglect, abuse, or prejudice. Discovery tends to focus on the process of elimination based on trial and error.

In a simple form, discovery is often employed as a process that encourages students to manipulate or to experiment with objects (artifacts, relics, for example) or with events so that they might gain new insights into the nature of objects, events, and relationships. For example, students are encouraged to speculate about the nature and function of objects placed in a wastepaper basket by the teacher. The teacher placed these objects (potsherds, arrow points, nets, stone carved pieces) there to develop an activity called a "wastepaper basket excavation." Students are expected to "excavate" the basket and to describe and to speculate about the Indian society that produced and used these objects. From these objects the students are to infer something about the society and the life-style of the people. In a different activity, the teacher can copy pictures of appliances, tools, and farm implements from a 1905 Sears and Roebuck catalog. Students are encouraged to speculate about the function of the appliances and to make informal guesses about the times in which these appliances were in use. In some discovery activities, students can be asked to do some extended research to validate their speculations.

Critical Thinking

Critical thinking is a process that requires the use of reason and evidence to evaluate an event or a claim. This process is similar to a judicial process, a process used in courtrooms to validate various claims or counter claims. In other words, a critical thinking process is aimed at helping students identify and examine the basic assumptions and beliefs that influence human perceptions and behaviors based on the understanding that there are many crucial questions in life with many competing answers, of which some are objectively better than others. Therefore, critical thinking is considered a form of analytical thinking that will allow students to deal systematically with issues. The characteristics of critical thinking include the use of evidence, reasoned analysis of all sides of an issue, the identification of the values, beliefs and underlying assumptions, a search for additional information and a certain skepticism regarding the limitations of current knowledge.

According to Robert H. Ennis (1987), five key ideas are associated with critical thinking: "practical, reflective, reasonable, belief, and action" (p. 10). He goes on to define critical thinking according to the following statement: "Critical thinking is reasonable reflective thinking that is focused on deciding what to believe or do" (p. 10).

Critical thinking also may be described as a two-sided process in which students are taught (1) to analyze a message, behavior, belief, value, attitude, opinion, product, proposition, or statement by breaking it down into its most basic elements and to examine these elements according to some criteria or standard and (2) to make a judgment based on some standard or criteria about the meaning, truth, importance, and relativity of the message. For example, students might be asked to take a passage from a political speech or an advertisement for a new product and analyze the message in terms of its meanings, claims, and accuracy. In the first part of this process, students attempt to identify underlying assumptions, beliefs, and values regarding one side of an argument. In the second part of this process, students attempt to determine whether the claims are accurate and justified in light of evidence and analysis. The process of critical thinking is a helpful means for dealing with human values and the analysis of human behavior (Paul, 1981).

Propaganda Analysis

Closely related to critical thinking skills is the need for students to understand how influential forces attempt to gain public acceptance and action without any critical thought on the public's part. Persuasive statements or claims in publications, on radio or television, or in group meetings all call for thoughtful analysis. In the 1930s, with the writings of authors such as Stuart Chase and the publications of the Institute of Propaganda Analysis, a movement was started to prepare youth and adults to detect political and economic persuaders and their techniques. The result was the development of a list of seven approaches used by professional propagandists to influence the public (Chase, 1938). The seven "Tricks of the Trade" were entitled Name Calling, Glittering Generality, Transfer, Testimonial, Plain Folks, Card Stacking, and Bandwagon. Today, especially with the drastically increased impact of the visual media, there is even a greater need to teach young people how to detect the continuing stream of claims of highly vocal special interest groups, as well as that of fallacious commercial advertising. Social studies teachers make a significant contribution to the well-being of their students by helping them uncover the influences in their environment that encourage individual acceptance and action with no analytical thought or decision making on their part.

Issue-Centered Approaches

Debate continues over issue-centered education; but under current national circumstances the wisest way to promote the long-sought teacher use of inquiry and problem resolution is to urge and give examples of its values as a

CAN YOU REMAIN "CRITICALLY CORRECT" AND STILL EXPLORE THE VOLATILE SOCIAL ISSUES OF OUR TIMES?

Critical thinking analyses and their conclusions by students need to be carefully incorporated into a variety of social studies lessons. These strategies might include differing reports of historical events, conflicting political opinions, or the study of advertisements and the claims of news columnists. Would you be willing to adjust a typically content-oriented subject matter high school course to include such approaches? If yes, present an overall outline of such an issue-focused class. If not, explain in detail your reluctance to so organize a problem-centered offering.

prime strategy with or along with other and traditional settings at the junior and senior high school level. Several courses are now commonly organized or titled so that the problem approach can be used. These include some civics classes, world problems or regions offerings, and the declining contemporary or senior problems courses. Realistically, proponents of an issue-centered strategy cannot expect radical or thorough revision of the established social studies curriculum toward a full problem setting. Additionally, current contemporary developments in American society and education are tending to push more programs into traditional patterns. School curricula have always changed very slowly, and new ideas and arrangements frequently succumb to the traditional after short trials. It is apparent, therefore, that to build the fundamental competencies of critical thinking, problem resolution, and wise decision making, the proponents of the issue-centered inquiry setting need to emphasize a skill-oriented approach within or along with other settings. This should be forwarded as a strategy that materially reduces the time and the heavy attention to usual fact emphases and knowledge inculcation that so "turns off" a very large segment of students. Proponents need to underscore and give evidence from the serious conditions that affect human well-being of the need to considerably increase attention on the unresolved aspects of most of the topics being studied. Also, proponents need to demonstrate that the processes of skilled inquiry and problem resolution are crucial elements of learning for citizens of a free and democratic society that must be preserved. Citizens, parents, as well as teachers are in dire need of the theory and evidence that underscore the imperative value of a problems setting and strategies for the social education of America's youth. (The September/October, 1989, issue of *The Social Studies* featured a special section on issue-centered education. The hopes and thinking of five leaders in the movement, Shirley

Engle, Ronald Evans, Richard Gross, Byron Massialas, and James Shaver are included.)

CONCLUSIONS

In reading this chapter, you have learned that the success of program design rests ultimately on your planning and performance strategy. This chapter on instructional settings and approaches indicates a myriad of opportunities and responsibilities for the truly concerned and professionally prepared mentor to reach course goals and promote necessary student learning. All courses, units, and lessons call for significant teacher knowledge of this triad: (1) understanding pupils and their backgrounds; (2) subject-matter competence; and (3) command of a variety of learning approaches and materials.

A teacher from the same or a similar community or ethnic background as that of the students can gain respect and cooperation from many pupils. A magnetic lecture or dramatic storyteller may well interest many students in subject-matter content. A master instructor can use numerous approaches and related motivational materials to involve many students in learning. A teacher who is a model of good character and democratic values may help students reach even unstated goals and reap unexpected rewards.

Can the foregoing qualities be combined? Fortunately in a considerable number of instances, yes. In other situations, able and perceptive individuals, well prepared for the rigors of teaching, can successfully compensate for certain lacks or inadequacies. It should be clear, however, that the so-called "born" teacher with all the necessary qualities is very rare. For many teachers, improved productivity and increased subject-matter knowledge are needed, and this calls for substantial amounts of in-service disciplinary study. Considerable increases in initial state certification requirements are also needed, and particularly teachers with only minor concentrations in the social studies areas must extend their depth and breadth of subject-matter knowledge well beyond official requirements. For many beginning teachers or those transferring to different areas, a significant exposure to community and cultural conditions, as well as understanding of pupils living in these circumstances, is essential. And then, as an archer with a quiver full of varied arrows shaped to reach desired ends, the mentor needs the expertise to hit the multiple targets of the educational agenda. (How unfortunate is the too commonly noted assignment of unqualified personnel by school administrators to attempt to instruct in the complex social studies field.) Above all, teachers who are humane individuals with empathy for and recognition of the needs of children and youth may well make their most significant long-term educational contributions.

REFERENCES

Barth, J. L. (1990). *Methods of instruction in social studies education.* Lanthan, MD: University Press of America.

Beyer, B. (1973). *Inquiry in the social studies classroom: A strategy for teaching.* Columbus, OH: Charles E. Merrill.

Chapin, J., & Gross, R. E. (1973). *Teaching social studies skills.* Boston: Little, Brown.

Chase, S. (1939). *The Institute for Propaganda Analysis, The Fine Art of Propaganda.* New York: Harcourt, Brace.

Chase, S. (1986). *The tyranny of words.* New York: Harcourt, Brace.

Christensen, C. R. (1987). *Teaching and the case method.* Boston: Harvard Business School.

Cohen, E. (1986). *Designing group work: Strategies for the heterogeneous classroom.* New York: Teachers College Press.

Engle, S., & Ochoa, A. (1988). *Education for democratic citizenship: Decision-making in the social studies.* New York: Teachers College Press.

Ennis, R. H. (1987). A taxonomy of critical thinking disposition and abilities. In J. B. Baron & R. J. Sternberg (Eds.), *Teaching thinking skills: Theory and Practice* (pp. 9–26). New York: W. H. Freeman.

Gilliom, M. E. (1977). *Practical methods for the social studies.* Belmont, CA: Wadsworth.

Gross, R., Muessig, R., & Fersh, G. (Eds.). (1960). The problems approach and the social studies, Curriculum Series #9. Washington, DC: National Council for the Social Studies.

Hunkins, F. P. (1972). *Questioning strategies and techniques.* Boston: Allyn & Bacon.

Johnson, H. (1940). *Teaching history.* New York: Macmillan.

Margolis, H., et al. (1990). Using cooperative learning to facilitate mainstreaming in the social studies. *Social Education, 54:* 111–114.

Marsh, J. C. (1977). Local Community studies. In M. E. Gilliom (Ed.), *Practical methods for the social studies* (pp. 204–227). Belmont, CA: Wadsworth.

Massialas, B., & Cox, C. B. (1966). *Inquiry in social studies.* New York: McGraw-Hill.

Muessig, R. (1958). Using projective pictures. *Social Education, 22:* 250–252.

Paul, R. (1981). *Critical thinking.* Rohnert Park, CA: Sonoma State University, Center for Critical Thinking.

Pratt, D. (1980). *Curriculum design and development.* San Diego, CA: Harcourt, Brace, Jovanovich.

Rowe, M. B. (1986). Wait time: Slow down may be a way of speeding up. *Journal of Teacher Education,* (January/February): 43–50.

Sanders, M. N. (1966). *Classroom questions: What kinds?* New York: Harper & Row.

Saxe, D. W. (1991). *Social studies in schools: A history of the early years.* New York: State University of New York Press.

Schmuck, R., & Schmuck, P. (1975). *Group processes in the classroom.* Dubuque, IA: Wm. C. Brown.

Shaftel, F., & Shaftel, G. (1982). *Role playing in the curriculum.* Englewood Cliffs, NJ: Prentice-Hall.

Slavin, R. E. (1983). *Cooperative learning.* New York: Longman, Brown.

State Curriculum Commission (1962). *Social studies framework for the public schools of California.* Sacramento: California State Department of Education.

Sutro, E., & Gross, R. E. (1983). The five senses—Prime keys to the art and craft of teaching. *The Social Studies, 74,* 118–124.

Taylor, S. (1969). *Listening. What researchers say to the teacher* (publication #29). Washington, DC: National Education Association.

Wassermann, S. (1992). A case for social studies. *Phi Delta Kappan, 73,* 793–801.

12

The Evaluation, Selection, and Development of Instructional Materials

INTRODUCTION

In this chapter you will learn that textbooks and supplemental teaching materials traditionally have been used as the focus of instruction; however, today new technologies and materials are influencing the traditional patterns of instruction. These new techniques and materials often require multimedia presentations as well as computer applications. Teachers also face the demanding task of keeping pace with rapid changes in subject-matter emphasis and instructional orientations by selecting materials that seem most appropriate for their instructional programs and students. Subsequently, teachers are required to review, assess, select, and revise materials from within a wide range of items available for classroom instruction. Under this condition, teachers should develop a systematic means for performing these tasks to avoid costly mistakes.

Even though the textbook is the most widely used single instructional resource, reading skills tend to pose learning problems for many students. You will find that this problem stems in part from the structure of textbooks. Gunter, Estes, and Schwab (1990) contend that textbooks often lack a connected narrative to interest students.

> . . . the books in which they *learn to read* differ from the books in which they are asked to *read to learn*. How so? Under pressure to convey vast amounts of information, instructional texts leave out "the story" which would make information interesting and memorable. Unless instructional materials are chosen wisely and used discriminately, the result is boredom for learners. (p. 50)

In spite of the limitations of textbooks, Banks (1985) suggests that textbooks do have virtues:

> Most social studies textbooks are well-organized, readable, attractively illustrated, and contain important if highly selective information. The social studies as presented in the textbook is the best social studies curriculum that many students ever experience. (p. 225)

In general, textbooks are different from other types of materials in that they are designed to be self-contained learning resources. Characteristically, social studies textbooks consist of descriptive narratives that are structured around concepts, skills, values, and supportive content that are selected especially for students by grade level. Textbooks contain a great many and varied learning aids such as maps, charts, illustrations, documents, pictures, drawings, study questions, and explanatory notes. Most textbooks are also accompanied by supplemental resources specifically designed for textbook instruction including posters, transparencies, workbooks, pictures, filmstrips, films, charts, and teacher guides.

An important instructional decision you are required to make in planning a course of study is the extent to which you will use the textbook as a primary or secondary resource within the instructional program. Beginning teachers typically use the textbook as the primary means of instruction, especially while they are developing their courses, units, and lessons. More experienced teachers tend to use the textbook as a secondary source in conjunction with commercial and teacher-constructed materials. Master teachers tend to use a wider range of supplemental and teacher-constructed materials because experience has taught them to recognize both the benefits and the inadequacies of textbook-centered instruction.

Textbook Instruction

An awareness of strengths and weaknesses can help teachers determine the role of textbooks in instruction. As early as 1896 the conferees of the Committee of Seven wrestled with the role of textbook instruction in the history classroom. According to Saxe (1991),

> The conferees considered the textbook a valuable tool for those teachers without "wide training, long experience, and, in addition, daily opportunity carefully to examine the field and to search out the nature of the problems that he [sic] is

called upon to discuss." Indeed, this qualification was apparent to many prospective history teachers given a catalog of their own qualifications. To such teachers the textbook was an absolute essential teaching aid. "Without the use of the text," emphasized the conferees, "it is difficult to hold the pupils to a definite line of work." Additionally, "within the covers of one book, however, it is impossible to bring together one hundredth part of the materials which any careful historical writer would examine for himself before coming to a conclusion." On the one hand, the textbook brought unity, continuity, and historical mindedness; on the other hand, the textbook was incomplete, prone to lead students to accept generalizations as facts, and, by the unwitting teacher's erroneous emphasis on fact accumulation, foster an unhealthy dulling of historical appreciation. (p. 69)

Many concede that textbooks are ideal for class instruction because they are a standardized source of information for all students. With a textbook pacing chart or guide, the teacher is able to lead students through the instructional program in a timely fashion. In addition, most textbook companies have attempted to produce materials that are attractive and structured to help students become independent learners. The self-contained organizational structure of the textbook usually promotes student learning through a comprehensive instructional design that provides for additional background information, reflective thinking ideas, questions designed to measure comprehension, activities for skill development, and practice and reference citations that help coordinate textbook instruction with related instructional supports such as workbooks that accompany the textbook.

During the first weeks of instruction, many experts recommend that the teacher take time to provide students with a textbook orientation. For students to use their textbooks effectively, whether used as a primary or secondary source, they must possess certain basic reading and study skills associated with locating and using information, interpreting various types of illustrated information such as maps and charts, and the ability to think critically about the events, processes, and relationships presented within the written narrative. Because of the extent of textbook-dependent instruction, students should be taught how to read, comprehend, and utilize the social studies textbook. Banks (1985) points out the importance of previewing the use of the textbook:

> The teacher should explain the parts of the book to students, including the front-matter [sic] (title page, table of contents, preface, etc.) and the end matter (the appendixes, glossary, index, and other special features). The teacher should explain the purpose of each of these sections of the book and ask the students to complete a number of activities. . . that will help them to increase their skills in using the textbook. (p. 229)

This type of orientation will help students locate topics and particular elements of information within the textbook(s) and to pursue textbook topics through further study and research in monographic literature and primary sources.

CAN YOU HELP YOUR STUDENTS LEARN TO USE THEIR TEXTBOOK THROUGH TEXTBOOK ACQUAINTANCE LESSONS?

Develop a one- or two-period lesson to introduce students to the use of their textbook. Include explanations of how such books should be read for different purposes—such as content knowledge, specific item reference, overview, main ideas, or review.

Textbooks are designed to communicate a great amount of information specifically for youthful learners; in addition, they are designed so that the *concept load* (number of concepts per page pertaining to the level of difficulty or complexity of presentation) is appropriate according to grade-level reading norms. Nerbovig (1970) lists other advantages of using textbooks:

> The advantage of using the learners' texts lies in their convenience and their common elements of agreement with what is being studied in various localities by learners at the same grade level and the same subjects. . . . Learners' texts can be useful: (1) as definers of scope (though one need not necessarily use the text sequence), and (2) as a reference for learners during the learning phase of the unit [also, (3) for review purposes]. (p. 20)

On the other hand, Nerbovig (1970) recognizes that textbook instruction has certain weaknesses.

> Their disadvantage lies also in their generality: their tendency to "survey" or give an overview of the field, though the authors of some of the newer texts have made real efforts to provide for depth, for comparison and contrast of known and unknown, and even for varied levels of difficulty. Except for coincidence, however, they do not have local information. Neither can textbooks include the most current materials. (p. 20)

Also, because of attempts to cover a broad scope of subject matter, textbooks frequently lack the motivational and enriching elements needed to enhance student interest, thus leading to the criticism that textbooks contain little in the way of human interest. Students often find the textbook too difficult to read, which requires the teacher to make interventions such as attempting to use several textbooks with varying reading levels to supplement the regular classroom textbook. Also, because of students' poor reading ability, motivational problems, and the size and weight of some large social studies texts, critics charge that it is futile to expect students to read the textbook outside of the classroom. As a consequence of these weaknesses, many teachers are not able to address the development of many concepts and skills and other goals associated with the higher levels of thinking as applied to social issues. (Students are likely simply to parrot back the textbook rather than reason their way through its content.) In addition, textbooks tend to be out-of-date even before they reach the classroom; consequently, teachers are required to supplement the textbook with changes due to recent discoveries and events. (Standard textbooks usually are adopted for a five-year period, and when textbooks are replaced, they may be as much as ten years out of date. For example, political and geographic changes take place so rapidly that before the ink is dried on a map, territorial boundaries have changed, new nations have emerged, and name changes have occurred.) In spite of this concern, William E. Patton (1980) suggests that out-of-date textbooks can be a source of valuable supplemental information for current creative instructional use. Textbooks from the past are considered especially valuable in regard to the visuals, cartoons, and graphs. In addition, critics assert that textbooks often contain stereotypical points of view that reflect past attitudes or perspectives of the roles of men, women, and children in society. Today as in the past, critics contend that social studies textbooks have never been of a high quality and that in recent years they appear to be becoming even more mediocre. (In Texas, for example, textbook critics report that social studies textbooks contain numerous factual errors—such as that the atomic bomb was dropped during the Korean conflict and that the U.S. House of Representatives impeached Richard Nixon.) In recent years, critics have charged that social studies textbooks do not provide a "proper" ethnic or gender balance, thus depriving students from various cultural backgrounds of role models or perspectives.

In defense of these charges, publishers and authors of textbooks suggest that textbooks never have been designed as a single instructional approach or materials source. According to Banks (1985),

> Many of the poor teaching practices associated with textbooks result more from the way they are used rather than from the nature of textbooks themselves. The authors, editors, and publishers of textbooks do not intend them to be the only source of information when teaching the social studies. Common statements such as, "My social studies book is too long for me to cover in one year" or "I think I will be able to cover my textbook this year" indicate the extent to which many teachers regard the textbook as the curriculum. (pp. 224–225)

In spite of the many problems associated with the textbook, textbooks remain the most single important learning resource in the social studies classroom (Researchers report that students are engaged in textbook-related activities 75 to 90 percent of the time they spend in a social studies classroom (Wade, 1993).

Textbook Selection

By accepted practice, the selection of textbooks and supplemental materials should be based on the instructional needs of students according to their learning attributes and program needs. In some states, local school districts and even individual teachers are allowed to select grade-level and subject-matter textbooks as well as supplemental materials, whereas in some other states, textbook selection begins at the state level allowing local school districts only limited choices. The teachers' role in material selection has varied over time; however, as school districts have become large and complex public institutions, teachers have become less able to influence the selection of their textbooks. On the other hand, textbook publishing has become big business with millions of dollars at stake over the adoption of a single textbook. Consequently, textbooks are designed to appeal to the concerns of decision makers who have the power to influence the selection process. Paradoxically, teachers often are provided little opportunity to participate in this process, but are required to implement programs put into place by others who are more distantly removed from their classroom or school setting.

To add injury to insult, in the recent past textbook authors were encouraged to develop "teacher proof" instructional materials that would be taught according to a prescribed structure and format. In some cases, programmed instruction formats were used as a means of locking the teacher into a sequence of steps that would be followed in planning and presenting instruction. While an effective approach, programmed instruction is based on a process similar to that found in a cookbook in which a recipe is used to achieve a desired final result (or product). To some extent, this approach was based on the assumption that average classroom teachers were unable to develop an effective program of instruction or materials of their own. In addition, a programmed approach also is viewed as an effective means of standardizing the curriculum across a school district or a state. As a consequence, textbooks often reflected a highly programmed format that teachers and related instructional materials were expected to technically execute. In general, these instructional programs were organized around pre-identified objectives (essential elements) and performance tests that greatly influenced the content, emphasis, and format of instructional programs as well as the textbooks.

For some teachers, the highly structured instructional approach was unsatisfactory because structured programs often did not adequately address local conditions and the individual needs of their students. Faced with this situation, teachers began to modify these structured approaches with teacher-constructed and supplemental materials that were deemed more suitable for the needs of their students. While considered somewhat subversive by authoritative forces, these modifications seemed justified in light of the traditional role of the teacher as the classifier, interpreter, and modifier of instruction. This issue was addressed in an important education book written by Postman and Weingartner (1969), who borrowed a phrase from Ernest Hemingway that suggested that to be effective in the classroom, teachers needed to develop a built-in "crap detector" (p. 2) so that they could separate the essentials of instruction from superfluous practices imposed by institutional bureaucrats.

As applied to education, effective teachers must have intuitive insights and be willing to act accordingly. According to Gagne, Briggs, and Wager (1992), this ability is an important attribute when evaluating instructional materials, especially in light of unproven learning claims; as in reality, "few publishers have actually validated the effectiveness of their materials" (p. 304). Therefore, teachers must diligently review and evaluate instructional materials and attempt to modify mandated materials when they prove to be ineffective with students. But more important, teachers should attempt to acquire textbooks and supplemental materials that they can use to overcome the inadequacies and weaknesses of a single textbook approach. The use of a multiple-textbook/multimedia approach is considered an effective means of both addressing the requirements of imposed mandates while at the same time meeting local needs and desires.

Since parental choice and site-based management have gained in popularity and acceptance, school district officials expect teachers to provide instruction in the knowledge of basic essentials and skills and at the same time to offer "customized" instructional programs that appeal to parents and students. As a result, social studies teachers are expected to make curriculum choices and to develop curriculum programs that teach the essentials of history, government, geography, and other areas and at the same time provide programs that appeal to the special interests of students. For example, in one school setting or level, the social studies program might emphasize a particular discipline or approach such as history and geography with an emphasis on cognitive thinking skills, whereas in another situation the social studies program might focus on citizenship education with an emphasis on developing cooperative learning skills that would be applied to participation in community projects. Under these circumstances, social studies teachers are expected to continuously review and assess the status of their offerings and to make appropriate changes by regularly developing new programs, approaches, and materials.

Selection Criteria

Decisions regarding the selection of a textbook often are made by committees assigned the task of choosing one textbook from among a limited list of books. The methods of selection range from formal lists of pre-established criteria to various unspecified factors such as use of illustrations and color, similarity to current adoption, author name recognition, book and chapter titles, supplemental resources, size of print, results of reading samples, and book length. To more uniformly expedite the textbook selection process, a criteria-based process is preferable to an informal process. An important activity within the selection process is the identification of a list of criteria or preferred textbook characteristics. Therefore, textbook selection ideally should rest on a set of pre-selection criteria that can be used in identifying appropriate textbooks and supplemental materials. These criteria should serve as a means for evaluating the relative strengths and weaknesses of a wide range of materials. Many criteria will pertain to specific subject-matter topics and features that grade-level or subject-matter teachers would like to have included in their textbooks. In addition to subject-matter features, some general criteria can be applied to any textbook regardless of subject matter or discipline. For example, the following general criteria were developed by Gunter et al. (1990):

The criteria we choose as important in evaluating instructional materials are: (1) emphasis, (2) unity, (3) coherence, (4) repetition and elaboration, (5) appropriate vocabulary, (6) audience appropriateness, (7) format, and (8) caliber of questions.

- *Emphasis* is related to the components of instruction or the concepts, skills, and values that have been selected as the basis for learning the subject matter.
- *Unity* is related to the direction or the thrust of the book so that all topics and related materials are "orchestrated" toward the achievement of learning the subject. Unity often is achieved through the use of a comprehensive outline upon which the book was developed.
- *Coherence* is related to the level of idea comprehension or to the level of cognitive ability that is required in order to interpret the ideas that are presented in the book as well as the extent to which ideas are interrelated or connected.
- *Repetition and elaboration* is related to the extent to which new content (concepts, skills, and values) is connected to past learning as well as to the extent that the new content is re-addressed or reinforced throughout the text.
- *Appropriate vocabulary* is related to the idea that vocabulary should be suitable for students according to their academic ability.
- *Audience appropriateness* is related to the author's realistic knowledge and consideration for the students who will use the textbook.
- *Format* is related to layout of the textbook, including the use of illustrations, special type, use of color, etc., to emphasize important ideas in order to enhance comprehension.
- *Caliber of questions* is related to the use of various types of questions as a means of motivating student interest and to evoke the higher levels of cognitive thought. (A review of the questions contained in the textbook is a useful barometer for helping to determine the quality of a textbook.) (pp. 51–52)

Many states and districts have developed helpful rating guides for selection committees or individual teachers to use in choosing texts and other learning materials. Valuable analyses of current textbooks are available to teachers from professional sources such as the annual publication of the American Textbook Council, 275 Riverside Drive, New York, NY 10115.

CAN YOU AVOID CHOOSING THE WRONG TEXTBOOK?

Examine five textbooks published for a course you are to teach. Can you identify their strengths and weaknesses without testing these books with students? Why or why not? With a particular class in mind, which of these texts would you most favor using and which is least satisfactory? Why might you need a list of selection characteristics or criteria to help guide your choice? Explain. (See King pp. 38–41.)

Textbook Modification

Once a textbook has been assigned for a particular course or grade level, teachers should attempt to determine textbook suitability in light of student reactions and overall learning results. Once selected, materials may require modification or revision to make them more accurate and more useful or more presentable. According to Dick and Carey (1978),

> There are two basic types of revisions you will consider with your materials. The first is changes that need to be made in the content or substance of the materials to make them more accurate or more effective as a learning tool. The second type of change is related to the procedures employed in using (presenting) your materials. (p. 181)

To a large extent, learning in the social studies requires relatively high abilities in reading and comprehension, which serve as the primary basic learning skills of the social studies; therefore, the first concern of the teacher is the students' ability to read and understand the textbook. Some of the reading problems that students encounter in connection with the textbook include poor vocabulary development; an inability to understand questions; an inability to paraphrase the textbook; a lack of interpretive skills related to maps, charts, and tables; an inability to locate information in the textbooks as well as an inability to use the textbook as a source of information; an inability to recognize important information or to recognize organizational patterns contained within the textbook; and an inability to concentrate on the written narrative because of frequent and minor distractions (Turner, 1980).

Various tests such as the one developed by Edward Fry (1977) have been used by teachers to determine the reading level of their textbook, while other processes have been used to indicate student reading ranges within a class according to grade level and chronological age. Wilson Taylor (1953) developed the "cloze" test as a means of determining whether students were able to

DOES CREATIVE TEACHING RELY ON CREATIVE RESOURCES?

Many creative teachers do not base their courses on textbooks and use texts only as common basic references for the students. Such teachers need a rich collection of supplemental resources. Select a unit you plan to teach and begin to gather references and examples of available materials that you could use. Where will you look for these resources? Keep a specific list for future use.

read their assigned textbooks. Textbooks that prove to be somewhat inappropriate in terms of the capabilities of students will require supplemental resources to accommodate textbook weaknesses. In the case of modest or normal difficulties due to reading problems, Donald O. Schneider and Mary Jo McGee Brown (1980) have recommended that teachers develop study guides using a three-phase strategy to help students read and comprehend the textbook based on: (1) a prereading phase, (2) a reading phase, and (3) a postreading phase. In severe cases in which the textbook exceeds students' capabilities, it may have to be set aside in favor of more appropriate supplemental materials. In addition, some students will need materials that are more in-depth and sophisticated because of their special interests and talents.

Assuming that the textbook will be the primary instructional source, teachers should attempt to conduct a thorough review of the text and to list units and topics (concepts, skills, and values) that they will emphasize throughout the year. Such a review is helpful in formulating a course rationale and course objectives, but more important, such a review will help pinpoint the need for additional materials. In addition, this procedure will help teachers make certain decisions regarding what may be passed over in favor of content to be developed in-depth, thereby helping to identify topics that will require supplemental materials including teacher-constructed items. One valuable continuing assignment related to textbook content, emphases, and recency is to have the class monitor and record current events and developments from other sources and then ask them to write a new final chapter to the text.

As part of instructional design and development, beginning teachers should be taught to produce a series of teaching units. In most situations, the textbook is divided into self-contained teaching units as a general organizational pattern. While teachers may wish to reorganize these units, most supplemental resources provided by the textbook publisher are developed around this organization, including homework assignments, tests, and workbooks. In addition, teachers may wish to develop certain resource units (special topic units) that are not included in the textbook. Resource units may be used to help meet the

FOR A NEW BEGINNING HAVE YOUR STUDENT WRITE THE ENDING

As suggested previously, a valuable assignment for individuals or committees is to have students examine the last chapter(s) of their textbook and ask them to write updated items that reflect recent or current happenings and new or extended information about the period or content. Develop a set of directions for students in writing a new final chapter for their text.

special needs of students, to enhance the textbook program, or to allow teachers to pursue special interests. Typically the resource unit, often developed by a team of instructors, refers to a rich collection of materials from which teachers draw more limited and focused teaching or learning units. In addition, resource units might be used to help students focus on certain knowledge, skills, or value topics that the teacher deems essential in light of student needs.

While most textbooks include a relatively wide range of learning activities, teachers may wish to develop additional learning activities to supplement textbook instruction. For example, teachers may decide to develop an important course project or a series of special activities related to textbook content. Such activities may include simulation games, socio-dramas, scrapbook projects, library research projects, and other activities that require special resources and planning considerations. In addition, an instructor could decide to survey community resources to plan related field trips or to arrange for guest speakers with special knowledge of a topic or skill. Also, teachers may wish to arrange for related media that correspond to the topics in their textbooks from school and curriculum library sources. In some situations, teachers may organize a classroom library center of both nonfictional and fictional books that are appropriate to the topics in the textbook.

The classroom library often contains additional textbooks for the same course of study, thus providing students with multiple textbooks that help to eliminate the weaknesses of a single textbook. In addition, this approach offers a more complete and balanced study of topics and events. The use of additional textbooks can provide a cross-referenced source of information, and certain weaknesses, such as those related to shallow content, can be eliminated. Also, the classroom library should include other sources of reference information including some basic college textbooks, dictionaries, atlases, and biographical sources, as well as books on special topics that may enhance student interest in the course of study.

Supplemental Materials

Instructional materials are important because they can enhance textbook instruction by providing valuable additional materials; however, before purchasing supplemental materials, teachers should identify a list of specific needs that are not being met by the classroom textbook. As a rule of thumb, the selection of supplemental materials should be subject to the same type of scrutiny applied to textbooks to assure that high quality materials will be selected. The appropriateness of supplemental materials should be determined in regard to the extent to which the supplemental materials focus on the topic (in terms of breadth and depth of coverage) as well as according to the level of difficulty that was established by predetermined student needs and attributes. As was the case with textbooks, the quality of supplemental materials can be determined by the following criteria: accuracy, timeliness, presentation, production standards, and format or layout, as well as the physical nature of the materials. In addition, when selecting materials for a social studies instructional program, teachers should choose materials that:

- Promote a motivational impact
- Contain additional information that is not included in the textbook
- Create a more realistic presentation of a topic, event, or process
- Increase the students' interest in the subject matter
- Update the textbook with timely information
- Provide a change of pace from textbook instruction
- Offer a variety of technologies and presentation formats not contained within the textbook
- Help to meet the specialized needs of individual students not addressed within the textbook

In some instances, teachers find supplemental material of such value that they use them instead of a textbook. This is particularly possible if adequate funds are available or if textbook purchasing funds can be used for these resources.

Acquired Materials

Displays of supplemental materials commonly are found in exhibits at state and national professional meetings. In addition, school districts and teachers receive catalogues and advertisements pertaining to a wide range of instructional materials. Teachers normally do not have difficulty locating materials;

they do have difficulty keeping abreast of what is available, assessing quality, and choosing between comparable alternative items. (Also, too frequently, sufficient funds are not available for such purposes.) These difficulties are due, in part, to the wide range of materials that are available currently in the form of reference books, workbooks, visual media, maps, globes and charts, and software products. Professional journals are regular sources of reviews and advertisements of valuable new publications and learning materials. The sources and reviews of many professionally constructed supplemental materials are found in educational journals including publications such as *Social Education* and *The Social Studies* and in journals that address teaching subject areas such as *The Journal of Geography* and *The History Teacher*.

Reference books such as encyclopedias are appropriate for high school students as quick and handy references, and encyclopedias can be used to supplement textbooks by providing charts, tables, graphs, and related sources. High school students also benefit from the use of more in-depth reference sources such as statistical abstracts, specialized dictionaries, reprints of articles, almanacs, brochures, and specialized in-depth books that explore a single subject or issue. Student specialized reports, written and oral, should usually call for at least three such extra references.

Workbooks often are provided by publishers as a textbook supplement. A well-developed, purposeful workbook can be useful as an instructional aid. However, poorly developed workbooks can lead to abuses, such as the wasting of valuable instructional time. While workbooks tend to be popular with many teachers, poorly developed workbooks do little to advance instructional goals. More often than not, workbooks require little more than the completion of time-wasting "hunt-and-find" exercises in which students fill in large numbers of blanks in sentences taken directly from the textbook. Perhaps a better alternative resource would be teacher-designed worksheets that address a specific element of content (concept, skill, or value) or other written tasks developed in connection with specific goals of instruction that are part of teacher-developed unit and lesson assignments.

Visual media supplements such as pictures often are used to promote students' interest in a topic. As was the case with other forms of media, criteria standards should be used in the selection process; moreover, visual media should be selected on the basis that they will be used to help students learn or develop specific elements of content. Therefore, visual media should never be "fill-ins" but should always be linked as directly as possible to the class calendar. According to Hetzner (1977),

> Media experiences should be coordinated with the curriculum and designed to (1) promote the acquisition of procedural skills, (2) allow students to practice individual and group decision making, (3) challenge belief systems, and (4) develop skills that are transferable to a wide range of situations. The purely illustrative use of media is secondary to their use in posing situations that motivate students to engage willingly in problem solving. (p. 229)

The old adage that "a picture is worth a thousand words" is especially appropriate within the instructional setting. Pictures can be used to convey a more accurate image of a place, person, event, or process than can be conveyed in a prose description. Overhead projectors, film projectors, video cassette players, and slide projectors are used to present a variety of visual media, while audio equipment such as tape recorders and compact discs are used to present audio media. Time lines and wall charts are useful media for helping students gain a sense of chronology of an event or a process over time. Posters can be used to convey a single idea or a focused message that is reinforced again in the classroom. In addition, bulletin board posters can be used to encourage good work, remind students of rules, promote positive attitudes, and help students to avoid common mistakes. When designed and developed by students, posters can be used to teach values and attitudes by promoting behaviors related to desired aspects of social conduct—especially the "do's" and "don'ts" of human behavior.

Cartoons (caricatures, etc.) are a form of visual media that provides students with expressed opinions regarding social, economic, or political issues. In many cases the issue is well known to students and the cartoon expresses an irony or poignant point in a satirical message. Political cartoons, often in the form of public criticism, are used to express an opinion regarding the performance of a public figure. As such, these cartoons are used as a form of ridicule which is considered an appropriate form of expression within a democratic society. From a critical thinking perspective, students can be taught to interpret, analyze, and evaluate the subtle messages contained within cartoons. In this regard, students can be assigned the task of expressing their own opinions on an issue creating their own cartoons.

Student involvement in producing supplemental materials provides excellent motivation and learning opportunities. Photographing, assembling, and presenting slide projects have proved valuable innovations. (See Bower, Lobdell, & Swenson [1994] for some excellent ideas for incorporating visuals and activities into your standard history course.) Visual media are especially appropriate when used in connection with the study of current affairs; the study of a historical event is well served through the analysis of political cartoons of the day.

Films and video media have the advantage of recreating an event or process within a realistic setting. The greatest advantage of film media is that it combines seeing and hearing within an action setting. Also, films can encourage student participation and interaction within an instructional setting by directing students to follow the unfolding of an event through eyewitness reports. Because of the length of commercial films, teachers have frequently been frustrated in attempting to use feature-length movies. The advent of the video copy, which can be edited easily and used piecemeal, now provides teachers with a resource especially appealing to students that also can avoid expensive rental and shipping costs, as well as the complexities that can beset school movie projectors. Johnson and Vargas (1994) provide an illustration of the valuable power of using five outstanding examples of the many striking films that are now available on tape. Filmstrips and slides provide many of the same advantages as films while allowing teachers the added advantage of a "stop action" feature by which they can direct student attention to selected points of interest. Transparencies offer many of the same advantages, especially in providing a visual form of information that helps teachers focus student attention on a specific topic or detail of instruction. Graphs, charts, tables, and maps—often in the form of transparencies—can be used to promote classroom discussion. Textbook companies often provide transparencies that are designed specifically for use with the textbook. Maps, globes, and charts are important social studies teaching resources that help students form key concepts and develop numerous skills. At the same time, maps, globes, and charts can be used as the basis for learning activities in which students complete tasks related to important social studies skills. For example, globes help students realize the shape and the relationships that exist on the surface of the earth, while maps often represent an area of the earth on a flat surface that can be studied in greater detail. Various types of charts are used to present information in summary form that is striking and revealing. (Working from text or atlas maps, students can construct and profit from producing large-scale wall maps on paper sheets, cardboard, or on the chalkboard for classroom use.)

Software programs can be used to enhance instruction and promote learning in an alternative textbook setting. Current computer technologies and media allow teachers to use computers as instructional aids in connection with video discs and video cassette recorders. For example, computers with compact disc (CD-ROM drive) capability can provide encyclopedic amounts of information in data base form that can supplement instructional information using narrative and audiovisual resources on almost any social studies topic. For example, as a multimedia approach, interactive video allows teachers to instantly present a map or picture in connection with a historical event. In addition, students can use this media to explore a question or problem through a programmed format that may be coordinated with the teacher's presentation or related to a textbook assignment. Also, these new technologies allow students to generate live-action reports by creating their own videotapes on subjects pertaining to the local community. Computers in the classroom are now providing pupils with new alternative learning formats in addition to or in place of the textbook.

While now considered to be a standard form of technology, television was once heralded as a potential breakthrough in improving learning. To develop the use of television in the classroom, several extensive and expensive programs, often extending beyond individual school districts and even across state borders, were mounted. This medium was seen as a way to bring well-planned and even dramatic learning experiences to small and isolated schools where there is often a lack of helpful instructional materials. Statewide, regional and local public TV and radio networks now offer a great variety of such learning opportunities. (See Chapter 11 for additional descriptive ideas on the use of classroom television.)

Teacher-Constructed Materials

Teachers are capable of producing some of the most effective instructional materials because these materials tend to more closely address the needs of their students. These materials serve diverse purposes such as highlighting issues and events, describing processes, and making comparisons. For example, most schools contain equipment and materials from which teachers and students can construct transparencies, slides, video tapes, and bulletin board displays, posters, and activity sheets. These materials are used to support classroom learning activities, for assignment purposes, or as an aspect of project work. The production of display and instructional materials often requires the use of special equipment such as the opaque projector, duplicating equipment, laminating equipment, and various assembly tools and materials. Through making supplemental and project materials and in using related equipment, students learn numerous valuable skills.

Teachers often collect articles and illustrations in labeled file folders for eventual instructional use. Some teachers have even developed data bases (3 x 5 index card boxes or files of ideas stored on a computer) to collect and organize information they may use for instruction at some future date. If the data base is kept on file cards, each card contains a single idea or item of information (with bibliographic or descriptive notations). These entries are filed according to some type of classification or heading such as "The American Revolution," "Civil Rights," and "Labor Unions." Data files allow for additional entries and for changes in organization since each card is easily relocated within the data base structure. Some teachers keep file folders so labeled to hold news and magazine clippings, previous student reports, and other such items valuable for future student reference and projects. If the data

CREATING YOUR OWN CLASSROOM RESOURCE
AND REFERENCE FILES

Is there such a collection in your social studies department office or in the materials drawers in the school library? How can students be encouraged to contribute to the development of such a resource?

base is kept on computer files, individual filenames can serve as classification headings.

As teachers grow in experience and knowledge of learning resources, they should develop a collection of folders or data files related to a wide range of topics that they might teach. These will contain valuable resources for future units and lessons. Mentors can draw on sources such as newspapers, magazines, professional journals, and commercial advertisements. Teachers can encourage students to submit clippings, articles, and pictures that would be of value for student reports, individual assignments, and group projects as well as being valuable to themselves.

CONCLUSIONS

In this chapter you have learned that inappropriate materials are finding their way into social studies classrooms due in part to a lack of decision-making authority at the local level. According to Gunter et al. (1990),

> Many of the learning problems that students face in schools can be traced to the difficulty of the textbooks and resource materials they are asked to use. No matter how appropriate the rationale for your course or the objectives of a lesson you want to teach, if the textbook materials are inappropriate, learning will be impeded. Furthermore, given the range of interests and abilities of students in a typical classroom, no single information source can possibly serve every student. (p. 63)

Consequently, one of the greatest challenges facing you as a classroom teacher is to find specific ways to improve your instructional programs by using more effective learning materials. Because of the mandated educational demands combined with an array of bureaucratic chores in connection with an overcrowded curriculum, teachers are sometimes left wondering how they will be able to make such improvements.

In spite of this notion, you and your fellow teachers are, in reality, the only ones who can address the local and individual needs of your students. To address local and individual needs, however, teachers must be willing to go beyond the limits of the imposed restrictions and limitations by developing processes and materials that are designed to bring balance within their instructional programs. In other words, teachers are often caught up in rigors of a narrow-focused, test-driven, and mandated program. In spite of these conditions, professional teachers strive to provide an instructional balance in their classrooms by acquiring supplemental instructional materials that will broaden the learning experiences of their students.

More importantly, by using a combination of materials, you should be able to satisfy imposed instructional demands and, at the same time, meet many of the special needs of your students. In other words, you have learned that the key ingredient in the balanced instructional approach is the "right mix" of learning experiences that results from a variety of carefully selected materials that are specifically designed to offset the limitations of textbook-centered programs. All in all, one of the most professional aspects of teaching is associated with the day-to-day instructional judgments and decisions that teachers make as they select instructional approaches and materials to use in presenting content to students.

Because good teaching and learning rely on the selection of instructional materials, these materials should, at best, correspond to the realities of local classroom needs. Therefore, teachers must be willing to improve programs by finding ways to evaluate, select, and modify textbook and supplemental materials. Because of the growing trend toward school-based management, teachers are being asked to take on greater responsibilities for their instructional programs and materials. These responsibilities suggest that as a classroom teacher you also must be willing to stay abreast of new materials, to upgrade your instructional design and planning skills, and to directly participate in decisions related to program design, including all aspects of materials selection and development.

REFERENCES

Banks, J. A. (1985). *Strategies for the social studies*. New York: Longman.

Black, H. (1967). *The American school book*. New York: Wm. Morrow.

Bower, B., Lobdell, J., & Swenson, L. (1994). *History alive! Engaging all learners in the diverse classroom*. Menlo Park, CA: Addison-Wesley.

Dick, W., & Carey, L. (1978). *The systematic design of instruction*. Glenview, IL: Scott, Foresman.

Fry, E. (1977). Fry's readability graph: Clarification, validity, and extensions to level 17. *Journal of Reading, 21*, 242–252.

Gagne, R. M., Briggs, L. J., & Wager, W. W. (1992). *Principles of Instructional Design* (4th ed.). Fort Worth, TX: Harcourt, Brace, Jovanovich.

Gunter, M. A., Estes, T. H., & Schwab, J. H. (1990). *Instruction: A models approach*. Boston: Allyn & Bacon.

Hetzner, D. (1977). Media. In M. E. Gilliom (Ed.), *Practical methods for the social studies* (pp. 228–275). Belmont, CA: Wadsworth.

Johnson, J., & Vargas, C. (1994). The smell of celluloid in the classroom: Five Great movies that teach. *Social Education, 58*, 109–113.

King, D.C. (1977). "Social studies texts: How to recognize good ones and survive bad ones." *Learning, 5*, 38–41.

Nerbovig, M. H. (1970). *Unit planning: A model for curriculum development*. Worthington, OH: Charles A. Jones.

Patton, W. E. (1980). Updating the outdated in textbooks. In W. F. Patton (Ed.), *Improving the use of social studies textbooks* (Bulletin 63, pp.

1–8). Washington, DC: National Council for the Social Studies.

Postman, N., & Weingartner, C. (1969). *Teaching as a subversive activity*. New York: Dell.

Saxe, D. W. (1991). *Social studies in the schools: A history of the early years*. New York: State University of New York Press.

Schneider, D. O., & McGee-Brown, M. J. (1980). Helping students study and understand their social studies textbooks. In W. F. Patton (Ed.), *Improving the use of social studies textbooks* (Bulletin 63, pp. 9–20). Washington, DC: National Council for the Social Studies.

Taylor, W. L. (1953). Cloze procedures: A new tool for measuring readability. *Journalism Quarterly*, (Fall 1953, pp. 415–433).

Turner, T. N. (1980). Making the social studies textbook a more effective tool for less able students. In W. F. Patton (Ed.), *Improving the use of social studies textbooks* (Bulletin 63, pp. 21–26). Washington, DC: National Council for the Social Studies.

Wade, R. C. (1993). Content analysis of the social studies textbooks: A review of ten years of research. *Theory and Research in Social Education, 21*, 232–256.

Assessing Instructional Effectiveness and Learning Outcomes

INTRODUCTION

Indications of how well an instructional product or system performs are best obtained from systematically gathered evidence. The means of gathering, analyzing, and interpreting such evidence are collectively called methods of *evaluation*. . . .(Gagne, Briggs, & Wager, 1992, pp. 331—332)

In this chapter you will learn that evaluation includes the decisions and judgments that teachers make regarding the quality of instruction and learning materials, approaches, and outcomes of student achievement as a result of instruction. As a component of design, evaluation helps teachers to (1) assess the effectiveness of their teaching and (2) make grading decisions related to student achievement. Instructionally, assessment can be used for the following purposes:

1. *The clarification of assumptions.* Assumptions regarding the underlying reasons for instruction.
2. *The clarification of learning processes.* Ways of thinking that are needed by students for instructional purposes.
3. *The induction of self-motivated learning.* Learning through the development of one's own abilities and desires.
4. *The establishment of learning standards.* Standards that are used to measure the achievement of instructional goals.
5. *The assessment of cumulative results.* A comprehensive measurement that includes all aspects of instruction, but especially course or unit goals.

6. *The assessment of instructional effectiveness.* To determine the extent to which the instructional program was successful in meeting the goals of teaching.

Before discussing instructional design related to the assessment of teaching, certain important technical terms should be addressed and clarified. Because the terms *test, measurement,* and *evaluation* will be used throughout this chapter, the following definitions are provided by Gronlund and Linn (1990):

> A *test* is "An instrument or systematic procedure for measuring a sample of behavior"; a *measurement* is "The process of obtaining a numerical description of the degree to which an individual possesses a particular characteristic"; and *evaluation* is "The systematic process of collecting, analyzing, and interpreting information to determine the extent to which pupils are achieving instructional objectives." (p. 5)

Evaluative approaches and programs are the product of four important instructional processes, which usually include the development of a systematic plan of action, the identification of clearly stated evaluation objectives, the use of appropriate techniques of evaluation, and the wise use of test results.

Developing a Systematic Plan of Evaluation

A systematic plan of evaluation is a vital part of any instructional program. This plan serves as a blueprint for coordinating the collection of assessment information. Therefore, a systematic plan of action is developed to schedule various measurements that will help in monitoring teaching and achievement. A plan of action is usually grounded in an evaluation process that reflects a philosophical position regarding the purpose of instruction. An important design decision pertains to the selection of a *rationale* statement that addresses the conditions of assessment.

Evaluation Rationale

Typically, a rationale statement is based on one of two evaluation approaches: *criterion-referenced evaluation* or *norm-referenced evaluation*. A criterion-referenced rationale is based on the belief that instruction and evaluation should reveal the extent to which each student's achievement has met performance standards (for example, "70 percent correct"). The norm-referenced rationale is based on the extent to which student achievement is measured against the achievement of a large group of representative students with similar attributes (Borich, 1992). For instance, if the teacher decides that assessment outcomes should be based on measurements that sort students according to levels of achievement, a norm-referenced evaluative approach would be appropriate. On the other hand, if the teacher decides that assessment outcomes should be based on measuring the extent to which students have achieved preset instructional goals, a criterion-referenced evaluation approach would be appropriate (Pratt, 1980). Instructionally, the results of evaluation would then be used to assign grades and to make changes in the program. In addition, the decision of whether to use a criterion-referenced or a norm-referenced approach influences the evaluation practices that will be used in design. This decision affects the patterns of instruction, basic relationships, and the schedules of various assessments for monitoring effectiveness and learning outcomes.

Subsequently, instructional evaluation often is classified according to certain assigned tasks that are related to making decisions and monitoring effectiveness. This classification typically includes diagnostic testing, formative evaluation, and summative evaluation, which often serve the following purposes: (1) the diagnosis of student readiness for instruction, (2) in-progress or formative assessment as an indication of learning while instruction is taking place, and (3) a final assessment of student achievement of the goals of instruction (Pratt, 1980).

Developmentalists tend to support the idea that readiness and pacing are important factors in determining the extent to which new subjects can be easily learned. In addition, the principles of readiness include the idea that a certain amount of prior instruction should precede the teaching of a new subject. Therefore, some form of diagnostic testing is necessary to measure the status of current knowledge and entry behaviors, or the students' level of social studies knowledge, skills, and values that pertain to the topic of instruction. Dick and Carey (1978) point out the importance of identifying entry behaviors.

> If you have identified specific entry behaviors, then it is in your best interest to measure these prior to having students begin instruction so you know whether they have the entry behaviors which you identified as important. If you have no explicit entry behaviors for a particular set of instructions, then, of course, you will have no test. (p. 90)

In criterion-referenced testing, readiness tests should be determined by the teacher's instructional objectives. Therefore, design is based on a behavioral objective design model. **Behavioral objectives** are instructional objectives that are based on an observable behavior related to the object of instruction that the student should be able to express or demonstrate in some measurable fashion. An example might be, "To list three reasons why the Civil War began."

However, if the teacher is certain that students are well prepared for a new topic or skill and if the teacher is certain that students have no prior knowledge of the topic, there is no need for diagnostic testing. When diagnostic testing is required, it can take many forms, ranging from a diagnostic instrument, often referred to as a pretest, that evaluates the minimal levels of specific items of information, skills, or values. Teachers might select a few general items from a posttest scored according to the *50 percent rule*. According to this rule, minimal readiness levels are attained when the class as a whole is able to answer approximately half of these items correctly before beginning instruction. If the whole class does not meet this standard, additional preparatory instruction would be indicated.

Formative (in-progress) testing provides information pertaining to the completion of a certain amount of instruction. The main purpose of formative assessment is to indicate teaching weaknesses and misunderstandings in order to make midstream corrections. According to Gagne et al. (1992),

> Evidence of an instructional program's worth is sought for use in making decisions about how to revise the program while it is being developed. In other words, the evidence collected and interpreted during the phase of development is used to *form* the instructional program itself. (p. 335)

Therefore, formative evaluation is closely associated with the development of instructional programs and plays a functional role in determining the extent to which one program, approach, or set of materials is superior to another program, approach, or set of materials. As a result, formative evaluation tends to consist of several stages of evaluation (or points of judgment) within the systematic plan of evaluation. According to Smith and Ragan (1993), formative evaluation should consist of four evaluation stages: "(1) design reviews, (2) expert reviews, (3) learner validation, and (4) ongoing evaluation" (p. 389).

Summative evaluation attempts to measure student achievement once instruction has been completed. A norm-referenced approach would sort students according to a range of results from the highest score to the lowest score. A criterion-referenced approach would measure the extent of change in student behaviors in light of the objectives of the unit or course. Kemp (1985) describes how test items are related to instructional objectives:

> It is customary to derive test items from the objectives, with subject content or task items being used for detail. Once you are satisfied with the extent of completeness of the learning objectives, you are ready to develop ways for evaluating them. (p. 161)

As Gross, Messick, Chapin, and Sutherland (1978) point out, one of the main purposes of summative results is to award grades according to the achievement of the instructional objectives.

> Summative evaluation means a rounding up of the results of instruction. This
> phase of evaluation occurs at termination points of units or courses. . . .The pur-
> pose of summative evaluation is to measure and interpret the students' progress
> in a global fashion. The results are benchmarks or guideposts to future instruc-
> tional planning and interpreted data about student learning that can be commu-
> nicated to parents and students. (pp. 62–63)

Validity and Reliability Standards

As an aspect of systematic planning, assessment items should meet the standards of validity, reliability, and usability. All test instruments are assessed
according to these three important criteria or standards in which "The term
validity refers to an instrument's truthfulness, *reliability* to its consistency and
usability to its practicality" (Green, 1975, p. 137). Kemp (1985) also explains
that a test is valid when

> it specifically measures what was supposedly learned in terms of the subject con-
> tent or task as specified by learning objectives for the unit or topic. (p. 175)

Kemp further states that "Reliability refers to the ability of a test to produce
consistent results whenever used" (p. 177).

The validity of a test is based on the assumption that the instructional program (course, unit, or lesson and its related materials) is valid; therefore, test
validity can be determined by comparing each of the test items with the corresponding elements from within the program. The closer the correlation
between test items and the elements of instruction, the greater the relative
validity of the test. Hopkins and Stanley (1981) describe validity as

> a measure is how well it fulfills the function for which it is being used. Regardless
> of the other merits of a test, if it lacks validity in the information it provides it is
> useless. (p. 76)

With the use of behavioral objectives, instructional designers use another type of validity called *content validity*. Content validity determines the degree to which test items correlate with instructional objectives. Also, the use of a certain type of test item involves a form of validity known as *construct validity*. Construct validity relates to the extent to which the form, content, and structure of a test influence the results on the test. Langdon (1973) further defines and describes the validation processes for improving teaching:

> Validation has been aptly described as a "debugging" process. It can be viewed as either a post-design or in-process method of designing activity, depending on time and need for implementation. Hopefully, it would be the latter. More specifically, validation is testing to see that the students who have experienced an instructional design have in fact learned. Where learning has not been effective, under validation procedures, the instruction is revised and tested again until learning is effective. (p. 9)

A reliable test is a test that provides approximately the same results every time it is administered to students. Thus, a reliable test provides consistent results with the same or similar group(s). Therefore: "A reliable (accurate) instrument is one which is consistent enough that subsequent measurements give approximately the same numerical status to the thing or person being measured" (Green, 1975, p. 143).

Test and item reliability are affected by the form and the structure of the test or test item. For example, an error in a test item would affect its reliability, and should students not be able to apply some part of the test, such as a map key, test reliability also would be affected. Bad wording is a common source of unreliability of tests and test items. In addition, the emotional and physiological condition of students taking the test could affect test reliability. For example, if the students were cold, hungry, angry, or fearful, test results could be affected. An extremely long test or a complex test or test item could also cause fatigue and discourage students. Various types of coefficient strategies are often used to determine test reliability. Test reliability is increased when numerous test items are included rather than a small number of items. It is possible that a reliable test may not be a valid test; for example, a test given to American history students would not be valid with world history students. At the same time, a test that is valid should also be reliable because reliability and validity are interrelated.

The intended use of a test or test item will be different according to whether a criterion-referenced approach or a norm-referenced approach is used. A process called **item analysis** is commonly used to identify defective test items. In addition, item analysis can be used to address the relative difficulty of levels of test items as well as the ability of test items to discriminate between stu-

WHAT CAN YOU DO ABOUT CONFUSED TEST RESULTS?

Test item analysis also is valuable in determining the effectiveness of a teacher's instruction and the quality of test items. If generally poor students do very well on a test, what are the possible implications? If typically strong students do poorly on several items, what steps should you take before establishing a final grade?

dents with knowledge and students without knowledge. Therefore, the overall function of item analysis is to determine the effectiveness of each test item regarding whether or not it is answered according to its intended use (Gronlund & Linn, 1990, pp. 244–258). The purpose of item analysis for norm-referenced test items is mainly to detect if test items discriminate between high and low achievers, whereas the purpose of item analysis for criterion-referenced test items is mainly to determine if test items are effective in measuring the extent to which a goal of instruction was achieved.

Identification of Evaluation Objectives

Identifying a set of evaluation objectives is a useful way to help teachers integrate an evaluation process within an instructional program. As a general rule, it is important to consider the instruction and evaluation together so that evaluation becomes an important aspect of teaching. In addition, the development of evaluative objectives is a useful means for identifying the type of assessment techniques that will be employed in an overall teaching plan. For this purpose, Gronlund and Linn (1990) have identified some general principles that relate to the identification of evaluation objectives. They include specifying:

- *Exactly what is to be evaluated according to a recognized priority*. In developing a social studies unit, the teacher would carefully describe what will be evaluated. Evaluation is more than a random sample of the content presented to students since it differentiates between what is important and what is ancillary. In addition, this instructional task has the added benefit of helping the teacher clearly identify the intended learning outcomes.

- *The types of assessment instruments that will be used before, during, and after instruction.* These instruments would be used to diagnose prior student knowledge, the formative development of learning during instruction, and the summative results of students achievement following instruction.
- *The types of evaluation items that will be developed in accordance with selected measurement instruments.* As part of this process, the teacher should consider the strengths and weaknesses of assessment items (such as true/false, multiple-choice matching, essay, checklist, and so forth) in accordance with the overall goals of instruction.
- *A variety of evaluation techniques to be used in measuring student learning.* For example, knowledge is best measured through the use of objective tests, while skill development is best measured with performance exercises. In addition, higher levels of thinking, as well as critical thinking, are better indicated on essay tests. Consequently, a comprehensive evaluation program demands the use of varied types of measurements, and a well-planned test requires a variety of test items.
- *Evaluation approaches that do not rely on pencil-and-paper tests but include such items as assorted assignments, performances, activities, observations, and interactions with individual students.* While tests offer helpful indications of learning, they are not as accurate or as precise as some would think. All tests include measurement errors that are difficult to detect, such as students' guessing on a true and false test or the inclusion of semantic clues that some students detect while others do not. Therefore, evaluation objectives should include a variety of elements in addition to tests and standard test items.
- *Means to improve instruction once instruction has taken place based on the idea that information gained through evaluation should be used to revise instruction.*
- *The factors and weighing of those factors that will be used to determine student grades.* Some of these factors include test scores, assignments, performances, and tasks. In addition, the evaluation objectives should include the means that will be used to record and report student grades. (pp. 6–10)

Once evaluation objectives have been identified and stated, the teacher is ready to begin the task of test construction. Because of the variety of techniques available for test construction, a review of the techniques of evaluation is in order.

Techniques of Evaluation

Evaluation techniques vary according to instructional needs; therefore, in assessing the effectiveness of instruction and achievement results, the assessment items should be appropriately matched to the type of instructional component (concept, skill, or value) that is being assessed. For example, techniques that are used to evaluate cognitive learning (for example, knowledge of facts) often rely on the collection of numeric data gathered on objective tests.

Techniques that are used to evaluate the extent to which a skill has been acquired often are based on observational and performance techniques. On the other hand, scales and priority lists are sometimes used as indicators of attitudes and value acquisition, whereas complex learning related to the acquisition of in-depth knowledge or advanced intellectual skills is often evaluated through various forms of the essay test.

Cognitive Objectives and Objective Test Items

The development of objective test items that measure cognitive learning related to the acquisition of information (facts, concepts, and generalizations) requires rigorously applied procedures. According to Green (1975), rigor in test construction can be enhanced by the following processes: "(1) the . . . careful analysis of objectives, of course content, and of texts to determine test content; (2) . . . administration to a representative sample of the target population; (3) . . . item analysis and item editing and revision to eliminate faulty items; (4) . . . the establishment of standardized scores which represent the levels of performance of the sample of the population or the criterion group to whom the test was administered" (p. 56).

Because objective test items require specific responses to a statement, they often are limited to the recall items of information. The advantage of objective test items is their ability to provide valid and reliable measures of student learning over large amounts of material. Objective test items include true/false items, matching or ranking items, multiple-choice items (or variations of multiple-choice items), and short-answer or completion items.

True/False Items

True/false items commonly are used to measure learning because they are easy to construct; however, the ease of construction is often the result of the teacher's taking items verbatim from the textbook or worksheet. In addition, these items often allow guessing with a relative high probability (50–50 chance) of guessing the correct answer. A problem arises when true/false items require a great amount of qualification to be true, thus suggesting the answer. The following example does *not* require such lengthy qualifications.

Example:

_F_ The Clinton administration favored decreased taxes in order to reduce the national debt.

True/false items have the advantage of being easy to construct and efficient to administer. Because students are able to respond quickly to these items, more items can be included on a given test. Consequently, a greater sample size can be collected, which increases the validity of the test. In constructing true/false test items, it is recommended that:

- The entire statement should be either true or false.
- Minutia should not be the basis for a false answer.
- The statement should be short and clear.
- The statements should not be taken verbatim from the textbook.
- Negative statements should be avoided.
- Quantitative statements should be used rather than qualitative statements (for example, "Five people were killed in the attack" rather than "Some people were killed in the attack").
- Controversial statements include a source (for example, "Judge Jones ruled busing as unacceptable").

See Kelly (1958), Green (1975), and Gronlund and Linn (1990) for a detailed explanation and description of these processes, as well as other general sources related to the development of tests and measurement in education.

Some teachers try to avoid the weaknesses of true/false testing by having students correct items they have marked "false." To avoid guessing, others may, for example, take two points off an error but only one point off for leaving an answer blank. Test experts hold different opinions on such modifications. The teacher really concerned about the deficiency of true/false questions may be wise to avoid their use.

Multiple-Choice Items

Multiple-choice items are preferred by experts to most other forms of objective test items, mainly because these items allow teachers to measure higher levels of thinking ability and the guess factor is more limited. At the same time, multiple-choice items tend to be difficult to construct because all alternative options or distracters must be plausible answers. A multiple-choice item consists of a stem, the correct answer, and a set of alternative choices or distracters.

Example:

1. In the upper midwest, which state has the largest population of Native Americans?
   a. Iowa
   b. Wisconsin
   c. Minnesota
   d. Indiana
   e. Illinois

In constructing multiple-choice test items, it is recommended that:

- Necessary instructions for students should be included.

- The central issue or problem should be stated in the stem.
- Alternative choices should be short statements (correct answer should be the same length as the other detractors).
- Pattern responses such as A, B, C, D, E and A, B, C, D, E should be avoided.
- The stem should be stated in positive rather than negative terms.
- Controversial statements should include an expert source ("According to the Secretary of Education").
- A given test item should not suggest the answer to another test question.

Matching Items

A matching item is an abbreviated form of a multiple-choice item. Typically, these items consist of two columns in which items in the first column are to be matched with items in the second column.

Example:

Column A
_____ 1. The Stamp Act
_____ 2. The Boston Tea Party
_____ 3. Lexington/Concord

Column B
A. Minutemen
B. "Mohawks"
C. Committees of Correspondence
D. Sons of Liberty

Matching items have the advantage of saving space, and they are efficient because they allow students to respond to a relatively large number of items in a short period of time. Matching, however, is characterized as a process of elimination, and once several matches are made the remaining answers may be guessed. Therefore, it is recommended that at least one more foil in the second column be included to avoid guessing on the last items to be matched. Also, the following recommendations are suggested by experts:

- The number of items in a column should not exceed ten elements in one question.
- Both the statements and the response items in each column should be homogeneous in nature (for example, a list of countries might be matched by a list of agricultural products).
- The columns should be relatively short and concise.
- The premise statements (the statements to be matched by the responses in the right column) should be arranged for clarity, and the responses should be arranged alphabetically or chronologically.
- All responses in the right column should be on the same page.

Short-Answer Items

The most common type of short-answer item is a completion item in which a statement with an important idea is left blank so that students can add a specific factor of information to the blank space.

Example:

The cotton gin was invented by _____ .
The war of _____ was caused in part by the impressment of seamen.

Short-answer items are easy to construct when simple recall answers are required. When higher cognitive elements are to be measured, however, completion items are difficult to construct. One part of this difficulty results when unexpected answers that have some merit are given. At the same time, short-answer items are well suited for responses that require students to demonstrate knowledge of a definition. While these items may contain context clues, they also limit students' ability to guess as compared to true/false items. The following recommendations are given for constructing a short-answer test item:

- The phrase or statement should include enough information to inspire the knowledgeable response.
- Syntax clues should be avoided.
- The length of the blank space should be uniform and not broken into segments.
- Each correct answer should receive one test point (the required completeness of response should be established prior to giving the test to students).
- Short-answer test items should be reserved for measuring information recall.

WHEN CAN A WRONG ANSWER BE RIGHT?

If a student can give a rational reason for his or her "wrong" answer, what procedure would you follow in resolving the issue which would satisfy the student as well as the rest of the class?

Rearranged and Ranking Items

Rearranged items, similar to multiple-choice, have an added variation that requires respondents to rearrange the factors according to some order (sequence or chronology).

Example:

1. Reorder the countries of Chili, Argentina, and Brazil by size of geographic area ranging from large to small.
   a. Chili, Argentina, and Brazil
   b. Argentina, Brazil, and Chili
   c. Brazil, Argentina, and Chili
   d. Brazil, Chili, and Argentina
   e. Chili, Brazil, and Argentina

In constructing rearranged items, it is recommended that the string of items to be rearranged be limited to three items. In such queries students may be asked to arrange items by size, importance, length, or time sequence. The only satisfactory way to employ such lists is in groups of three; otherwise, accurate marking is impossible.

Example:

Place the following events leading to the Civil War in proper order by checking the middle occurrence:
John Brown's Raid (√)
Kansas-Nebraska Act
Election of Lincoln

CAN YOU MAKE A CASE FOR COMBINATIONS?

What are the arguments for balancing objective-type items with an essay section(s) in a unit test?

Assessing Complex Achievement Through Essay Tests

Essay items are often used to evaluate the results of complex learning related to the higher levels thinking in the social studies. At the same time, essay questions are often poorly crafted, which diminishes the potential value of this type of assessment. The advantages of this type of assessment are significant. They encourage students to express their ideas and indicate students' ability to demonstrate their analytical skills, detect cause-and-effect relationships, develop hypotheses, formulate conclusions, defend decisions, reveal depth of knowledge, comprehend complex ideas, and organize and integrate information. In addition, essay questions help students develop their ability to organize the elements of a topic and to improve writing competencies such as spelling. Also, as a result of writing essay answers, students' word use competencies are enhanced by the application of newly acquired special words, terms, and concepts, especially when applied to a given situation, setting, or problem.

The disadvantages of essay tests include that they are difficult to evaluate and score. Even though some essay tests focus on a very limited aspect of subject-matter content, teachers often write questions that are open to various responses and interpretations. Also, two of the most limiting factors in administering essay tests are the amount of time that is needed to correct and grade students' responses and the question of how to deal with spelling and syntax errors.

To avoid subjectivity in evaluating student essays, teachers should outline or write out sample answers. Such answers might include complete examples and explanations or those that are minimally sufficient. This helps ensure against charges of unfair grading.

Open-ended and generally stated essay questions are a form of the *extended response* essay question. This type of question allows students wide-ranging freedom in selecting, organizing, and writing an answer using all the information and resources that they can muster in response to the question. They are particularly helpful in promoting students' ability to express themselves in writing and in revealing the extent of their knowledge of a comprehensive topic. Depending on teacher goals for a class, such examinations may be designated as "open-book" and students allowed to use texts or other references. The problem with extended response questions is that they allow wide-ranging responses that are difficult to evaluate and score. To correct this deficiency, *restricted response* questions reflecting specific goals are recommended. Restricted response essay questions limit students' responses. At the same time, however, restricted response questions tend to defeat an important advantage of the essay question, which is to allow students greater freedom of response.

Examples:

Extended: What should the American government do about Japanese trade policy?

Restricted: Should the federal government restrict the import of Japanese automobiles in light of recent information about dumping surplus production in the United States market? (Be sure to consider the effects of restricted trade policy on American exports to Japan.)

Assessing Skills Through Performance and Observation Techniques

Teachers should remember that pencil-and-paper tests are only one part of an evaluation plan. Numerous other assessment techniques are related to performance tasks and observation as well as a host of informal insights that are gained by constant contact and classroom interaction. From homework and committee assignments to oral work and book reports, teachers have many opportunities to assess pupil progress. Even behaviorally stated objectives can and should be assessed according to performance activities as well as various types of teacher observations. Formally planned performance assessments require specific task performances that will be observed and recorded by the teacher. As with other assessment techniques, performance/observational assessment techniques also contain certain biases. In particular, observation techniques are threatened by focusing intensely on just one aspect of performance. According to Green (1975),

> Unfortunately, however, observation-evaluators often fail to observe all the important elements of the performance; they may permit the total evaluation to be influenced unduly by one aspect which biases their judgment, or they may direct their attention to different elements in each of several consecutive performances. Check lists and rating scales are important tools, which can help the observer-evaluator overcome problems such as those noted above. (p. 100)

Pencil-and-paper tests may not be an appropriate way to evaluate the extent to which students have acquired or mastered a skill. Techniques such as observation and product analysis may be more meaningful ways to ascertain skill achievement. These two techniques require that students actually demonstrate the extent to which a target skill has been acquired or mastered.

Performance Observation

Performance-observation evaluations are commonly associated with evaluating the extent to which students have mastered newly acquired knowledge and skills. In the social studies, geographic skills related to map work are often evaluated on the basis of the student's ability to demonstrate these skills. A simple means of exercising performance observation is to ask the class or an individual student to demonstrate learned knowledge and skills through performance. Wiggins (1993) explains:

The word *perform* in common parlance means to execute a task or process and to bring it to completion. Our ability to perform with knowledge can therefore be assessed only as we produce some work of our own, using a repertoire of knowledge and skills and being responsive to the particular tasks and context at hand. (p. 202)

Checklists and Rating Sheets

Checklists and rating sheets are a systematic way to record student progress through a frequency or rating format in which specific behaviors are recorded when observed. Rating sheets are relatively easy to construct and can be used to measure a wide range of skills that are based on the direct observation of specific performances. Moreover, checklists and rating sheets help to limit biases and to improve assessments that otherwise plague unspecified observations. Most checklists and rating sheets include lists of important behaviors that the teacher identified as important elements in the acquisition or mastery level of skill development. Therefore, certain patterns of responses can be diagnostic as well as indicate acquisition level of mastery.

Notes, Diaries, and Logs

Observations could be recorded in the form of notes, diaries, or other forms of writing. In addition, teachers may use observational techniques regarding student responses to specific learning tasks. For example, observation may be used to indicate students' readiness to learn a new concept or skill. Comments regarding students' attitude toward the learning task, the status of their study habits, expressions of their social skills, and their ability to perform prerequisite tasks are just a few examples of topics of interest to the teacher. Summary notes regarding students with particular learning problems are especially helpful in assessing those problems. In addition, teachers can use anecdotal notes to record unanticipated behaviors and results that were not included on checklists or rating sheets. Because of bias, experts often recommend that teachers refrain from overgeneralizing or making conclusions about the behavior of individual students.

Product Assessment

In addition, the results of student work in the form of products can be collected for evaluation purposes. Product evaluation should be based on a specific set of criteria and specified standards that are clearly communicated ahead of time. By collecting a systematic sample of student work, the teacher is able to detect any changes in student work. These patterns may pertain to the whole class or to individual students. Samples of student work should include pupil notebooks, completed worksheets, student projects, reports, and other types of student assignments that require the completion of a specific task(s).

In recent times, school districts have begun to use student portfolios in addition to or instead of tests in measuring achievement. This change is an

IS SELF-CORRECTION A GOOD IDEA?

Why should students mark their own test papers rather than being asked to mark those of other students? If this approach is taken, what precautions should be taken to control students' temptation to ignore mistakes?

attempt to encourage better quality work and higher standards for students in what is being termed "alternative assessment" or "authentic assessment." Typically a portfolio would include specific examples of student work including written work, map work, and completed tasks that are designed to demonstrate the students' ability to perform more complex tasks. Portfolio assessment has some weakness related to the scoring process. Also, portfolio evaluation is time consuming and sometimes unreliable. In addition, in some states, portfolio assessment has been claimed to indicate poor levels of performance and has been used to call for higher instructional standards (see *The Dallas Morning News*, Education Section, March 23, 1993).

For many generations teachers have been over-dependent on the results of paper-and-pencil tests that concentrate on the memorized production of factual content. Often such tests are clearly unreliable and invalid. Few teachers take the time and effort to construct truly satisfactory examinations; yet such measures frequently are the major source of evaluation and grading. To promote a more appropriate and broader base for evaluation, especially as it relates to the assessment of important skill competencies and attitudinal and value growth and application, the following limitation is recommended:

Conventional testing of knowledge gained from pencil-and-paper instruments should not constitute more than 20 percent of any evaluation program.

Assessing Values and Behaviors Through Analysis and Reasoning Approaches

Educators often complain that it is difficult to construct evaluation items for the affective domain (for example, the domain of values, attitudes, and emotions). Value and attitude instruction is ultimately aimed at helping students confront and deal with values and attitudes rationally and logically rather than emotionally. Thus, we are measuring the ability of students to deal rationally with a given situation by helping them confront the consequences of values and attitudes on behavior and on the consequences of various actions. Regarding the study of values related to objects and actions, assessment should focus on the ability of students to recognize the effects of values and attitudes on behavior. Students should understand the relative benefit (or worth) of objects and actions to one's welfare and well-being as well as to other persons involved. Values have been assessed by such techniques as self-reporting inventories, story completions, and role playing. Analytical exercises in which the student clarifies an issue by ordering elements according to a priority are also helpful. In situations where social issues involve two-party conflicts, solutions are proposed by first identifying the underlying values and attitudes that contribute to the issue or by proposing a solution that can be defended according to some overriding value position.

Scales

Self-reporting inventories are often based on a scale in which the students register their attitudes toward an object, idea, or activity.

Example: Social Studies Activities Scale

Task Work	Liked Task	Okay Task	Disliked Task
1. map work	X		
2. oral reports		X	
3. worksheets			X

Story Completion and Role Plays

Also, attitudes may be assessed by having students complete a story or add an ending to the story. Typically, story completion rests on a criterion related to student's ability to comprehend the nature of the social issue or conflict and to deal with it reasonably and effectively. Prior to the story completion exercises, the student would receive instruction regarding the use of democratic processes or some form of moral reasoning that could be generally applied to almost any situation involving controversy or conflict. This instruction can be completed individually or in a group through class discussions, in committees, or in paired exercises between two pupils. A valuable modification here is to have students role-play the possible conclusion(s) to the story, event, or problem being studied. Precise evaluation is difficult, but teachers can gain valuable insights into pupil beliefs and attitudes by observation and from subsequent class discussion of the action. When such skits or role plays are employed, they can be especially helpful in formative evaluations, indicating emphases and options that may be in order for an entire class or the needs of certain members.

Priority Lists

In the study of drug abuse, students might be asked to list important reasons for *not* using drugs and then to rank the listed reasons according to their importance. Following this task, each student would be asked to justify his or her list. The basis for evaluation would rest on the ability to develop a list of priorities and to present rational reasons for the order of the priorities according to personal, group, and societal concerns. According to Girod (1973), values and attitudes should not be assessed in the same manner as cognitive performances for the following reasons:

> With attitudinal objectives we defeat our purpose if we tell students that they are to perform certain behaviors consistent with selected attitudes. Attitude objectives are not performance objectives in that we will evaluate the worth of a student in terms of his attitudes. Rather, we are assessing our worth. To retain that fine balance between the students' honesty and their desire to please it seems only useful to not state specific attitudinal statements to students. (pp. 87–88)

Self-Evaluation

Students can be a source of assessment provided that the assessment is based on specific criteria with set standards that are communicated to students prior to its execution. With an "assessment form" based on graded variation standards, students can present the completed form to the teacher as the basis for discussing their achievements and the quality of their work. An advantage of student self-evaluation is that it encourages them to think about their responsibilities related to various learning tasks. A problem with self-evaluation is that some students are unrealistic about the quality of their work. Bright students may underrate themselves. Less successful students may tend to upgrade their performance. However, studies of self-evaluation indicate that correlations between students' and teachers' marks are .60 to .80, certainly high enough to justify self-grading, especially since students learn from such opportunities.

CAN YOU SUGGEST WAYS TO COUNTERACT THE NEGATIVE ASPECTS OF SELF-EVALUATION?

Explain some steps you can take to avoid the difficulties that lead some teachers to be negative about most aspects of student self-evaluation.

Test Development Guidelines

The following suggestions are included to help teachers construct better tests:

1. The vocabulary of directions should be clear, concise, and appropriate for students.

2. Test directions should be included for each section of the test in which different test items are clustered.

3. When possible, try out the test on some representative students before administering the test for achievement purposes.

4. All students should take the same test at the same time and be allowed ample time to complete the test.

5. Emphasize items related to your key goals, including statewide and national essentials.

6. Include assessment items related to skills and attitudes and values as well as subject-matter content.

7. Avoid the following test item elements: trivial items, spelling errors, and poor sentence structure; trick questions; compound questions (questions with multiple parts); suggestions or clues; identical textbook language; parallel items in which one question suggests the answer to another question; and words such as *always, never, surely,* and *forever.*

8. Group test items by type, such as true/false and multiple choice, and arrange according to difficulty beginning with easier items.

9. Review test items for the inclusion of higher thinking levels and for a variety of question types.

10. Scramble the responses of true/false and multiple-choice items so that they do not fall into patterns, such as the chronology in which the material was presented.

11. Be sure the question has a clear answer that is obvious to the knowledgeable student.

12. Develop a test bank from which different forms of the test can be constructed. Attempt to prepare at least two versions of the test for security purposes so that students taking a makeup test do not gain an advantage over the other students. This helps to limit the importance of communication between students from different class periods.

13. Complete an item analysis on each item to eliminate items that are too easy or too difficult. Item analysis is done after the test is administered to evaluate each test item in regard to whether all students missed or passed the item.

14. Group work is often evaluated according to results, products, or presentations. In addition, teachers sometimes attempt to evaluate each group on its ability to cooperate, stay on task, fulfill individual responsibilities, and

convey positive attitudes when groups or committees were meeting. Cooperative learning, for example, tends to be very valuable in encouraging students to help each other meet their responsibilities. Stronger students often tutor weaker students in the various aspects of the assignment. In a cooperative learning activity, the teacher may evaluate the performance of a randomly selected group member; therefore, every student must be prepared to represent the group as a whole.

Wise Use of Test Results

Test results should play an important role in designing instruction and evaluating instructional outcomes. Therefore, a systematic plan of action should be developed at the same time courses, units, and lessons are being planned in order to monitor and modify instruction, identify a specific set of evaluation objectives that can be used to develop an evaluation program, identify the type of assessment items to be used to measure achievement, and to establish assessment schedules according to course, unit, and lesson placement. An assessment schedule would be used to place diagnostic, formative, and summative instruments within the overall plan of instruction. Test results from these instruments would be used to perform specific functions.

The results of diagnostic tests, for instance, should suggest that either the current instructional program is or is not compatible with the experiences and abilities of students. In addition, diagnostic results might help to identify students who are underachieving in light of their indicated potential ability. In general, test results also can provide teachers with a certain level of confidence that current programs are compatible with students' abilities and that students will most likely be able to achieve the goals of instruction. In a more refined sense, test results can identify areas that need a greater instructional emphasis.

Monitoring changes in student behavior through test results is an important means of deciding whether suitable instructional progress is being made and whether certain additional changes in instruction might further enhance the rate of learning (Airasian, 1971). In-progress test results should be used to make decisions about (1) the effectiveness of the instructional materials, (2) the instructional techniques and the methods used to present instruction, and (3) the activities, assignments, and learning tasks that are being used to help improve student behaviors by reinforcing ideas, skills, and values. During instruction it is important that teachers attempt to detect those errors and misunderstandings that hinder learning.

Achievement results often associated with summative tests or posttests should, in part, also be used as an indication of the extent to which goals of

DOES DRILL PRODUCE MASTERY?

Some educational theorists hold that the failure of students to attain key lesson objectives calls for reteaching until evaluation reveals subject-matter mastery. When a student in your class fails to reach the objectives, how will you handle this situation?

instruction were achieved by the class as a whole and by each individual student. In addition, achievement results can help teachers make decisions about changes that need to be made to help address specific student needs. For example, summative test results might suggest that either remedial or enrichment instruction should be implemented. Also, if diagnostic and summative test results are available, a comparison of these test results can suggest the extent to which instruction was effective as a means of changing each student's behavior; thereby, each student's entry behavior is compared with his or her exit behaviors. Criterion-referenced tests are particularly appropriate for measuring the extent to which students were able to achieve the intended objectives of instruction.

Discriminating between low and high achievers, on the other hand, often provides a defensible means of assigning grades. Grades that result from normative measurements (often objective tests with numerical results measured according to a specified statistical standard), frequently are considered more valid and reliable (or less biased) than other forms of assessment. In addition, norm-referenced test results should provide a reasonable amount of competitive, challenging, stimulating, and motivated learning. In addition, norm-referenced test results are based on grading standards in which past performance is used as an indicator of future performance. Norm-referenced grading standards usually are based on a bell-shaped curve that statistically distributes scores over a very large population. The center of the bell-shaped curve is a point that identifies the mean (the average of all scores), median (the midscore), and the mode (the most frequently recorded score). From this point, the scores above the central point and below the central point are measured in terms of standard deviations. Grades ranging from A to F are frequently assigned according to this distribution:

A = 7% of the cases
B = 24% of the cases
C = 38% of the cases
D = 24% of the cases
F = 7% of the cases

To Curve or Not to Curve—What Are the Conditions?

Normative tests that include grading a class on a bell curve can have severe liabilities. Explain why and indicate under what conditions such grading may be appropriate.

Before using such an approach, teachers must consider its appropriateness in terms of the size of the class and the spread of ability levels in the groups of students being tested.

Another common practice of many teachers is to develop a grading curve based on the distribution of correct responses for each test. By constructing a frequency distribution of results, the teacher constructs a distribution of grades based on estimated categories of results. The skewed curve often is used to reflect the local population, community, or student body. The flexible curve often is criticized because of grade inflation, but it is defended on social or political grounds. The top of the distribution is assigned the grade of "A" and the bottom of the distribution is assigned a grade of "F." Scores falling in the middle receive grades of "B" through "D."

    A = 20% of the cases
    B = 30% of the cases
    C = 30% of the cases
    D = 15% of the cases
    F = 5% of the cases

Teachers frequently use a fixed standard based on a percentage of correct answers or points gained as a result of grading. For example, the distribution of grades might be based on the following percentages:

    94% correct or better = A
    86–93% correct = B
    78–85% correct = C
    70–77% correct = D
    69% and below correct = F

Instructors using such fixed standards often justify their use on the bases of their knowledge of the fundamental subject matter being taught and tested as well as on their knowledge of typical student performance and of the individuals in the group being tested. Many teachers, however, wish they had the time,

CAN YOU MAKE AN OPEN OR A SHUT CASE FOR OPEN-BOOK EXAMS?

Some teachers frequently give open-book exams or use test questions submitted by students. Can you defend the use of both of these procedures?

aid, setting, and educational regulations that would allow them to evaluate every pupil's progress separately as the unique individuals of varying backgrounds and environments that characterize each member of a class.

Regardless of the grading standard used, a single grade does not adequately represent all of the elements that contribute to learning achievement. In spite of this condition, instructional outcomes are almost always reduced to a single grade. Subsequently, it is important to relate the symbolic meaning of the grade to specific instructional meanings. Moreover, when the primary purpose of grading is aimed at improving future learning, some of the more punitive aspects of grading should be reduced. It is recommended that, where possible, single-letter grades be accompanied by at least brief teacher comments. These statements explain and enlarge on the single report of achievement and also encourage student progress.

CONCLUSIONS

In this chapter you learned that evaluation can be used for instructional purposes as well as measurement; therefore, in developing a plan of action or an assessment blueprint, teachers should consider learning goals. For example, assessment items can require that students apply their knowledge and skills to a variety of situations, and as a result, new information is acquired and new skills are further refined. In addition, you learned that the use of assessment items can help promote higher levels of thought such as the analysis, synthesis, and judgment of social events and issues. Also, you learned that assessment can be used to further student understanding of the specific components of social studies content including concepts, skills, and values. In this regard, the use of assessment can help broaden and deepen student experiences related to knowledge acquisition, skill applications, and value study.

Motivation is greatly influenced by the process and the outcome of evaluation. Therefore, it is important that the possible punitive aspects of evaluation be controlled so that students are not threatened but are challenged by the prospects of taking a test or by its outcomes. Consequently, you need to begin to perceive varied evaluation procedures as important positive components of instruction that you can use to help students to fully achieve their individual potentialities. In other words, evaluation should help students to pinpoint their misunderstandings and to suggest changes that can help them overcome deficiencies in knowledge and skill. Also, students should realize that assessment can help them identify specific avenues for further achievement and recognize that every individual has the potential for continual growth. In this regard, Gronlund and Linn (1990) suggest that grade reports can be made more meaningful "when the report (1) clarifies the instructional objectives, (2) indicates the pupil's strengths and weaknesses in learning, (3) provides information concerning the pupil's personal-social development, and (4) contributes to the pupil's motivation" (pp. 244–258). As Ralph Tyler once told one of the authors of this book, "The true purpose of evaluation is not to discover if pupils have done their work, but to find what the work has done for the pupils."

REFERENCES

Airasian, P. W. (1971). The role of evaluation in mastery learning. In J. H. Block *Mastery learning and practice* (pp. 77–88). New York: Holt, Rinehart & Winston.

Borich, G. D. (1992). *Effective teaching methods* (2nd ed.). New York: Macmillan.

Dick, W., & Carey, L. (1978). *The systematic design of instruction*. Glenview, IL: Scott, Foresman.

Gagne, R. M., Briggs, L. J., & Wager, W. W. (1992). *Principles of instructional design* (4th ed.). Fort Worth, TX: Harcourt, Brace, Jovanovich.

Girod, G. R. (1973). *Writing and assessing attitudinal objectives*. Columbus, OH: Merrill.

Green, J. A. (1975). *Teacher-made tests* (2nd ed.). New York: Harper & Row.

Gronlund, N. E., & Linn, R. L. (1990). *Measuring and evaluation in teaching* (6th ed.). New York: Macmillan.

Gross, R. E., Messick, R., Chapin, J. R., & Sutherland, J. (1978). *Social studies for our times*. New York: John Wiley & Sons.

Hopkins, K. D., & Stanley, J. C. (1981). *Educational and psychological measurement and evaluation* (6th ed.). Englewood Cliffs, NJ: Prentice-Hall.

Kelly, E.J. (1958). "Appraising and measuring the attainment of democratic citizenship competencies." In Gross, R.E., and Zeleny, L.D. (eds.) *Educating citizens for democracy*. New York: Oxford University Press (pp. 517–559).

Kemp, J. E. (1985). *The instructional design process*. New York: Harper & Row.

Langdon, D. G. (1973). *Interactive instructional designs for individualized learning.* Englewood Cliffs, NJ: Educational Technology.

Pratt, D. (1980). *Curriculum design and development.* San Diego, CA: Harcourt, Brace, Jovanovich.

Smith, P. L., & Ragan, T. J. (1993). *Instructional design.* New York: Macmillan.

Wiggins, G. (1993). Assessment: Authenticity, content, and validity. *Phi Delta Kappan, 75,* 200–214.

PART FIVE

Design-Based Instruction

DESIGNING, DEVELOPING, AND IMPLEMENTING COURSES, UNITS, AND LESSONS

What teacher practices, planning patterns, and presentation cycles can be followed in developing an effective and systematic approach to instructional design, development, and implementation for the social studies?

In Part Five of your textbook, you will learn to address important preinstructional preparations including rules and arrangements that can be planned and implemented in instruction. To some extent these factors include an awareness of certain practices that you can follow to provide more effective instruction. Included in effective instruction is an understanding of the teacher's role in establishing a positive learning environment, which includes knowledge of the learning attributes of students and a management system that can be developed to support the instructional program. In addition, the effective social studies teacher must be able to handle special concerns related to subject-matter content, such as dealing with controversial issues. Consequently, the social studies teacher must recognize that controversy is a normal aspect of social studies instruction and that effective social studies teachers are able to act in ways that result in constructive experiences for students, parents, and administrators.

The design, development, and implementation of instructional programs is often carried out according to certain patterns and cycles. These patterns of planning and cycles of presentations are based on formats that have been developed to provide systematic instruction for students in light of subject-matter characteristics and student needs. Formats often are based on certain design principles such as those identified by Tyler and Taba, including the principles of scope, sequence, continuity, and integration as well as the rhythmic instructional presentation cycles suggested by various individuals including Madaline Hunter.

An outgrowth of planning patterns and presentation cycles is specific steps in model form that can be followed in developing a systematic approach to curriculum design, development, and implementation. We have termed the process *design-based instruction*. Design-based instruction is an outgrowth and extension of design, which is briefly described by Smith and Ragan (1993) in the following statement:

> The term **design** implies a systematic planning process prior to the development of something or the execution of some plan in order to solve a problem. Design is distinguished from other forms of planning by the level of precision, care, and expertise that is employed in the planning process. Designers employ a high level of precision, care, and expertise in the systematic planning of a project because they perceive that poor planning can result in serious consequences, such as misuse of time and other resources. . . . Specifically, instructional designers fear that poor instructional planning can result in poor, inefficient, and unmotivated learning—a consequence that can have serious long-term effects. (p. 4)

In our design-based instructional model, you will learn to extend a systematic nine-step model in facilitating the design, development, and implementation of courses, units, and lessons. According to design-based instruction, instructional planning and implementation begins as you address certain basic questions regarding (1) the purposes and goals of instruction in terms of curriculum mandates, (2) the characteristics of the subject matter and the learning characteristics and needs of students who will be the recipients of instruction, (3) the pedagogical means (such as strategies, activities, materials, and assessments) that are available in achieving purposes and goals, and (4) the identification of changes of behavior that can indicate and be used to measure the extent to which learning has taken place. The design model provides a step-by-step guideline that will help you address these questions by helping you develop and implement the products of design in the form of courses, units, and lessons.

14

Meeting Needs and Providing Effective Instruction

INTRODUCTION

Effective teaching is often determined by societal standards, expectations, and perceptions. For example, in some traditional societies a good teacher is one who passes on cultural knowledge, including legends and myths about the people and their origins. In ancient Egypt a good teacher was expected to possess important knowledge regarding religious beliefs and practices, accounting systems, and the system of writing. In the eighteenth and nineteenth centuries in the United States, a good teacher was expected to teach the essential basic skills of reading and writing, elements of Latin grammar, arithmetic, and spelling and to serve as a moral role model for students.

During the early decades of the twentieth century, effective teachers were considered by progressives to be those who believed that the purpose of education should be to motivate students to reach their full potential as related to Dewey's idea of growth. In the following quotation, Lawrence A. Cremin (1965) interprets Dewey's view of education and student growth as described in Dewey's 1916 volume entitled, *Democracy and Education:*

> The key to this particular form of education lies in Dewey's conception of "growth," a term that has been much abused by his disciples and critics alike. Growth, he tells us, is "constant expansion of horizons and consequent formation of new purposes and new responses." Therefore, when he argues that education is a continuous process of growth, having as its aim at every stage an added capacity for growth, he is merely saying that the aim of education is to make not citizens or workers or soldiers or even scientists, but human beings who will live life to the fullest, who will never stop expanding their horizons, reformulating their purposes, and modifying their actions in light of these purposes. Given this conception of growth, a democracy can be defined simply as a society in which

each individual is encouraged to continue his education throughout his lifetime. (p. 19)

In the 1970s and last decades of the twentieth century, the definition of effective teaching shifted to a behavioral model in which a good teacher is expected to be able to change student behavior by systematically applying a model(s) of effective instruction that enhances student learning according to specifically stated pre-instructional class goals (as opposed to the varied individual growth of each student). According to Borich (1992),

> In the last two decades a revolution has occurred in the definitions of good teaching. We have seen that defining good teachers by community ideal proved unrealistic on the job and in the preparation of teachers. We have seen how teachers' psychological characteristics proved to be poorly related to what teachers actually did in the classroom. This directed researchers to study the impact that specific teachers' behaviors had on the specific cognitive and affective behaviors of their students. The term good teaching changed to *effective teaching*, and the research focus shifted from studying teachers to studying their effects on students. (pp. 4–5)

Teacher effectiveness, according to this approach, is verified by student performance, or the ability of students to perform certain tasks or demonstrate certain behaviors as a result of instruction. In other words, the outcomes of instruction should be asserted ahead of time and should be measured according to certain types of evidence (such as test results, products, or performance of processes) which indicate that students have successfully achieved what is being claimed or predicted by the teacher. Both of these more contemporary approaches (Dewey's concept of education as growth and the more contemporary concept of education as predicted outcomes), whether in separate or in combined forms, require that teachers process or collect background information pertaining to the instructional program and students' attributes before instruction begins.

Gathering Pre-Instructional Background Information

Educators have long recognized that all students do not have the same abilities, experiences, maturity, motivation, and readiness to learn. Therefore, teachers need to take some time and effort to assess student attributes and readiness before they determine the extent to which special instructional programs are needed to help address special student needs. For example, the need for remediation may exist because students have learning difficulties or lack essential knowledge or skills necessary to succeed with a particular program of instruction. While an assessment of student needs may not necessarily be used in the development of a curriculum program, it should be considered when presenting the instructional program for a particular student population. Ultimately, the purpose of gathering pre-instructional background information is to assist students in achieving their full potential (or growth toward that potential) in the face of all kinds of personal, social, and cultural limitations. Thus, it may be argued that the need for information about students and programs exists in order to help students "grow" in an educational sense; or helping students achieve certain predicted outcomes that must begin by reconciling students' needs with the requirements of the educational program. Subsequently, even before a course begins, it is recommended that teachers gather available information on the characteristics of their students.

Information for Reconciliation

The process of reconciliation is of particular importance when the teacher is to implement or present the course of study. Therefore, background information should include knowledge of the characteristics of the instructional program as well as information pertaining to students enrolled in the course. We have recommended that, prior to implementing a course of study, teachers should gather information by performing the following tasks:

- Inspect records pertaining to students' ability to deal with social studies content in order to identify the learning needs of their students. (A review of information provided by guidance counselors is valuable in helping teachers better understand their students' personal and social situations and backgrounds.)

- Review student learning strengths and weaknesses in reading and comprehension, which are necessary skills in any proposed instructional program. (A survey may include discussions with previous teachers and parents and a review of school records; also, individual student interviews are very helpful, especially as students are asked to read and explain a sample reading from the course textbook.)

- Study state, school, and department (or grade level) instructional mandates pertaining to social studies knowledge, skills, and values. (An inventory of assigned textbook and supplemental materials for the course of study should be included as well as a critique of key content elements—concepts, skills, and values—that are to be emphasized throughout instruction.) In addition, the teacher should attempt to list possible learning experiences and activities that will provide students with a practical or applied exposure to the elements of content (concepts, skills, and values) to be presented in units and lessons.

• Consider the means of assessment and approaches that can be used to monitor and measure instructional effectiveness and student achievement. (The development of an overall plan of evaluation should play an important role in reconciling course content requirements with student attributes and needs.)

These types of background information should be used to determine whether an instructional program, as currently envisioned, can be implemented in light of student attributes, abilities, and needs. According to Smith and Ragan (1993), teachers "who omit this step may find themselves designing instruction that simply cannot be implemented (or learned)" (p. 27). This information is, of course, invaluable in designing course units.

Entry Behaviors, Pretesting, and Readiness

Design experts such as Gagne, Briggs, and Wager (1992) often refer to this type of information as an indication of *"entry behaviors."*

> The purpose is to determine which of the required enabling skills the learners bring to the learning task. Some learners will know more than others, so the designer must choose where to start instruction, knowing that it will be redundant for some but necessary for others. (pp. 24–25)

When teachers are unfamiliar with the students coming to their classes at the beginning of the year, gathering information about these students should be attempted including the possible use of pre-instructional diagnostic tests based on expected social studies content, skills, and values. Also, as the school year progresses, teachers may wish to pretest (use a diagnostic measure) to determine the extent of "readiness" for subsequent instruction. According to Tanner and Tanner (1980),

> Over the years the principle that schools shall meet individual differences has persisted; but the theoretical ideas concerning means have undergone change. One such concept is readiness, which means "the capability for successfully performing certain learning tasks". . . . Today researchers find development to be the result of experience (past stimulation and learning) as well as maturation. (p. 423)

When *readiness* is not indicated (on diagnostic instruments such as a *pretest*), additional background instruction may be recommended as a means of providing essential knowledge or skills considered basic to instruction on a new topic. Student interviews and questions are valuable sources of information regarding student readiness for new instruction.

Pretesting is a helpful way to determine whether or not students already possess extensive knowledge about the topic, as well as deciding whether or not additional instruction is needed before beginning the unit. A simple means of pretesting the class on a new topic would be to select a set of sample test questions from the unit or course test (the more general questions that the "average person on the street" would likely know). Another means of pretesting would be to select key elements of content (concepts, skills, or values) from the course or unit and ask students to explain or describe these elements. In the case of concepts, students might be asked to give an example of the concept (for example, a *progressive tax*), while skill assessment may be pretested through a student explanation or demonstration of a process (for example, locating a city on a map). As a rule of thumb, some experts suggest that approximately half of the class should demonstrate correct responses on the pretest items as an indicator of "readiness" for instruction.

Serving Students with Special Needs

As was previously stated, experienced teachers realize that their students are not the same in abilities, experiences, maturity, motivation, and readiness to learn; therefore, a great deal of the teacher's time and effort is spent in addressing the special needs of students. Some students in almost every class will have remedial as well as advanced instructional needs. In recent years, teachers also have become aware of the cultural needs of their students. Remedial enrichment and cultural needs tend to rely on certain instructional strategies that are aimed at addressing special needs.

Since the passage of Public Law 94-142, students with various types of special physical and learning needs are entering, or being *mainstreamed* into regular social studies classrooms. "Mainstreaming applies the principle of inclusion as opposed to exclusion of students with handicapped conditions" (Herlihy & Herlihy, 1980, p. 2). Various instructional approaches have been recommended as a way to help students with special needs deal with social studies content: rewriting the textbook, homogeneous and heterogeneous groupings, the development of new courses, and individualized approaches. After reviewing all considerations, many social studies teachers have attempted to use more individual approaches for those students with special learning needs (Gregory, 1980). Such personal assignments especially seem to work quite well in connection with a learning center or classroom "lab" setting. If funds are available for teachers aides, they often can prove helpful, as do some parent volunteers.

Remedial Needs

The need for remediation exists because some students simply are not ready for instruction; therefore, these students need some additional instruction before they enter current studies. The need for remedial work is based on diverse factors; for example, such needs may be the result of school absence or low ability and may be a continuous problem regardless of the amount of special help. On the other hand, remedial needs may be the result of poorly developed skills or lack of experience with the subject matter, problems that may be more easily overcome with special attention to lesson reviews, strengthening needed skills, or developing subject-matter knowledge. The problem for the teacher is to develop a systematic remedial program for helping students with diverse needs to better cope with instruction.

The first step in developing a remedial program for students with special needs is the diagnosis of special needs. Remedial problems in the social studies often are related to an inability to read the material comprehensively. Consequently, many of the strategies recommended for students with reading problems would be appropriate for students needing remedial work in the social studies. Another element that must be addressed is the conditions under which this remedial work is to take place. Ideally, the best remedial work occurs under the direct supervision of the teacher. Realistically, this type of supervision may not be possible, as the teacher must manage the whole class and time does not allow for such an arrangement when there are several remedial students in the same classroom. An alternative would be to develop a general remedial social studies program for students who lack preparation and skill development with special emphasis on developing reading and comprehension skills. This program would consist of special materials and instructions that are prepared for students and executed in a special learning center established for this purpose. This approach works especially well when a teacher's aide or the student's parents are available to help supervise and instruct students working in a learning center. The materials for this center should be varied to meet the special needs of students, yet be keyed to the current social studies program that is being taught to the class. The advent of numerous programmed and video exercises and drill and review type learnings that are now available for use in classroom computers and monitors can be ideal sources of aid for remedial instruction. Teachers need to keep abreast of their growing availability. In sum, remedial work should be carefully developed and systematically applied to address students' weaknesses.

A variety of materials can be tailored to meet the needs of each student. Much has been written about teaching and reaching the poor learner and the disadvantaged; but few suggestions exist specifically for the social studies. An interesting and sympathetic discussion of the problems involved can be found in a volume by Selakovich (1970) which he dedicated to "the kids in the back row."

Gifted and Talented Needs

The need for enrichment exists because some students have the ability to do more sophisticated work than the typical or average student. In this situation, the problem is to provide students with content instruction at a level that challenges their unique abilities, experiences, and knowledge. The need for enrichment exists because some students have advanced learning needs that exceed those of the other students in the classroom. As was previously stated, the need for enrichment can result when students have the ability to handle more mature content than the typical student. This need is especially critical when the ability to do more sophisticated work is coupled with an advanced knowledge of the subject matter.

Gifted and talented students tend to grasp instruction more easily and in a shorter period of time than do the average students. Consequently, these students tend to finish their tasks earlier and more easily than do other students. Regular classroom assignments often do not challenge these students, and they tend to become bored and distracted when kept at the same pace as other students. Unfortunately, many teachers respond to this situation by piling on more of the same type of work in order to keep these students busy. In recent years, it has been found that many of the gifted and talented students are "students at-risk" for dropping out of school because of the tedium of routine classroom instruction. The problem for the teacher is to provide these students with content instruction at a level that challenges their unique abilities.

Enrichment strategies are somewhat similar to remedial strategies in that the ideal instructional setting would be a direct teacher-to-student interaction in which the teacher guides the pupils into advanced studies that appeal to

What Factors Make the Difference Between Quality Tasks and Time-Wasting Tasks?

Most social studies classes are organized on a heterogeneous basis; even in classes that are grouped, there are more differences than similarities between students. Therefore, a major design problem for teachers is to develop a program that includes units and lessons that motivate and reach as many students as possible. What specific actions can you take to ensure that your course meets these varied needs?

their special interests and talents. As with remedial students, teachers often do not have enough time to take care of the special needs of gifted and talented students in a regular classroom unless a special instructional program with related learning materials is developed that parallels the regular social studies course, but at a more advanced level.

Students may be talented in narrow and special areas, although they may not be identified as "gifted" by the conventional measures such as IQ tests. Teachers should strive to discover students with these capabilities, for if allowed to "flower," they can contribute to motivation and learning and enrich an entire class experience. Everything from hobbies and unique foreign backgrounds to artistic and technical skills that relate to course subject matter can be found in most classes. On occasion gifted students will bring these interests to the attention of the teacher who should remain open to incorporating such creative opportunities into individual or class units and lessons.

In conclusion, it is important to note here that it is not only the gifted who frequently become bored with the standard program as it is too often delivered. After many years of teaching experience with children and youth, we have found that topics, options, and assignments developed for the gifted often hold great appeal for the bulk of students in a class. The implications of this fact to those designing units and lessons are clear.

Learning Centers

By establishing special learning centers, for example, an alternative program and materials can replace or supplement the standard history or government course. Teacher-constructed instructional materials that serve specific learning needs are often presented and taught in a classroom learning center. The most effective learning center materials are those that address individual and group needs, especially, those needs that are aimed at remedial and gifted learning and the development of skills. Most commonly, these skills will relate to improving reading, writing, and map abilities that are essential to helping students learn social studies content. In addition, learning centers should support regular classroom instruction, especially as it relates to enriching course, unit, and lesson instruction.

Because of the variety of possible activities, learning center functions should coincide with regular classroom instruction. In addition, the learning center should allow for maximum flexibility of use and function. The learning center can be used for a particular function beyond daily classroom instruction. For example, once a month the learning center might serve as a library center for a week, and during the same month the learning center might function as a listening center (equipped with tape recorders and headphones) where students may select and play tape recordings related to a unit of instruction. Also, each time a new unit of instruction is introduced, a series of motivational activities correlated to the course, unit, or lesson might be made available to students according to pre-identified categories of student interests (for example, technology, transportation, dress, and customs). Toward the close of topical instruction (course or unit), the learning center might be used as a project center in which students develop materials that will be used in a culminating activity. The purpose of the learning center will also determine the type of furniture and equipment as well as the materials placed in the learning center. Learning centers are often used for one or more of the following purposes: remedial study, enrichment study, skill development, project work, silent reading and writing, problem solving, assessment, research, committee work and cooperative learning groups, panel report preparation, tutoring sessions, and independent study opportunities for the gifted.

With units that include significant amounts of individualized and small-group work, provisions for these are very important. For various assignments, the existence of a separate room, adjacent to the classroom or next to the school library, may be most helpful. However, in most instances, learning centers have to be established in the secondary classroom. This facility is somewhat isolated from the rest of the classroom and usually contains at least a table, four or five chairs, and possibly counters, cabinet space, and media equipment. Individual study centers, on the other hand, may consist of individual study carrels that are arranged for student use. By surveying classroom areas, a teacher should be able to determine the best location for a learning center, keeping in mind, that a certain amount of classroom separation is recommended for best results. The teacher is responsible for establishing learning center procedures and rules as well as the overall supervision of the learning center. Supervision and management are important teacher responsibilities, including student training and the operation and care of equipment. The teacher role in designing a learning center begins by considering its location, arrangement, and supervision. Supervision begins by establishing a set of rules and procedures that will govern the operation of the learning center.

Rules and procedures should be posted so that students are aware of the teacher's expectations, and as a rule of thumb, the teacher should be able to observe and interact with the students while they are working in the learning center. Regardless of all other considerations, the most important factors that determine the success or the failure of the center as a learning experience are the instructional materials and activities that will be developed for the center.

Where space does not make such areas feasible in the classroom, it is sometimes possible to develop these in school libraries or adjacent rooms. School librarians are very knowledgeable and helpful in advising, developing, and providing materials for either type of learning center.

Culturally Diverse Needs

Social diversity due to cultural differences may need to be addressed within the instructional program. Therefore, the student's social background and experiences should be considered, along with levels of ability and the possession of basic literary skills when designing or planning a program of instruction. The need for multiethnic studies originates with the varied conditions under which children in American society live. Since the 1960s there has been a growing curriculum trend in which school districts are attempting to modify or balance their instructional programs to include studies that focus on ethnic and cultural diversity. As a result of this trend, the study of history has steadily moved toward a focus on social history rather than political history. To some extent, various social groups have always been represented in social studies textbooks; however, this representation has mainly focused on European groups who migrated to North America. In more recent times, textbook writers have also been concerned about including information on non-European groups. This concern, when carried to a narrow interpretation, suggested that multiethnic studies should focus on African Americans, Native Americans, Asian Americans, or excessively non-European groups (Simms, 1980). In response to this narrow perspective, others have proposed that ethnic studies include all groups, including all European-American groups such as German Americans, Irish Americans, Scandinavian Americans, and Italian Americans.

James Banks (1990) views ethnic studies as a curriculum reform movement rather than as an attempt to balance the social studies curriculum.

> Rather than viewing ethnic studies as an addition to the regular social studies curriculum, it should be viewed as a process of curriculum reform. . . . As such, it can result in the creation of an innovative curriculum based on new assumptions and new perspectives. (pp. 219–220)

In opposition to this perspective, other educators have argued that it is not possible to include almost every ethnic group in the United States as a focus of the social studies curriculum. Therefore, curriculum planners at the state and local level often provide ethnic studies as electives based on those ethnic groups that are substantially represented within their state or school populations. As a consequence of this policy, school districts with large minority populations are encouraged or required to develop ethnic and cultural studies just for those particular groups. For example, bilingual education includes a great deal of ethnic instruction that would address a Mexican-American population. In California, Asian studies would be included along with Mexican-American studies. At the same time, states such as Minnesota with a large Scandinavian population seldom require instruction in the Scandinavian languages or the study of Scandinavian culture; however, elements of such heritage are often included in conventional social studies courses and community activities. Therefore, ethnic studies as generally practiced tend to focus on non-European cultures and are justified on the basis that much of the content of American history is, in reality, based on a European orientation because the majority of American citizens share that heritage regardless of racial background.

The overall goal of cultural studies is to help students recognize the value of diversity within the mainstream of American culture and to reduce ethnic and racial tensions by recognizing the value of cultural differences. Because of the nature of these goals, ethnic studies often are viewed as another form of ethno-nationalism that tends to rely on certain elements of indoctrination. However, the pre-anthropology education that emerged in the 1960s tended to provide a more scientific means of studying cultures according to the concepts and methodologies of a behavioral science. This approach is attractive mainly because it tends to be less ethnocentric and provides a means for comparing cultures according to well-founded categories and principles. For example, in an anthropological approach, students might be encouraged to combine the study of cultural history with ethnographic case studies.

In addition to ethnic studies, gender studies began to appear in the social studies curriculum in the early 1970s and continued to advance throughout the last decades of the twentieth century. The women's movement included elements of civil rights such as in the cases of discrimination within employment and school activities. These cases fell under Title IX of the Education Amendments, which were adopted by the federal government and applied to the public schools.

Also, by 1971 the National Council for the Social Studies was beginning to address this issue of social education. As far as the social studies curriculum was influenced, larger school districts began to offer elective courses on women's studies as well as various minicourses. According to Carney (1980), increasing attention was given in courses and units to women and their expanding roles in society.

Most of these changes in the school curriculum have tended to be in the form of elective courses in women's history and/or women's studies. This has been due, in part, to the multimedia, interdisciplinary nature of most of the instructional materials that came on the market. (p. 48)

Over the past several decades, many social studies teachers have encouraged their students to investigate the role of women in the affairs of the world, nation, state, and community. By the early 1990s, substantial numbers of women were holding high appointed and elected offices, suggesting that a more balanced gender approach would eventually characterize social studies content as a consequence of changes currently taking place in American society.

Separate classes or minicourses established at one time to focus, for example, on "Black Culture," "Our Hispanic Heritage," or "Women in United States History," have tended to disappear because of their limited coverage and the lack of time and space in the established social studies curriculum.

Behaviors and Practices of the Effective Teacher

Beginning in the 1960s and 1970s, educational researchers probed into teaching behaviors and practices that helped to promote effective teaching. For example, Rosenshine and Furst (1971) attempted to identify teacher behaviors that are positively correlated with student learning by compiling over fifty research reports on effective teaching. They divided effective behaviors (variables) into three categories, including "most promising," "somewhat promising," and those variables with "little or no support." (Many studies, including those of Rosenshine and Furst, Dunkin and Biddle, Cruickshank, Medley, Gage, Borich, Good, Emmer and Evertson, Stalling, and Porter and Brophy are summarized in Donald R. Cruickshank (1990, pp. 69–82). In his book, *Effective Teaching Methods*, Gary D. Borich (1992) organized these variables into lists of essential practices for effective teaching. Having reviewed Borich's categories, we have listed below the selective successful practices as a guide for teachers who wish to provide effective instruction in their social studies classrooms. (It is important to note here that research findings can and do conflict from one study to the next; thus, you should be cautious and judicious in interpreting and applying recommendations stemming from limited research studies. At the same time, educational research is an ongoing process that requires repeated studies and applications with differences arising out of local conditions and sometimes undetermined variables. Therefore, as more research is completed in the field of teaching effectiveness, certain conclusions can be substantiated as consistently effective and should be incorporated into regular teaching practices.)

1. *Lesson clarity.* Clear and precise presentation is essential for comprehension. This practice relates to the clarity of presentation (lesson delivery) as a means of communicating content to students.

2. *Instructional variety.* Varied lesson strategies and activities affect student motivation. This practice relates to presentations that include a range and variety of strategies and activities, including impromptu questions, use of examples, changes of pace, and variety of materials.

3. *Task orientation.* Staying on task provides for efficiency. This practice relates to the amount of time (minutes, hours, weeks, or months) that the teacher will spend on the focus or theme of the lesson, unit, or course.

4. *Student engagement.* Uninterrupted learning time promotes learning. This practice relates to the amount of time (minutes or hours) that students spend engaged in a specific learning process without disruptions, distractions, or interruptions (the fewer the distractions the better).

5. *Structured instruction.* A structured instructional cycle can be used to aid student comprehension. This practice relates to the idea that by providing a structured presentation—for example, lesson opener, lesson body, and lesson closure—students will be better able to focus on the important elements of content being taught.

6. *Cognitive development activities.* Thinking encourages comprehension. This practice relates to the use of strategies and activities (such as asking questions or a series of questions, that is, as according to Bloom's taxonomy, etc.) as a means of aiding student comprehension.

7. *Expanding (extending the knowledge or skill base) processes.* By recognizing underlying relationships comprehension can be improved. This practice relates to the use of strategies and activities (such as student research and reporting methods) as a means to further explore an event, concept, skill, or value.

8. *Building for student success.* Student self-confidence supports achievement. This practice relates to the teachers' ability to foster student confidence in their ability to achieve learning success as well as to clear expectations of learning attainment.

9. *Student participation and contributions.* Student participation motivates interest. This practice relates to the belief that student participation in the teaching/learning process promotes the desire to learn the subject matter.

10. *Teacher affect.* Teacher enthusiasm is a source of student motivation. This practice relates to the level of the teacher's commitment (thereby enthusiasm) for the subject-matter content as a stimulus for student interest.

During the stages of instructional design and development each one of these practices should be considered, but when presenting instruction to students the first seven are considered very essential. Research evidence may not be as

Can You Evaluate Your Own Strengths and Weaknesses in Terms of Effective Teaching Traits?

Review some of the literature on characteristics of teacher effectiveness. Which qualities or practices do you believe you particularly need to consider and activate to improve your own effectiveness as an instructor?

strong for the last three, but in your authors' opinions, teaching will be unsuccessful unless these factors are in evidence.

Establishing a Positive Learning Environment

The learning environment, which depends mainly on the personal and professional attributes of the teacher, suggests that standardization in instruction is mainly a myth. The personal attributes that the teacher brings to the classroom include knowledge and personality factors such as energy level, social skills, ability to interact, affection toward others, and emotional stability. Also, because every individual is unique, students in the same classes will have various reactions and different social experiences due to these differences. In addition, the other students (a corporate social body referred to as a class), also are unique individuals who will profoundly influence the teacher and the behavior of other class members. More important still, the development of a positive social relationship between teacher and students is a key factor in determining the social environment of the classroom. Developing positive student relationships can play an important role in motivating and promoting learning. Because the personal attributes of the students also play an important role in establishing and maintaining the social environment of the classroom, the teacher should attempt to promote positive relationships between students.

The professional attributes of the teacher include knowledge of the subject matter, ability to communicate subject matter, ability to use instructional technology, ability to develop and present instruction, ability to evaluate and revise instruction, interest in professional growth and development, and a high level of dedication to classroom responsibilities and tasks. An attitude of professionalism is an important teacher characteristic that should be encouraged and nurtured by all school officials as a means of promoting a more effective instructional environment for students. This factor, more than any other, may help to establish an attitude of respect between teacher and student. It can inspire a "mutual admiration society" for teachers and students, and as a consequence, produce a desire to work toward worthwhile and admirable goals. For this to happen, teachers must feel good about their work and themselves, and they must be recognized and praised for their efforts and accomplishments. Unfortunately, most teachers feel that their efforts go unnoticed except by a few of their more supportive students, as well as by some administrators. As a result, teacher morale often tends to be low, which in turn is detrimental to the entire learning environment.

In particular, it is important that teachers develop a sense of ownership regarding their instructional programs. In part, this sense of ownership comes with the realization that they are responsible for modifying the curriculum and courses of instruction to meet the needs of their students. Therefore, the classroom environment is influenced by instructional programs to the extent that they are suitable to the current student audience, and only the classroom teacher can adequately fulfill this important responsibility. But to modify and improve a course of study, the teacher must possess certain design, development, and presentation skills as those described in this text. In addition, the learning environment is influenced by the instructional materials the teacher selects to present content to students. When standard classroom materials prove to be inadequate, as is commonly the case, the teacher must be able to provide more appropriate supplemental materials or to construct certain materials for specific instructional needs (see Chapter 12).

In an era of increasing national standards and assessment, these vital prerogatives of teachers in their schools and classrooms can be threatened. One of the most personal evidences of teachers' responsibility is revealed by the kind and amount of teacher-student planning that is characteristic of individual classrooms. This can provide evidence of the ultimate and intimate final application of design for learning, which should be in the hands of the individual teacher. This belief stems, of course, from the roots of progressive education. In practice, it can and should forward course aims and objectives and the learning of basic content. (Many publications are available on numerous aspects of joint planning and learning in the classroom. An influential early work with many examples is H.H. Giles [1941].) Course aims and objectives are best attained by able and knowing instructors who shape their lessons via cooperative learning experiences with their students. In reaching established standards, the effective teacher can plan some aspects of instruction by using the 5 *"W's"* and the *"H"* guidelines. That organizing

CAN YOU APPLY THE 5 "W's" AND THE "H"?

Why are teacher/student planning opportunities frequently overlooked by instructors? As you plan activities for a specific unit, indicate where and how you can incorporate the 5 "W's" plus "H" of pupil participation into your program.

includes discussion, student suggestions, voting, and shared decision making according to the who, what, where, why, when, and how of units and lessons. In this procedure, the teacher can help to include students in a democratic process so frequently overlooked in our schools. This procedure also gains students' acceptance of the learning assignment because they have had personal input into it.

The learning environment consists of physical and psychological factors that can influence students' emotional responses to instruction (see Chapter 10). Therefore, the learning environment of the classroom and school should be purposely designed and developed to psychologically support and promote the goals of instruction. For example, as a part of pre-instructional consideration, the teacher should attempt to organize instruction in the most attractive light or at least to showcase the currency of the topic. A bulletin board should have specific instructional purposes. It can, for example, showcase a current topic or unit. The instructional program should attempt to meet expectations of students, parents, and school officials, just as the teacher should project a classroom image that attempts to meet high professional and community expectations (Gunter, Estes, & Schwab, 1990).

In a similar vein, the physical arrangement of the room should motivate learning according to the instructional setting, such as whole-group, small-group, technical setting, or creative setting. (See Chapter 11, "Setting and Characteristic Strategies.") Most teachers are well aware that they should change the physical arrangements of the classroom to provide students with the best possible working environment in which to complete learning tasks of a particular type. In other words, teachers should have developed several room arrangement plans in which one arrangement is used for one instructional setting (lecture) and another different room plan for another setting (group discussion setting). In addition, an individualized setting and a small-group setting (that is, classroom library setting or learning center) may consist of a special reserved area of the room where students go to perform certain assigned tasks such as student research with selected reference materials.

CAN YOU DESIGN THE IDEAL CLASSROOM ARRANGEMENT?

Increasingly in our school rooms, rigid rows of desks are being replaced with other seating arrangements. If you had your choice, what pattern would you prefer (chairs and tables, seating like the British Parliament, or others)? Indicate the positive reasons as well as any possible limitations that might accompany such an arrangement.

Classroom Management

Classroom management is an important aspect of instructional planning that should be planned and developed as a standard aspect of design. A system of management should reflect such concerns as the nature of the instruction, the desires of the teacher, school policies, the characteristics of students, and environmental and equipment features of the classroom. The principles of effective classroom management would be aimed at establishing an atmosphere of mutual respect based on a set of classroom rules that reflect the teacher's behavioral expectations for students. Therefore the management system would include provisions for (1) developing a set of classroom rules and procedures, (2) training students in their classroom and school responsibilities, (3) monitoring student behavior, (4) consistently applying rules, and (5) rewarding or recognizing students for cooperation and achievement.

Also, the teacher should include rules and procedures that will be followed throughout the school year pertaining to managing the instructional setting and classroom relationships. These rules and procedures should be appropriate for the age and characteristics of the students. Also important are provisions for communicating and explaining the teacher's expectations to students. Usually, these procedures will include (1) general rules governing routine matters such as attendance, seating arrangements, the management of materials, asking questions, and interacting with other students and (2) specific rules that reflect the instructional conditions and changing instructional settings. Procedures also might include items such as respecting others, extending courtesies to others, paying attention, respecting property, completing assignments, using materials and equipment, and learning center rules. Other things to be considered include whole-group rules, individual study rules, seating, rules of conduct, assignments, student to teacher relationships, student to student relationships, conduct, group arrangements, etiquette and courtesy (classroom manners), conflict resolution, conduct outside the classroom, rewards and punishments, contact with parents and administrators, communications, classroom maintenance of materials (storage, distribution, and clean-up of materials), and arrangement and rearrangement for instruction. As suggested previously, much of this should be accomplished with teacher-pupil planning.

Classroom rules and procedures should be agreed upon, stated orally, and posted in the classroom. Reasons should be given as to why these rules are important and should be obeyed for the benefit of every student. In addition, after the first week of class, students should be given opportunities to comment on the rules and to make suggestions for modifications that are reasonable and appropriate. In addition, provisions should be made regarding the consequences of violating rules and procedures and for displaying inappropriate behavior. But no violations should ever be punished with school work or educational assignments.

At the beginning of the year, the teacher should consistently apply rules and procedures by monitoring, enforcing, recognizing, and rewarding compliance. Some systematic form of record keeping should be used to help the teacher and students monitor management policies. The development of some form of record keeping is a useful means for monitoring the extent to which individual students have met their classroom responsibilities. In many situations, aspects of these procedures and monitoring can be carried out by pupils and recorded in their notebooks. Monitoring should be used as the basis for the rewards and the withholding of rewards in recognition of students who meet their classroom responsibilities.

A reward system should be developed that is meaningful and appropriate to the age and grade characteristics of students. Such a system might include the use of verbal and written praise, special privileges such as the selection or choices of assignments, the use of symbols and token rewards, and other forms of recognition when students demonstrate desired behaviors and achievements. Educational games, free reading time, acknowledgments, meaningful praise, reports to parents, signed letters from the teacher or principal, name and picture recognition (places of honor bulletin boards and student of the row and week) are a few examples of reward programs for students. In addition, students should be allowed to redeem their violations of rules and policy through some specific optional task or service related to the operation of the classroom.

Dealing Effectively with Value Controversies

Students frequently indicate a lack of interest in social studies because the topic is or seems to be far removed from their experiences or concerns. For many youngsters, having to study content that they don't understand as being currently important and personally useful makes the subject matter meaningless and boring. This is one reason that teachers should always enable students to share valuable and even personal relationships with the subject matter. Such opportunities exist not only in current events but also in much traditional content if the teacher will take the time and thought to link long-term as well as the more immediate consequences of events. To draw parallels between former or distant affairs with the present scene and related problems is a process that promotes student suggestions. (For sixty examples of the relationship of historical developments to current, personal, social, political, or economic problems, see Gross and Zeleny [1958, pp. 78–79].) At such points, the social studies lesson can "catch fire." This holds true as students consider conditions affecting their lives on which they may hold strong attitudes and which have been receiving attention in the media. Wherever there are strong, varying positions on these developments, teachers make their lessons come alive by purposely raising such issues and related queries for the class. They have then entered the arena of controversy.

Teachers should be prepared to deal with controversial issues and to have a command of pertinent instructional processes. As a first step, the teacher should determine whether the topic is appropriate either as a current event, a one day's lesson, or as a unit of instruction, depending on course goals. The teacher must prepare to teach the lesson and decide whether it is possible to present all sides of an issue. The motivational value of troublesome issues cannot be questioned; but successful employment of appropriate strategies is essential. It is, for example, very important to eliminate conditions that might bring charges of imbalance or one-sided treatment, of subjectivity, of propagandization, and of the squelching of opposing or minority opinions.

Several studies have revealed that numerous teachers, especially at the elementary grade levels, concerned about these charges and administrative and parental displeasure, often do not introduce potentially controversial lessons and also avoid considering these issues even when raised by class members. This is especially unfortunate because lists of topics which school administrators prefer that teachers refuse to treat often parallel those that are of high interest to students. In recent years in many school districts there has been an increasing tendency to permit and even promote frank schoolroom treatment of "hot" topics. Public support has grown for the discussion of topics such as teenage pregnancy, drug use, and local race relations—issues that were often taboo a few years ago.

Nevertheless, teachers should consider guidelines for introducing and handling controversial issues without unfortunate results. Gross (1964) has proposed the following guidelines for planning the study of controversial issues:

1. Preparing students through background, reading, and study.
2. Providing adequate time for thorough analysis.
3. Identifying and discussing core values that are likely to surface in connection with the issue.

4. Establishing ground rules for decorum and respect for different points of view.

5. Ensuring balance and objectivity as best as possible on the part of both teacher and students.

6. Informing the administration, fellow teachers, and parents about the assignment and how you intend to handle the value issue properly.

7. Encouraging students to draw their own conclusions and, where possible, providing opportunities for pupil or class action as a result of their decisions.

Further instructional suggestions to help teachers succeed in effectively organizing and teaching such lessons and units include the following:

1. Initially it is very important to carefully define the problem with the class.

2. During consideration of a problem, the teacher should help the class examine measures tried at other times and places in resolving a similar problem and urge them to discover the reasons for previous success or failure.

3. The teacher may provide or ask students to generate alternative solutions and then consider carefully whether the solutions will actually address the basic or immediate causes of the problem.

4. Students should discuss whether the favored solutions might cause new or greater problems and whether they think the students or the groups they represent would abide by the final conclusion agreed upon by the class.

Valuable ideas for handling controversy in the classroom also appeared in a special issue of *Social Education*, April, 1975. (See also Kelly [1989].)

A common query in connection with the handling of controversial issues is whether the teacher should give his or her opinion on the problem. In light of many years of teaching experience on the part of these authors, we have concluded that the mentor should not try to appear neutral on serious issues. The teacher should conduct open and objective discussion of these issues; but depending on the instructor's relationship with the class and on the knowledge that the students have about the teacher, in a friendly but charged environment, the teacher should be free to present his or her views, with the reasons thereof, at a most appropriate time. To avoid influencing students, many teachers hold that they should postpone presenting their opinions until individuals in the class have had the opportunity to make up their own minds. (Some students may admire or fear and therefore follow the teacher's opinion; others may reject teacher views as those of disliked parent substitutes.) It is our hope that the views of the teacher would be considered as just one more fair and adult reference by the pupils and therefore not be overly influential in affecting pupil conclusions. When mentors are understood to be joint seekers of the best solutions, even though they have their own initial opinions, the viewpoints of teachers should not have undue impact.

CAN YOU MAKE A LIST OF TABOO SUBJECTS FOR TODAY'S SCHOOLS?

Does the school or district in which you are teaching (or may teach in the future) have a policy statement on the handling of controversial issues? If not, can you discover why not? In the community environment of this school are there any topics or problems that are taboo for school treatment? Explain why or why not such taboos are justified. Can you find out if in your school in recent years any instructor has had difficulties related to the treatment of a controversial issue in class? What are the implications of your information?

We believe that the infusion of contrary views and of opinionated conclusions concerning elements in all social studies courses is to be expected. Openly stated, diverse opinions promote regular examination of many topics that are commonly treated uninterestingly in an established and unquestioning manner. Such deviations from the norm and the traditional approach may do more than anything else to stir pupil interest and ultimately involve them in vital learnings that bring substantial personal growth and civic contributions.

In spite of increased public and parental support for including the study of serious problems in the school curriculum, some teachers continue to carry out self-censorship concerning such topics. Teachers, especially if new in a school system, may be concerned about the propriety of instruction about particular issues. They should inquire if there is a school or district policy, established by the school board, which underwrites the treatment of controversies in classes as being appropriate. If such a policy does not exist, sample statements are available from state and national educational organizations or from other school systems. Teachers, in league with administrators and concerned parents, need to promote the establishment of clear policies that guarantee the right of the learners to learn as well as the freedom of teachers to teach.

CONCLUSIONS

In this chapter you learned that the role of the teacher in effective instruction and in program development should not be underestimated. Simply put, teachers play the most critical role in teaching/learning processes. Therefore, teachers must be prepared to take on more of the responsibilities related to planning and executing instruction. Tanner and Tanner (1980) note the importance of teacher involvement in planning:

> Throughout the twentieth century we have learned repeatedly that, in the last analysis, there is no substitute for the intelligent participation of the teacher in curriculum improvement. Yet in the closing decades of the twentieth century, the teacher's role still has not been well conceptualized. (p. 623)

Since the late 1960s, there has been a growing trend toward teachers becoming little more than "didactic technicians" in which they are expected to precisely implement a series of functions to execute a program that has been planned by local and state officials. At last, community leaders and state officials are concluding that the responsibility for effective teaching must increasingly rest with teachers, thus requiring that they be given more authority in determining school and classroom programs and policy. As a result, educational leaders are recognizing that enforcement of programs and standards from the top-down has not worked. Consequently, the role of teachers is shifting to direct professional involvement in the formulation of educational policies and instruction.

Throughout this book we have taken the position that the top-down micromanagement approach was doomed to inevitable failure because of the local needs of varied populations whose learning needs can be known only by teachers. We have attempted to provide a model for training teachers for those responsibilities associated with designing, developing, and presenting effective instruction whether in the form of standard programs that must be modified or in the creation of unique one-of-a-kind programs.

As part of this process, we have stressed that teachers should be aware of their roles and responsibilities in dealing with those classroom and social factors that influence instruction. These factors relate to basing instructional effectiveness on measured student results, gathering background information on the needs and learning attributes of students, addressing students' needs when presenting a program of instruction, becoming aware of and implementing research results that pertain to teacher effectiveness, establishing a positive learning environment, establishing a supportive classroom management system that promotes and rewards learning, and applying sound practices for dealing with controversial issues that arise in social studies topics.

REFERENCES

Banks, J. (1990). *Teaching strategies for the social studies*. New York: Longman.

Borich, G. D. (1992). *Effective teaching methods*. New York: Macmillan.

Carney, L. J. (1980). Responses to sexism: Two steps forward and one back? In R. L. Simms & G. Contreras (Eds.), *Racism and sexism: Responding to the challenge* (Bulletin 61, pp. 45–63). Washington, DC: National Council for the Social Studies.

Cremin, L. A. (1965). *The genius of American education*. New York: Vintage.

Cruickshank, D. R. (1990). *Research that informs teachers and teacher educators*. Bloomington, IN: Phi Delta Kappa Educational Foundation.

Gage, N. L. (1972). *Teacher effectiveness and teacher education: The search for a scientific basis*. Palo Alto, CA: Pacific Books.

Gagne, R. M., Briggs, L. J., & Wager, W. W. (1992). *Principles of instructional design* (4th ed.). Fort Worth, TX: Harcourt, Brace, Jovanovich.

Giles, H. H. (1941). *Teacher-Pupil Planning*. New York: Harper & Brothers.

Gregory, G. P. (1980). Modes of instruction. In J. G. Herlihy & M. T. Herlihy, *Mainstreaming in the social studies* (Bulletin 62, pp. 34–41). Washington, DC: National Council for the Social Studies.

Gross, R. E. (1964). *How to handle controversial issues* (How-to-do-it series, 14). Washington, DC: National Council for the Social Studies.

Gross, R., & Zeleny, L. (1958). *Educating citizens for democracy*. New York: Oxford University Press.

Gunter, M. A., Estes, T. H., & Schwab, J. H. (1990). *Instruction: A models approach*. Boston: Allyn & Bacon.

Herlihy, J. G., & Herlihy, M. T. (1980). Why mainstream. In J. G. Herlihy & M. T. Herlihy, *Mainstreaming in the social studies* (Bulletin 62, pp. 2–8). Washington, DC: National Council for the Social Studies.

Kelly, T. (1989, October). Leading class discussions for controversial issues, *Social Education, 53*, 368–370.

Rosenshine, R., & Furst, N. (1971). Research on teaching performance criteria. In B. O. Smith (Ed.), *Research in teacher education* (pp. 69–70). Englewood Cliffs, NJ: Prentice-Hall.

Selakovich, D. (1970). *Social studies for the disadvantaged*. New York: Holt, Rinehart & Winston.

Simms, R. L. (1980). Pluralism: Historical roots and contemporary responses. In R. L. Simms & G. Contreras (Eds.), *Racism and sexism: Responding to the challenge* (Bulletin 61, pp. 9–21). Washington, DC: National Council for the Social Studies.

Smith, P. L., & Ragan, T. J. (1993). *Instructional design*. New York: Macmillan.

Tanner, D., & Tanner, L. N. (1980). *Curriculum development: Theory and practice* (2nd ed.). New York: Macmillan.

15

Designing Courses, Units, and Lessons

INTRODUCTION

In this chapter you will be given the opportunity to apply some of the guidelines and respond to the queries raised in the previous chapters. Also, you will learn that the design, development, and presentation of instruction rests on certain design features that influence the basic characteristics and the patterns of teaching that will be used to impart subject-matter content to students. For example, the scope of learning represents the breadth and depth of an instructional program. **Scope** is determined by certain decisions regarding the needs to be addressed and the best means for addressing those needs.

Scope is an endemic problem that all teachers face and must make decisions about when planning courses, units, and lessons. Gunter, Estes, and Schwab (1990) describe the challenge that scope presents to teachers:

> Every teacher is faced with the frustration of having too much to cover in too little time. There is an ever-present danger that in the hope of teaching much, the teacher may fail to take the time to teach well. Since all the conceivable content and information related to a course cannot be covered within the time frame of a course, choices have to be made as to the actual breadth and depth. (pp. 38–39)

Sequence often is described as the order that will be used in implementing an instructional program or course. History courses are typically taught according to a chronological order, while most social science courses are taught in a topical order. One design decision that is commonly associated with sequence is whether to use a deductive organizational pattern or an inductive organizational pattern. The *deductive organizational pattern* begins with a general study of an idea and proceeds to specific cases of the idea. For example, government is usually taught from the federal system to the local system (general to specific). The *inductive organizational pattern* begins with a specific item, idea, or case study and proceeds to a general set of conditions or circumstances (for example, from specific incidents to a generalized study of related cases). It is generally assumed that the order of instruction tends to influence student comprehension; therefore, instructional planning should be based on the most logical sequence of presentation to promote learning. Skill development usually is based on a series of related skills that must be learned either prior to or after learning the target skill. For example, before participating in a problem-solving exercise, students should be skilled in a step process in which they identify the problem, formulate a hypothesis, and proceed to test the hypothesis in order to draw a conclusion. As a rule of thumb, sequencing also is based on the idea that new instruction should be grounded in previous learning.

Continuity relates to sequence, but specifically confronts the issue of how long a subject should be taught within an instructional program. Continuity confronts the issue of how often a topic should be addressed within the entire K–12 curriculum of the school (Doll, 1970; Taba, 1962). In this case, continuity addresses the issue of articulation (communication of a topic) from one grade level to the next within the curriculum. Continuity also involves a concern for the length of time that will be given to a topic or subject within a course of study, unit, or lesson. It pertains to the extent to which a topic will be emphasized within a course in accordance with its related units or lessons.

Integration addresses the extent to which a field of knowledge is connected with other fields of knowledge. An integrated instructional program usually provides instruction in two or more disciplines at the same time. For example, a teacher might teach geography with history as an integrated course; integration allows the teacher to make connections between the two subjects. In a related approach, two subjects are taught together in a two-hour block of time. For instance, American history and American literature might be taught in a two-hour block, thus allowing the teacher(s) to make connections between history and literature. These same basic characteristics (scope, sequence, continuity, and integration) of the curriculum are fundamental characteristics of courses, units, and lessons.

You will also learn that the final product of curriculum design work is an official document usually called a *framework*, which includes lists of courses that will be taught according to assigned grade levels. The curriculum framework can be thought of as a sort of grand design that is accepted as the official educational program for an entire state or a school district. The framework is in the form of a scope and sequence pattern that is influenced by a stated curriculum rationale which contains the grounds on which the entire program will be ideologically developed and justified.

The examples of scope and sequence patterns shown in Figure 15-1 have greatly influenced the social studies.

The scope and sequence design patterns of the curriculum are the work of important curriculum committees and influential individuals. Recall, for example (Chapter 2), the 1916 National Education Association Commission on the Reorganization of Secondary Education—Committee on the Social Studies greatly influenced the secondary pattern of courses for the high school. Later,

Grade (Sequence)	Scope
K–3	Study of self, home, family, school, neighborhood, and community
4th	State and local or regional emphasis with an introduction to history, geography, and economics.
5th	American history with an emphasis on early period to Civil War (may include some elements of government)
6th	Cultural studies with an emphasis on world regions and world cultures
7th	State history and geography
8th	U.S. history and government with an emphasis on the period after the Civil War
9th	Civics, world geography, or state history
10th	World history or modern history
11th	U.S. history
12th	Contemporary problems related to the study of government, economics, psychology or sociology, and social science electives

Figure 15-1. Scope and sequence pattern for social studies.

Paul Hanna (1963) proposed a social studies pattern of courses called an "expanding-communities" design which suggests that each larger component community be studied in sequence by the child. The scope and sequence shown in Figure 15-2 was proposed for elementary education.

Hanna justified his scope and sequence pattern of courses in the following rationale statement:

Figure 15-2. The "Expanding-Communities" pattern of social studies courses.

Grade	Emphasis
1	1. The child's family community
	2. The child's school
2	3. The child's neighborhood community
3	4. The child's local communities: country, city, county, metropolis
4	5. The child's state community
	6. The child's region-of-states community
5	7. The U.S. national community

We hold that there is merit in providing all youth first with experiences that help them see the larger warp and woof of the cultural patterns within which they live; we advocate in the beginning school grades the wholistic [sic] study of men living in societies; we believe that such a beginning makes possible later in the secondary and/or collegiate grades a profitable separation of the several social science and historical threads into special courses for more intensive and meaningful study. (p. 191)

The Origins and Application of Design Models

Courses, units, and lessons are designed according to certain models that have been selected by school officials or by the teacher. Models of design and instruction have existed for many years and have been used to provide a systematic means for identifying and developing the major elements of instruction and thereby helping solve basic organizational problems. In addition, models provide for an orderly program of instruction that is in the form of sequential steps.

Origins of Design Models

The models approach to designing, developing. and executing instruction has its roots in the work of early twentieth century educators who were interested in the work of John Dewey. Dewey was concerned with the use of inquiry within the precollegiate instruction. As a result of their interest in Dewey's work, H. H. Giles, S. P. McCutchen, and A. N. Zechiel (1942) attempted to develop improved programs of instruction in connection with the Eight-Year Study (1933–1941). The purpose of their study was to help free the secondary curriculum from its college-preparatory orientation. The Eight-Year Study addressed four questions pertaining to:

- The identification of objectives
- The selection of means for attaining identified objectives
- The organization of means
- The evaluation of learning outcomes

According to Giles, McCutchen, and Zechiel, "the four fundamental questions or problem areas are represented as interdependent determinants: Objectives, subject matter, methods and organization, and evaluation" (p. 2). Subsequently, the Giles, McCutchen, and Zechiel report of 1942 contained the model of instruction that was not linear (see Figure 15-3).

This model was further advanced by the work of Ralph Tyler (1949) and Hilda Taba (1962). Tyler, for example, explored four fundamental questions that eventually worked into a four-step linear curriculum model. His model included the following sequential steps:

1. The identification of objectives
2. The selection of the means to obtain these objectives
3. The organization of the means for obtaining the objectives
4. The evaluation of outcomes (p. 1)

Taba (1962) credited Tyler's work as being the inspiration for her expanded linear model, which included the following seven steps:

Step 1:   Diagnosis of needs

Step 2:   Formulation of objectives

Step 3:   Selection of content

Step 4:   Organization of content

Step 5:   Selection of learning experiences

Step 6:   Organization of learning experiences

Step 7:   Determination of what to evaluate and of the ways and means of doing it

For many years curriculum specialists have used models in developing instructional programs for subject areas including the social studies. Design models also have been used in developing these programs and in producing instructional materials. At the same time, it should be noted that the linear models of Tyler and Taba were not intended for the purpose of carrying out instruction, as these models were inappropriate for this purpose because they were designed only for planning purposes.

Accepted Design Practices

Most experts agree that there are four important design factors: (1) the intended subjects or learners who will receive instruction or training, (2) the

Figure 15-3. The Giles, McCutchen, and Zechiel model.

Objectives

Subject Matter

Methods and Organization

Evaluation

purposes or goals that are to be accomplished as a result of instruction, (3) the means or methods that are to be used in presenting subject matter, content, or skill, and the activities that are to be used to reinforce subject matter, content, or skill, and (4) the assessment or plan of evaluation that will be followed in determining the effectiveness of instruction and the extent to which the instructional objectives have been accomplished (Joyce & Weil, 1972).

According to Smith and Ragan (1993), the designer begins the design processes by asking three basic questions: Where are we going? How will we get there? How will we know when we have arrived? To answer these questions, the designer goes through three processes, including analysis, the identification of a strategy, and evaluation. Smith and Ragan report that over forty related models of instruction have been developed for use in educational settings. In general, all of these models are organized as a series of steps that the designer follows in developing an instructional program.

Kemp (1985) has further delineated these factors to include ten basic elements. Many of these same elements are similar to the ones listed under the teacher's responsibilities and tasks.

1. Assess *learning needs* for designing an instructional program; state *goals, constraints*, and *priorities* that must be recognized.
2. Select *topics* or *job tasks* to be treated and indicate *general purposes* to be served.
3. Examine *characteristics of learners*, or *trainees*, which should receive attention during planning.
4. Identify *subject content* and analyze *task components* relating to stated goals and purpose.
5. State learning *objectives* to be accomplished in terms of subject content and task components.
6. Design *teaching/learning activities* to accomplish the stated objectives.
7. Select *resources* to support instructional activities.
8. Specify *support services* required for developing and implementing activities and acquiring or producing materials.
9. Prepare to evaluate *learning* and *outcomes* of the program.
10. Determine preparation of learners or trainees to study the topic by *pretesting* them. (p. 11)

The elements listed by Kemp contain some of the key ingredients that can be used to develop a systematic plan of instruction for the social studies. Teachers are concerned with the design, development, and execution of courses, units, and lessons but often without benefit of a model. However, in recent years, steps in systematically planning and executing models of instruction have been developed for teachers as a means of promoting mastery learning. These programs are based on "direct instruction models" that outline specific processes, sequences, or sets of steps.

Step 1	Step 2	Step 3	Step 4	Step 5	Step 6	Step 7	Step 8	Step 9
Identify program goals	Analyze subject matter	Identify needs and entry behaviors	Select Content Elements	Write performance objectives	Develop criterion-referenced tests	Develop strategies and activities	Present instruction	Revise instruction

Figure 15-4.   Design model for social studies instruction based on Dick and Carey's model (1978).

A Design Model for the Social Studies

The planning model shown in Figure 15-4 was developed by the authors for teachers to use in social studies instruction as they design their courses, units, and lessons. This design model is patterned after a model suggested by Dick and Carey (1978); however, several changes have been made to better accommodate social studies content and to include elements related to the presentation of instruction.

Model Components

The nine model components include:

1.   Identifying program goals. Program goals often are presented in the form of desired outcomes that address concerns such as societal needs, the needs of students, subject-matter focus, learning conditions, and the range of activities and materials that will be experienced by students. (These goals are sometimes in a narrative form and are described in a *rationale statement* that is used to justify the program of instruction.) The identification of goals is very helpful as the first step in organizing a program of instruction because the current status of the educational programs and conditions can be synthesized with selected educational values and outlooks. Goal setting is important since goals provide motivation for teachers and students; goals can help strengthen teacher morale and confidence in their ability to accomplish what is expected; goals are communicated ahead of time so the teachers and the students know exactly what is to be accomplished; goals as the target or outcome of instruction can be organized, planned, and scheduled; goals can be used to assess what has been accomplished in a program; goals can be used to break old patterns of instruction and move instruction out of well-worn ruts; and goals can provide the means for teacher self-evaluation.

   2.   *Analyzing subject-matter content.* Subject-matter content is usually organized and presented in instructional materials such as the textbook, supplemental items, and other media. An analysis of subject matter contained in the textbook and related materials helps to reveal the important topics that students will encounter during instruction. In addition to the textbook and supplemental materials, course study guides and state or local documents may contain mandated "essential elements" that students are expected to acquire as a result of instruction.

   3.   *Identifying needs and entry behaviors of students.* Prior to instruction, teachers should become familiar with their students' background knowledge and learning styles. This information is used to determine the level of students' "readiness" for instruction, including their ability to perform basic learning functions such as reading, writing, and communicating. While entry level behavior should *not* solely dictate the nature or direction of the instructional program, when deficiencies are detected, the teacher may be wise to develop additional remedial instructional experiences for all or a portion of the class. These "special" experiences may be treated separately or they may be integrated into the regular program of instruction.

   4.   *Selecting content elements.* The social studies contains a range of approaches and disciplines and many important content elements (concepts, skills, and values). Instructional objectives tend to reflect the selection of approaches, disciplines, and content elements. In addition, the range and level of difficulty of selected topics (concepts, skills, and values) tend to establish the level of instructional difficulty in accordance with the perceived abilities and needs of students. In the recent past, curriculum design experts have tended to emphasize subject-matter elements as a pattern within the curriculum such as in the case of the "spiral curriculum." (During the curriculum reform era known as "the new social studies," several social studies projects were based on a spiral design which, in turn, was based on a set of key concepts that were used in a repeated and continuing pattern to structure an entire social studies curriculum.)

   5.   *Writing performance objectives.* Lists of specific objectives are formulated as behavioral statements that are used to help determine the kind of learning experiences that students will encounter, as well as the type of assessment (evidence) that will be used to suggest the extent of instructional effectiveness. Performance objectives consist of components that help to clarify and specify the instructional objective (target) and the means and indications that will be used to achieve the objective.

   6.   *Developing criterion-referenced tests.* Criterion-referenced tests (referenced to instructional objectives) serve basic functions including in-progress (formative) assessments that help to determine the extent to which students are making progress in achieving the objectives and the final (summative) assessment which should indicate the extent to which students have achieved instructional objectives as a result of instruction. In addition, assessment results may be used for grading purposes. Assessment can also be used to analyze the effects of instruction and to pinpoint any weaknesses or possible areas of the lesson or unit that call for revision.

7. *Developing instructional strategies and activities.* Instructional objectives also help determine which activities and strategies are needed in order to help achieve instructional objectives. Consequently, strategies and activities should be related to important objectives and subject-matter content so that these experiences will provide students with meaningful learning encounters that reinforce course content.

8. *Presenting instruction.* The ultimate proof of any well-designed program of instruction (curriculum, course, unit, or lesson) is its successful presentation to a representative group of students. In an ideal situation, a representative group of students may be used as in a field trial for the program. In a regular classroom, new courses, units, and lessons should be evaluated regularly to make changes deemed effective.

9. *Revising instruction.* Instructional programs can be improved and strengthened by revisions that result from presenting content to students; therefore, student performance and reactions are the best sources of information regarding what techniques, practices, and materials work best in the classroom.

Design Criteria

As a general rule of practice, the design, development, and execution of courses, units, and lessons should meet certain standards of good planning. By applying these standards or criteria, teachers are somewhat assured that their untested programs will have the best probability of success. Thus, these criteria can be used as a checklist for detecting certain flaws in aspects of planning. The following criteria are recommended as a means of assessing the program construction of social studies courses, units, and lessons:

1. *Consistency.* This criterion is often considered the single most important factor in determining the effectiveness of instructional design and development. Each of the parts of instruction must be correlated and interrelated; therefore, the parts or components of instruction should be based on a certain uniform congruity. In other words, objectives, elements of content, and assessment should be directly related in all respects of design, development, and execution. The "rule" of consistency is violated when some unaccounted for item (a topic, for instance) is allowed to influence instruction or assessment. These irregular items often are independent or detached from the systematically planned elements of content. For example, during class the teacher has emphasized the duties of the president in nominating individuals for the U.S.

Supreme Court, but on a related quiz the teacher also asks students to explain the role of the president in naming ambassadors to foreign nations. Consistency can be determined by examining each component of instruction for out of place elements of content. In addition, there should be consistency between the design and development of instruction and the presentation of instruction.

2. Appropriateness. This criterion helps teachers provide instruction that is appropriate to students' needs, to their entry behaviors, and to overall course design. At the same time, appropriateness also suggests that students will be encouraged to progress from one level of understanding to a more advanced level of understanding.

3. Accuracy. This criterion is associated with the subject-matter content of courses, units, and lessons. Information and subject-matter content that is presented to students should be accurate or factually correct. Also, when a social issue is presented in class, teachers should make sure that they provide adequate and balanced information in their presentation and in the resources they make available to students.

4. Substantiveness. This criterion is associated with the importance of the subject matter in light of instructional objectives. Because of the vast amount of information that exists on any given social studies topic, the teacher is required to select which content to include. Substantive issues should be emphasized.

5. Creativity. This criterion is related to the teacher's ability to provide unique activities that help motivate learning. The use of creativity in the instructional setting can encourage students planning and participation in various learning activities.

6. Attractiveness. This criterion is related to the extent to which the presentation of various instructional materials is attractive so that the materials will help promote student learning. In addition, attractiveness is an important aspect of the entire classroom setting. Factors related to environment and setting include displays, use of varied strategies and activities, pictures, maps, and media that help promote student interest and learning activities.

The Purpose and Justification of Instruction

A **rationale** is a statement that outlines the purpose of instruction (sometimes referred to as *mission statement*). This statement is used to justify instruction in light of the cognitive, social, and physical needs of the student as well as content. In addition, a rationale statement often includes a theoretical perspective regarding the nature of learning and the means to be used to present subject matter to students. A rationale statement may identify the overall instructional goals and serve as the guideline for selecting and developing instructional materials for courses, units, and lessons. In developing a rationale statement for courses, Oliver (1977) suggests that teachers might address some of the following concerns:

> the social, cognitive, and physical background and current needs of students
>
> the emphasis on content (e.g., discipline(s) such as history, government, geography, etc.)
>
> the instructional approach or subject field tradition to be incorporated into the program of instruction (e.g., social science, reflective thinking, citizenship, etc.)
>
> the content elements to be emphasized (e.g., knowledge, skills, and values)
>
> the learning principles that will be used in acquiring information or changes in behavior (e.g., objectivist or cognitivist, intuitive inquiry, etc.)
>
> the type of evaluation strategy that will be used to indicate instructional effectiveness and student achievement. (pp. 366–370)

As stated above, a social studies rationale might indicate several instructional approaches such as disciplinary approaches, intellectual skills approaches, and citizenship approaches. These factors are often described in curriculum guides and are intended to reflect a perceived societal need such as drug education, vocational training, or the study of global perspectives. Also an instructional rationale might describe specific student needs such as the need for remedial studies for less knowledgeable students or enrichment needs for gifted students. In summary, a typical rationale statement consists of two or three paragraphs that provide (1) specific goals and reasons for developing the program of instruction, (2) the logical basis behind adopting particular goals, (3) the reason for including certain aspects of content rather than other aspects of content, and (4) the basis for identifying instructional objectives.

Section One: Course Design

Courses are usually designed and developed by teachers in connection with a course study guide that is commonly prepared by a district committee or curriculum supervisors. Normally a course study guide will contain a rationale statement, instructional objectives, lists of course and supplemental materials, and a course outline. Pacing schedules, a calendar of events, and test schedules may also be included. The teacher's task is to develop the course specifics by organizing, developing, and integrating the various components of the course. This process may be aided by the use of a course design model such as the one shown in Figure 15-4.

The Application of a Course Design Model

In the following example, the nine-step design model is applied to the development of a secondary school government course. Included with each step are some examples of materials, processes, and activities that may be used in designing, developing, and presenting a hypothetical American government course.

Step 1: Identifying Course Goals

The identification of course goals often centers on themes and topics that will be addressed within the course. The overall course goals may be reflected in the course title and be further clarified in statements pertaining to curriculum requirements such as lists of important topics, skills, and values that are contained in a curriculum framework. Course goals may be even further clarified in the form of a course *rationale* statement that describes rather than lists the desired outcomes of the course. With these characteristics in mind, a teacher can use the following example to illustrate course goals in the form of a rationale statement (recall that design attempts to answer the questions Where are we going? How will we get there? How will we know when we have arrived?):

> The "American Government" course will emphasize the structure and organization of government throughout American history, including the influences that led to its foundation and development. Related to the foundation of American government are the conditions that led to the writing of the Constitution including the Articles and the Bill of Rights. An important aspect of the study of American government is the civil liberties that were included in the Bill of Rights and the responsibilities of the citizen in light of these rights. Amendments and the reasons for their adoption will be included.
>
> The structure and organization of American government will be explored in regard to the checks and balances that are deemed essential for a stable representative democracy. In addition, students will explore each of the branches of the federal government and its functions, duties, and responsibilities to the citizens of the nation. Through the study of the structure and the organization of the federal government, students will learn the role of the citizen as participant in the public affairs of the nation, state, and local government.
>
> The study of local and state government is aimed at helping students compare various types of government organizations and the functions and services that they perform in health, education, police protection, and the regulation of commerce. Finally, students will be encouraged to study the problems of democratic government and to review various recommendations for reforming government to make it more efficient. Each component of the course will be assessed through a variety of tasks, performances, products, and criterion-referenced tests, which will be used to measure instructional effectiveness and student achievement.

Step 2: Analyzing Subject-Matter Content

When designing a course of study, the teacher should examine the materials that will be used in the instructional setting. Usually, these materials will include teacher resources and references and the materials that will be used by students. In most cases the school district authorities will provide teachers and students with textbooks and related supplemental materials that often are keyed to the course study guide. In addition, the teacher may wish to provide related materials that support instruction. The following are examples of materials and aids used in the presentation of the course of study:

Example: "American Government"

Standard Materials	Supplemental Materials	Related Materials
textbook	transparency kit	pamphlets
teacher's guide	filmstrip kit	picture sets
test booklet	district films	charts
workbook	study guide set	political map set
selected maps		review questions
		videocassettes
		personal slides

An analysis of instructional materials is helpful in identifying important ideas and elements of content (concepts, skills, and values), which also may reflect course instructional objectives and suggest strategies and activities and types of assessments that might be developed in connection with the course of study.

Step 3: Identifying Needs and Entry Behaviors

Before beginning a course, the teacher will want to gather information on students' learning needs, especially in connection with the prerequisites of the course. This information might include information regarding the ability, knowledge, and interests of each student. In some situations, the teacher should develop a diagnostic pretest that can provide information on the background knowledge of students related to the theme and content of the course.

Example: Identifying Needs and Entry Behaviors

Background Information	Pretesting	Interviews and Surveys
discussion with previous teachers	tests items designed to indicate basic skills	getting acquainted interview
cumulative file	tests items designed to indicate background knowledge in social studies	survey on interests and goals, hobbies, and past experiences
discussion with counselors		

Background Information	**Pretesting**	**Interviews and Surveys**
discussion with parents	tests items designed to indicate current knowledge of program elements	discussion on course interests related to topics and units
profiling learning strengths and weaknesses and level of self-confidence		discussions on preferred approaches and activities

Step 4: Selecting Content Elements

The selection of content elements (key concepts, target skills, and core values) will emphasize various aspects of the course. Identifying and listing content elements help the teacher emphasize them throughout the course. Therefore, by listing the important concepts, skills, and values at the beginning of the year, students are alerted to key items that warrant special attention, and they will realize that these elements will appear repeatedly throughout the units and lessons of the course.

Example: List of Content Elements Related to a Course

Key Concepts	**Target Skills**	**Core Values**
sovereignty	interpreting charts	equality
public policy	interpreting tables	freedom
federal system	locating information	due process
civil liberties	writing reports	rights
civil rights	constructing time lines	responsibilities
majority rule	analyzing an issue	democracy
ratification	passing a bill	impartiality
executive	conflict resolution	discrimination
legislative	interpreting symbols	
judicial		

Furthermore, content elements can be organized within a course outline and can be arranged on a course planning calendar. The course outline serves as an applied intermediate step between the identification of the important topics and the development of units; therefore, a course outline would include unit themes as important headings in the course outline. Once the course outline has been developed, it can be correlated with a course calendar. The planning calendar is also an intermediate step between the identification of content elements and the further development of a course plan in which course units and specific lesson plans are developed. The calendar helps the teacher make the transition between planning instruction and executing instruction. The following examples illustrate the scheduling of units within a course structure:

Example: General Course Outline by Units of Instruction

Unit 1   Foundations of Government
Unit 2   Civil Rights and Civil Liberty
Unit 3   Federal Government
Unit 4   The Executive Branch
Unit 5   The Judicial Branch
Unit 6   The Legislative Branch
Unit 7   Participation in the Affairs of Government
Unit 8   State Government
Unit 9   Local Government
Unit 10   Government Reform

Example: Course Planning Calendar

Unit 1	Sept. 7 - Oct. 1	Foundations of Government
Unit 2	Oct. 2 - Nov. 1	Civil Rights and Civil Liberty
Unit 3	Nov. 2 - Dec. 2	Federal Government
Unit 4	Dec. 3 - Dec. 23	The Executive Branch
Unit 5	Jan. 12 - Feb. 2	The Judicial Branch
Unit 6	Feb. 3 - March 2	The Legislative Branch
Unit 7	March 3 - April 5	Participation in the Affairs of Government
Unit 8	April 6 - April 20	State Government
Unit 9	April 21- May 2	Local Government
Unit 10	May 3 - June 8	Government Reform

Step 5: Writing Performance Objectives

Performance objectives are used to help direct the instructional program toward goals and outcomes so that students will acquire specific learning behaviors as a result of instruction. As compared to unit and lesson objectives, course objectives take a relatively long period of time to achieve. For example, the teacher may want students to develop the ability to construct a series of comparative organizational charts of various governmental organizations at the federal, state, and local levels. The following are examples of course objectives:

Example: Course Objectives

Desired Student Behaviors	Object of the Behavior
To describe	civil liberties and civil rights as an aspect of American government

Desired Student Behaviors	Object of the Behavior
To apply	the methods used by political scientists to measure public opinion regarding a current public issue
To distinguish	between the role and function of the three branches of government
To evaluate	the extent to which culture influences voting patterns in urban centers of American cities
To construct	a series of comparative organizational charts related to federal, state, and local governmental structure

Step 6: Developing Criterion-Referenced Assessments

Criterion-referenced assessments are used to indicate the extent to which specific course objectives have been achieved as a result of instruction. Therefore, course design and development require a comprehensive evaluation plan in which assessment items are correlated with specific course objectives. Whenever behavioral objectives are used in designing and planning a course of study, the comprehensive evaluation plan should include formative tests and a summative test that monitor and measure instructional effectiveness and student achievement. According to such a plan, formative tests would be scheduled at periodic intervals, usually after the completion of a unit, while the summative test would be scheduled at the end of the course.

Example: Comprehensive Evaluation Plan

Formative Assessment	Summative Assessment	Possible Assessment Strategies
Periodic tests	Final course test	1. Diagnostic testing
		2. Formative testing
		3. Summative testing

    a. for instructional effectiveness (by criterion-referenced strategies)
   — portfolio
   — checklists
   — written reports
   — direct observations
   — performance
   — activities
   — self-assessment

    b. for achievement (by norm-referenced strategies)
   — multiple-choice tests
   — essay tests

Step 7: Developing Course Strategies and Activities

Once course objectives have been identified, teachers can plan course strategies and learning activities. The development of course strategies and activities should correlate with course objectives (Nerbovig, 1970). Course strategies include the main instructional settings in which content will be presented to students. For example, the teacher might decide to use a cooperative small-group setting as an alternating strategy with whole-group teacher presentations. Course activities include selected learning experiences that students will participate in at the opening and close of the course as well as those major course projects that will be executed sometime during the course. Activities are an essential aspect of social studies learning because the activities or learning tasks are important means of affecting changes in behavior (that is, acquisition of a new skill), and these changes would influence both the short-term and the long-term behavior of the student.

For example, secondary school students might work on a term paper throughout the course, and the paper would be presented in final form at the end of the term. In other situations, learning activities may take several weeks to complete, and they can take the form of a class, group, or student project. The government class may take a field trip to Washington D.C. to gain firsthand experience in the physical and operational nature of the federal government in March. During the course, the students learned about the structure of the federal government, its operations, and the relationship between the executive, legislative, and judicial branches of government. After returning from Washington, students are required to construct displays and to write reports on their Washington experiences. These experiences are then compared with the impressions acquired from their studies prior to the field trip.

Example: Course Strategies and Activities

Course Objective	Instructional Strategy	Learning Activity
To construct a series of comparative organizational charts related to federal, state, and local governmental structure	Project setting	Students will construct a series of three comparative governmental charts.

Step 8: Presenting Course Instruction

In presenting a course of study to students, teachers may wish to follow a pattern of direct instruction in which they introduce, present, and close the course. The opening of the course may provide general information about the course to students and give the teacher the chance to gather information about student knowledge and readiness for the course. Items addressed at the opening of the course may include a course overview or explanation of the purpose and major features of the course, a pretest that may help to determine student readiness for the course, or an opening activity that promotes student interest in the course.

The body or core of the course provides a thematic structure or framework that consists of units. At the close of a course, students are encouraged to participate in some type of culminating activity that reviews and reinforces course objectives. The culminating activity may be in the form of a project or experiences that help to tie together content and to review the important instructional components presented during the course. In addition, the course review and reinforcement should help prepare students to address the summative evaluation instrument that will be used to indicate instructional effectiveness and student achievement.

Example: Course Presentation Cycle

Opening the Course	Presenting the Core of the Course	Closing the Course
Overview	Components for course instruction in the form of units of study	Culminating activity
Pretest	Course strategies	Course review and reinforcement
Motivating activity	Course activities	Final course assessment

Step 9: Revising Instruction

Following instruction, the teacher should analyze the results of instruction and revise course elements based on the data and insight gained as a result of presenting the course to students. Throughout the course, the teacher may wish to keep a log of impressions and reactions to instruction along with recommendations for revising the course. More important, at or near the close of the course, the teacher should attempt to pull together and interpret all assessment information that has been accumulated from formative unit tests and the final course test. By continually correlating test items with specific course objectives, the teacher should attempt to determine the extent to which each course objective was achieved. Through this analysis, the teacher should make a list of instructional weaknesses and difficulties. In addition, the teacher may wish to compare the entry behaviors of students with their exit behaviors to determine the extent to which student behavior has been modified by instructional experiences. Finally, the teacher should re-examine each course objective in light of outcomes to assess the clarity and the reasonableness of these objectives.

Section Two: Unit Design

Unit planning is an important aspect of course development and is an important responsibility of the teacher. Most teachers have developed special units to supplement their regular textbook programs and thereby are familiar with the modularized format of the unit. In some situations, units have served as a type of minicourse that was developed by teachers with some special purpose in mind.

The unit of instruction has its roots in the instructional revolution that began during the Progressive Era. Progressive reformers wanted a more scientific education for American society that was aimed at helping children develop a systematic understanding of the topics, issues, and processes that were to be taught. John Dewey often is associated with the origins of the science of education movement and his views on thinking caused others to advance unit instruction. According to Nerbovig (1970),

> Elizabeth Berry credits both John Dewey's and Johann Friedrick Herbart's thinking as being the basis of unit work; especially Dewey in his "How We Think" in which the use of a problem, performing its analysis and solution, are [sic] suggested as profitable. Henry Morrison also was an early proponent of unit preparation and use; he recommended that unit study should proceed through the phases of exploration, presentation, assimilation, organization, and recitation. Berry credits Morrison as having improved upon the Herbartian steps of preparation, presentation, comparison, generalization, and application. (p. 3)

Following World War II, educators were wrestling with important decisions regarding what subjects should be taught in the schools and with organizational issues aimed at making instruction more efficient and effective. Again, the unit of instruction was seen as an essential structure of presenting information to students, especially in light of the rapid expansion of knowledge that was taking place in all disciplines. Nerbovig (1970) again points out that

> Subject matter experts as well as curriculum leaders see the unit as a way of bringing order to the many concepts, generalizations, skills and attitudes from the "knowledge explosion" that are available to be taught. (p. 4)

Social studies units can be classified according to four major types. Each type serves a special purpose in social studies instruction.

1. *Resource units.* These units are usually developed by a committee of teachers or can be written by an individual instructor for his or her use or for other teachers. Resource units may be produced commercially by textbook companies or by governmental organizations and local or private agencies. The resource unit is *not* meant to be taught as such but provides the resources on

which teachers can draw for their own instructional needs. Therefore, a resource unit may not be related to a specific class or grade level, but is meant to be a rich source of suggested ideas, aids, activities, materials, references, films, and games. Consequently, the resource unit has many more ideas and materials than the teacher could possibly include as a standard teaching unit.

2. *Textbook units.* These units are designed to be taught sequentially according to the order of the textbook or course guides. In addition to textbook lesson plans, the unit worksheets and supportive activities are important unit items. For example, an American history course would be divided into units for instructional purposes. Each unit presents a segment of the course that has been organized according to a teacher's prescribed unit format. In addition to the textbook, the teacher has developed supplemental materials and collected additional resources that may supplement or to some extent replace the standard classroom textbook. These units are sometimes referred to as teaching or learning units.

3. *Special topic units.* These units are developed by the teacher to convey a body of information related to a special social studies topic. These topics may reflect a contemporary problem that has arisen because of certain unfolding events not addressed in the curriculum or course study guide. In addition, a special topic unit may be needed to address certain instructional needs related to the community. For example, students living in a petroleum-producing area may benefit from a special unit that explores the history, technology, and impact of the oil field. In addition, special topic units for the social studies include other important issues related to contemporary American society such as

multiethnic studies,

education for sex equality,

career education,

law-related education,

global education, and

environmental and energy education

4. *Skill units.* Units that deal with specific social studies skills. These units are designed to help students develop skills that will help them become more effective learners. For example, a social studies teacher might develop skill units in reading, writing, and inquiry in the social studies. In addition, students may need additional skill development in a content area of the social studies such as gathering and illustrating information or making comparisons in chart form. Since the mid-1980s, geography skills have re-emerged as an important social studies concern, and as a result, social studies teachers are developing special skill units designed to help students acquire a variety of map skills.

In most instructional settings, the unit of instruction is comprised of a relatively large segment of instruction. Normally units may run from two to four weeks. Teachers often combine more than several textual chapters into their single units. The components of the unit include important instructional elements such as resources, objectives, elements of content, patterns for organization, learning experiences, schedules of instruction, and the assessment instruments. Like the course of study, units of study can be developed according to the nine-step design model presented earlier (Fig. 15-4) in this chapter. Therefore, this model can be used to help teachers plan and present units by following the sequenced steps of our model.

The Application of the Design Model in Unit Form

Teachers can use the nine-step model as the basis for unit design, development, and presentation. As in the American government course example, the model will be applied to the development of a unit of instruction that was identified previously as the course unit entitled, "Civil Rights and Civil Liberties."

Step 1: *Identifying Unit Goals*

The title of the unit, "Civil Rights and Civil Liberties," suggests that this unit will focus on the rights of the citizens in regard to the Bill of Rights. The title also may suggest that students will study "rights" as protections under a variety of circumstances involving the citizen and governmental actions. This focus is further clarified by a review of the unit materials that are provided as the basis for instruction. In addition, the teacher may develop a unit *rationale statement* that may provide a justification for the unit, but also to help identify unit goals. While a unit rationale is, to some extent, a product of the course rationale, the unit statement tends to be more explicit about the overall goal(s) of the unit. For example, the unit rationale statement for "Civil Rights and Civil Liberties" might declare:

> The "Civil Rights and Civil Liberties" unit will emphasize the First Amendment of the Bill of Rights with special emphasis on religious freedom, free speech, freedom of the press, and the freedom of assembly. In addition, the unit will focus on the judiciary process known as "due process of the law" and the related amendments to the Bill or Rights that pertain to civil liberties, the rights of the accused, and the practices that ensure a fair trial and the right to privacy.
>
> In addition, this unit will emphasize the concept of "equal protection under the law" as it has been applied to important court cases. Special attention will be paid to various groups who have sought to gain equal recognition and protection under the law through the civil rights movement that spans the period of time from the end of World War II up to the present time.

Step 2: Analyzing Subject-Matter Content

One of the most important initial steps in unit development is the identification and analysis of instructional resources. Unit resources are available from a variety of sources within and outside the school. In a situation where the textbook is the main source of subject-matter content, the teacher should carefully review the chapter that pertains to civil rights and civil liberties to determine the need for additional supplemental materials including readings, documents, films, and case studies. The unit should contain a unit bibliography in which the sources of supplemental materials are identified and described. We recommend that the bibliography be classified according to those materials to be used exclusively by the teacher and those to be used by students within the instructional setting.

Example: Unit Resources

Teacher Resources

Center for Civic Education, *We the people . . . the citizen and the constitution*, Calabasis, California: The Center, 1993.

Graber, Doris A., *Mass Media and American Politics*, 2nd ed., Congressional Quarterly, 1984.

Kaplan, H. (ed.), the delicate balance II: *Our Bill of Rights.* Chicago; American Bar Association. 1994

Kluger, Richard, *Simple Justice*, New York: Knopf, 1976.

Student Resources

Printed Resources:

Lewis, Anthony, *Gideon's Trumpet*, New York: Random House, 1964.

Audio Visual:

Criminal Justice and a Defendant's Right to a Fair Trial, 60-minute film, Films, Inc. Wilmette, IL.

Eyes on the Prize (Six 60-minute videos), PBS Videos, Alexandria, VA.

Civil Rights: Yesterday, Today, Tomorrow (filmstrip), Guidance Associates, Communication Park, Mount Kisco, NY.

Step 3: Identifying Needs and Entry Behaviors

Before beginning unit instruction, the teacher may need to collect information regarding student knowledge related to "Civil Rights and Civil Liberties." To some extent, this information has been collected at the beginning of the year in connection with course prerequisites of the subject-matter topics and skills. Unit prerequisites that may be addressed in a unit pretest might be used to determine student readiness for unit instruction; however, a unit pretest is not needed in situations in which the teacher is aware of the students' learning attributes and background knowledge. The following items might appear in a unit pretest related to our unit on "Civil Rights and Civil Liberties":

Example: Unit Pretest

In the blanks, label each of the following statements as true (T) or false (F).

_____ 1. The mayor of our city can provide a Christmas tree for city hall.
_____ 2. The principle of our school can write and deliver a morning prayer.
_____ 3. You can ignore a school rule that violates your beliefs.
_____ 4. You can yell "fire" in a theater if you feel like it.
_____ 5. You can print a story about a school board member if you have evidence.
_____ 6. Libel and slander mean the same thing.
_____ 7. If your rights have been violated, you can participate in a riot.
_____ 8. A judge can decide if a law applies to a certain group of people.
_____ 9. Evidence acquired by accident cannot be used in court.

(As a rule of thumb, true and false items can be used in a pretest, but should be generally avoided in formative or summative assessments because of validity and reliability problems.)

Step 4: Selecting Content Elements

Content elements include important unit concepts, skills, and values that will be highlighted and emphasized throughout the presentation of the unit. These elements can be identified through the development of a unit outline in which important subject-matter elements are identified; in most cases a topic (or conceptual) outline will be developed.

Example: Unit Outline

I. Civil Rights
   A. The Bill of Rights
      1. The Constitution and the Bill of Rights
      2. Review of First 10 Amendments
         a. Religious Freedom
         b. Freedom of Speech
            (1.) Protection of Speech
            (2.) Limitation on Actions
            (3.) Symbolic Speech
            (4). Obscene Speech
         c. Freedom of Assembly
         d. Other Freedoms
   B. The Historical Struggle for Civil Rights
      1. Property and Citizenship Rights
      2. Indentured Servant and Slavery
      3. Expanding Citizenship Rights
   C. The Civil Rights Movement
      1. Black Americans and Post Civil War Struggles

    2. The Civil Rights Movement and Education
    3. The Civil Rights movement in the 1960s
    4. Civil Rights and Public Policy
 II. Civil Liberties
    A. The Citizen and the Government
    B. Exercising First Amendment Rights
      a. School Prayer
      b. Slander in the Press
      c. Politically Correct Speech (speech codes)
    C. Due Process and Civil Liberties
    D. The Rights of the Accused
    E. Trial by Jury
    F. Cruel and Unusual Punishment

The outline, once complete, can be organized into a unit planning calendar, which is a convenient intermediate step toward scheduling instruction and developing individual lesson plans. The planning calendar also serves as an intermediate step between the identification of unit content and the further development of lesson plans. (As was previously recommended in connection with courses, teachers may wish to provide students with a copy of the unit planning calendar to help them organize their notebooks. The planning calendar also could be used to help open lessons and to provide students with an overview of instruction.) Moreover, the unit planning calendar is an important means for sequencing instruction. Most of all, the planning calendar serves the important function of bringing the unit together into a total unit design or structure which includes:

1. The instructional elements that will open the unit (overview, pretest, and motivating activity)
2. The instructional elements that will serve as the core of the unit, including the components of content—concepts, skills, and values; the instructional strategies; and the learning activities
3. The instructional elements that will be used to close the unit—the culminating activity, review and reinforcement activities, and the final unit assessment

Example: Unit Planning Calendar

Week #1

Day 1
Unit Opener

Day 2
I. *Civil Rights*
  A. Bill of Rights
    1. The Constitution and the Bill of Rights
    (Review of first ten Amendments)

Week #1

Day 3
(continue with ten Amendments)
       a. Religious Freedom
       b. Freedom of Speech
           (1.) Protection
           (2.) Limits on Actions
           (3.) Symbolic Speech
           (4.) Obscene Speech

Day 4
    B. The Historic Struggle for Civil Rights
       1. Property and Citizens' Rights
       2. Indentured Servants and Slavery
       3. Expanded Citizens' Rights

Day 5
The Civil Rights Movement
The Civil Rights Movement and Education

Week #2

Day 6
II. *Civil Liberties*
    A. The Citizen and the Government
    B. Exercising First Amendment Rights

Day 7
    C. Due Process and Civil Liberties
    D. The Rights of the Accused
    E. Trial by Jury

Day 8
Unit Culmination
Trial Simulation

Day 9
Unit Culmination
Trial Simulation

Day 10
Final Unit Assessment

The content elements contained in the outline and instructional planning calendar may be further selected for presentation in concept, skill, and value form. This process will be illustrated in lesson design later in this chapter.

Step 5: Writing Performance Objectives

Unit objectives are related to those of the course in the sense that they help to advance the development of course objectives. Therefore, while stated in the same manner as course objectives, unit objectives are more specifically focused on smaller segments of content (such as topics, events, concepts, skills, and values). Unit objectives may be derived from the unit rationale and from the theme of the unit. In general, unit objectives tend to focus on certain instructional trends (such as themes, concepts, and skills) that are addressed throughout the unit; at the same time, unit objectives help to tie the unit together because the activities used to open and close the unit are correlated to unit objectives. In addition, unit assessment items are correlated to unit objectives. The following are examples of unit objectives:

Example: Unit Objectives

Desired Student Behaviors	Object of the Behavior
To describe	the First Amendment as protection of individual rights in connection with religion, speech, press, and assembly
To apply	the judiciary process known as "due process of the law" to a variety of situations and circumstances
To summarize	the rights of the accused by relating these rights to a trial situation
To analyze	the ways in which "equal protection under the law" have been applied to selected individuals and groups within American society
To dramatize	a simulated trial situation based on a student's script that focuses on freedom of speech and speech-action

Step 6: Developing Criterion-Referenced Assessments

Criterion-referenced unit assessments are used to determine the extent to which instruction was effective in achieving unit objectives. Assessments administered during instruction are termed "informative" or "in-progress" assessments, while assessments administered at the close of the unit covering all unit objectives are called "summative" assessments. In addition, the summative test may be used, in part, to assign individual grades as an indication of individual achievement. Both formative and summative evaluations should measure student learning of the unit objectives. While student learning is often measured in the form of a pencil-and-paper test, other forms of evaluation should be used to measure effective instruction, including a combination of measurements. (An over-reliance on tests in assigning grades can be a serious weakness in the evaluation plan. See Chapter 13.)

Example: In-Progress Test Items

1. The first ten amendments to the Constitution are collectively called:
    a. civil liberties
    b. pure speech
    c. the Smith Act
    d. Bill of Rights
    e. the free exercise clause

2. Religious freedom is guaranteed in:
    a. the First Amendment
    b. the Declaration of Independence
    c. Virginia Statute of Religious Liberty
    d. *Marbury v. Madison*
    e. the Fourth Amendment

3. Symbolic speech is a type of expression where:
    a. the rules of silence are imposed
    b. objects and actions replace words
    c. regardless of the action, the message must be honored
    d. crude jesters are better than words
    e. anything goes and is legally permitted

4. Before the Civil War, this famous court case affected the status of slaves:
    a. Dred Scott
    b. *Brown v. Brown*
    c. *Plessy v. Ferguson*
    d. *Scott v. Sanford*
    e. *Mapp v. Ohio*

5. Civil disobedience was a civil rights strategy used to:
    a. free the slaves before the Civil War
    b. reconstruct the South after the Civil War
    c. help desegregate the South after World War II
    d. help unify India and was borrowed from Martin Luther King
    e. pass the Civil Rights Act of 1964

Step 7: Developing Unit Strategies and Activities

Unit strategies are learning experiences that engage students in the subject-matter content of the unit. These strategies along with subject-matter content truly represent the "heart" of the unit. Using several unit strategies or combinations of strategies is desirable when teaching for an extended period of time in order to maintain student interest in the unit. For example, specific unit strategies might be used to motivate learning, to introduce the unit, to culminate the unit, and to review and reinforce the unit. By determining the most desirable instructional setting for the unit (especially in light of the unit subject matter), the instructor can more easily identify specific instructional strategies that would be most effective for unit instruction. Unit activities may be used to open, develop, and close the unit. Moreover, unit activities are used to help develop content elements (concepts, skills, and values) to be emphasized within the unit. A unit activity placed at the beginning of the unit may be used to motivate student interest in the unit, whereas a unit activity placed at the end of the unit may review and reinforce content that was taught during the unit.

Example: Unit Strategies and Activities

Instructional Strategies	Activities and Projects
Whole-group setting: lecture discussion	*Unit opener:* guest speaker
Small-group setting: cooperative learning	*Unit body:* scrapbook written report mobile panel presentation role play
Simulated setting: socio-drama simulated trial case studies	
Individual setting: library study	*Unit closer:* simulated trial
Problem setting: problem solving	

Step 8: Presenting Unit Instruction

In presenting a unit of study to students, the teacher may wish to follow a pattern suggested previously, in which the unit is introduced, presented, and closed. As part of an introduction to the unit, the teacher may wish to provide a unit overview that orients students to the unit. As a general rule, the purpose of the unit overview is to provide a detailed explanation of the theme of the unit, a brief description of the important components of content (concepts, skills, and values), and a preview of topics and unit activities and projects. In addition, teachers may explain unit grading and reporting practices that they will follow to determine a unit grade. The teacher also may wish to gather information regarding the students' readiness for unit instruction. In some situations, a unit pretest may help to determine students' readiness, especially when there are prerequisite requirements such as knowledge of certain topics or skills. The introductory phase of unit presentation may include a motivating activity designed to enhance student interest. For example, interest in the unit might be enhanced through a dramatic reading from a novel devoted to aspects of government, such as *All the Kings Men,* or through the presentation of a film such as *Due Process of Law Denied* from the *Ox Bow Incident.*

Unit subject matter will be presented in connection with a related series of lessons that address selected subject-matter topics. These topics may be organized around key concepts, target skills, and core values related to the course of study. The means of presentation will include lesson strategies and activities that are selected to provide students with meaningful learning experiences.

Toward the close of unit instruction the teacher may wish to involve students in a culminating activity that reviews and reinforces the important elements of subject-matter content that were presented during unit instruction. This review may be used to help students recognize relationships between related ideas that have been presented. In addition, the teacher should help prepare students for some form of unit evaluation. Unit assessment helps to determine the extent to which unit objectives have been acquired by students as a result of instruction.

Example: Unit Presentation Cycle

Opening the Unit	Presenting the Core of the Unit	Closing the Unit
Overview	Concepts, skills, and values	Culminating activity
Pretest	Lesson strategies	Unit review and reinforcement
Motivating activity	Lesson activities	Final unit assessment

Step 9: Revising Instruction

Soon after the results of instruction have been determined, the teacher may wish to review the unit for weaknesses in design, development, and presentation. This review may indicate that some changes should be made in various aspects of the unit, including unit objectives, materials, strategies, activities, and assessment. This review may also suggest changes for the treatment of a subsequent unit. In addition, teachers may wish to keep a daily log to record their immediate reactions to the effectiveness of various elements of instruction.

Section Three: Lesson Design

The social studies teacher's essential responsibilities of designing, developing, and presenting lessons are often met through varied practices according to school district policy. Planning formats tend to range from a loose type of planning calendar to a highly structured format in which certain instructional elements must be addressed. In general, no single planning and presenting format is accepted by all school officials; therefore, in some situations, school policy might dictate that a certain lesson plan format must be used; in more situations, lesson plan formats are left to the discretion of individual teachers. In recent years there has been a growing awareness that lesson plans should include both design and execution features to help guide the development and presentation of the lesson. For many teachers, lesson plans are a necessary aspect of presenting classroom instruction because they may contain the minute-by-minute schedule of instruction that can be used as a reference guide for carrying out classroom activities. Because the nine-step model (Figure 15-4) contains provisions for designing, developing, and presenting instruction, it also can be used to help teachers develop lesson plans.

The Application of the Design Model in Lesson Plan Form

As was the case with course and unit design, in most instructional situations, lesson design is developed around course materials and study guides that have been provided by school officials, as well as those units and special materials developed by the teacher. Lesson design, for example, is directly tied to the course and unit design since lessons are the specific means through which courses and units are presented over the duration of the school year. According to the nine-step model, a lesson plan should include certain opening or pre-instructional activities such as prior student preparation, behavioral objectives, elements of content (concepts, skills, and values), instructional strategy(ies), lesson activity(ies), a sequenced procedure for presenting the lesson to students, and closing activities including aspects of evaluation, lesson feedback, next assignments, and provisions for revising the lesson.

Step 1: Identifying Lesson Goals

The theme of the lesson may suggest the overall lesson goal and clarify the overall purpose and justification of the lesson. Day six from the previously presented American government unit has been selected to illustrate the use of the nine-step model in designing, developing, and presenting a lesson. The theme of the lesson is "Exercising First Amendment Rights." The lesson rationale declares that:

> Citizens (students) should become familiar with the applications and limitations of their First Amendment rights.

Step 2: Analyzing Subject-Matter Content

Prior to instruction, it is generally recommended that teachers make a list of the materials including textbook pages and instructional materials (transparencies, etc.) needed for presenting the lesson as well as materials pertaining to student tasks, activities, and assignments. These materials should be listed on the lesson plan to remind the teacher that these items need to be prepared prior to instruction, usually at least one day in advance of instruction.

Example: Review of Lesson Materials

Textbook and Related Materials	Instructional Materials	Materials for Student Tasks and Activities
textbook reading assignment pp. 170–180	transparencies pictures chalkboard checklist	student notebooks

Step 3: Identifying Needs and Entry Behaviors

Before lesson instruction, the teacher should try to determine student readiness for the lesson and to prepare students for the lesson by asking questions pertaining to their understanding of First Amendment rights. For example, the students might be asked some of the following questions before instruction:

1. Can the government make laws that would lead to the establishment of a national church? Why or why not?

2. What and on what basis are the types of aid that government can provide for church-affiliated schools?

3. How are speech and "speech-plus" different concerning what is acceptable to the courts?

4. Why would First Amendment rights be important to individuals living in a democratic society?

Student responses might help the teacher decide whether students are ready for this lesson, whether additional preparation is needed, or if aspects of the lesson need to be emphasized.

Step 4: Selecting Content Elements

Content elements include important lesson concepts, skills, and values that will be highlighted and emphasized throughout the presentation of lessons. These elements were originally identified in the unit outline and scheduled for instruction in the unit planning calendar.

Example: Lesson Content Elements

Category	Classification	Specific Elements
Concept list	Freedom of speech	pure speech speech-plus speech codes sedition defamation libel and slander
	Freedom of press	censorship prior restraint injunction obscenity source protection
	Freedom of assembly	pickets parades strikes speech disruption riots
Skill list	Categorizing	acceptable and unaccept- able speech press and assembly
Value list	Prizing	speech, press, and assembly in a democratic society

Step 5: Writing Performance Objectives

Lesson objectives are also related to course and unit objectives in the sense that they help to advance the development of course and unit objectives. The format of lesson objectives is the same as that for the course and unit. Lesson objectives are more specific in regard to unbiased elements or conditions (behavior, object of the behavior, task conditions, and acceptable performance standards). In addition, the teacher may wish to distinguish between the use of **primary** and **secondary objectives** (supportive or enabling objectives or related objectives that clarify and support the development of the primary lesson objective). Once formulated, the primary lesson objective may be used to guide the development of the lesson plan.

Example: Lesson Objectives

Objective	Desired Student Behavior	Object of the Behavior	Task Conditions	Performance Standard
Primary objective	to Describe	First Amendment freedoms —speech, press, and assembly	whole-group setting based on teacher presentation and discussion	Each student will be able to provide an example of First Amentment rights and a completed T-Chart
Secondary objective	to Categorize	First Amendment rights— speech, press and assembly (according to acceptable and unacceptable classifications)	whole-group activity (Chalkboard T-Chart)*	
Secondary objective	to List	three reasons why First Amendment rights are important in a democratic society	individual notebook entry	completed notebook entry

*A T-Chart is a convenient means for illustrating a comparison of characteristics in which the horizontal line is divided by a vertical line thus forming a T. One side of the T represents "acceptable" while the other side represents "unacceptable" expressions of First Amendment rights.

Step 6: Developing Criterion-Referenced Assessments

At or near the close of the lesson, the teacher should assess the extent to which lesson objectives have been achieved. Criterion-referenced lesson assessment could focus on some type of objective correlated student feedback once the lesson has been completed.

Example: Lesson Feedback

Lesson Objective	Performance Standard	Feedback
Primary objective	Each student will be able to provide an example of First Amendment rights in a whole-group setting.	A checklist will be used to record individual student contributions.
Secondary objective	Students in a whole-group setting will fill in a chalkboard T-Chart.	Each side of the T-Chart will contain six items.
Secondary objective	Each student will make a notebook entry listing three reasons why First Amendment rights are important in a democratic society.	The teacher will quickly check each student's three notebook entries.

Step 7: *Developing Lesson Strategies and Activities*

Lesson strategies consist primarily of teacher-centered activities related to the presentation of the lesson. The selection of appropriate strategies can greatly influence student understanding of social studies subject matter. Lesson activities should provide students with learning experiences directly related to the theme or topic of the lesson. Activities are the means through which an objective can be implemented; therefore, activities are used in conjunction with instructional objectives. It is normal to include several different strategies and activities for a single class hour.

Example: Lesson Strategy

Lesson Objective	Strategy
Primary lesson objective	*Whole-group setting:* teacher presentation lead class discussion
Secondary objective	*Whole group:* direct the T-Chart activity
Secondary objective	*Individual setting:* supervise written notebook entry

Example: Lesson Activity

Activity	Purpose	Student Instruction in Sequential Order	Some Expected Outcome
Chalkboard T-Chart activity	to categorize First Amendment Rights — speech, press, and assembly (according to acceptable and unacceptable classifications)	1. Review textbook section on First Amendment Rights. 2. Make a list of speech, press, and assembly actions as described in the textbook. 3. Categorize each action according to its acceptability in described incidences and court cases using violence as a decision-making criteria. 4. Participate in the construction of the chalkboard T-Chart	At least six acceptable actions will be listed under each side of the T-Chart. *Right Side:* Acceptable First Amendment Right Actions (e.g., debate, wearing arm-bands, picketing, marching, reporting, attending public and private meetings) *Left Side:* Unacceptable First Amendment Actions (e.g., sedition, call for a violent over-throw of legitimate government, false fire alarm, slander, and obscenity)

Step 8: Presenting Lesson Instruction

Prior to lesson instruction, teachers should give students an overview of the lesson, thereby providing them with a detailed explanation of the lesson and its elements (concepts, skills, and values as well as the general procedure of the lesson) and its importance to them. Often this includes a one- or two-paged handout for their notebooks. The body of the lesson would include the main elements of instruction that would be used in meeting lesson objectives. In closing the lesson, teachers should work with the students on a review or summary of the lesson with special emphasis on important content elements (concepts, skill, and values). In addition, teachers should take the time to acquire student feedback on their understandings acquired as a result of instruction.

Example: Lesson Cycle

Lesson Opener	Procedure or Order of the Lesson	Lesson Closure	Lesson Feedback
Introduction: review motivator attention getter overview	Sequential order of the lesson and estimated amount of instructional time	Summary: review reinforcement	Feedback strategy: quiz oral questions examples explanations
"Can the government stop a suspected terrorist from going on TV to make a speech against the President of the United States?"	Teacher Presentation and discussion (estimated 20 minutes) Chalkboard T-Chart activity (estimated 20 minutes) Individual notebook entry (estimated 10 minutes)	"Today you learned that First Amendment rights include freedom of speech, press, and assembly and related responsibilities."	"Give an example of why First Amendment rights are important to individuals in a democratic society."

Step 9: Revising Instruction

Soon after the lesson has been completed, and after considering student feedback, the teacher should review and alter any aspects of the lesson that will help improve acquisition of the objectives. As an ongoing practice, teachers should review and clarify all behavioral objectives and analyze and possibly modify the components of the lesson (concepts, skills, values, activities, and strategies). As a routine practice, the teacher should note all recommended changes on the lesson plan as a reminder and for future reference and for possible alterations in the next lesson.

Simple One-Page Lesson Plan

Most schools expect their teachers to develop lesson plan forms that in some fashion specify how they will be used in presenting the content of instruction.

Lesson plans enable teachers to execute instructional parts of their professional responsibilities. In addition, lesson plans help make the teacher instructionally more effective. Moreover, the lesson plan is required for those times when the teacher is absent and a substitute instructor takes the class. The lesson plan shown in Figure 15-5 will help you learn to fulfill this responsibility and at the same time to develop daily lesson plans based on some of the design principles emphasized throughout this volume. (Appendix A contains a more complex and extensive lesson plan, which includes more in-depth design training and is suggested for use by experienced teachers who are interested in adopting a more complete approach to instructional planning and presentation.)

CONCLUSIONS

In this chapter, you learned that even though you only indirectly influence the design and development of the social studies curriculum, you do exercise a great deal of influence over design, development, and implementation of courses, units, and lessons. One of the myths of education is the myth of standardization. The myth of standardization is based on the assumption that course titles indicate students will be presented with the same or similar courses of study. In reality, a course of study should be identified by the teacher's name such as "Ms. Smith's American History" or "Mr. Jones' American Government," thus indicating the extent to which the teacher influences a course of study, including how subject-matter content will be presented and interpreted. In other words, student learning experiences are greatly determined by each teacher's knowledge, training, preferences, world view, experiences, and personality. In 1983, Gross and Dynneson made the following observation:

> Course titles tend to report on the general framework of the social studies curriculum without giving much detailed information on the specifics of the course. Also, two teachers teaching from the same framework can vary the emphasis of their instruction so that there is little similarity between what takes place in one classroom and another classroom. Frameworks and scope and sequence charts are poor predictors of the actual practices of teachers. . . . More often than not, they [instructors] teach from highly structured textbooks, which include some of the features of these frameworks; but they may actually be teaching a variety of courses under the same course title. A more accurate picture of the status of the social studies may be found in a careful examination of social studies textbooks and particularly, of the behaviors of individual teachers. (p. 11)

Course, unit, and lesson design planning and implementation stems from decisions that teachers make prior to the beginning of instruction. By crafting

Lesson Plan
Course:
Unit:
Lesson:

Review:	Introduction or Motivation (Opener):	Evaluation: (How will student learning be assessed? Specific items related to objective(s) attainment.) Quiz questions, written work, quality of oral statements, and pupil self-evaluation)
Aims and Objectives: (stated in form: "To describe the five key responsibiities of the Federal Reserve")	Procedures: (Can include outline of content, queries, activies, and lesson steps)	Lesson Reminders for the Teacher: (Why didn't something work satisfactorily?)
	Conclusion (Closure):	Revisions for Future:
Needed Materials:	References:	Assignments:

Figure 15-5. Sample lesson plan.

a rationale statement teachers are able to limit the boundaries of instruction, more precisely identify learning goals, identify the processes and procedures that will be followed in presenting subject matter, and stipulate specific learning outcomes that students should achieve as a result of instruction. Although the rationale statement is used to justify instruction, it also is an important means for designing teaching and for selecting the elements that will be emphasized within the instructional settings. Recall, a rationale statement is used to help identify course, unit, and lesson objectives, the components of instruction, the organization of instruction, and the evaluation plan.

Originating with the rationale statement, objectives are the specific manifestations of the rationale statement which can be thought of as an instructional road map for reaching the end point of teaching. In addition, objectives are used to identify the elements of content (concepts, skills, and values) that will be emphasized during the lessons as well as the components of instruction (strategies, activities, etc.) that can be used to present and to reinforce content. Finally, objectives provide the means for determining the extent to which a program of instruction effectively increased students' knowledge.

The setting of instruction, which includes both the physical and social environment, is designed to help reinforce the establishment of the objectives. The physical environment includes everything from room arrangement to the visual materials used to reinforce learning ideas, skills, and values. The social environment includes the development of friendly and respectful relationships within the classroom. Moreover, the instructional setting is designed to promote learning by enhancing student interest in the subject matter and in the various activities by encouraging student participation in the teaching/learning process and by promoting the development of positive social relationships.

The management system should help to promote learning and provide for an orderly and structured learning environment. Classroom rules should be attuned to, or appropriate for, the subject matter. Also, the management system should provide a means for engaging students in learning activities. In addition, classroom rules should reflect the type of interactions that are expected within the instructional setting. For example, the rules of management can include a code of conduct for discussing a controversial contemporary social problem. Also, the rules of conduct should include the processes that will be followed when handling instructional materials and equipment as well as the "put-away" and "clean-up" responsibilities of students. In other words, the management system should reflect the subject matter, the goals of instruction, and the types of activities that are normally associated with the subject-matter content. Much of this can be well accomplished via teacher-pupil planning activities.

It is imperative that as a future social studies teacher you are knowledgeable of social studies content, but also well trained in the principles of course design and construction. The nine-step model, the various elements of course design, and the various examples that were presented in this chapter were aimed at helping beginning and experienced teachers learn to plan courses, units, and lessons for successful teaching. Also, this model and these guidelines were aimed at helping teachers to make their courses, units, and lessons more meaningful to students. Quality social studies instruction for the nation's students rests ultimately on the ability of individual teachers to plan and execute programs that will advance the learning needs of students. These needs may be known only to the classroom teacher who interacts with the student daily; therefore, to be successful, the teacher must be able to transform the course content into a format that is effective for instruction and then arrange the presentation of the course content in ways that invite student learning. It is imperative that you move beyond isolated, day-to-day, textbook assignments and questioning sessions that turn potentially interesting learning experiences into continuing deadly hours for disinterested and uninvolved students. The well-constructed unit and purposeful lessons that can accrue from a well-designed course are the major factors in successful social studies education. More importantly, you—the well-educated, well-trained, and inspired social studies teacher—hold the key to the development of instructional programs that can truly assure student learning within the classroom setting.

REFERENCES

Dick, W., & Carey, L. (1978). *The systematic design of instruction*. Dallas, TX: Scott, Foresman.

Doll, R. C. (1970). *Curriculum improvement: Decision-making and process* (2nd ed.). Boston: Allyn & Bacon.

Giles, H. H., McCutchen, S. P., & Zechiel, A. N. (1942). *Exploring the curriculum*. New York: Harper.

Gross, R. E., & Dynneson, T. L. (1983). *What should we be teaching in the social studies?* (Fastback 199). Bloomington, IN: Phi Delta Kappa Foundation.

Gunter, M. A., Estes, T. H., & Schwab, J. H., (1990). *Instruction: A models approach*. Boston: Allyn & Bacon.

Hanna, P. R. (1963). Revising the social studies: What is needed? *Social Education, 27:* 190–196.

Joyce, B., & Weil, M. (1972). *Models of teaching* (also in a more recent 4th ed., 1992). Englewood Cliffs, NJ: Prentice-Hall.

Kemp, J. E. (1985). *The instructional design process*. New York: Harper & Row.

Nerbovig, M. H. (1970). *Unit planning: A model for curriculum development*. Worthington, OH: Charles A. Jones.

Oliver, A. I. (1977). *Curriculum improvement: A guide to problems, principles, and process* (2nd ed.). New York: Harper & Row.

Smith, P. L., & Ragan, T. J. (1993). *Instructional design*. New York: Merrill/Macmillan.

Taba, H. (1962). *Curriculum development: Theory and practice*. New York: Harcourt, Brace, & World.

Tanner, D., & Tanner, L. N. (1980). *Curriculum development: Theory and practice* (2nd ed.). New York: Macmillan.

Tyler, R. W. (1949). *Basic principles of curriculum and instruction*. Chicago: University of Chicago Press.

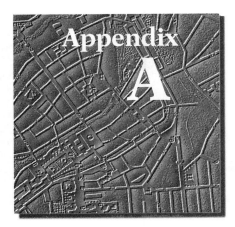

A Design Lesson Plan
Workshop for Teachers

The design lesson plan workshop for teachers is intended to help teachers expand their instructional skills by refining their ability to more precisely plan and execute instruction. Once these skills are acquired, teachers may choose to apply these skills in any number of settings and to any variety of planning forms already available within their schools. But for the purpose of training, the following lesson plan is recommended because it is divided into two basic parts so that teachers will distinguish between the planning phase and the presentation phase of design and development. In addition, the two-page approach is intended to help teachers learn to coordinate these two activities so there is total consistency between these two phases (see pages 381 and 384).

Part I: Planning Page

The planning page of the lesson plan contains several parts that should be considered when developing a lesson plan. While some of these components are essential for all lesson plans, other elements are optional and are used according to the desires of the teacher. For example, every lesson plan should have at least one objective and all instructional lesson plans need at least one content element (concept, skill, or value). At times, teachers may want to have more than one primary objective or a combination of primary and secondary objectives. At other times, teachers may want to use all or a combination of content elements.

Lesson Plan Parts

The following items are contained on the *planning page* of the lesson plan. These items are developed prior to the scheduling and presentation of the lesson to students. Again, it is important to remember that, according to this format, there should be complete consistency between the planning page and the presentation page of this lesson plan.

1. *Prior student preparation.* At the teacher's discretion, a lesson may be based on a task that was assigned prior to instruction. When this is the case, the teacher will simply identify the task. For example, the teacher might note that students were to read textbook pages 125–128 before the lesson and consider long-term results of the event treated. Prior preparation can include reading assignments, worksheets, study questions, or a review of handouts. (Note that there is a direct connection between "Prior Student Preparation" and the "Assignment" component contained on page 2 of the lesson plan.)

2. *Lesson theme.* Each lesson should be given a title according to its function, theme, or application. Because lesson plans are usually an aspect of a broader instructional unit, each lesson should be given a title indicating its overall purpose or theme. Most lessons will have an instructional purpose related to subject-matter content. In these situations, the lessons may be given a content theme title such as "The Geography of Illinois."

3. *Instructional objectives.* Each lesson will contain at least one instructional (or procedural) objective related to the overall plan of instruction. At the same time, it is common for a lesson plan to contain several objectives; however, the lesson plan is somewhat restricted by an allotted period of time—usually a class period. (You learned in Chapter 9 that instructional objectives can be written according to different formulas. They also relate to various parts that include the behavior and the object of the behavior.) The following lesson plan form contains four elements of which two are considered essential (the behavior and the object of the behavior). In addition, two optional components include "Task Condition" and "Performance Standard." The "Task Condition" may designate that students will be working in small groups or individually in the library, for example, while the "Performance Standard" may be used to indicate a level of performance that the teacher expects of the students in order to determine that the objective has been successfully achieved. For instance, a teacher may state that, "Following instruction, each student will be able to list three basic causes of the Civil War." This expectation may be used to reveal if students can differentiate between basic and immediate causes of the conflict.

In addition, instructional objectives can be classified as primary or secondary (supportive or enabling) objectives. Each lesson plan must have at least one primary objective that indicates the overall goal of instruction. The primary objective simply says that, "Following instruction, this is what the student will be able to do." Secondary objectives are stated when a lesson plan sequence is to be used to accomplish the primary objective. For example, in acquiring a target skill, students will have to be able to perform a sequence of steps that they will learn through observing a demonstration of the skill followed by supervised practice and repeated applications to a variety of situations. In this situation, the teacher often uses the primary objective (which in essence states that following instruction the student will be able *"to perform the skill"*). In addition, the teacher may use several secondary objectives to indicate the skill learning sequence, which includes, for example, observing the teacher perform the skill, practice, and transfer to another situation.

4. Subject-matter elements. Instructional lessons need to include at least one or more subject-matter elements (concepts, skills, or values). Procedural lessons (such as a unit opener, closure, and evaluation lessons) normally may not contain typical subject-matter elements. Subject-matter elements are briefly reviewed next:

Concepts. Recall that social studies concepts often are in the form of one-word ideas that have been selected for introduction, emphasis, application, or clarification and usually are derived from disciplinary content (such as history, government, geography, or economics). Such concepts might include, for example, "transportation," "taxation," "Copperhead," "forty-niner," and "apartheid." The ideas, events, places, and persons appear in textbook chapters and often are the focus of instruction. We recommend that the concept be stated and clarified for instructional purposes. For example: *forty-niner* (concept—prospector, California, 1849, routes, population shifts, economic consequences, etc.)

Skills. Recall that skills consist of learned processes that students are expected to learn and even master through the processes of practice and application. Skills often are used in applying processes or in expressing social studies ideas and information in the form of charts, graphs, tables, maps, reports, or dramatic presentations. Social studies skills are presented in the form of basic skills such as reading, writing, and other forms of communication, including motor skills related to illustrating (drawing or acting out) events and processes. In addition, skills include complex skills used in cognitive development and critical thinking tasks and activities such as problem solving, discovery, and analysis. Because skills follow certain patterns in which the teacher usually attempts to demonstrate the skill followed by student practice and transfer, these lesson plan forms often follow a pattern that was described earlier. In addition, skills often are used in connection with the lesson activity, assignments, tasks, group work, and project work. Once skills are introduced (initial practice), they are often reinforced so students can continue to refine them (continued practice) and in time become competent in their use or application (mastery). As was the case with concepts, skills should be clarified within the lesson plan. For skills, we recommend that you identify the typical skill sequence that the students would execute in applying the skill. For example, *making a time line* (skill) might involve these steps: (1) draw a ten-inch horizontal line, (2) divide the line into twenty equal segments, (3) label each segment according to five-year periods beginning with 1950 and ending with the year 2000, and (4) locate the list of events for inclusion.

Values. Recall that social studies values include beliefs, attitudes, virtues, and aesthetics and are related to the ethical and moral conduct of individuals, groups, and society as a whole. Values often are addressed from an analytical perspective in which students are encouraged to discuss or study an event by identifying and analyzing the values that influenced human behavior and decision making. Because values may be both explored and acquired as a result of studying social studies content, the teacher should identify the value that will be the focus of instruction and be able to clarify its focus within the lesson setting. In a history classroom, for example, the teacher might like students to focus on the personal value(s) that Lincoln addressed in dealing with the slavery issue. Therefore, the teacher may clarify the lesson by encouraging students to identify Lincoln's values as applied to the emancipation proclamation. According to this approach, students are encouraged to analyze Lincoln's statements and actions in light of the slavery issue. For example, if students studied the value of *Lincoln's beliefs*, they would (1) identify values related to his actions and (2) analyze how those values influenced his decision to sign the Emancipation Proclamation and (3) explain why the slaves in the border states were not freed at that time.

5. *Instructional components.* These components are the planning and organizational skills that the social studies teacher uses in designing and presenting instruction to students. In addition to instructional objectives and motivational concerns, these components include strategies, activities, materials, and the means or plan of evaluation that will be used to determine the extent to which the teacher's instructional objectives have been attained as well as the extent to which students have reached the desired level of achievement.

Strategies. Each instructional lesson will identify the instructional strategy that the teacher will use in presenting the subject-matter content to students. For example, the teacher might simply list lecture, discussion, and role playing as the means of presenting content or supervising a student task. (Recall that Chapter 11 contained a large number of strategy settings and means or methods that are appropriate to the social studies teacher.)

Activities. We recommend that, if possible, each lesson contain an activity related to the *primary objective* of the lesson plan. It is important to keep in mind that hands-on activities are important in helping students more realistically learn concepts, skills, and values. Therefore, even at the secondary level, social studies instruction should be centered on activities so students have an opportunity to apply what they have read, heard, or learned in some related form. Pupil involvement is crucial in promoting learning.

Materials. Materials should be listed to remind the teacher that certain materials may be required in the execution of a lesson and thus arranged for or duplicated ahead of time. Lesson materials include handouts and media such as films or tapes and projectors, transparencies, and instructional kits.

Lesson Plan Format

Part I: Planning Elements

Prior Student

Preparation: _____

_____

Lesson Theme: _____

Instructional Objectives:

Observable Behavior	Object of the Action	Task Condition
1. Primary Objective		
Performance Standard		
2. Secondary (supportive/enabling) Objective		
Performance Standard		
3. Secondary (supportive/enabling) Objective		
Performance Standard		

Subject-Matter Elements (list or outline and clarify):

Concept(s) List:

Skill(s) List:

Value(s) List:

Components of Instruction:

Strategy(ies) (teacher action):

Activity(ies) (student experiences):

Material(s) List:

Part II: Presenting Page

The presenting phase of the lesson plan contains several parts (opener, lesson schedule, closure, evaluation, and revision) that should be considered in the presentation of a lesson. The presentation of instruction follows a cycle based on the teachers' need to provide students with (1) an introduction to the lesson, including a concern for motivating or arousing student interest; (2) a body of the lesson that is scheduled according to a pacing schedule and lesson sequence; and (3) a closure that is designed to review and reinforce important subject-matter ideas, events, and processes. It also allows teachers to acquire feedback from students to see if they understood the key points presented in the lesson. Finally, the presentation phase of the lesson provides a place for teachers to make comments regarding some possible changes or improvements for the lesson next time it is taught. It may end with a specific assignment for the end of the day.

1. *Lesson opener.* The opener provides a motivation for and introduces or orients the student to the lesson. In most lessons, teachers present an overview of the lesson, a teasing question or puzzle (motivator), and an explanation of their expectations as a result of instruction. When the lesson is a continuation of the day before, a review of the initial part of the lesson by the students or teacher would be in order. (We suggest that the teacher state the primary objective from Page I as an aspect of the lesson opener, as this helps to promote consistency throughout the lesson.)

2. *Order of the lesson.* The order of the lesson is the schedule or chronological sequence that the teacher will follow in presenting the body of the lesson. The body of the lesson usually contains the subject-matter content (the teacher's outline and related questions for students may be included) and the instructional activities that will promote the learning of the concepts, skills, and values that are the focus of the lesson. The teacher estimates the length of time that will be allowed for the presentation of and activities for each segment of the body of the lesson. Time allotments usually do not include opener, closure, or evaluative procedures. Generally, the estimated pacing schedule should not be allowed to dictate instruction, but it should serve as an instructional aide. Lessons should be carefully and precisely planned, but taught flexibly according to the demands of the situation.

3. *Lesson closure.* Teachers use the lesson closure to review and reinforce key subject-matter elements. In some situations, teachers use it to help prepare students for an assignment, task, or even an assessment. Most of all, the closure should tie together the various subject-matter elements by helping students form connections between events, ideas, or the steps of a process. (We suggest that the teacher again state the primary objective from Page I as an aspect of the lesson closure because this helps to promote consistency throughout the lesson.)

4. *Lesson feedback.* Lesson feedback gives teachers an opportunity to listen to students' interpretation of the key elements that were presented during the lesson. It is especially helpful in detecting misconceptions or misunderstandings that occurred because of distractions that might have interfered with the presentation of the lesson, thus providing the teacher with a chance to correct, adjust, or clarify concepts, skills, or values.

5. *Lesson enhancement.* The lesson enhancement is a convenient way to change, refine, or improve the lesson soon after it has been taught. Suggested changes might include the elements of subject-matter content, a reformulation of the primary or secondary objectives, changes in instructional media and materials, or modifications in activities. By making notations immediately after presenting the lesson, the teacher can continually improve the instructional program and the presentation and activities.

As teachers gain experience and become familiar with the subject matter and the pupils and class, highly detailed lesson plans may become less necessary. Nevertheless, thought and time devoted to pre-planning and lesson development and execution are called for in all instances. "Teaching extempore" or "off the cuff" is clearly non-professional. (See Conklin, 1971; Flouris, 1983; Kellum, 1969; and Zahorik, 1975.)

Lesson Presentation

Part II: Presentation Cycle

Lesson Opener: (introduction, review, motivator, attention getter, overview, restatement of the primary objective)

During this lesson, you will _____

_____

Order of the Lesson:

Estimated Time   Sequential Steps

_____|_____
1.

_____|_____
2.

_____|_____
3.

_____|_____
4.

_____|_____

Lesson Closure: (review, reinforcement, summary, emphasis, restatement of the primary objective)

During this lesson, you learned _____

_____

Assignment:

_____

Lesson Feedback:

"What did you learn?"

"Explain the following..."

"Give an example of ..."

Lesson Enhancement:

Next time I teach this lesson, I will make the following changes _____

_____

Lesson Plan Activity

Purpose

The purpose of this activity is to construct a lesson plan according to the two-page lesson plan format by dealing with the following situation and by answering the following questions.

Situation

As a new teacher, you have decided that your seventh-grade students need to know some of the important characteristics of five Texas metropolitan centers, including Houston, Dallas/Ft. Worth, Austin, San Antonio, and El Paso.[1] You have decided that it is important for your students to be aware of the locations of these cities and of their most important economic functions; therefore, in planning a fifty-minute lesson you will need to answer the following questions.

1. What prior lesson preparation, if any, do your students need?
2. What will be your lesson theme?
3. What primary and supportive objectives are to be achieved as a result of instruction?

   Are there any special task conditions or special arrangements (such as library work or small group work) under which students will work?

   Are you going to use a prior set of performance standards to indicate that students have achieved the objective? If so, what are your standards?

4. In teaching about the location and function[*] of the five cities, what concepts, skills, and/or values will you focus the lesson on? How will you clarify each element so that your meaning is clear?
5. What strategy(ies) will you (the teacher) use in presenting the content to your students?
6. What activity will you develop as a means of providing students with a working experience related to the primary objective(s) and the elements (concepts, skills, and values) listed above?
7. What materials and resources will be required to execute this lesson?
8. How will you open the lesson so that students will preview what is coming and know what is expected?
9. What will be the order of your lesson and how much time will you allow for each step or phase of the lesson?
10. How will you close the lesson so that students will review the important concerns that were raised during the lesson?

---

[*] To clarify the functions (or economic characteristics) of each city, you may wish to check a general source, such as an encyclopedia, for each city's main economic activity—for example, Austin's economic base tends to focus on political activity and education, while Houston is a port city with oil refineries. Also, it may prove helpful to construct a brief outline as a guide to concept, skill, and value development.

11. What assignment (if any) should be made in preparation to the next lesson related to the metropolitan areas?

12. What questions will you ask students to find out their current level of understanding regarding the content taught?

Sample Lesson Plan Questions and Lesson Plan

Situation

As a new teacher, you have decided that your seventh-grade students need to know some of the important characteristics of five Texas metropolitan centers, including Houston, Dallas/Ft. Worth, Austin, San Antonio, and El Paso.[1] You have decided that it is important for your students to be aware of the locations of these cities and of their most important economic functions; therefore, in planning a fifty-minute lesson you will need to answer the following questions.

1. What prior lesson preparation, if any, do your students need?

   Read pages 277–288 in the textbook

2. What will be your lesson theme?

   Cities of Texas

3. What primary and supportive objectives are to be achieved as a result of instruction?

   Primary Objective: To locate major metropolitan cities of Texas on a map
   Secondary Objective: To label Houston, Dallas/Ft. Worth, Austin, San Antonio, and El Paso
   Primary Objective: To list the major economic characteristics of each city listed above
   Secondary Objective: To design a set of map symbols to represent the economic characteristics of each city and place them on the map

Are there any special task conditions or special arrangements (such as library work or small group work) under which students will work?

   No

Are you going to use a prior set of performance standards to indicate that students have achieved the objective? If so, what are your standards?

   City locations and symbol associations must be accurate

4. In teaching about the location and function of the five cities, what concepts, skills, and/or values will you focus the lesson on? How will you clarify each element so that your meaning is clear?

Concepts List
    City: densely populated, civic center, regions, zones, and traffic patterns
    Economic activity: trade, markets, finance, shipping and receiving, manufacturing, tourism, and culture
Skills List
    Location: (1) reference map (2) locate and label Houston, Dallas/Ft. Worth, Austin, San Antonio, and El Paso on Texas outline map
    Symbol construction: (1) List the two or three economic activities for each city (e.g., Austin: political activity and education) (2) create a map symbol for each economic activity (e.g., draw a truck to symbolize transportation)
    Map key: (1) create a map key referencing symbol with economic activity (2) locate symbols on the map according to appropriate urban activity
Values List: none

5. What strategy(ies) will you (the teacher) use in presenting the content to your students?

    Teacher presentation
    Demonstration with transparencies
    Activity supervision

6. What activity will you develop as a means of providing students with a working experience related to the primary objective(s) and the elements (concepts, skills, and values) listed above?

    "Texas map project"

7. What materials and resources will be required to execute this lesson?

    Prepared transparencies, 25 Texas outline maps, overhead projector, pointer, colored pencil sets

8. How will you open the lesson so that students will preview what is coming and know what is expected?

    During this lesson you will study five major cities in Texas—Houston, Dallas/Ft. Worth, Austin, San Antonio, and El Paso—in regard to their location and important economic functions. An important activity will focus on locating these cities on a Texas outline map, creating a map key and symbols that will be used to represent the main economic activity of each city.

9. What will be the order of your lesson and how much time will you allow for each step or phase of the lesson?

    a. 10 minutes: review textbook pages 277-288 and list the main economic activities of the five cities

    b. 10 minutes: teacher demonstration with transparencies for locating Austin, Texas, including the creation of symbols for political activity and education

c. 30 minutes: map development activity in which students locate the five cities on their maps, including the creation of a map key and symbols representing economic activity

10. How will you close the lesson so that students will review the important concerns that were raised during the lesson?

During this lesson you studied five major cities in Texas—Houston, Dallas/Ft. Worth, Austin, San Antonio, and El Paso—in regard to their location and important economic functions. An important activity focused on locating these cities on a Texas outline map, creating a map key and symbols that were used to represent the main economic activity of each city.

11. What assignment (if any) should be made in preparation to the next lesson related to the metropolitan areas?

Read textbook pages 289-291

12. What questions will you ask students to find out their current level of understanding regarding the content taught?

Where is El Paso located within the state of Texas and what are its main economic activities?

Lesson Plan Format (Part I—Planning Elements)

Prior Student Preparation: Read pages 277 - 288 in the textbook.

Lesson Theme: Cities of Texas

Instructional Objectives: Observable Behavior	Object of the Action	Task Condition
1.	*Primary Objective*		
	To locate	major metropolitan cities of Texas on the outline map	
	Performance Standard	Accuracy of location	
2.	*Secondary (supportive/enabling) Objective*		
	To label	Houston, Dallas/Ft. Worth, Austin, San Antonio, and El Paso on the outline map	
	Performance Standard	Accurately label	
3.	*Primary Objective*		
	To list	the major economic activities of the five cities	
	Performance Standard	Correctly list and place two to three activities (in symbol form) per city on a map key and outline map	
4.	*Secondary (supportive/enabling) Objective*		
	To design	a set of map symbols to represent the economic activities of each city	

Subject Matter Elements:

Concepts List:

City: densely populated, civic center, regions, zones and traffic patterns

Economic activity: trade, markets, finance, shipping and receiving, manufacturing, tourism and culture

Skill List:

Location: (1) reference map, (2) locate and label Houston, Dallas/Ft. Worth, Austin, San Antonio, and El Paso on Texas outline map

Symbol construction: (1) List the two or three economic activities for each city (e.g. Austin: political activity and education) (2) create a map symbol for each economic activity (e.g. transportation = ⌐o—o⌐o—o)

Map Key: (1) create a map key referencing symbol with economic activity (2) locate symbols on the map according to appropriate urban activity

Values List: None

Instructional Strategy (teacher action): Teacher presentation, demonstration with prepared transparencies, and activity supervision.

Activity Description (student experience): "Texas Map Project"

Material List: Prepared transparencies, 30 Texas outline maps, overhead projector, rulers, and sets of colored pencils.

Lesson Presentation (Part II—Presentation Cycle)

Lesson Opener: Introduction, review, motivator, attention getter, and overview

During this lesson you will study five major cities in Texas – Houston, Dallas/Ft. Worth, Austin, San Antonio, and El Paso – in regard to their location and important economic functions. An important activity will focus on locating these cities on a Texas outline map, creating a map key and symbols that will be used to represent the main economic activity of each city.

Order of the Lesson:

	Estimated Time	Sequential Steps
1.	10 minutes	review textbook pages 277 - 288 and help students list the main economic activities of the five cities.
2.	10 minutes	present the teacher demonstration with transparencies for locating Austin, Texas, including the creation of symbols for political activity and education
3.	30 minutes	supervise map development activity in which students locate the five cities on their maps, including the creation of a map key and symbols representing economic activity

Lesson Closure: Review, reinforcement, summary, and emphasis

During this lesson you studied five major cities in Texas – Houston, Dallas/Ft. Worth, Austin, San Antonio, and El Paso – in regard to their location and important economic functions. An important activity focused on locating these cities on a Texas outline map, creating a map key and symbols that were used to represent the main economic activity of each city.

Assignment: Read textbook pages 289 - 291

Lesson Feedback: Where is El Paso located within the state of Texas and what are its main economic activities?

Lesson Enhancement:
The next time I teach this lesson, I will make the following changes: _____

_____

_____

Developing the Sample Lesson Activity

Situation

To complete the lesson plan, the teacher needs to develop the lesson plan activity pertaining to studying the five major cities of Texas. Recall that according to the sample lesson plan, a 30-minute activity called the "Texas Map Project" was identified but not developed. This activity can be planned for instructional use in the following manner.

As a matter of practice, teachers often keep activity files (often called resource files, sometimes provided by textbook publishers) that are correlated to courses, units, and lessons. Even when the social studies textbook is replaced, these files remain a valuable component of supplemental instruction, as they tend to address specific topics that are commonly taught regardless of textbook adoption. In addition, the development of separate activity files is an ideal means of enhancing any instructional program, as these activities may serve as the basis for major as well as minor projects and/or activities that provide direct involvement (or hands-on experiences) for students. A typical resource file includes:

- A standard file folder (upon which the name of the activity is stated on the folder tab)
- A descriptive paragraph explaining the purpose of the activity in reinforcing classroom instruction (this statement, written for another teacher, attempts to relate the activity to the primary objective(s) of the unit or lesson as well as to the major subject matter elements of the unit or lesson (concepts, skills, and values)
- A set of specific instructions for students in a step-by-step sequence so that these directions are made available to students as an aid to help them complete the activity
- Finally, the activity file contains an example of a completed activity that is somewhat representative of the hoped-for expectations of the teacher. Because activities should result in some type of end-product, the teacher should develop an example of what this student product might resemble. In addition, this example might serve as a model to students as well as a standard of performance.

The following items were developed to illustrate the contents of a typical file based on the activity developed from the previous workshop.

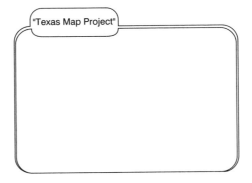

"Texas Map Project"

Activity Description

The purpose of this activity is to provide students with a form of direct experience with the two primary objectives of this lesson. These objectives pertain to the location of major metropolitan cities and associating them with their major economic characteristics. In addition, this activity is designed to help students expand their understanding of large cities as metropolitan areas, especially in regard to specific economic activities. At the same time, this activity should help students acquire and apply basic map skills related to the use of the map key, especially in reference to the interpretation and use of map symbols.

Activity Directions for Students

The following sequence of steps is included to help you complete the "Cities of Texas" map project.

1. On a sheet of notebook paper, list the five cities: Houston, Dallas/Ft. Worth, Austin, San Antonio, and El Paso (leave some space for additional writing).
2. Review pages 277-288 in your textbook and after each city listed on your notebook paper make a list of the economic activities that are characteristic of that city.
3. For each economic activity on your list, draw a symbol or a picture, such as a truck to depict the movement of goods on a highway, or a ship to represent international trade coming into a port city such as Houston.
4. Turn in your textbook to the map on page 278, and in reference to this map, locate the five cities of Texas by placing a dot and printing the name of the city near the dot. Accuracy counts.

5. In the left hand corner of your outline map under the standard map key, draw a box large enough to include an additional key called an "economic activity key." (You may want to draw this box with light pencil marks so that adjustments can be made.)

6. Within the margins of the "economic activity key" box, draw each of the economic symbols and list the economic activity that it represents (see item #3 above).

7. Next to each city on the map, draw the symbols that represent a major economic activity for that city. (Major means that this activity employs a great many people and generates a great deal of financial activity for this city. Minor employment and financial results should not be represented. For example, all of these cities have universities, but Austin is particularly influenced by the main campus of the University of Texas.)

8. Put your name on your completed maps and place them in the "turn in" box on my desk.

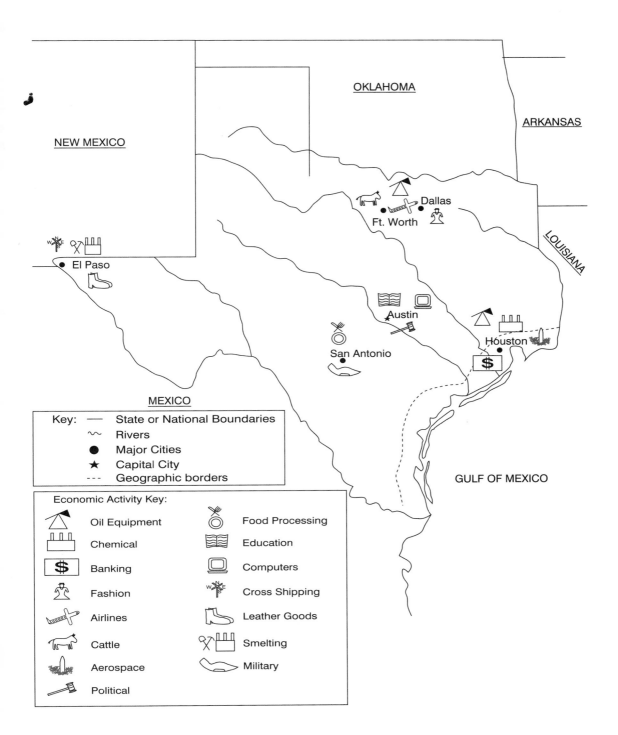

OKLAHOMA

ARKANSAS

NEW MEXICO

Dallas

Ft. Worth

LOUISIANA

El Paso

Austin

Houston

San Antonio

MEXICO

Key:
— State or National Boundaries
~ Rivers
● Major Cities
★ Capital City
--- Geographic borders

GULF OF MEXICO

Economic Activity Key:

Oil Equipment

Food Processing

Chemical

Education

Banking

Computers

Fashion

Cross Shipping

Airlines

Leather Goods

Cattle

Smelting

Aerospace

Military

Political

395

REFERENCES

Conklin, R. (1971). Why are lesson plans always incomplete? *Clearing House, 40:* 67–71.

Flouris, G. (1983). Instructional design in the social studies. *The Social Studies, 74:* 128–132.

Kellum, D. (1969). The planned lesson as an art form. *The Social studies: Myths and realities.* New York: Sheed & Ward.

Zahorik, J. A. (1975). Teachers' planning models. *Educational Leadership, 33:* 134–139.

Appendix B

Unit Planning Workshop for Teachers

Developing the Training Unit

As a result of working with students using many of the principles recommended throughout this book, we have been found that pre-certification teachers and experienced teachers can be trained in many of these practices in workshops or in-service settings. At the same time, the success of any similar type of instructional experience rests on careful pre-workshop arrangements related to the duplication of materials and the assembly of content resources. In addition, to be successful, the workshop leader must be familiar with and be able to demonstrate and give examples of each aspect of the unit development process described in the following steps.

Unit Development Process

Step 1: Participants will be assigned appropriate social studies topics according to grade-level interests and disciplinary concerns in accordance with workshop materials. Participants may work in small groups of two or three or they may work alone.

Step 2: Participants will begin to develop the training unit by searching for information on the unit topic by consulting some general resources such as reference and encyclopedia sources. Next, the search may proceed by identifying books and supplemental resources including kits, films, slides, and so forth. These resources will be divided into two bibliographic categories: one category that will provide reference materials for the teacher (including special references, college-level textbooks, adult monographs, and reference materials) and a second category that will consist of resources that the student will hypothetically encounter during instruction. Remember that this is a training and not a teaching unit, so no students will encounter these materials. The second category of materials may include several grade-level textbooks, maps, charts, pictures, and films that will also appear in the material section of lesson plans. (As a rule, stronger units tend to include a greater variety of materials because these materials are used for instruction and serve as the basis for activities and projects.) Typically, when developing a teaching unit, the participants should be instructed to formulate a *rationale* statement (see Chapter 6); however, for training purposes the inclusion of this important planning factor may be left to the discretion of the workshop leader.

Step 3:   Participants will develop an instructional outline that consists of *seven* major parts or are designated by seven Roman numerals (I., II., III., etc.). Each of the seven disciplines of the social studies disciplines (history and the six social sciences) will be assigned a Roman numeral according to the order (sequence) determined by each participant. Using the resources described in Step 2, the participants will develop the subparts of the outline (following the rules of the topic outline).

Step 4:   Once the outline has been completed in Step 3, the participants will be asked to construct a planning calendar (see the sample unit that follows) based on a 10-column format. The purpose of the planning calendar is for planning a presentation structure. Days 1, 9, and 10 are designated as *procedural lessons* for the purpose of opening (Day 1) and closing (Days 9 and 10) the unit. Days 2 through 8 are designated as *instructional lessons*, and the instructional outline from Step 3 (Roman numerals I through VII) is placed in the seven center columns for Days 2 through 8, one separate column for each discipline. In addition, for structuring the lesson plan, a completed planning calendar will help the participants identify lesson plan objectives. Therefore, participants should be asked to review each of the columns and, in some symbolic way (*), select the topics or identify related skills and values that will be emphasized during instruction.

Step 5:   Participants will identify a list of five or more unit objectives that will reflect the overall aims of instruction. Unit objectives for a *teaching unit* are directly related to course objectives and to course and unit rationale statements, but because this is a *training unit* and the product may be too fragmented and shallow to use for teaching purposes, a rationale statement is optional. In addition, unit objectives should reflect the theme (title) of the unit as well as those subject-matter elements (concepts, skills, and values) that will be strongly emphasized throughout the unit. Finally, learning experiences, such as an important unit project, may be stated as a unit objective.

Step 6: Participants will develop an assessment plan and related assessment and test items that will be used to (a) measure student readiness (pretest) for instruction, (b) indicate the teaching effectiveness midway into the unit (in-progress indicators), and (c) verify that unit and lesson objectives have been attained (summative measure) according to some reasonable standard of achievement. The assessment plan should contain a variety of means of measuring effective instruction. Student performance and achievement will be measured on items that are keyed to specific unit and daily objectives. Included with the assessment plan should be an overall assessment rationale for assigning unit grades. The assessment rationale should be included in the overview of the unit, which for students will be addressed on Day 1.

Step 7: Participants will plan opening and closing activities that will include (a) a motivating activity to open the unit and (b) a culminating activity to review and reinforce the most important concepts, skills, and values that were emphasized during the unit. The opening activity should be an attention-getting activity that promotes student interest in the unit; the closing activity should bring the unit to a timely end and also help to prepare students for the final unit assessment.

Step 8: Participants will develop the opening lesson (Day 1) of the unit (following the lesson plan directions and format contained in Appendix A). This particular lesson contains three important introductory parts that include (a) an overview for students that describes the main characteristics of the unit including essential content, skills, and values to be learned as well as the method for determining a unit grade, (b) the pretest that was developed to determine whether or not students are "ready" for unit instruction or whether some type of prior instruction is necessary, and (c) the motivating activity that was developed in Step 7 for encouraging student interest in the unit. Because this is a procedural lesson rather than a content lesson, the lesson plan may be in a shortened form and may not contain subject-matter elements (see the following sample unit for guidance).

Step 9: Participants will construct the seven instructional lessons for Days 2 through 8. Each lesson should be based on the planning calendar developed in Step 4 with the addition of the development of lesson objectives, clarification of the subject-matter elements, the components of instruction, and lesson presentation cycle as clarified in Appendix A. It is important that participants check on the *consistency* between lesson plan elements so that unrelated items are not added. (For example, a new concept should not be added to the presentation part of the lesson plan.) Check to see that the secondary objectives are related to the primary objective and that the subject-matter components are reflected in the primary and secondary objectives. Also, check to see that there is consistency between page 1 and page 2 of the lesson plan. For example, the primary objective of the lesson should be reflected in the lesson opener and closure.

Step 10: At this time, participants should be ready to organize the culminating lesson around an activity (see Step 7) that will bring all of the important content elements together for a final review and for reinforcement. (For example, the final result or product of an ongoing unit activity might be presented, displayed, and discussed. In another situation, an activity might be planned in which an encompassing product can be used to review the history and social science perspectives of a topic such as a team-planned display.) This activity should be used to focus attention on the key instructional elements that are related to the goals and objectives of instruction, especially in preparation of the final assessment.

Step 11: The final lesson of the unit should be a procedural lesson that is aimed at assessing student achievement according to the plan of assessment described in Step 6. Most important, all test items should be specifically correlated to the unit objectives to assure that these test items are appropriate and consistent with unit objectives. By correlating each item with a unit objective, the participant can audit the assessment to see that unrelated test items were not accidentally included in the assessment, thus assuring a valid correlation between instruction and assessment.

Step 12: Each participant should sketch or lay out an instructional bulletin board that can be used with some aspect of the unit, such as in illustrating a concept, skill, or value for the opening or closing activity or for a specific instructional lesson.

Finally, when planning a training unit, participants should be aware that estimates of presentation time are usually unrealistic since the training lesson will likely contain more activities and content than can be delivered in a 50- to 55-minute instructional period. At the same time, it is important to help teachers learn to improve their instructional pacing skills; therefore, participants should be encouraged to develop a pacing schedule as part of planning while recognizing that this schedule should be flexible, as it serves as a general guide.

Developing the Sample Unit

The following sample unit was written by a pre-certification social studies teacher and was based on the principles, processes, and recommended practices as imparted in this book and in conjunction with the guidelines established in Appendix A. This unit is aimed at seventh grade social studies (state studies). The unit is not a teaching unit, but a *training unit* in that it consists of sample lessons from each of the seven disciplines (history and the social sciences) and three procedural lessons (one lesson aimed at "opening" the unit and two lessons aimed at "closing" the unit). The opening unit lesson includes the means for providing students with an overview, pretest, and motivating activity. The closing lessons include a lesson for culminating the unit with an activity in preparation for the final unit assessment on the following day. Consequently, this unit is appropriate *for training purposes* because of its shallow coverage or sampling nature; thus, the unit as it is currently constructed probably is not appropriate for instructional purposes. In other words, the unit focus is on learning planning skills and procedures rather than on content presentation. This fact becomes obvious when it is understood that each of the seven disciplines will be represented by a 50-minute sample lesson (including a 15- to 20-minute activity that supports the primary lesson objective).

Also, because this is a training unit rather than a teaching unit, the *rationale* for the unit, as far as the methods instructor is concerned, centers primarily on teaching design and planning skills. The content aspects of the rationale focus mainly on helping teachers experience some aspect of planning for each of the seven social studies disciplines.

An important goal of training is to encourage workshop participants to develop units based on a variety of important supplemental materials rather than the standard classroom textbook. As a result, this unit is *not* textbook centered, but contains information from many valuable and related sources, including supplemental instructional materials, monographic books, and journals.

The student who developed this sample unit[*] had very little actual classroom experience in working with students for which her unit was designed; therefore, some aspects of the unit may not be as appropriate as those units developed by experienced classroom teachers or within a different setting (other than this workshop). These differences tend to represent the differences that result between theory and practice, differences that commonly occur in undergraduate social studies methods courses that are not field based. At the same time, a prime goal of the workshop was to train inexperienced teachers in an instructional design system that could be easily transferred to a full range of actual grade levels and subject-matter subjects for the social studies classroom.

As was stated previously, the main purpose of the unit development workshop was to train pre-certification and experienced teachers in the techniques of effective instruction that have been emphasized throughout this book. The unit presented should suggest the extent to which novice teachers can begin to become effective instructors as a result of training.

Sample Unit Overview

This seventh grade social studies unit is designed to examine aspects of Texas history, anthropology, sociology, psychology, economics, government, and geography. The unit will begin with a pretest on Texas to assess the students' background. If 50% of the students get 50% of the pretest items correct, then the teacher will proceed with the unit.

---

[*] Reprinted by permission of and modified and revised by Maudine D'Laine Young, The University of Texas of the Permian Basin, 1994.

The unit examines Texas in terms of the seven social studies disciplines. Each lesson is followed by a supporting activity. On the first day, there will be no instructional lesson; however, the class will participate in a motivational activity in which they create a salt map of Texas.

The instructional lessons begin with a brief study of anthropology by describing the first Texans and how they lived. The supporting activity focuses on the Apache Indians and their uses for buffalo.

With the topic of Texas history, the students learn about the important provisions of the Treaty of Guadalupe Hidalgo and explain how it affected Texas. Students also dramatize the negotiations and signing of the treaty.

The unit also looks at the geographical regions and rivers of Texas. This lesson is supported by a map activity. Closely related to geography is Texas economics. As a supporting activity, students will participate in a learning center and identify items either as commodities or as natural resources, and then list the uses for each item.

In this unit, the teacher will also introduce students to the three main branches of Texas government and their functions. As an activity, the students will brainstorm a proposed bill and list the steps required to make the bill into a law.

The sociology and psychology lessons focus on the Texas Rangers and their functions. The students are asked to create a recruiting poster for the Rangers and to illustrate and describe an event in the life of one Texas Ranger, N. A. Jennings.

As a review of the unit and as reinforcement of material already covered, students are asked to put together a bulletin board using as many of the unit activities as possible.

Students will also take a test midway through the unit and a final or summative test at the completion of the unit.

Texas Social Studies Resource Unit

Unit Objectives

Behavior (Thematic Objectives)	Object
1. To identify	the first groups of people who lived in Texas and how they lived
2. To identify	Texas geographical regions and rivers
3. To describe	the functions of the three branches of Texas government
4. To describe	the characteristics of the Texas Rangers
5. To identify	economic resources of Texas
6. To examine	events involved in the annexation of Texas
7. To examine	the effects of the Mexican American War on Texas

Student Overview

This unit covers the seven areas of Texas social studies.

First you will take a short quiz to find out what you already know about Texas. Everyone will then participate in an activity in which you will plan, design, and construct a salt map.

The first topic we will consider is anthropology. You will create an activity that focuses on the ways Apache Indians used the buffalo.

You will also study the history of Texas. We will discuss in class several events that are important in Texas history. One of those events is the signing of the Treaty of Guadalupe Hidalgo, which you will role-play as the supporting activity.

This unit also focuses on two closely related topics: geography, which deals with the earth and its resources, and economics, which deals with how we use those resources. You will be expected to identify certain regions and rivers, as well as the uses for commodities and natural resources of Texas.

You will learn the functions of the branches of government in Texas. You will be expected to brainstorm a bill or proposed law and list the steps required for the bill to become a law.

The last two instructional lessons focus on the Texas Rangers. You will study them as a group and look at the life of one Texas Ranger, N. A. Jennings. Finally, you will create an exciting recruiting poster for the Rangers and illustrate and describe an event in the life of N. A. Jennings.

You will also plan, design, and construct a bulletin board displaying many of the activities you have done during the unit.

Midway through the unit, you will take a quiz to see if you are learning the material. On the last day, you will also take a final test over the entire unit. Half (50%) of your unit grade will come from the completion of the daily activities. Thirty percent (30%) of your unit grade will come from effort and participation. The remaining twenty percent (20%) of your unit grade will be made up of the mid-unit quiz and the final unit test.

Instructional Outline: Texas

I. Anthropology
   A. The first immigrants
   B. The American Indians
      1. Caddos
      2. Apache
II. History
   A. The Louisiana Purchase
   B. The Treaty of Guadalupe Hidalgo
   C. Texas secedes from the Union
   D. Reconstruction
III. Geography
   A. Plains
      1. Coastal plains
      2. High plains
      3. South plains
      4. Climate
   B. Mountains
      1. Guadalupe Mountains
      2. Chisnos Mountains
   C. Plateaus and canyons
   D. Rivers
      1. Rio Grande
      2. Colorado River
      3. Brazos River
      4. Red River
      5. Pecos River
      6. Sabine River
   E. The Texas coast

  IV. Economics
      A. Population and major cities
          1. Austin
          2. Houston
          3. San Antonio
          4. Dallas/Ft. Worth
      B. Farming
          1. Cotton
          2. Fruits and vegetables
      C. Ranching
          1. Cattle
          2. Sheep
          3. Goats
      D. Natural Resources
          1. Oil
          2. Natural gas
   V. Government
      A. The Texas Constitution
      B. The governor
      C. The legislative system
      D. Texas judiciary
          1. Municipal courts
          2. Justice of the Peace
          3. County Court
          4. Court of Civil Appeals
          5. Court of Criminal Appeals
          6. District Court
          7. Texas Supreme Court
      E. The election process
  VI. Sociology
      A. The Texas Rangers
      B. Functions of the Texas Rangers
          1. Mexican raiders
          2. Battling the Indians
      C. The Six-Shooter
      D. Present functions
 VII. Psychology
      A. N. A. Jennings, Texas Ranger
          1. The early years
          2. Signing on with the Rangers
      B. Battles with the Mexicans
          1. Laguna Madre
          2. Los Cuevos Fight
      C. Rangers' social life
          1. Poker playing

2. "Snipe" hunting
D. Reorganization of the Rangers
    1. Law and order established
    2. Old command disbanded

Unit Planning Calendar Week One (Part One)

DAY 1	DAY 2	DAY 3

Pretest
 	
Unit Overview
 	
Motivating Activity
(salt map)
	I. Anthropology
	
	  A. The first immi-
	     grants
	
	  B. The American
	     Indians
	
	    1. Caddos
	
	  *2. Apache
		II. History
		
		  *A. The Louisiana
		     Purchase
		
		  *B. The Treaty of
		     Guadalupe
		     Hidalgo
		
		  C. Texas secedes
		    from Union
		
		  D. Reconstruction

Materials	**Materials**	**Materials**
25 copies of pretest, resource book, text-books, photographs of Texas, salt, corn starch, food coloring, water, cardboard, butcher paper, pencils, tooth-picks, mixing bowl, old shirts, scissors, tape, markers	brown paper bag, markers, crayons, brown yarn, popsicle sticks, paper, pencil	cardboard paper-towel rollers, butcher paper, markers, construction paper, glue, cotton balls, scissors, clear tape, Karo Syrup, worn jackets and boots

Unit Planning Calendar Week One (Part Two)

DAY 4	DAY 5

III. Geography
  *A. Plains
    1. Coastal plains
    2. High plains
    3. South plains
    4. Climate
  B. Mountains
    1. Guadalupe
    2. Chisnos
  C. Plateaus and canyons
  *D. Rivers
    1. Rio Grande
    2. Colorado
    3. Brazos
    4. Red
    5. Pecos
    6. Sabine
  *E. The Texas coast
	Mid-unit test
	IV. Economics
	  A. Population and major cities
	    1. Austin
	    2. Houston
	    3. San Antonio
	    4. Dallas/Ft. Worth
	  *B. Farming
	    1. Cotton
	    2. Fruits and vegetables
	  *C. Ranching
	    1. Cattle
	    2. Sheep
	    3. Goats
	  *D. Natural resources
	    1. Oil
	    2. Natural gas

Materials	**Materials**
25 copies of map 25 handouts of color key, map colors	25 copies of mid-unit test, cotton clothing, wool clothing, beef, fruit and vegetables, peanut butter, motor oil, plastic, gas heater, leather boots, gas lamp

Unit Planning Calendar Week Two (Part One)

DAY 6	DAY 7	DAY 8

V. Government
  A. The Texas Constitution
  *B. The governor
  *C. The legislative system
  *D. Texas judiciary
    1. Municipal Court
    2. Justice of the Peace
    3. County Court
    4. Court of Civil Appeals
    5. Court of Criminal Appeals
    6. District Court
    7. Texas Supreme Court
  E. The election process
	VI. Sociology
	  *A. The Texas Rangers
	  *B. Functions of the Texas Rangers
	    1. Mexican raiders
	    2. Battling the Indians
	  C. The six-shooter
	  D. Present functions
		VII. Psychology
		  *A. N. A. Jennings, Texas Ranger
		    1. The early years
		    2. Signing on with the Rangers
		  *B. Battles with the Mexicans
		    1. Laguna Madre
		    2. Los Cuevos Fight
		  *C. Rangers' social life
		    1. Poker playing
		    2. "Snipe" hunting
		  D. Reorganization of the Rangers
		    1. Law and order established
		    2. Old command disbanded

Materials	**Materials**	**Materials**
posterboard, markers, 25 copies of handout	chalkboard, chalk, markers, posterboard, crayons, scissors, construction paper	drawing paper, pencil, crayons, markers, glue, scissors, writing paper

Unit Planning Calendar Week Two (Part Two)

DAY 9	DAY 10
Culminating activity (bulletin board)	Summative test
Materials	**Materials**
All unit activities, butcher paper, construction paper, markers, crayons, scissors, stapler, staples	25 copies of summative test

Lesson Plan Format

Prior Student Preparation: _____

_____

Lesson Theme: Texas Unit Introduction

Instructional Objectives:

Observable Behavior	Object of the Action	Task Condition
1. *Primary Objective*		
To respond	to pretest	
Performance Standard	40% rule	
2. *Primary Objective*		
To ask	questions regarding student overview and the unit	
Performance Standard		
3. *Primary Objective*		
To participate	in the design and construction of a salt map of Texas	
Performance Standard	initial	

Instructional Components:

Concepts List:

Skill List: Mapping: locate, draw, label, identify regions, cities, rivers

Value List:

Instructional Strategy (teacher action): Administer pretest, present student overview, answer questions regarding overview and unit, and give guidance and instruction during construction of the salt map.

Activity Description (student experience): Participate in design and construction of a salt map of Texas.

Material List: Resource books and textbooks with maps and photographs of Texas, salt, corn starch, food coloring, water, large piece of cardboard, butcher paper, pencils, toothpicks, large mixing bowl, old shirts, scissors, tape, markers

Lesson Presentation (Cycle)

Lesson Opener: Introduction, review, motivator, attention getter, and overview

During this lesson you will: respond to a pretest, listen to student overview, ask questions regarding the overview and the unit, and participate in the design and construction of a salt map of Texas.

Sequential Steps of Lesson:

	Estimated Time	Order of Lesson
1.	10 minutes	pretest
2.	10 minutes	student overview, address questions on student overview and the unit
3.	25 minutes	students plan and construct a salt map of Texas

Lesson Closure: Review, reinforcement, summary, and emphasis
5 minutes

During this lesson you learned to: *respond to a pretest, listen to the student overview and ask questions regarding the overview and unit, and participate in the design and construction of a salt map of Texas.*

Assignment: _____

_____

_____

Lesson Feedback:
"What did you learn?"
"Explain the following. . . ."
"Give an example of. . . ."

Lesson Enhancement:
The next time I teach this lesson, I will make the following changes: _____

_____

_____

Day 1 Lesson Activity

Motivating Activity

Description: The purpose of this activity is to motivate students to become interested in the unit on Texas. Students will be expected to participate in the design and construction of a salt map of Texas. The map will depict many of the things they will learn in the unit: locations of rivers and geographic regions, Texas borders, and major cities. It will also identify locations in which commodities are produced and natural resources exist. Students will gain this information from resource materials available to them while they are planning the map. By working in cooperative groups this activity will also promote good social relationships with other members of the class.

Directions:

1. Divide into two cooperative groups
   Group One: Combine mixture of salt, corn starch, and water until you form a workable paste.
   Group Two: Cover the cardboard with butcher paper and draw an outline in the shape of Texas on the paper.
2. Both groups will come together and decide what colors will indicate the different geographical regions and bodies of water.
   Group One: Color the paste with food coloring.
   Group Two: Make the labels to go on the maps out of small pieces of paper, taped to toothpicks.
3. Group Two: Apply the paste to the cover and mold to conform to the outline of Texas.
4. Group One: Place the labels in their appropriate locations following the maps from the resource materials as a guide.
5. Let map "set up" in a dry, warm place.

Motivating Activity: Salt Map

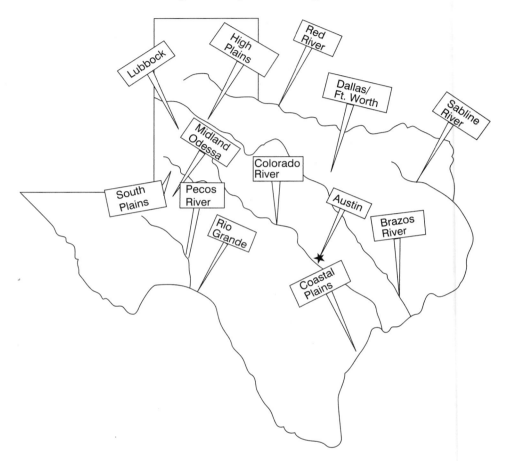

Unit Pretest

Directions: Answer each question briefly in the spaces provided. Raise your hand if you have any questions.

1. What is the capital of Texas?_____
_____

2. Who is the highest elected official in Texas?_____
_____

3. What animal did the Texas Indians hunt for food and survival?_____

4. Was Texas ever a part of Mexico?_____
_____

5. What is one of the most important crops raised by farmers in Texas?_____

Circle the correct answer.

6. The high plains are found in
   a. West Texas
   b. North Texas
   c. East Texas

7. The part of Texas that meets the Gulf of Mexico is called the
   a. peninsula
   b. coast
   c. border

8. The men who fought the Mexicans and Indians to make Texas safe are called the
   a. Texas Rangers
   b. Lone Stars
   c. Texas Police

9. Texas is a
   a. country
   b. county
   c. state

True or false?

10. _____Is Texas the largest state in the United States?

In the blanks, respond to the following question.

11. From your prior knowledge, describe the job of the Texas Ranger on the Texas frontier.

_____
_____
_____
_____
_____
_____
_____

Pretest Key

1. Austin
2. the governor or George W. Bush
3. buffalo
4. yes
5. Any of the following answers is acceptable: cotton, grapefruit, rice, oranges
6. b
7. b
8. a
9. c
10. c

Lesson Plan Format

Prior Student Preparation: _____

_____

Lesson Theme: Texas Anthropology

_____

Instructional Objectives:

Observable Behavior	Object of the Action	Task Condition
1. *Primary Objective*		
To describe	characteristics of the first people in Texas	
Performance Standard		
2. *Primary Objective*		
To describe	characteristics of the basic lifestyle of the Apache Indians	
Performance Standard		
3. *Secondary (supportive/enabling) Objective*		
To create	a "buffalo hide" depicting drawings of three ways in which the Apache Indians used the buffalo	
Performance Standard		
4. *Secondary (supportive/enabling) Objective*		
To describe	the three uses of buffalo in a descriptive paragraph	
Performance Standard		

Instructional Components

Concepts List: Indians: natives, original people
Nomads: move, wander, roam
Hunter: arrows, bow, spears, buffalo, pursue game

Skill List:

Value List:

_____

Instructional Strategy (teacher action): Lead discussion on first Texans and the Apache Indians; give guidance during student activity.

_____

Activity Description (student experience): Create a "buffalo hide" depicting three ways in which the Apache Indians used buffalo.

_____

Material List: Brown paper bags, markers, crayons, brown yarn, ice cream sticks, paper, pencil

Lesson Presentation (Cycle)

Lesson Opener: Introduction, review, motivator, attention getter, and overview

During this lesson you will: *describe characteristics of the first people in Texas, describe the characteristics of the life-style of the Apache Indians, and create a "buffalo hide" depicting three ways the Apache Indians used the buffalo.*

Sequential Steps of Lesson:

	Estimated Time	Order of Lesson
1.	10 minutes	Teacher will lead discussion on the first people in Texas.
2.	15 minutes	Teacher will lead discussion on the characteristics and life-style of the Apache Indians.
3.	20 minutes	Students will create a "buffalo hide" depicting three ways in which the Apache Indians used the buffalo. Students will write a descriptive paragraph for each use.

Lesson Closure: Review, reinforcement, summary, and emphasis
       5 minutes

During this lesson you learned to: *describe the characteristics of the first people in Texas, describe the characteristics of the life-style of the Apache Indians, create a "buffalo hide" depicting three ways in which Apache Indians used the buffalo, and describe each use for buffalo in a descriptive paragraph.*

Assignment: _____

_____

_____

Lesson Feedback:

"What did you learn?"   What did you learn about the first Texans?
"Explain the following. . . ."   For what purposes did the Apache use buffalo?
"Give an example of. . . ."   What is a nomad?

Lesson Enhancement:
The next time I teach this lesson, I will make the following changes: _____

_____

_____

DAY 2

Lesson Activity

Description: The purpose of this activity is to help students develop a better understanding of the Apache Indian culture. Students will use information learned in class discussions and their own creativity to make a "buffalo hide" depicting three ways in which the Apache Indians used the buffalo. This activity will demonstrate the resourcefulness of the Apache tribe and encourage students to cultivate an interest in learning more about anthropology and Texas history.

Directions:

1. Tear a brown paper bag so that the edges are frayed.
2. Using a pencil, crayon, or marker, draw three ways in which the Apache Indians used buffalo.
3. Use the point of a pencil to poke three holes through each side of the "hide."
4. Cut two, 1-foot pieces of brown yarn.
5. Place two ice cream sticks on either side of the "hide."
6. Lace the yarn through the "hide" and around the ice cream sticks, leaving slack between the "hide" and the sticks.
7. Tie the yarn tightly to the ice cream sticks every time you wrap it around so that it will not come loose.
8. When you have completed your drawings, write a descriptive paragraph for each of the uses you drew. Do this on a separate sheet of notebook paper.

Buffalo Hide

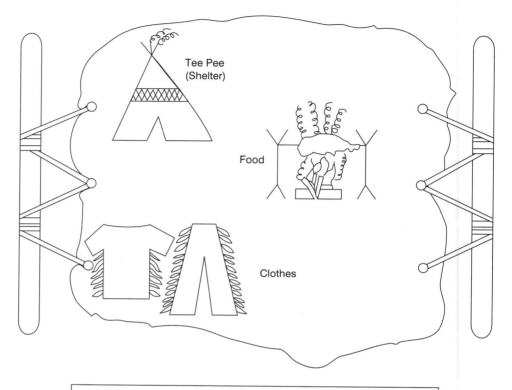

Tee Pee
(Shelter)

Food

Clothes

Buffalo Hide

The Apache Indians used buffalo in many ways. They used the buffalo hides to make their houses. Their houses are called tee pees. They tanned the hide so that water could not get in. They were warm in the winter. The Indians could open the flap and let breezes in so they would be cool in the summer. The tee pees were big enough for 6 to 8 people to sleep on the floor.

The Apache Indians also used buffalo hides for meat to eat. The women would cut up the meat into small pieces and smoke it over a fire. Then they would hang the meat out in the sun to dry. This provided them with meat all winter when they couldn't find animals to kill.

Thirdly, the Indians used buffalo hides for clothes. They would tan the hides, and the women would cut them and sew clothes. They wore only shirts and pants in the winter. The women wore dresses made out of the hides. In the summer the men wore little pieces of hides around the waist. Kind of like a little skirt with slits up each side.

Lesson Plan Format

Prior Student Preparation: _____

_____

Lesson Theme: Texas History

_____

Instructional Objectives:

Observable Behavior	Object of the Action	Task Condition
1. *Primary Objective* 　To list	the basic provisions of the Louisiana Purchase and its implications for Texas	
Performance Standard		
2. *Primary Objective* 　To list	the basic provisions of the Treaty of Guadalupe Hidalgo	
Performance Standard		
3. *Secondary (supportive/enabling) Objective* 　To participate	in writing the provisions of the Treaty of Guadalupe Hidalgo	
Performance Standard		
4. *Secondary (supportive/enabling) Objective* 　To participate	in the dramatization of the signing of the Treaty of Guadalupe Hidalgo	
Performance Standard		

Instructional Components:

Concepts List: Treaty: compromise, settlement, negotiate, United States, Mexico, Texas, provisions

Skill List:

Value List: Cooperation: compromise, listening, work together, common goals, mutual benefit

Instructional Strategy (teacher action): Lead class in discussion of the Louisiana Purchase and Treaty of Guadalupe Hidalgo; guide students during the activity.

Activity Description (student experience): Participate in writing the provisions of the Treaty of Guadalupe Hidalgo, and participate in role-playing the signing of the Treaty.

Material List: Cardboard paper-towel rollers, butcher paper, markers, construction paper, glue, cotton balls, scissors, clear tape, Karo Syrup, worn jackets and boots

Lesson Presentation (Cycle)

Lesson Opener: Introduction, review, motivator, attention getter, and overview

During this lesson you will: *list the basic provisions of the Louisiana Purchase and its implications for Texas, list the provisions of the Treaty of Guadalupe Hidalgo, and participate in the writing and dramatization of the Treaty of Guadalupe Hidalgo.*

Sequential Steps of Lesson:

	Estimated Time	Order of Lesson
1.	5 minutes	Teacher will lead discussion on the Louisiana Purchase.
2.	15 minutes	Teacher will lead discussion of the Treaty of Guadalupe Hidalgo.
3.	20 minutes	Teacher will guide students in writing the provisions of the Treaty and organizing and constructing "costumes."
4.	10 minutes	Students will dramatize the negotiations and signing of the Treaty of Guadalupe Hidalgo.

Lesson Closure: Review, reinforcement, summary, and emphasis
          5 minutes

During this lesson you learned to: *list the basic provisions of the Louisiana Purchase and its implications for Texas, list the provisions of the Treaty of Guadalupe Hidalgo, and participate in the dramatization of the Treaty of the Guadalupe Hidalgo.*

Assignment: _____

_____

_____

Lesson Feedback:
"What did you learn?"
"Explain the following. . . ."
"Give an example of. . . ."

Was Texas a part of the Louisiana Purchase?
What did the Treaty of Guadalupe Hidalgo end?
Who were the United States and Mexican leaders during this period?

Lesson Enhancement:
The next time I teach this lesson, I will make the following changes: _____

_____

_____

Lesson Activity

Description: The purpose of this activity is to help students understand the effects of U.S. foreign policy on Texas history. Students will use information gained from class discussions to list the basic provisions of the Treaty of Guadalupe Hidalgo. Students will use their creativity to dramatize the signing of the treaty by playing the roles of government leaders from the United States, Mexico, and Texas. This activity fosters students' ability to work well with others and to help them understand how world affairs affect what is happening in Texas.

Directions:

1. As a class and on your own paper make a rough draft of the basic provisions in the Treaty of Guadalupe Hidalgo.
2. Determine which student will do the writing on the large piece of butcher paper.
3. Have the student write basic provisions of the Treaty of Guadalupe Hidalgo on the butcher paper.
4. The teacher will determine who will play what roles in the dramatization.
5. When the roles have been determined, the class will formulate a written dialogue or script.
6. One person should be chosen to write out the script in dialogue form.
7. Students with major speaking parts should quickly review their parts.
8. Both male and female students enjoy getting into "costume" using cotton as beards. Attach the cotton to the face with a dab or two of Karo Syrup.
9. Use construction paper to make the worn jackets into "uniforms" by adding bars and stars to the shoulders and breast pocket. Medals can also be made out of construction paper.
10. Students should be dressed in dirty old boots and hats to represent those who have been fighting.
11. Places everyone . . . Action!

THE TREATY OF GUADALUPE HIDALGO

This document hereby decrees that the war between the United State of America and Mexico has ended on this day in eighteen hundred and forty-eight. These United States are to receive some 500,000 thousand square miles of territory previously occupied by the Mexicans. The United States will pay Mexico a sum of $15 million. And from this point on, the boundary between the United States and Mexico will be drawn at the Rio Grande. All land on the other side of the Rio Grande shall belong to Mexico. All land north of the Rio Grande belongs to Texas or the United States.

February 2, 1848

Santa Anna	President James Polk
President	General Zachary Taylor
Mariano Paredes	General Winfield Scott

Lesson Plan Format

Prior Student Preparation: _____

_____

_____

Lesson Theme: Texas Geography

Instructional Objectives:

Observable Behavior	Object of the Action	Task Condition
1. *Primary Objective*		
To discuss	the plains and various rivers of Texas and their characteristics	
Performance Standard		
2. *Secondary (supportive/enabling) Objective*		
To identify	the plains and various rivers of Texas on a map and color the map according to the color key	
Performance Standard	continuing practice	

Instructional Components:

Concepts List: Plain: flat, level, open land

Skill List: Mapping: identifying, locating,
                                          coordinates latitude, longitude

Value List:

Instructional Strategy (teacher action): Lead the discussion on the Texas plains and various rivers and guide students during the activity.

Activity Description (student experience): Identify the plains and various rivers on the map and color the map according to the color key.

Material List: Handout of Texas map and color key, map colors

Lesson Presentation (Cycle)

Lesson Opener: Introduction, review, motivator, attention getter, and overview

During this lesson you will: *discuss the various rivers and the plains of Texas, identify them on a map, and color the map according to the color key.*

Sequential Steps of Lesson:

	Estimated Time	Order of the Lesson
1.	20 minutes	Teacher will lead a discussion on the plains of Texas, various rivers, and their characteristics.
2.	25 minutes	Teacher will guide students as they identify plains and rivers and color a map of Texas.

Lesson Closure: Review, reinforcement, summary, and emphasis
5 minutes

During this lesson you learned to: *discuss the plains and rivers of Texas and their characteristics and identify and color a map of Texas according to the color key.*

Assignment: _____

_____

_____

Lesson Feedback:

"What did you learn?"   What kind of soil is found on the coastal plains?
"Explain the following. . . ."   Who built homes near rivers and why?
"Give an example of. . . ."   What does *Rio Grande* mean?

Lesson Enhancement:
The next time I teach this lesson, I will make the following changes: _____

_____

_____

_____

DAY 4

Lesson Activity

Description: The purpose of this activity is to give students a better understanding of the geographical regions of Texas so that they will be well informed of their surroundings. Students will also develop a better understanding of the cultures and economics of the area. Students will use resource materials available and class discussion to complete the map.

Map Exercise

1. Color The High Plains Region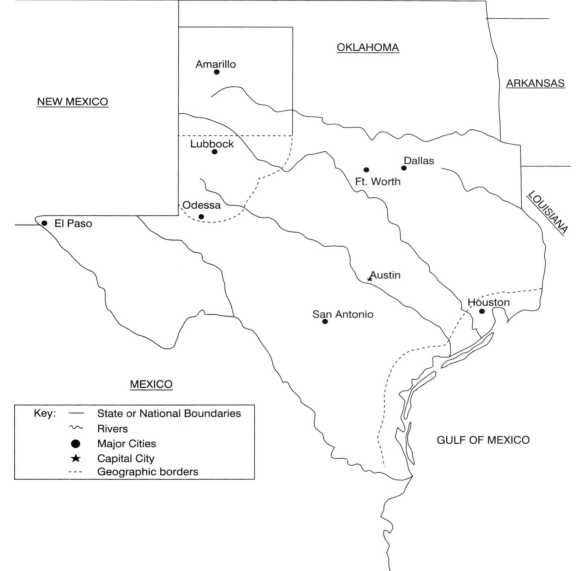
2. Color The South Plains Region
3. Color The Coastal Plains Region
4. For each river, write its name beside it:
   Rio Grande, Colorado, Brazos, Pecos, Red, and Sabine

OKLAHOMA

ARKANSAS

NEW MEXICO

Amarillo

Lubbock

Dallas

Ft. Worth

Odessa

LOUISIANA

El Paso

Austin

Houston

San Antonio

MEXICO

Key: — State or National Boundaries
      ⌇ Rivers
      ● Major Cities
      ★ Capital City
      - - - Geographic borders

GULF OF MEXICO

Map Exercise: Answer Key

1. Color The High Plains Region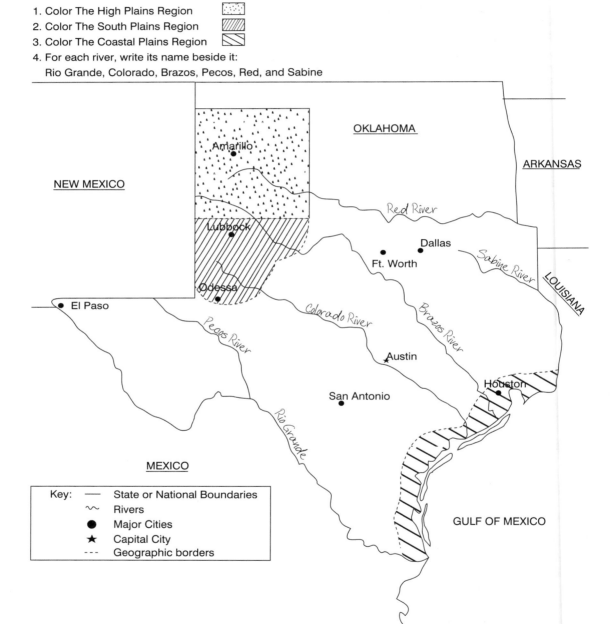
2. Color The South Plains Region
3. Color The Coastal Plains Region
4. For each river, write its name beside it:
   Rio Grande, Colorado, Brazos, Pecos, Red, and Sabine

Lesson Plan Format

Prior Student Preparation: _____

_____

_____

Lesson Theme: Texas Economics

_____

Instructional Objectives:

Observable Behavior	Object of the Action	Task Condition
1.		
Primary Objective		
To respond	to the mid-unit test	
Performance Standard	50 percent rule	
2.		
Primary Objective		
To describe	commodities and resources of Texas	
Performance Standard		
3.		
Secondary (supportive/enabling) Objective		
To identify	commodities and resources of Texas at the learning center	
Performance Standard		

Instructional Components:

Concepts List: Resources: advantages, assets, capital
             Commodities: goods, trade, products, produce

Skill List:

Value List:

Instructional Strategy (teacher action): Lead discussion on commodities and resources of Texas; guide students at the learning center.

Activity Description (student experience): Identify and describe the important commodities and resources of Texas at the learning center.

Lesson Presentation (Cycle)

Lesson Opener: Introduction, review, motivator, attention getter, and overview

During this lesson you will: *respond to a mid-unit test, describe commodities and resources of Texas, and identify those commodities and resources in a learning center.*

Sequential Steps of Lesson:

	Estimated Time	Order of the Lesson
1.	10 minutes	Students will respond to mid-unit test.
2.	20 minutes	Teacher will lead discussion on commodities and resources of Texas.
3.	20 minutes	Students will identify and describe the important commodities and resources of Texas and their uses at the learning center.

Lesson Closure: Review, reinforcement, summary, and emphasis
     5 minutes

During this lesson you learned to: *respond to a mid-unit test, describe commodities and resources of Texas, and identify commodities and resources of Texas at the learning center.*

Assignment: _____

_____

_____

Lesson Feedback:
"What did you learn?"   What types of things are grown or raised in Texas?
"Explain the following. . . ."   What are natural resources?
"Give an example of. . . ."   In what ways do we use cotton?

Lesson Enhancement:
The next time I teach this lesson, I will make the following changes: _____

_____

_____

Material List: Cotton clothing, wool clothing, beef, fruit and vegetables, peanut butter, can of motor oil, plastic, picture of a gas pump, picture of a gas heater, leather boots, gas lamp

DAY 5

Lesson Activity

Description: The purpose of this activity is to help students understand how the resources of Texas are used for economic gain and to develop creative ways to find more and better ways to use our resources and commodities. This lesson also teaches the basic economic theories of capitalism and free enterprise on which the united States operates. Students will use personal experiences and information from class discussions to identify commodities and resources from the learning center.

Directions:

1. Look at each item at the table and determine its importance and whether it is a commodity or a natural resource.
2. Divide a sheet of paper into two columns.
3. In the first column, write the name of the item and label it as a commodity or a natural resource.
4. In the next column, list some traditional uses for the item and any new ones you might be able to think of.

The Learning Center

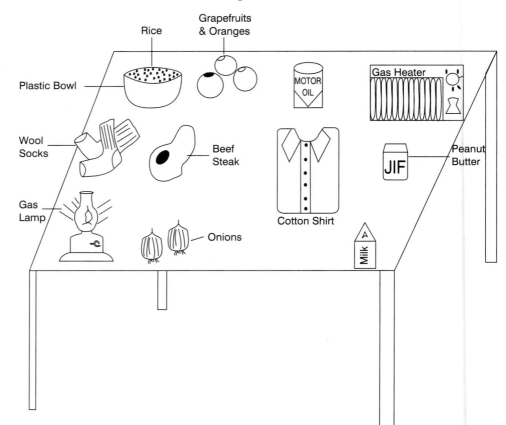

Rice

Grapefruits & Oranges

Plastic Bowl

MOTOR OIL

Gas Heater

Wool Socks

Beef Steak

Peanut Butter

JIF

Gas Lamp

Cotton Shirt

Onions

Milk

The Learning Center Activity

ITEM	USES
Rice—commodity	food
oranges—commodity	food
grapefruit—commodity	food
motor oil—natural resource	Motor oil is used in cars and as a lubricant for other engines.
gas heater—natural resource	Natural gas is used to heat homes and in portable heaters, stoves, and hot water heaters.
socks—wool from lambs—commodity	Wool is used for clothes—coats, sweaters, gloves, socks, hats, mufflers, skirts, and pants.
lambs—commodity	Lambs are also used for meat to eat.
beef steak—commodity	Cattle are used for food and beef. Leather from cattle is used for clothes—coats, boots, belts, gloves.
cotton shirt—commodity	Cotton is used to make all sorts of clothes and household items, such as sheets, towels, curtains, and mops.
peanut butter—commodity	Peanuts are used for food for humans and for cattle. The oil from peanuts is used for cooking oil.
onions—commodity	food
plastic—is made from petroleum which is a natural resource	all kinds of plastic goods, rubber, electricity, and fuel for cars
gas lamp—natural gas is a natural resource	heating homes, stoves, as fuels for transportation, gas grills

Mid-Unit Test (In-progress)

Directions: For each of the following questions, circle the correct answer. If you have any questions, raise your hand.

1. What river divides Texas from Mexico?
   a. Sabine River
   b. Guadalupe River
   c. Rio Grande

2. Which Indian tribe that we studied hunted buffalo?
   a. Karankawa Indians
   b. Tejas Indians
   c. Apache Indians

3. The plains usually have which characteristic?
   a. flat, open space
   b. many mountains
   c. many trees

4. Who selects the governor of Texas?
   a. the voters of Texas
   b. the President of the United States
   c. the Texas House of Representatives

Fill in the blanks with the correct answers.

5. Name two commodities produced in Texas and one natural resource. _____

   _____

6. A person who rules over a courtroom is called a _____.

7. The _____ ended the war with Mexico and made _____ the boundary between Texas and Mexico.

8. We use cattle for _____.

9. Texas was not a part of the _____ which doubled the size of the United States.

10. Indians and pioneers used to establish their settlements near _____.

Mid-Unit Test Key

1. c
2. c
3. a
4. a
5. cotton, oranges, grapefruit, rice, oil, natural gas
6. judge
7. Treaty of Guadalupe Hidalgo; Rio Grande
8. food, beef, and meat
9. Louisiana Purchase
10. Rivers

Lesson Plan Format

Prior Student Preparation: _____

_____

Lesson Theme: Texas Government

_____

Instructional Objectives:

Observable Behavior	Object of the Action	Task Condition
1. *Primary Objective*		
To describe	the functions of the three branches of government	small-group work
Performance Standard		
2. *Secondary (supportive/enabling) Objective*		
To participate	in writing a bill, or proposed law	
Performance Standard		
3. *Secondary (supportive/enabling) Objective*		
To list	the steps required for the bill to pass and become a law	
Performance Standard		

Instructional Components:

Concepts List: Democracy: vote, election, government by the people, majority rule
Representative government: legislature, House of Representatives, Senate, Governor

Skill List:

Value List: Democracy: vote, election, government by the people, majority rule, lobby

Instructional Strategy (teacher action): Teacher will lead discussion of the three branches of Texas government and guide students during the student activity.

Activity Description (student experience): Students will divide into cooperative groups and write a bill or proposed law. Students will then list the steps required to make the bill into a law.

Material List: Posterboard, markers, handout on steps required to make a bill a law

Lesson Presentation (Cycle)

Lesson Opener: Introduction, review, motivator, attention getter, and overview

During this lesson you will: *describe the functions of the three branches of Texas government, participate in writing a bill or proposed law, and list the steps required to make the bill a law.*

Sequential Steps of Lesson:

	Estimated Time	Order of the Lesson
1.	15 minutes	Teacher will lead discussion on the functions of the three branches of Texas government.
2.	10 minutes	Students will divide into cooperative groups and write a bill or proposed law.
3.	10 minutes	Students will list the steps required for the bill to become a law.
4.	15 minutes	Student groups will present their bills or proposed laws to the class for discussion. [Note: In an *actual* teaching situation, this lesson would include the evaluation of results.]

Lesson Closure: Review, reinforcement, summary, and emphasis
      5 minutes

During this lesson you learned to: *describe the three branches of government and their functions, participate in writing a bill or proposed law, and list the steps required to make a bill a law.*

Assignment: _____

_____

Lesson Feedback:
"What did you learn?"   What is meant by "checks and balances"?
"Explain the following. . . ."   What is a "veto" and who uses it?
"Give an example of. . . ."   How does someone become a senator or representative?

Lesson Enhancement:
The next time I teach this lesson, I will make the following changes: _____

_____

_____

DAY 6

Lesson Activity

Description: The purpose of this activity is to enable students to develop a better understanding of the ways Texas government works and laws are made. This activity also teaches basic democratic values essential to good citizenship. Through class discussion and a handout, students are able to formulate a bill and list the steps required to make the bill into a law.

Directions:

1. Divide class into four cooperative groups.
2. Give each group a large posterboard.
3. Ask everyone in each group to write down their own idea for a bill.
4. Each person in the group will read his or her idea and state the reasons the idea should become a law.
5. Each group will discuss each idea and determine which one they are going to use.
6. The group will then decide who will write the idea for the bill at the top of the large posterboard.
7. Each member of the group will take turns writing the steps required to make a bill a law using the handout they have been given.
8. Be prepared to discuss these with the rest of the class and give the reasons your bill should be a law.

How a Bill Becomes a Law

Summary: A bill that is approved by the House of Representatives, the Senate, and the governor becomes a law.

Step 1: The bill is read before the entire House of Representatives or the Senate.

Step 2: A committee decides whether the bill would make a good law. Then the committee votes to send the bill either to the House of Representatives or to the Senate.

Step 3: The first branch to hear the bill (either the House of Representatives or the Senate) votes on the bill, and if the majority approves, then the bill goes to the other branch to be voted on.

Step 4: Once the bill has been approved by both the House of Representatives and the Senate, it goes to the governor.

Step 5:   If the governor signs a bill, then it becomes a law.

Step 6:   If the governor does not think the bill would make a good law, he or she can veto the bill or refuse to sign it. Then the bill cannot become a law unless two-thirds of the House of Representatives and the Senate vote to override the governor's veto.

How a Bill Becomes a Law

BILL: All school buses in the state of Texas must be equipped with seatbelts for all students.

How this bill will become law:

1.   It will be read before the House of Representatives.

2.   Then a committee will decide that it is a good bill and it goes to the Senate.

3.   The Senate votes whether it should be a law or not, and they think it should. The majority approves.

4.   The bill then goes to the House of Representatives and they vote on it. They think it is a good bill too, and the majority approves it.

5.   The bill now goes to the governor, who says it is a good bill and should be a law. The governor could veto the bill, which would mean it would have to go back to the House and Senate and win two-thirds approval from both to override the veto. But the governor likes the bill and signs it. Therefore, now our bill is a law.

Lesson Plan Format

Prior Student Preparation: _____

_____

Lesson Theme: Sociology, The Texas Rangers

Instructional Objectives:

Observable Behavior	Object of the Action	Task Condition
1. *Primary Objective*		
To describe	characteristics and events associated with the Texas Rangers	
Performance Standard		
2. *Primary Objective*		
To list	characteristics and functions of the Texas Rangers on the chalkboard	
Performance Standard		
3. *Secondary (supportive/enabling) Objective*		
To participate	in making a recruiting poster for the Texas Rangers	
Performance Standard		

Instructional Components:

Concepts List: War: fight, battles, opposing forces, conflict
Texas Rangers: lawmen, peace, mounted, special agents
Laws: rules, guidelines, order

Skill List:

Value List: Cooperation: compromise, work together, respect, mutual benefit, common goal

Instructional Strategy (teacher action): Lead discussion on the characteristics and functions of the Texas Rangers and guide students while they list these characteristics and functions on the chalkboard and work on student activity.

Activity Description (student experience): Students will work in cooperative groups to make a recruiting poster for the Texas Rangers.

Material List: Chalk, chalkboard, markers, posterboard, crayons, scissors, glue, construction paper

Lesson Presentation (Cycle)

Lesson Opener: Introduction, review, motivator, attention getter, and overview

During this lesson you will: *describe the characteristics and functions of the Texas Rangers, list these characteristics and functions on the chalkboard, and participate in making a recruiting poster for the Texas Rangers.*

Sequential Steps of Lesson:

Estimated Time	Order of the Lesson
1. 15 minutes	Teacher will lead discussion on the Texas Rangers.
2. 5 minutes	Teacher will supervise students while they list the characteristics and functions of the Texas Rangers on the chalkboard.
3. 15 minutes	Students will work in cooperative groups to make a recruiting poster for the Texas Rangers.
4. 10 minutes	Each group will present its poster to the class for discussion.

Lesson Closure: Review, reinforcement, summary, and emphasis
5 minutes

During this lesson you learned to: *describe the characteristics and functions of the Texas Rangers, list those characteristics and functions on the chalkboard, and participate in making a recruiting poster for the Texas Rangers.*

Assignment: _____

_____

Lesson Feedback:

"What did you learn?"   Why were the Texas Rangers formed?
"Explain the following. . . ."   Were the Rangers always the "good guys"?
"Give an example of. . . ."   What are the present functions of the Rangers?

Lesson Enhancement:
The next time I teach this lesson, I will make the following changes: _____

_____

_____

DAY 7

Lesson Activity

Description: The purpose of this activity is to help students understand how Texas was settled and in what kind of conditions the people of Texas lived. This activity will help students understand the culture of the Texas Rangers and the danger involved in their everyday lives so Texans can live in peace today. Using information learned in class discussion and their own imaginations, students will create an original recruiting poster for the Texas Rangers.

Directions:

1. Divide class into four cooperative groups.
2. Each group will have a piece of posterboard.
3. Each group member will be responsible for creating a slogan for the recruiting poster for the Texas Rangers.
4. Discuss each word or phrase and decide on three or four to go on the poster.
5. Write the slogans on the poster.
6. Brainstorm a quick illustration to go with the slogans.
7. Draw the illustration at the top of the posterboard.

Lesson Plan Format

Prior Student Preparation: _____

_____

_____

Lesson Theme: Psychology; N. A. Jennings, A Texas Ranger

Instructional Objectives:

Observable Behavior	Object of the Action	Task Condition

1. *Primary Objectives*
    To examine   the life of N. A. Jennings,
                     a Texas Ranger

    Performance Standard

2. *Secondary (supportive/enabling) Objective*
    To illustrate   an event in the life of N. A.
                     Jennings that was discussed in class

    Performance Standard

3. *Secondary (supportive/enabling) Objective*
    To describe   the illustrated event in a
                     descriptive paragraph

    Performance Standard

Instructional Components:

Concepts List: Texas Ranger: peacekeepers, law men and women, mounted, special agents, rebels
Laws: rules, guidelines, order
Frontier: unsettled, undeveloped

Skill List:

Value List:

Instructional Strategy (teacher action): Lead discussion on the life and events of N. A. Jennings.

Activity Description (student experience): Students will illustrate an event in the life of N. A. Jennings that was discussed in class and write a descriptive paragraph about the illustration.

Material List: Drawing paper, pencil, crayons, markers, glue, scissors, writing paper

Lesson Presentation (Cycle)

Lesson Opener: Introduction, review, motivator, attention getter, and overview

During this lesson you will: *examine the life of N. A. Jennings, illustrate an event of his life which was discussed in class, and describe the illustration in a descriptive paragraph.*

Sequential Steps of Lesson:

	Estimated Time	Order of the Lesson
1.	15 minutes	Teacher will lead class in discussion of N. A. Jennings, a Texas Ranger.
2.	15 minutes	Students will illustrate an event from the life of N. A. Jennings which was discussed in class.
3.	5 minutes	Students will describe the illustrated event in a brief descriptive paragraph.
4.	10 minutes	Students will present the illustrations and read paragraphs to the class for discussion.

Lesson Closure: Review, reinforcement, summary, and emphasis
5 minutes

During this lesson you learned to: *examine the life of N. A. Jennings, a Texas Ranger; illustrate an event from his life; and describe the illustrated event in a brief descriptive paragraph.*

Assignment: _____

_____

_____

Lesson Feedback:
"What did you learn?"   Did the Texas Rangers have an easy life according to Mr. Jennings?

"Explain the following. . . ."   What did Mr. Jennings do for fun?
"Give an example of. . . ."   Discuss one of the battles Mr. Jennings was involved in.

Lesson Enhancement:
The next time I teach this lesson, I will make the following changes: _____

_____

_____

DAY 8

Lesson Activity

Description: The purpose of this activity is to enable students to study the life of an individual who worked to shape Texas into the state as we know it. This activity motivates students to want to learn more about our state and its exciting past. The information for this activity comes from class discussion and the book by Mr. Jennings, *A Texas Ranger,* which the students have access to.

Directions:

1. Each student will decide on an event from the life of N. A. Jennings, who was discussed in class.
2. On drawing paper, illustrate the event. Use crayons, construction paper, markers or whatever you want to help your picture better illustrate the event.
3. When you have finished your illustrations, use a separate sheet of writing paper to write a paragraph describing the event.

The Life of N. A. Jennings

The Life of N. A. Jennings

    N. A. Jennings was young and didn't know what to expect. There wasn't a lot to do out in the wide open frontier. So when the Rangers weren't arresting Mexican horse thieves and raiders, the Rangers tried to have some fun. N. A. describes one of the first times he played poker, a card game, with the Rangers and he lost all of his money. The older, wiser Rangers tricked him into believing their cards weren't good so he would bet a lot of money. Everyone had better cards than N. A. did and he lost.

Lesson Plan Format

Prior Student Preparation: _____

_____

_____

_____

Lesson Theme: Texas Unit Culminating Activity

Instructional Objectives:

Observable Behavior	Object of the Action	Task Condition
1. *Primary Objective*		
To examine	the unit activities	
Performance Standard		
2. *Secondary (supportive/enabling) Objective*		
To create	a bulletin board using all the activities from the unit	
Performance Standard		

Instructional Components:

Concepts List:	Bulletin board: display, focal point, achievements, information
Skill List:	
Value List:	Cooperation: work together, compromise, common goals, mutual benefit

Instructional Strategy (teacher action): Lead class in review of all unit activities, guide students during the planning, organization, and construction of the unit bulletin board.

Activity Description (student experience): Plan, organize, and create a bulletin board displaying all the unit activities.

Material List: All unit activities, butcher paper, construction paper, markers, crayons, scissors, stapler, staples

Lesson Presentation (Cycle)

Lesson Opener: Introduction, review, motivator, attention getter, and overview

During this lesson you will: *review the unit activities and create a bulletin board using all of the unit activities.*

Sequential Steps of Lesson:

	Estimated Time	Order of the Lesson
1.	20 minutes	Teacher will lead the class in a review of the unit activities.
2.	10 minutes	Teacher will guide students during planning and organization of the bulletin board.
3.	20 minutes	Teacher will guide students during the creation of the bulletin board.

Lesson Closure: Review, reinforcement, summary, and emphasis
          5 minutes

During this lesson you learned to: *review the unit activities and create a bulletin board using the unit activities.*

Assignment: _____

_____

Lesson Feedback:
"What did you learn?"
"Explain the following. . . ."
"Give an example of. . . ."

What was your favorite thing in this unit?
Name some of the people we learned about in this unit.
Give an example of ways Texans make a living.
Who is the chief executive of Texas?

Lesson Enhancement:
The next time I teach this lesson, I will make the following changes: _____

_____

_____

_____

Culminating Activity

Description: The purpose of this activity is to review the most important material covered in this unit. This activity reinforces the main concepts, skills, and values taught during this unit. The culminating activity will refresh students' memories of the Treaty of Guadalupe Hidalgo, the geographic regions of Texas, the branches of government, and the life-style of the Apache Indians. Putting the bulletin board together in cooperative groups will continue to promote good social relationships and the ability to work with others, which is vital to the healthy development of young people.

Directions: Before beginning the planning and construction of the bulletin board, review all of the activities of the unit. Take the time to discuss lessons associated with each activity.

1. Divide the class into seven cooperative groups. Each group will be responsible for the activities from one discipline: history, geography, economics, anthropology, government, sociology, and psychology.
2. Each group will create a section of the bulletin board by selecting a sample from each of the activities. Select five to seven of each of the activities to go on the bulletin board.
3. Cover the bulletin board with butcher paper.
4. Staple the activities to the board in an attractive manner. You may want to "frame" the activities by putting a piece of construction paper behind it.

ACTIVITIES BULLETIN BOARD

Day 9

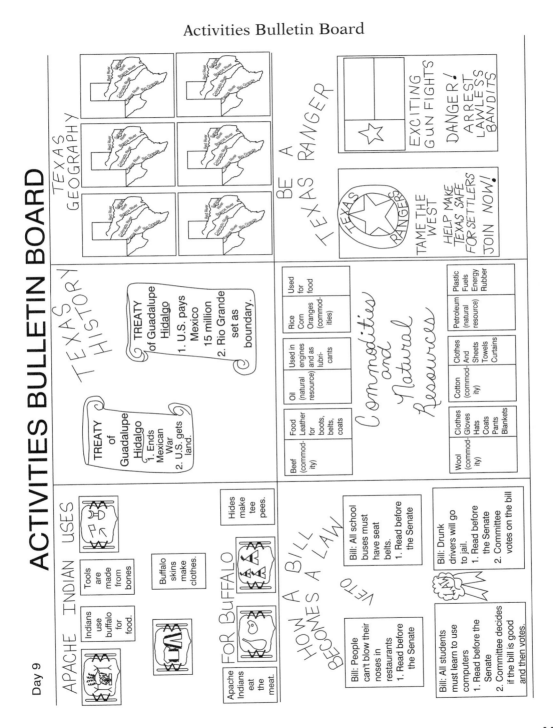

TEXAS GEOGRAPHY

BE A TEXAS RANGER

TEXAS RANGERS

TAME THE WEST

HELP MAKE TEXAS SAFE FOR SETTLERS

JOIN NOW!

EXCITING GUN FIGHTS

DANGER! ARREST LAWLESS BANDITS

TEXAS HISTORY

TREATY of Guadalupe Hidalgo
1. Ends Mexican War
2. U.S. gets land.

TREATY of Guadalupe Hidalgo
1. U.S. pays Mexico 15 million
2. Rio Grande set as boundary.

Commodities and Natural Resources

| Beef (commodity) | Food Leather for boots, belts, coats | Oil (natural resource) | Used in engines and as lubricants | Rice Corn Oranges (commodities) | Used for food |
| Wool (commodity) | Clothes Gloves Hats Coats Pants Blankets | Cotton (commodity) | Clothes And Sheets Towels Curtains | Petroleum (natural resource) | Plastic Fuels Energy Rubber |

APACHE INDIAN USES FOR BUFFALO

Indians use buffalo for food.

Tools are made from bones.

Buffalo skins make clothes.

Hides make tee pees.

Apache Indians eat the meat.

HOW A BILL BECOMES A LAW

VETO

Bill: All school buses must have seat belts.
1. Read before the Senate

Bill: Drunk drivers will go to jail.
1. Read before the Senate
2. Committee votes on the bill

Bill: People can't blow their noses in restaurants
1. Read before the Senate

LAW

Bill: All students must learn to use computers
1. Read before the Senate
2. Committee decides if the bill is good and then votes.

449

Lesson Plan Format

Prior Student Preparation: Completion of the unit activities.

Lesson Theme: Texas Unit Summative Text

Instructional Objectives:

Observable Behavior	Object of the Action	Task Condition
1. *Primary Objective*		
To respond	to summative test	
Performance Standard	70% rule	

Instructional Components:

Concepts List:

Skill List:

Value List:

Instructional Strategy (teacher action): Teacher will administer the summative test.

Activity Description (student experience):

Material List: Summative test

Lesson Presentation (Cycle)

Lesson Opener: Introduction, review, motivator, attention getter, and overview
During this lesson you will: *respond to a summative test.*

Sequential Steps of Lesson:

	Estimated Time	Order of the Lesson
1.	45 minutes	Teacher will administer the summative test.

Lesson Closure: Review, reinforcement, summary, and emphasis
5 minutes

During this lesson you learned to: *respond to the summative test.*

Assignment: _____

_____

Lesson Feedback:
"What did you learn?"
"Explain the following. . . ."
"Give an example of. . . ."

Lesson Enhancement:
The next time I teach this lesson, I will make the following changes: _____

_____

_____

Summative Test

Directions: Fill in the blanks with the correct answers.

1. The first invaders of Texas came during the last great _____.

2. The coastal plains of Texas meets with the _____.

3. Texas is the leading producer of _____, which is a commodity.

Circle the correct answer.

4. The Apache Indians relied on what animal for survival?
   a. deer
   b. buffalo
   c. rabbit

5. This river serves as a border between Texas and Louisiana.
   a. Concho River
   b. Rocky Mountain River
   c. Sabine River

6. The mission of the Texas Rangers was to make Texas
   a. preserved
   b. safe
   c. a country

7. The first Texans were Indians.   *True* or *False*

8. The Treaty of Guadalupe Hidalgo ended the war with Spain.   *True* or *False*

9. The United States paid $15 million for the land that is now Texas.   *True* or *False*

10. The Rio Grande was set as the boundary between Texas and Mexico in the Treaty of Guadalupe Hidalgo.   *True* or *False*

11. The Texas Rangers were foot soldiers.   *True* or *False*

Fill in the blanks with the correct answers.

12. In the Apache tribe the _____ were responsible for cleaning and skinning the animals killed on a hunt.

13. If the governor refuses to sign a bill, it is called a _____.

14. Both the _____ and the _____ must approve a bill before it goes to the governor.

15. The Permian Basin produces oil, which is a _____.

Circle the correct answer.

16. The high plains are located in what part of Texas
   a. North
   b. West
   c. Central

17. The Texas Rangers' main form of protection was the

    a. whip
    b. shot gun
    c. six-shooter

18. The President of the United States when the Treaty of Guadalupe Hidalgo was signed was

    a. James Polk
    b. Zachary Taylor
    c. Santa Anna

Fill in the blank.

19. The three branches of Texas government are the legislature, the governor, and the _____
    _____.

20. The area of social studies that examines the uses of geographic resources is _____.

Summative Test Key

1. Ice Age
2. Gulf of Mexico
3. cotton
4. b
5. c
6. b
7. False
8. False
9. False
10. True
11. False
12. women
13. veto
14. Senate and House of Representatives
15. natural resource
16. a
17. c
18. a
19. judiciary
20. economics

Sample Unit Bibliography

TEACHER RESOURCES

Anderson, A. N., Wooster, R. A., Armstrong, D. G., Stanley, J. R. (1993). *Texas and Texans*. Westerville, OH: Macmillan/McGraw-Hill.

Davis, K. C. (1990). *Don't Know Much About History*. New York: Avon Books.

Dobie, J. F. (1955). *Up the Trail from Texas*. New York: Random House.

Duval, J. C. (1935). *Early Times in Texas*. Austin: The Steck Company.

Eichner, J. A., Shields, L. M. (1983). *Local Government*. New York: Franklin Watts.

Fehrenbach, T. R. (1968). *Lone Star: A History of Texas and the Texans*. New York: American Legacy Press.

Freedman, R. (1985). *Cowboys of the Wild West*. New York: Clarion Books.

Jennings, N. A. (1959). *A Texas Ranger*. Austin: The Steck Company.

Kaltsounis, T. (1982). *The World and Its People: States and Regions*. Morristown, NJ: Silver Burdett Company.

King, A. V., Dennis, I., Potter, F. (1981). *The U.S. and the Other Americas*. New York: Macmillan Publishing Company.

Klein, S. (1981). *Our Country Today*. New York: Scholastic Book Services.

Mayhill, M. P. (1965). *Indian Wars of Texas*. Waco, TX: Texian Press.

Pettus, B. E., Bland, R. W. (1976). *Texas Government Today*. Homewood, IL: The Dorsey Press.

Senesh, L. (1973). *Our Working World: Cities*. Chicago: Science Research Associates, Inc.

Senesh, L. (1973). *Our Working World: Regions of the U.S.* Chicago: Science Research Associates, Inc.

Veninga, J. F., Bennett, G., Lich, G. E., Buehger, W. L., Calvert, R. A., Williams, C. (1990). *Preparing for Texas in the 21st Century*. Texas Committee for the Humanities.

STUDENT RESOURCES

Anderson, A. N., Wooster, R. A., Armstrong, D. G., Stanley, J. R. (1993). *Texas and Texans*. Westerville, OH: Macmillan/McGraw-Hill.

Baker, D. W. C. (1991). *A Texas Scrapbook*. Austin, TX: Texas State Historical Association.

Fehrenbach, T. R. (1968). *Lone Star: A History of Texas and the Texans*. New York: American Legacy Press.

Gille, F. H. (1985). *Encyclopedia of Texas*. 2nd ed. Michigan: Somerset Publishers.

Holley, M. A. (1990). *Texas*. Austin, TX: Texas State Historical Association.

Jennings, N. A. (1959). *A Texas Ranger*. Austin, TX: The Steck Company.

Kaltsounis, T. (1982). *The World and Its People: States and Regions*. Morristown, NJ: Silver Burdett Company.

Klein, S. (1981). *Our Country Today*. New York: Scholastic Book Services.

Mayhill, M. P. (1965). *Indian Wars of Texas*. Waco, TX: Texian Press.

Silverthorne, E. (1990). *Christmas In Texas*. College Station, TX: Texas A&M Press.

Webb, W. P. (1935). *The Texas Ranger*. Austin, TX: University of Texas Press.

About the Authors

Thomas L. Dynneson

A native of Minnesota, Thomas L. Dynneson served in the Air Force during the Korean War and later earned a B.S. in Business Administration from Macalester College. After a short career with Ford Motor Company, he completed a teaching certificate and taught history, international affairs, geography, and civics in junior high and high schools in Colorado and Minnesota. In 1965, Dynneson received a Coe Fellowship in history at Macalester College, where he completed his M.Ed. in 1968. Dynneson received another Coe Fellowship in history from Stanford University in 1968, and earned his Ph.D. from The University of Colorado in 1972.

In 1972, after teaching for one year at Coe College in Cedar Rapids, Iowa, Dynneson was invited to become a founding faculty member at The University of Texas of the Permian Basin, where he currently serves as a Professor of Education.

During the past fifteen years, Dynneson has been invited four times to Stanford University as a visiting scholar. He has presented many papers, published numerous articles and research monographs, and co-edited and authored or co-authored many books, including *Pre-Collegiate Anthropology: Trends and Materials*, *What Should We Be Teaching in the Social Studies*, and *Social Science Perspectives on Citizenship Education*. Dynneson, who is included in *Who's Who in America*, is currently working on manuscripts about the western and American history of education related to the evolution of the civic culture.

Richard E. Gross

Richard E. Gross has been responsible for the programs in social studies curriculum and instruction and teacher education at Stanford University for the past 35 years. Before his professorial appointment at Stanford's School of Education in 1955, he served at Florida State University and previously taught high school history and government. Gross earned his bachelor's and master's degrees at the University of Wisconsin (Madison) and his doctorate at Stanford University.

Gross is the author, co-author, and editor of many books at the elementary, secondary, and college levels. He has served as a consultant to school districts across the United States and has been an international consultant in the Netherlands, Denmark, Spain, Morocco, and Hong Kong. He has mounted workshops at Stanford for national social studies leaders and has organized in-service programs for the United States Military Dependent Schools in Europe and Asia.

Gross has served as a guest professor at the University of Wisconsin, Monash University (Australia), and the University of Frankfurt (Germany). He has been a USIA lecturer in Europe and served as a visiting Fulbright lecturer in teacher education at Swansea University College (Wales). He also has worked as chief Consultant for the California State Department of Education Curriculum Committee. A founder of the Florida and California State Social Studies Councils, Gross is a past-president of the National Council for the Social Studies (1966-67) and is a recipient of a variety of research and instructional awards.

Index